Kazakhstan in the Making

Contemporary Central Asia: Societies, Politics, and Cultures

Series Editor: Marlene Laruelle, George Washington University

At the crossroads of Russia, China, and the Islamic world, Central Asia remains one of the world's least-understood regions, despite being a significant theater for muscle flexing by the great powers and regional players. This series, in conjunction with George Washington University's Central Asia Program, offers insight into Central Asia by providing readers unique access to state-of-the-art knowledge on the region. Going beyond the media clichés, the series inscribes the study of Central Asia into the social sciences and hopes to fill the dearth of works on the region for both scholarly knowledge and undergraduate and graduate student education.

Titles in the Series

Kyrgyzstan beyond "Democracy Island" and "Failing State": Social and Political Changes in a Post-Soviet Society, edited by Marlene Laruelle and Johan Engvall
Afghanistan and Its Neighbors after the NATO Withdrawal, edited by Amin Saikal and Kirill Nourzhanov
Integration in Energy and Transport: Azerbaijan, Georgia, and Turkey, by Alexandros Petersen
Kazakhstan in the Making: Legitimacy, Symbols, and Social Changes, edited by Marlene Laruelle

Kazakhstan in the Making

Legitimacy, Symbols, and Social Changes

Edited by
Marlene Laruelle

LEXINGTON BOOKS
Lanham • Boulder • New York • London

Published by Lexington Books
An imprint of The Rowman & Littlefield Publishing Group, Inc.
4501 Forbes Boulevard, Suite 200, Lanham, Maryland 20706
www.rowman.com

Unit A, Whitacre Mews, 26-34 Stannary Street, London SE11 4AB

British Library Cataloguing in Publication Information Available

Library of Congress Control Number: 2016950707
ISBN: 978-1-4985-2549-7 (cloth : alk. paper)
eISBN: 978-1-4985-2548-0

♾™ The paper used in this publication meets the minimum requirements of American National Standard for Information Sciences—Permanence of Paper for Printed Library Materials, ANSI/NISO Z39.48-1992.

Printed in the United States of America

Contents

Acronyms

APK	Assembly of the Peoples of Kazakhstan
BTA	TuranAlem Bank
DEKKO	dombra, estrada, küi, komputer, and oryndaushi
DMK	Democratic Choice of Kazakhstan Party
DPNI	Movement Against Illegal Immigration
DUMK	Religious Board of the Muslims of Kazakhstan
EEU	Eurasian Economic Union
ENRC	Eurasian Natural Resources Group
FIG	financial-industrial group
FSB	Russian Federal Security Service
GDP	gross domestic product
GNPF	Kazakh State National Pension Fund
IPS	Institute of Political Solutions
KEGOC	Kazakhstan Electricity Grid Operating Company
KIMEP	Kazakhstan Institute of Management, Economics and Strategic Research
KNB	Kazakh National Security Committee
KZT	Kazakh Tenge
MITI	Japanese Ministry of International Trade and Industry
MP	Member of Parliament
OSCE	Organization for Security and Co-operation in Europe
SAPF	Kazakh State Accumulative Pension Fund
SME	small- and medium-size enterprise
SSGPO	Sokolov Sarbai Mining Production Association

SSR	Soviet Socialist Republic
TB-LNNK	Tēvzemei un Brīvībai-LNNK (For Fatherland and Freedom-LNNK)
TNG	Trans Neft i Gaz

Introduction

Marlene Laruelle

In less than two decades, Kazakhstan has become one of the best-known success stories of Central Asia, perhaps even of the entire Eurasian space. The country's burgeoning economy had an impressive growth rate of about 7 percent a year—until the 2014 economic slowdown. Kazakhstan alone produces about two-thirds of the gross domestic product of all Central Asia and positions itself not far behind Russia in terms of GDP per inhabitant. The country has adopted a so-called multivector foreign policy, which includes a strategic alliance with Russia, a growing partnership with China, and good relations with the United States and Europe. It has become a world leader in debates on denuclearization and presents itself as a bridge linking the Western, Muslim, and Asian worlds, with several sophisticated branding strategies such as new the Western-style university, and hosting the world expo Astana-2017.

However, the domestic picture looks more contrasted. The Kazakhstani authorities have been slow to avoid Dutch disease and to move away from an excessive specialization in raw materials exports, especially oil. The institutionalization of state structures and political parties remains weak, unable to compete with the ultra-personification of power around the "father of the nation," President Nursultan Nazarbayev. Neopatrimonial practices and endemic corruption undermine the justice system and the state administration, as well as the education system. Residents of the hinterlands and provincial cities did not benefit from the rising living standards of the 2000s, and they made their dissatisfaction known during the Zhanaozen event of December 2011 and the land reform protests of spring 2016. Since 2014, the economic crisis has hit Kazakhstani standards of living hard, especially the poor and middle classes, and partly undermined popular support for Nazarbayev and his "stability and prosperity" discourse.

Kazakhstan's emergence as the economic driver of the Central Asian region and a strategic power in Eurasia has led to many policy-driven publications. These works came from U.S. think tanks (Martha Brill Olcott's *Kazakhstan: Unfulfilled Promise*, Washington, DC: Carnegie Endowment for International Peace, 2002, or Ariel Cohen, *Kazakhstan: The Road to Independence Energy Policy and the Birth of a Nation*, Washington DC: The Central Asia and Caucasus Institute, 2008), or from international financial institutions such as the IMF, World Bank, and Asian Development Bank, with leading research done, for example, by Richard Pomfret on Kazakhstan's agricultural reforms and resource nationalism and Johannes Linn on Kazakhstan's role in regional integration.

While Kazakhstan has often been in the policy spotlight, scholarly knowledge of Kazakhstani society is much more modest. The reasons for that are multiple. In the 1990s the academic community working on Central Asia mostly focused on Uzbekistan, then seen as the main regional power, and on Tajikistan, then in the middle of a bloody civil war. In the 2000s, the massive opening of Kyrgyzstan to Western, especially United States, interests contributed to a growing literature on Kyrgyz society, while the end of the civil war in Tajikistan attracted scholars looking at post-civil war reconstruction processes. Paradoxically, Kazakhstan was partly passed over, not considered a typical "Central Asian" society by scholars with an Oriental studies background, and neglected by those focusing on Russia and the transformation of "Sovietness" in the whole region. This situation is even more surprising because historians working on the Kazakh steppes under Tsarist domination and during the first decades of the Soviet power were particularly visible in the history field.

Several well-received monographs shaped the scholarly landscape on contemporary Kazakhstan. Edward Schatz's *Modern Clan Politics: The Power of "Blood" in Kazakhstan and Beyond* (Seattle and London: University of Washington Press, 2004) looked at Kazakhstan as a case study for exploring the role of genealogical affiliations in building political networks. Sally Cumming's *Kazakhstan: Power and the Elite* (London and New York: I.B. Tauris, 2005) offered a sociological approach to the country's elites, their processes of co-optation, and the interaction between that individual level and the broader post-Soviet institutional construction. Bhavna Dave's *Kazakhstan: Ethnicity, Language, and Power* (London: Routledge, 2007) explored the role of language in building new legitimacies, both for the regime itself and for the state's national identity. Some works took account of the fact that Kazakhstan is the only state in Central Asia with statistically important minorities (accounting for half of the population in the 1990s), for instance, Alexander Diener's *Homeland Conceptions and Ethnic Integration among Kazakhstan's Germans and Koreans* (New York: Edwin Mellen Press,

2004), and Marlene Laruelle and Sebastien Peyrouse's, *Russians in Kazakhstan. National identities and New States in the Post-Soviet Spac*e (in French and Russian, Paris: Maisonneuve & Larose/IFEAC, 2004).

Beyond these foundational works, the scholarly literature on contemporary Kazakhstan has been enriched by many articles that can be grouped into three main categories. First, a large body of research deals with the "nature" of the Kazakhstani political regime, particularly the close intertwining of political networks and business circles, making Kazakhstan a fruitful case for the study of neopatrimonialism or patronage politics (Barbara Junisbai, Edward Schatz, Assel Tutumlu, Pauline Jones Luong, Sally Cummings). A second group of work is devoted to the nationhood process, looking at the official policy of promoting a Kazakhstani ideology and the tensions between different identity repertoires, at the ethnic repatriation programs, and the narrative on Islam (Anatoli Khazanov, Diana T. Kudaibergenova, Yves-Marie Davenel, Alexander Diener, Gaelle Lacaze, Marlene Laruelle, Maria Omelicheva). A third body of literature, more original and specific to Kazakhstan, emerged thanks to political geographers and anthropologists who explored the construction of the new capital, Astana, and its meaning for the population (Nathalie Koch, Mateusz Laszczkowski, Alexander Diener, Adrien Fauve). The rural world, changing social conditions, important labor migration flows, the disappearance of the industrial fabric, and—paradoxically—Islam remain the poor stepchildren of our research. Things are changing, however, with renewed interest from scholars on these understudied aspects of Kazakhstan (Alima Bissenova, Wendell Schwab, Ulan Bigozhin, Tommaso Trevisani, Bhavna Dave, etc.), and several new monographs are on their way. Many important names have not been mentioned in this schematic list, and I apologize in advance for those not included here.

This edited volume offers a new perspective on the current research on Kazakhstan and the new trends in the social sciences that structure this research. It hopes to partly fill the gap by proposing new interpretative frameworks to study the current evolution of Kazakhstan around three main issues: the state, the nation, and the society. It is based on a conference organized in June 2014 by The George Washington University's Central Asia Program and the Uppsala Center for Russian and Eurasian Studies (UCRS) and funded by Riksbankens Jubileumsfond (RJ).

The first section of the volume addresses "the state" in Kazakhstan and offers four different approaches to comprehend how the Kazakhstani regime functions and legitimizes itself. Kazakhstan has been defined by Edward Schatz as an example of "soft authoritarianism" —compared to the "harder" regimes of Uzbekistan, Turkmenistan and, now Tajikistan. "The cement of soft authoritarian rule is an elite's ability to frame political debate, thereby defining the political agenda and channeling political outcomes. Soft authoritarianism relies more centrally on the means of persuasion than on the means of coercion, although coercion remains a part of the ruling elite's arsenal."[1] For Schatz, the regime functions thanks to the existence of a committed core of Nazarbayev supporters among the elites, the ability to mobilize the broader population thanks to enticements (a perceptible rise in living standards) and blackmail (the risk of losing the acquired wealth and stability), the occasional harassing and selective coercion of opposition groups, and managing information flows by preempting the emergence of competitive narratives. This section's chapters offer new explorations of these soft authoritarianism tools.

Assel Tutumlu offers a compelling analytical framework of authoritarian stability by analyzing how the Kazakhstani regime manages its rent revenues and balances predatory activities of the elites and the redistribution of social welfare benefits to the broader population. Specifically, she looks at how private pension funds were restructured into a single pension fund under state control in 2013. In the case of pension reform, the Kazakhstani authorities found solutions to the regime's three main dilemmas: balancing property rights and investment opportunities; financial credibility and debt repayment; and administrative discipline and information transparency. President Nazarbayev's decision-making process on pension reform shows that he had to take into consideration these three dilemmas and to walk a fine line between satisfying the population and accommodating the elites in order to keep them loyal to the regime.

The second chapter in this section, by Sebastien Peyrouse, analyzes the intra-elite level and investigates the regime's ability to master a subtle balance among three main interest groups: members of the presidential family, oligarchs, and technocrats. not only preventing one from dominating the others but as the arbiter of the "game" among these groups, avoiding one to dominate the others, but also distributing incentives and punishments. Over the decades, this equilibrium has been re-adjusted several times, with some family members repressed, some oligarchs dispossessed of their business empires, and technocrats promoted or obstructed in their career. As in Russia, the country faced, in the 2000s, a recentralization process under the Samruk-Kazyna sovereign fund, but it has now been forced to initiate a new wave of privatization and neoliberal measures in order to cope with the current economic crisis. The system established by the authorities seems fairly insulated from the country's economic ups and downs in terms of regulating the intra-elite competition, but this does not mean that it can manage easily the growing distrust of society on some specific issues such as land reform, the benefits of Eurasian Economic Union membership, and protecting the population from the current economic decline.

Conventional political science, which looks at institutions, elites, and explicit ideologies, is often excessively focused on a top-down logic and therefore misses a central aspect of the legitimacy question, that is, the interaction between the state and its citizens. Anthropology and cultural studies complement this missing layer of our analysis by focusing on the micro-level, on the informal, the implicit, the unsaid, and by looking at bottom-up phenomena.

In this framework, Mateusz Laszczkowski investigates how the erection of Astana as a fairy-tale city, marked by a futuristic urban landscape built from scratch and saturated with symbolism, creates a new space for state-society interaction in which citizens not only consent to domination, but internalize the symbols of domination. Defining this phenomenon as "magical authoritarianism," Laszczkowski addresses the quasi-religious charisma attributed to the figure of Nursultan Nazarbayev, often given almost supranatural powers, and the multiple implicit and non-textual registers that speak to the population. He thus demonstrates the level of sophistication that the authorities had to master in building legitimacy tools, probably a critical element to explain not only the durability, but also the popularity of Nazarbayev's regime and its personification of the nation.

Wendell Schwab and Ulan Bigozhin explore another aspect of the state construction in Kazakhstan, moving the cursor from the overstudied urban world to understudied rural regions. At the local level, legitimacy mechanisms are embedded in in-situ hierarchies of notables and share with the national level a relatively similar neopatrimonial logic, shaped by patron-client relationships. However, contrary to the national level, legitimacy at the local level does not rely on the futuristic fairy-tale narrative symbolized by Astana, but on more traditional codes often linked to Islam. Based on the case of the creation of a new shrine in a small city of southern Kazakhstan, Schwab and Bigozhin demonstrate how much the secular everyday space and the religious one are intimately articulated: as citizens use connections to find a patron—in that case to acquire the land where the supposed grave of a holy man is located—the same way God is to be addressed through a holy patron. The holiness of the shrine is validated not in the name of any kind of scripturalist reading of Islam but by the experiences of the shrine's "clients," who confirm that the holy man is a good patron for the community. The ability of state structures and civil servants to navigate the parallel interpretations of patronage, both political and religious, embeds state legitimacy into the social fabric.

Part two of this volume is devoted to the "nation" as an imagined community to be built by a mutually reinforcing process between the state and the elite on one side, and society on the other. Here also, dynamics are both top-down and bottom-up.

Diana T. Kudaibergenova offers a comparative study of Kazakhstan and Latvia, the two post-Soviet countries, aside from Russia, with the highest share of ethnic Russians in the population. She analyzes their two largely diverging trajectories in nation-building: while Latvia offers a more democratic political framework than Kazakhstan, Kazakhstani elites remain more flexible in shaping the national identity of the new state. By defining Latvian elites as nationalist elites, for whom ideology matters, and Kazakhstani elites as nationalizing ones, Kudaibergenova fruitfully demonstrates how nation-building is context-dependent and used by decision-makers as a tool to consolidate power, marginalize competitive elites, and get popular support. In the Kazakhstani case, the fact that the elites display inconsistent nationalization policies can be explained by the relationship to Russia and the need to pacify the Russian minority, but also by neopatrimonial mechanisms and the role of the informal in "making" politics.

Alexander Diener continues this discussion by examining the Kazakhstani narrative elaborated by the state since the early days of independence. Even if this Kazakhstani identity competes with the Kazakh one, and the authorities use both narratives depending on their audience, the Kazakhstani story has been the dominant scheme offered to the country's ethnic minorities and to the international community. This willingness to promote a civic-based patriotism has been constructed on several elements: obviously economic success and a developmental ideology, but also a patriotism based on the Soviet legacy of the "friendship of peoples," attachment to place and to the "small motherland" (*malaia rodina*), and the embodiment of the state by the president—Nazarbayev as father of the nation and protector of interethnic concord. However, difficulties in maintaining an easy and fast economic prosperity and the ongoing preparation for a post-Nazarbayev era could potentially jeopardize this Kazakhstani identity and the ethnic minorities' identification with it, and open the door to a shift into the state's identity narrative.

Marlene Laruelle's chapter complements the two previous ones by shedding light on the existence of a Kazakh ethno-nationalist landscape that, largely unsuccessful against Nazarbayev's ability to co-opt the narrative of nationhood and personify it, is nonetheless growing among younger generations. New networks of young activists, using social media platforms and navigating a rising Kazakh-speaking information space, has been able to alter the broader atmosphere in Kazakhstan. They scored successes with the Ukrainian crisis and Kazakhstan's accession to the Eurasian Economic Union and can rely on the social anxieties related to land reform and the fear of agricultural "colonization" by China. Their re-emergence after almost two decades of marginalization exemplifies the cultural and social transformations ongoing in the country in terms of language, relationship to the Soviet past, generational change, and the rural–urban divide. In the near future, Kazakhstan's "Kazakhness" will probably be the most dynamic identity trend to be incorporated, in one way or another, into state policies and could potentially challenge the political status quo.

In the last chapter of this section, Natalie R. Koch and Kristopher D. White help us deconstruct the essentialist framework of a Kazakh society shaped by "clan" divisions. Instead, they offer the notion of a specific regional identity, that of Southern Kazakhstan, as a sociocultural divide and a geographical imaginary. Through focus groups they decipher the process of "internal othering" and the structuring of culturally coded clichés—mostly stigmatizing, even if they may also display some positive criteria—about Shymkent, often described as Kazakhstan's "Texas."

The book's third section investigates the deep social and cultural changes ongoing in Kazakhstan. Largely open to the world, thirsty for international recognition and signs of success in globalization, but also shaped by profound re-configurations of both the urban and the rural social fabric, Kazakhstani society has been evolving over the last two decades, more so than the regime's apparent stability allows us to see. It formed a specific brand that combines cultural borrowings from abroad and calls for preserving national authenticity, an ongoing quest for modernity *and* for ancient-ness, for secularity *and* for religiosity.

Alima Bissenova addresses the subtle interplay between secular and religious authorities in finding shared interests and narratives that allow each to complement the other and avoid ideological competition or even distrust. By studying daily life, Friday prayers, and sermons at the Haziret Sultan mosque, the main mosque of Astana, she explores the birth of a "bourgeois Islam," adapted to the emerging middle classes, that presents itself as the "good" Islam, inculcating values that both the secular and the religious authorities validate. This Haziret Sultan brand can be defined as a successful combination of traditional Islamic orthodoxy, recognition by the world's *Ummah*, national traditions that shape "Kazakhness," and the state's efforts to modernize and advance the individual.

In her chapter, Megan Rancier delves into another aspect of the Kazakhstani society's will to merge symbols of traditions and modernity, the "Spirit of Tengri" music festival. The festival offers a unique insight into multiple ongoing processes of hybridization: reviving supposed traditional music and instruments, globalizing them into the trend of world ethnic music, making the final products marketable, etc. The "Spirit of Tengri" embodies the ability of some segments of Kazakhstani society to reap the benefits of the country's openness and to promote a new cosmopolitanism in tune with the quest for national identity. Indeed, the "Spirit of Tengri" offers a fascinating combination of local and global—glocalism—thanks to its reference to Turkicness:

this regional level, symbolized by the bands coming from across the Turkic world and by the reference to Tengri, the sky, a symbol of the pre-Islamic religion of the Turkic-Mongolian populations, allows participants to refer to the nation-state and at the same time to bypass it.

Last, but not least, Doug Blum concludes this book by exploring how the young generation of Kazakhstani citizens who has been trained abroad, specifically in the United States, manages the cultural changes that accompany a stay far from home. Their repertoire of normalcy, both in terms of values and social practices, relates to gender issues, body language, family and community ties, had to face important shifts. Each individual offers a unique combination of what he/she considers as attractive and offensive in the foreign culture, and what can be brought back home and adapted to local norms and values. This negotiation is a permanent one, sometimes successful, in terms of individual empowerment, but sometimes failing when people believe cultural borrowings will be rejected by their native environment. Blum's cultural anthropology approach allows us to move forward into the discussion about the so-called Bolashak generation—the thousands of young Kazakhs trained abroad thanks to the state-sponsored Bolashak scholarship program—and to move the cursor from the macro level—what will be the influence of this generation once they get the reins of power—to the micro one, showing the need for long and sometimes painful adjustments of cultural values and norms in Kazakhstan's fast-changing society.

NOTE

1. Edward Schatz, "The Soft Authoritarian Tool Kit: Agenda-Setting Power in Kazakhstan and Kyrgyzstan," *Comparative Politics* 41, no. 2 (2009): 203.

Part I

THE STATE: RULING MECHANISMS AND SYMBOLS

Chapter 1

The Rule by Law

Negotiating Stability in Kazakhstan

Assel Tutumlu

Multiple theories of authoritarian persistence have attempted to explain the durability of President Nursultan Nazarbayev's regime in Kazakhstan. Some attribute this success to economic growth and relatively large revenues from mineral rents.[1] Others claim that Nazarbayev's ability to mediate differences among clans and his capacity to keep "the house in order" have made him indispensable.[2] Lastly, some scholars point to Nazarbayev's ability to sideline potential opponents through electoral manipulation, leaving him the only viable candidate.[3] But not many scholars are able to explain the process of authoritarian stability. They fail to answer the question of how the authoritarian regime in Kazakhstan remains durable in both good and bad times. What logic drives the mechanism of political stability? How exactly does Nazarbayev negotiate and maintain control over his political position? This chapter provides an analytical framework of authoritarian stability. Authoritarian stability is a situation in which the same nondemocratic ruler stays in power regardless of the electoral law and relative domestic peace is maintained through the consent of the elites and population in economic booms and busts.[4] Although the framework can be applied to other countries, this chapter illustrates the workings of authoritarian rule through an in-depth analysis of the single case.

In order to proceed with the framework, this chapter makes a caveat that the framework applies only to regimes that govern through rule *by* law rather than those that govern through the rule *of* law.[5] These two terms identify modes of governing in neopatrimonial and developmental states respectively. Developmental states are those that are able to guide economic reforms by being the "rulemaker, rule monitor, and rule enforcer of first or last resort."[6] Developmental states are characterized by governance based on the rule of law in an authoritarian political setting. These regimes build political stability by ensuring strong economic performance and growth that is based on the equal application of fair and transparent procedure. Developmental states share strict discipline, indiscriminate application of regulations, and transparency in all three realms of law—making, monitoring, and enforcement. Bureaucratic discipline is derived from the fact that the government subjects itself to its own laws and abides by them. Rule of law ensures effective penalization of those officials and businesses that circumvent government regulations.

Japan in the 1980s, with strong power wielded by the Ministry of International Trade and Industry (MITI), is a good example of a developmental state. MITI's officials were able to ensure that laws regarding private property rights, government financial credibility, and administrative discipline all work toward economic growth and industrialization.[7] Rule of law ensured that government officials distributed property rights in a fair and transparent manner and that the government consistently managed financial resources without running into unsustainable debt. In addition, the rule of law enabled a transparent flow of information and smooth implementation of regulations from the top to the bottom of the government hierarchy. In practice, the rule of law enabled MITI officials to enforce their regulations by using subsidies and other forms of state support to fulfill the goals of economic development, industrialization, and growth and to reward competitive actors. In developmental Japan, formal laws were created, monitored, and enforced by regulators who were also subjects of these laws.

In neopatrimonial regimes, formal laws reflect the interests of small group(s) of elites that control government institutions in order to promote their personal interests, rather than public goods.[8] In these states, the authoritarian regime manipulates law as it deems fit. Law becomes an instrument used by the political regime to advance limited personal interests and to exempt the regime from its own set of regulations. Known as "rule *by* law," the concept depicts a situation in which the authoritarian regime stands above the law and arbitrarily applies regulations to fulfill political goals.[9] Law is made by the government, but selectively monitored and selectively enforced. Under such circumstances, formal law exists, but political and economic actors can never be certain when rules will be applied to them and when they will be spared from law enforcement.[10] This uncertainty enables the heads of authoritarian regimes to maintain their position above formal law and to invoke its principles whenever it is convenient. Thus, political stability in a neopatrimonial regime is ensured by balancing the relative power of the regime vis-à-vis the population and groups of elites in the country. Kazakhstan is a good example of a neopatrimonial state because uncertainly of law necessitates President Nazarbayev's continued grip on power to arbitrate and enforce regulations. By using law to its own advantage, the regime is able to award loyalists and punish anyone who might defy the regime.

Three major problems of governance result from uncertainty. First, uncertain application of law causes uncertainty in private property rights, because the regime can always accuse businesses and politicians who conceal their violations of formal regulations. Second, rule by law undermines a government's financial credibility since law can always be changed in a matter of days; for example, there is no long-term commitment to disciplined fiscal policy. Third, rule by law impedes administrative discipline because officials prefer to enrich themselves quickly, knowing that they can be arbitrarily fired, rather than building long-lasting administrative careers. Officials prey on businesses by using their political authority to extort financial benefits. Such activities are protected at each level of the government hierarchy by superiors who benefit from the predatory activities of their employees. If the regime wants to remain in power, it needs to carefully balance each of the governance problems (i.e., distribution of property rights, financial credibility, and administrative discipline) in a way that keeps groups of elites loyal and ordinary people content with the existing regime.

This chapter uses pension reform in Kazakhstan to illustrate an analytical framework of authoritarian stability. Pension reform is a good example: in August 2013 the state consolidated retirement funds from ten private institutions into a single government holding in order to access financial resources and distribute them among loyalist elites. It also freed key banks, owned by the loyalists, from subsidizing unprofitable pension funds. It ensured access to accurate information about the amount of money available in the funds and investment portfolios of each private entity, thus maintaining administrative discipline within the regime. Lastly, it assured people that their savings would be paid since the state guaranteed the safety of the money in their accounts.

FRAMEWORK OF AUTHORITARIAN STABILITY IN KAZAKHSTAN

It has been long noted that the standard distinction between authoritarianism and democracy does not provide us with adequate knowledge about the stability or persistence of various political regimes.[11] Instead, much of the recent literature has concentrated on studying institutions and patterns of governance in order to understand regime types and the nature of both authoritarian and democratic regimes. Specifically, institutional research has noted the peculiarities of rentier states, states that derive their revenues from rents, that is, revenues that governments get from manipulating access to public property. Unlike taxes, rent income creates incentives for governments to develop neopatrimonial regimes with strong patronage networks, clans, and crony capitalism.[12] The majority of this literature shows how elites capture economic benefits by controlling political power.[13] Rents have been linked to authoritarian persistence because money is spent on lawenforcement and security services that stifle dissent.[14] Rents have also been linked to corrupt distribution of public resources that enhance business dependency on political institutions. Furthermore, the lack of solidarity among civil society groups undermines the possibility of political change.[15]

Institutional research that relies on a neopatrimonial perspective reveals the importance of informal modes of elite recruitment and an incentive structure that rewards privilege and wealth over merit and professionalism.[16] For example, scholars show the hidden play of patron-client relationships between and within clans and interest groups, and how their under-the-table deals put pressure on economic growth and legitimacy.[17] This scholarship shows that formal laws distort the informal incentive structure that either consolidate or undermine authoritarian political system.[18] Although the description of the interplay between formal and informal laws is useful, it does not provide us with a systematic understanding of how and why the incentive structure works and persists over time. It gives us a broad but static picture of power organization and describes mechanisms that are used to sustain the regime in power without dynamism and/or any explanation of how the regime maintains power in both good and bad times.

Scholars who investigate patterns of governance in order to analyze how political regimes work have concentrated on studying how authoritarian regimes think about society and markets, looking into assumptions and theories that inform governmental policies. In my earlier work with Laura Adams, I identified two modes of governmentality in Central Asia. Specifically, the authoritarian regime in Kazakhstan has adopted a managerial, that is neoliberal, style of governance, whereas Uzbekistan followed a paternalistic, ordoliberal path that loosely resembles the governance values of European welfare states in the 1970s.[19] The governance perspective provides a comprehensive rationale behind the reform's design, an understanding of the scope and scale of government reform, and expected results. However, in practice, laws that have been written with much clarity and determination are not implemented according to their original mandate. In addition, local bureaucrats frequently subvert the reforms and find ways to escape the monitoring process. Regardless of these practices, the political regime remains stable since everyone benefits from the existing system. The regime derives domestic and international legitimacy in its discourse and, together with bureaucrats, extorts revenue from businesses in exchange for rents and bribes. People who work for these enterprises are also interested in securing employment and therefore support the existing system. However, similar to an institutional analysis of neopatrimonialism, governance and governmentality scholarship prevent us from understanding the dynamic nature of authoritarian persistence by offering an overall perspective on how the system works.

Instead, this chapter offers an additional view on authoritarian stability by concentrating on the dilemmas of governance and how authoritarian regimes deal with challenges to their political and economic stability. This chapter does not discount the importance of institutional or governance approaches, but rather seeks ways to complement existing research by analytically adding dynamism to the authoritarian exercise of power. In order to do so, this study first borrows from the literature on how authoritarian regimes avoid crisis points to theorize stability during bad times. Second, it relies on the rule by law scholarship to investigate ways that regimes solve challenges to authoritarian stability. Both bodies of scholarship are useful because they outline the main dilemmas of governance in nondemocratic regimes that are derived from balancing the predatory activities of the elites with the distribution of social welfare benefits to the broader population.

Neil Robinson's insight—that stability depends on the regime's ability to avoid the crisis point—is extremely fruitful for the research question. Robinson starts with the assumption that authoritarian regimes can collapse when their revenues are lower than the costs.[20] Robinson exemplified the crisis point with the formula of Revenues ≥ Costs, in which Costs consist of the amount of money needed to maintain loyalty of the clients (P) + the amount needed to maintain basic state functions (S) must be less than Revenue, which consists of the amount that can be appropriated by a neopatrimonial regime domestically (R) and borrowed internationally (C).[21]

$$\text{STABILITY} = (R + C) \geq (P + S)$$

Both the population and the bureaucrats need to be kept happy if the regime wants to stay in power. For example, if the budget is unbalanced due to the lack of rents and taxes and/or due to the inability to borrow capital abroad, then the ruler might face serious challenges from citizens who might be unhappy with the existing situation or from loyalists who may believe that their property are threatened and shift their allegiance to another candidate. With the crisis point in mind, regimes must constantly seek to balance between the interests of the people and the interests of loyalists, since both camps can present formidable challenges to the incumbent ruler. This understanding of the neopatrimonial structure and vulnerabilities also highlights that economic and political powers are merged within the regime. The political and economic stability of the regime depends on balancing the crisis point.

In the case of Kazakhstan, revenues for the neopatrimonial regime come from rents, taxes, and informal rollover (*otkat*),[22] as well as international loans that governments and affiliated businesses borrow utilizing sovereign guarantees. Revenue comes from two main sources: (a) businesses and individuals that pay taxes and rents and (b) businesses and individuals that benefit from subsidies as clients of specific bureaucratic officials in exchange for rollovers and that have permission to borrow abroad using government guarantees. This revenue has to cover the costs, that is the amount of money necessary to retain the loyalty of clients and provide minimal state functions; thereby satisfying both groups that could challenge authoritarian ruler. Costs in neopatrimonial regimes consist of (a) the expense of basic state functions, such as education, healthcare, defense, and other forms of public goods and (b) privileges and rewards for the loyalists, that is top-level bureaucrats who have the capacity to shift allegiance and support another political candidate. In other words, the stability of the authoritarian neopatrimonial regime of Kazakhstan is threatened when the regime's expenses exceed its revenues. When that occurs, either the people protest against the regime for failing to provide basic state functions or the loyalists from atop the bureaucracy rebel and start to form an opposition.

Once we have a framework for how stability is achieved and maintained, studies that analyze authoritarian persistence from the perspective of the rule by law become useful. To date, the rule by law literature has been mostly applied to the study of courts and judiciary politics in nondemocratic regimes to outline the dilemmas of stable governance. Specifically, this literature identifies three main dilemmas. The first deals with securing property rights and investment opportunities. Specifically, authoritarian regimes need to strike a balance between securing property rights against bureaucratic predation to ensure investment opportunities and economic growth while, at the same time, maintaining loyalty by selectively preying on private property rights and redistributing possessed assets among other elites.[23] In other words, political regimes need to assure investors and local businesses that their capital and business operations are secure, while simultaneously assuring loyalists that their status privileges and rewards are continuously expanded. If the regime fails to convince investors of the inviolability of their property rights, economic production and growth will halt—undermining the political stability of the regime. If the regime fails to convince loyalists that their neopatrimonial networks and privileges are secured, it may experience significant political perturbations, which may undermine the political stability of the regime. If we look back to the crisis point formula, the first dilemma depicts a number of ways that authoritarian stability might be challenged by loyalists on one side (P) or by people who may demand basic public functions (S), such as a guarantee of private property rights. In short, growing costs over revenues may destabilize the regime.

The second dilemma deals with the financial credibility of the regime and debt repayment. Specifically, the dilemma comes from the fact that authoritarian regimes that depend on rent constantly need to prove financial credibility to their investors because revenue from natural resources is highly unstable; thus the regime needs to protect domestic currency from financial fluctuations. Frequent changes in exchange rates impede the production process and the export of local products, including natural resources. Slow economic activities undermine authoritarian stability as the regime's revenues dwindle when international commodity prices are low. Low revenues create challenges from the population who may not be satisfied with the provision of public goods and/or the loyalists who would be unhappy with stagnant rewards for their political loyalty and support. As a result, the rulers are frequently borrowing money abroad or tapping into the resource revenues banked for a "rainy day" in a special fund. When prices are low, regimes can keep a stable exchange rate and prop up weak local currency values to make exports profitable and keep the population happy, while plugging state budget gaps with international credit. The rulers face particularly strong challenges to their authority when commodity prices are low and debt is high. In these circumstances, both the population and the loyalists may revolt to the growing costs over revenues.

The third dilemma deals with administrative discipline and information transparency.[24] Due to its very structure of authority, an authoritarian regime does not have adequate information about the behavior of officials in the lower ranks of state. Since every head of a government office appoints subordinates through corrupt practices (which may include the sale of office for a bribe or nepotistic appointments), they are interested in ensuring that their offices perform well on paper. As a result, when every boss covers up the corrupt dealings of their staff members, the authoritarian ruler progressively loses power at each level of government; central authorities cannot control and enforce discipline due to the lack of information and knowledge about local officials. Rife corruption may destroy social benefits, so the population may be willing to challenge the regime. On the other hand, enforcement may weaken the political support of loyalists who benefit from corrupt practices. As a result, the political stability of the regime depends on the ruler's ability to balance the situation in a way that selectively enforces the law to please the population and sets an example for other government officials without changing the structure of the system. In other words, by using rule by law, the regime selectively punishes officials to please the population while leaving most bureaucrats untouched.

By concentrating on dilemmas that challenge authoritarian regimes and on the ways regimes use rule by law to negotiate political stability, we will be able to achieve a better explanation of authoritarian persistence and hone the predictive capacity of regime durability by utilizing the proposed analytical framework. We expect the regime to maintain the balance between loyalists and the population by strategically distributing resources between the two groups. In times of crisis, we expect the regime to adopt two-pronged policies that can benefit both groups, rather than favoring one group over another.

Kazakhstan is a good case for testing this analytical framework because it is both neopatrimonial as well as rent-seeking. Although a much more robust study is necessary to show management of political stability throughout the twenty-four years of the regime, nonetheless, in order to show the mechanism of the framework, this chapter concentrates on a single case and evaluates the regime's activities in regard to restructuring private pension funds. Private pension funds have been banned; instead, the government pooled assets into a single state-controlled fund, the money of which sponsors domestic investments.

NEOPATRIMONIALISM IN KAZAKHSTAN

Every scholar of Kazakhstan has his or her own list of elite groups. Some scholars divide Kazakhstani elites based on their tribal affiliations.[25] Others prefer to divide the elites by their regional origin.[26] The most fruitful description of the elites comes from identifying the assets they own and the specific financial industrial groups (FIGs) they are affiliated with.[27] FIGs' assets are either controlled by Kazakhstani government officials and their affiliates or belong to foreign investors who work in the country with the permission of President Nazarbayev and his immediate associates, a circle of friends and family. Most of the FIGs are involved in extracting natural resources or providing services for the extractive industries. In exchange, Nazarbayev's regime receives formal and informal rents, stock shares, and taxes from these corporations. Although Nazarbayev's regime is the biggest beneficiary, the government officials who obtain tax revenues to pay for their projects and the people who receive salaries and employment through these arrangements do indeed support the neopatrimonial structure of the economy.

There are two key characteristics that make Kazakhstan neopatrimonial. First, governance in Kazakhstan is conducted in the interest of the few existing FIGs. Rather than seeing the process as a one-way street with the government giving orders to corporations, Nazarbayev's political regime understands the value of the "geese that lay golden eggs"; that is the extraction of natural resources, which includes both solid and liquid minerals. So the regime is engaged in providing the necessary legal framework and friendly environment for large extractive companies. For example, in 2013 the Eurasian Natural Resources Group (ENRC) faced a series of crises related to accusations of fraud and the resulting flight of most of its top officials.[28] In order to avoid criminal prosecution, ENRC's owners had to urgently delist company's shares from London Stock Exchange by buying back shares worth $6 billion. Since the government of Kazakhstan owned over 11 percent of the shares in the original company, it indirectly provided ENRC with funding that enabled company officials to escape criminal charges in the United Kingdom.[29] It is possible to consider this favor as a *quid pro quo* response to large corporate social responsibility expenses and substantial contributions to Nazarbayev's electoral campaigns throughout the years. In any case, the law was used to protect interests of FIGs in order to ensure their loyalty.

Second, the regime in Kazakhstan transfers control over large portions of the market to FIGs through preferential treatment. Large corporations that enjoy monopolistic status or oligopolistic competition (those that hold unrestricted control over domestic market share, helping them to occupy leading economic positions globally) are capable of providing stronger political and economic support. Thus, smaller domestic producers fail to compete with the global giants that are acquiring a growing number of Kazakhstani enterprises. For example, in 2005 the China National Petroleum Corporation acquired PetroKazakhstan with relatively mature fields, but the deal also gave it immediate control of 12 percent of the overall oil production in Kazakhstan.[30] It managed to enhance sixty-eight wells and keep the production rate at over 3.2 million tons by compensating with extraction from newly developed fields.[31] Overall, in 2008 Chinese companies already owned more than 11 percent of new deposits in Kazakhstan.[32] For Kazakhstan, it is easier to transfer property from smaller companies to bigger ones because it is easier to control a smaller number of large economic actors and to manage their potential conflicts. In turn, FIGs seek political stability and prefer to support the incumbent regime. In addition, FIGs have more investment capabilities, as well as distribution and global marketing networks that enable the smooth delivery of extracted resources to international markets. Property transfers are not inherently illegal and can take place within the legal structure. The regime may opt to nationalize enterprises due to alleged "violations of environmental regulations," only to be sold to bigger entities, or they could decide to grant preferential sales terms for the newly discovered fields. In both cases, the state violates private property rights in order to gain larger benefits.

However, the regime must keep control over social policies and labor security if it wants to continue to operate. With the exception of Samruk-Kazyna (protests took place in its subsidiaries), the ten largest corporations, in terms of production volume,[33] have experienced a growing number of labor protests and conflicts over salaries and safety records in the past five years.[34] Labor protests have also inspired national patriots to call for the nationalization of domestic industries, political sovereignty, and opposition to the Eurasian Economic Union with Russia and Belarus.[35] Although the regime has managed to impose strict punishment for instigating protests without prior approval by the government, tensions remain. In addition, in places where mineral deposits are reaching depletion, FIGs prefer to cancel production and move to other sectors, leaving workers and their families unemployed, stuck with large unpaid loans, and no prospects for the future. In order to prevent large-scale unemployment in geographically restricted and densely populated areas, Nazarbayev's regime must work with FIGs to negotiate their slow withdrawal and larger contribution into the social welfare.

Resource-rich Kazakhstan can be characterized as a neopatrimonial state with an economy dominated by FIGs that mainly derive their income from extractive resources and the service industries that facilitate their operations. However, the regime must also keep the population happy. In order to avoid reaching a crisis point, the regime first needs to negotiate property rights for the population and investment opportunities for loyalists. Second, the regime needs to negotiate financial credibility and repay its own debt. Third, the regime needs to ensure administrative discipline and access to accurate information. These three dilemmas provide us with an understanding of the context of authoritarian regimes. Authoritarian stability depends on the regime's capacity to solve these dilemmas. Rule by law is a way of negotiating authoritarian stability among the three dilemmas.

AUTHORITARIAN STABILITY: PENSION REFORM IN KAZAKHSTAN

In order to show how authoritarian regimes remain stable, I will examine the 2013 pension reform in Kazakhstan. Pension reform consisted of two parts. First, the government increased the retirement age for women from 58 to 63 years of age. The increase will take place over the span of ten years, gradually raising the retirement age by six months each year. Second, the government merged ten private pension funds into a single state-run entity. Before the reform, Kazakhstan had eleven pension funds with total capitalization of approximately €16.3 billion or about 11 percent of the GDP. Of these, ten private funds controlled about 80 percent of the total assets (see Table 1.1). As of January 1, 2013, around half of the population of Kazakhstan, or 8.4 million people, had contributed money to these pension funds. Most of the funds were established by the largest banks in the country. Most assets were invested domestically into safe government bonds. Eight out of the ten pension funds were established by banks. Banks are closely affiliated with FIGs, which were created to sponsor their financial activities.

However, private pension funds were losing money. The government prevented private pension funds from investing in risky assets, but the return rate

Table 1.1 Pension Funds in Kazakhstan Before Unification in 2013

Name of Fund	*Affiliation/Primary Shareholder*	*Capitalization (€)*	*Ownership*	*Links to Nazarbayev's Regime*
Astana	Sberbank	1 billion	Russian Federation	President's son-in law is member of the Board of Directors
PF of Halyk Bank	Halyk Bank	3.4 billion	Presidential Family	Daughter and son-in-law of Nazarbayev
GNPF, State National Pension Fund	Central Bank	16.3 billion	Government officials	Reports to the President
Grantum	Kazkom Bank	1.3 billion	Individuals + Samruk Kazyna National Welfare Fund	Government officials owned stocks after the bailout from financial crisis in 2010
Kapital	CenterCredit Bank	23 million	Individual + Kookmin Bank (South Korea)	
Otan	Altyn Zharnama + Individuals	10 million	Individuals	
UlarUmit	BTA Bank	64 million	Samruk-Kazyna National Welfare Fund	Government Officials acquired after bankruptcy and debt restructuring
Neftegas-Dem	Aktobe-Munai Finance + Individuals	12 million	Individuals	
Respublika	Tsesna Bank + Individuals	10.7 million		Owners: brother and son of the former Secretary of State
Atameken	Nur Bank	15 million	Presidential Family	Owners: another daughter and grand-son of the President
PF BTA	BTA Bank	47.7 million	Samruk-Kazyna National Welfare Fund	Government officials acquired after bankruptcy and debt restructuring

Sources: Kazakhstan Stock Exchange, www.kase.kz

on government bonds was far below inflation. As a result, funds began to seek regulatory changes by either requesting an increase in mandatory contributions, increasing pension age, or offering to relax regulations to allow more aggressive participation in international financial markets.

Government support for the pension reform and its implementation reflects three dilemmas that authoritarian regime needs to solve to create stability. First, the reform has to carefully balance property rights, that is the population's savings, with investment opportunities for loyalists and affiliated FIGs. Second, successful reform also has to reflect economic solvency. If the regime decides to use pensions as a source of domestic investment, it must ensure that the regime has enough financial credibility and control over the distribution of money into appropriate projects to make sure that funds are not only siphoned through corrupt mechanisms, but some of them translate into public goods. Third, in order to ensure implementation of the two components, the regime must balance the secrecy surrounding the informal asset distributions with access to adequate information and strong administrative discipline, which is difficult to have in a system where officials cover for each other's deeds because most are linked through personal ties.

To some observers, these dilemmas may represent a single process of ensuring policy implementation among multiple stakeholders, but each stage of the implementation requires a different set of skills and considerations. For example, it is possible to envision a combination of the first and second dilemmas being resolved in favor of the population, but without appropriate knowledge or control over asset distribution, the balance may tip in favor of the loyalists. Unfulfilled popular expectations may mobilize protests that threaten the stability of the regime. Similarly, if the regime conducts asset distributions in favor of the population but to the detriment of the loyalists, they may fight back and destabilize the political situation in Kazakhstan. Thus, the regime might offer loyalists additional investment opportunities in return for loyalty. In addition, the regime may not always experience all three dilemmas at the same time. Instead, government policy may address only one dilemma, depending on the specific circumstances. Thus, although the dilemmas may be seen as part of a single process, it is much more fruitful to keep them separate for greater analytical clarity.

The next section summarizes pension reform and then illustrates how the rule by law was applied to solve all three dilemmas.

Pension Reform and the Dilemmas

An accumulative model of pension funds was first introduced in 1998 and hailed as the most progressive retirement system in the post-Soviet space.[36] According to the new rules, the state no longer provided a public-defined benefit and, instead, asked every working citizen to provide for their own retirement during their employment years by reserving a mandatory contribution of 10 percent of their monthly salary. The reform was justified by the growing arrears (equal to over a 50 percent deficit) in the state pension fund, because businesses preferred to employ people informally, that is, outside of official payroll, to avoid mandatory payments. Illegally hired individuals also avoided paying extra money to the new State Pension Fund.[37] But legal employees had trouble making the contributions; the high inflation rate of 3,000 percent per year left little money for extra spending. Lastly, as 3 million people left Kazakhstan during the 1990s, every 100 workers had to sponsor 83 retirees, which was unsustainable. Furthermore, as many enterprises went bankrupt, the state hardly had money to cover social responsibilities.[38] By 1997 mass noncompliance caused a staggering KZT40 billion deficit ($530 million, KZT75.55 = $1 in 1997). The state decided to convert the solidarity system into an accumulative system with defined contributions. The model of the accumulative retirement system was borrowed from Chile, notorious for its pro-market reforms, after a government delegation visited the country in 1996.[39]

Besides establishing the State Pension Fund, the post-Soviet system allowed private actors to enter the market and provide asset management services, which by 2012 began to voice concerns over profitability and sustainability, particularly representatives of the National Bank of Kazakhstan, the Association of National Pension Funds, and Halyk Bank.[40] In order to stay active, the various funds had to invest in assets that outperformed the inflation and devaluation rates. Most of the funds were able to achieve impressive profit rates of 50 percent or more, but after the financial crisis of 2008, their gains began to decline.[41] As a result, critics complained about the strict regulation on where and how public money could be invested. Private owners showed that high inflation rates in the country "ate" most of the profits and that profit is only possible if the volume of mandatory contributions increased above 10 percent or if the retirement age is delayed.[42] As most of the money was invested in safe government-backed securities issued by the Kazakhstani state or bonds of national companies, the pension funds received relatively low or no returns depending on the macroeconomic situation of a particular year.[43] In order to profit, some of the funds used pension capital to sponsor affiliated businesses that invested in risky assets. These activities raised concerns over sustainability. Mismanagement of assets in many funds became apparent during the 2008 global financial crisis when contributors received statements showing negative balances for their accounts, and the government had to intervene with an indexing inflation coefficient and compensated some retirees for the investment losses.[44] Senator Omarkhan Oksikbayev publically stated that pension funds have more than KZT1 billion belonging to no one.[45] The minister of labor at that time also confirmed the statement and announced that more than 750,000 accounts were unused as employers had never transferred the money to these individuals.[46] Lastly, private funds took large commissions, as much as 15 percent on investment returns, swallowing 0.6 percent of income per year.[47] So despite somewhat lucrative opportunities, long-term macroeconomic indicators started to worry pension fund managers.

Dilemma 1: Private Property vs. Investment Opportunities

The new system had to balance the safety of retirement contributions with investment opportunities for the loyalists. The regime began by increasing the retirement age for women from 58 to 63 years, together with a significant decrease in the amount of social support provided for infants and new mothers.[48] Before the pension funds were combined, the regime felt already constrained by the fact that the population might feel dissatisfied with Nazarbayev's reforms. So when the government decided to merge pension funds into a single government-controlled entity with the potential of distributing assets worth around 11 percent of GDP, it had to carefully guarantee that retirement contributions would remain safe, but also that former pension funds have new investment opportunities.[49]

Obviously, FIGs did not want to see their pension funds taken by the government. So President Nazarbayev personally intervened and publically enforced the decision to restructure the country's pension system by July 1, 2013.[50] By resorting to rule by law, Nazarbayev's regime left no exemptions from participation for any group and enforced universal compliance. As a result, the regime adopted the reform despite social protests and resistance among FIGs as government officials hurried to provide adequate corrections in formal laws and as FIGs began negotiating the deals. In return, the largest of the eleven funds was offered buy-out schemes. For example, Grantum's assets were transferred to the government in exchange for shares of Kazkommertsbank (Kazkom), which the government had owned since the financial bailout in 2010. UlarUmit merged with State National Pension Fund (GNPF) and then joined the new State Accumulative Pension Fund (SAPF).[51] Now with the majority of assets in state hands, the government pressured smaller operators into joining SAPF by imposing deadlines.[52] However, the largest pension fund, Pension Fund of Halyk Bank, refused the government's buy-out schemes. Halyk Bank representatives did not want to acquire shares of BTA bank nor did they want to acquire three smaller banks in exchange for its pension fund. Instead, its managers wanted government compensation for the transfer of its assets. By November 2013, negotiations continued, with the government formally refusing to pay for the pension fund.[53] Halyk, which managed $7.8 billion in assets, agreed to transfer shares without government compensation. However, it recovered investments of KZT40 billion ($2.8 billion), which it paid as dividends to shareholders a year later.[54] Details of the mergers and negotiations over asset swaps rarely come under public scrutiny. Suffice it to say that although July 1, 2013, was set as an official deadline for SAPF, Halyk Bank transferred its assets in December 2014 when its operating license was finally revoked.[55]

In 2014, the SAPF appropriated $23 billion by merging the funds into a single entity.[56] The merger, enforced by the public decision of President Nazarbayev enabled the government to get control over public retirement savings while compensating the FIGs for asset transfers.

Dilemma 2: Financial Credibility and Debt Repayment

The regime had to decide how the pensions would be distributed and where they would be deposited in the interim. In order to answer this question, the regime had to walk a fine line between providing financial credibility to its investment projects while at the same time ensuring that pensions would be paid regardless of economic growth or future financial crises. So the regime decided not to invest public money abroad after seeing the devastating effects of the 2008 financial crisis, and the subsequent sovereign debt crisis in Europe proved to Nazarbayev that international investment into what seemed to be reliable government bonds could lose value in a matter of days. In addition, Kazakhstani economic growth rates have slowed down due to the low international prices on primary commodities and the shortage of credit for local enterprises. So there was an urgent need for liquidity in the domestic economy.

Nazarbayev, again, resorted to the rule by law and unilaterally declared that pensions must work for the benefit of the domestic economy and cover its needs. Investments in local infrastructure and industrialization projects are to provide the foundations for the development of the Kazakhstani economy and guarantee stability of return. Funds, according to Nazarbayev, should also be used to support small- and medium-size businesses and entrepreneurs.[57] Both the population and loyalists were promised that they would benefit from new projects from domestic investments. So the government was tasked with solving the second dilemma of guaranteeing financial credibility to loyalists and FIGs and debt repayment to the population.

The government had major problem with financial credibility. Previously, it had dipped into the National Fund for $10 billion to bail out banks that had borrowed short-term loans abroad and invested the money into long-term projects, such as construction. However, the banks never replenished the

National Fund. After 2008, many banks were burdened by nonperforming loans. By using the Samruk-Kazyna National Fund,[58] the government body that manages state interests in all economic sectors, the government distributed $10 billion to BTA Bank, Alliance Bank, Halyk, and Kazkommerts Bank on the condition that the money would be returned from future profits. But slow economic growth in Kazakhstan's key exporting partners resulted in decreasing economic growth, which in 2013 reached 5 percent a year, down from around 7 percent 2 years before that. So the challenge was: how to make public money work to boost economic growth without raiding the National Fund. The regime could not afford to do the same with pension funds without stirring mass protests. The new investment projects had to have a solid economic rationale and protection against potential failures.

Nazarbayev ordered the government to invest in industrialization projects and infrastructure. The head of the National Bank at that time, Kairat Kelimbetov, proposed using the money to create a mixed investment portfolio that included government-backed bonds with a 6 percent yield. Corporate shares of domestic blue chips would constitute another part of the portfolio.[59] Although it is hard to find enterprises with profitability above 6 percent, Kelimbetov suggested that the rigorous review process would avoid the problems that private pension funds faced when they lost money by investing in affiliated businesses with weak performance criteria.[60] Other parts of money could be used for funding domestic industrialization and infrastructure projects. Many observers met these statements with caution since the yield from infrastructure and industrialization projects typically is low and long-term.[61] For scholars, increased funding of the domestic economy might mean the loss of funds due to corruption, which could jeopardize the ability to pay pensions in the future.[62] In order to avoid these possibilities, SAPF was allowed to invest 20 percent of its portfolio in foreign securities, although investment in private equity and hedge funds are still restricted. New funds will be invested in industrialization projects administered through development institutions, such as the Development Bank of Kazakhstan. Funds will be used to support FIGs in the extractive industry through acquisition of their shares. Funds will also finance government debt by buying state-backed securities. Lastly, some funds will be used to buy stocks and bonds in foreign exchange markets. This time, the risks were much lower since SAPF assets increased the total capitalization of the National Bank to $120 billion or 60 percent of Kazakhstan's GDP and included $26 billion in gold and currency reserves as well as $66 billion from oil revenues that had accumulated in the National Fund. This large capitalization guaranteed macroeconomic stability and the ability to support industries in case of trouble.

This system of distribution protected public money from economic instabilities. It also provided investment opportunities to FIGs and loyalists, and it created a foundation for funding capital-intensive public goods, which benefit both the population and businesses.

Dilemma 3: Administrative Discipline and Information Transparency

The third dilemma deals with the actual implementation of the reform. In order to implement it properly, the regime had to clean up toxic assets, created through the transfer from the private pension funds. Then it had to ensure control from predatory officials who could squander public money.

Before accepting the investment portfolios of private pension funds, Nazarbayev's regime hired an independent auditor that verified the solvency and reliability of all the investments. At the end of this investigation, more than twenty companies declared default and SAPF lost around $600 million.[63] Some of the defaulted companies, such as Kazakhstan Kagazy, had attracted investments from various local and foreign funds, including Astana Oil and Gas, Ular Umit, GNPF, Grantum, Otan, and capital pension funds.[64] According to Tengri News, Kazakhstan Kagazy paid generous benefits to one shareholder, who happened to be a relative of the company owner, in the amount of $7.9 million and paid $2.3 million in compensation to company management.[65] In return, the debt was distributed among retirement accounts with contributors receiving statements with negative balance.[66]

After the clearing process, Nazarbayev's regime created a system in which the presidential administration has full control over the distribution of funds. Specifically, the Council for Management of Retirement Assets was formed under the auspices of the presidential administration and consists of government representatives, the National Bank of the Republic of Kazakhstan, members of financial markets, and independent experts. The president personally appoints individuals to the Council.[67] The Council is responsible for creating profit maximization strategies and issuing recommendations regarding investment restrictions and the overall security of the retirement funds.[68] The Ministry of Labor and Social Protection is responsible for paying retirement stipends. The National Bank, a government body independent of FIGs, is named as a managing entity responsible for investment strategies. So the system of oversight assumes that the Council suggests investments, and if the National Bank thinks that these types of assets are eligible for funding, it buys the stocks and bonds. But neither the Council nor the National Bank can unilaterally decide on investment opportunities.

The system enables administrative discipline. In case of conflicts, President Nazarbayev can intervene whenever necessary through the prerogative of the rule by law. Nazarbayev can always decide how the assets will be used and who gets what when, regardless of the formal legal procedure. In addition, the system enables the regime to acquire reliable and transparent information about the amount of funds available for investments, investment options, and projects. This last option is especially important for the stability of the regime, because it leaves the decision to support either the population or the FIGs in the hands of the regime.

For now, the reform has been relatively successful, with only a 0.4 percent default rate. In addition, as local banks are overwhelmed with nonperforming loans and toxic assets, they are unwilling to loan money to small- and medium-size enterprises (SMEs). The regime has recently decided that money from SAPF should be kept in the top ten local banks that can issue loans to SMEs.[69] Access to more loans can temporarily boost consumption and provide short-term benefits to people. By keeping personal control over the management of assets and creating a system of competing interests, Nazarbayev is able to decide on rewarding FIGs and/or the population and ensure the stability of his regime through the support of both groups.

CONCLUSION

This chapter shed light on the persistence of the authoritarian regime in Kazakhstan by focusing on the importance of the crisis point. To stay in power, President Nazabayev's regime has to ensure that revenues exceed costs and that the two principal groups that could potentially threaten political authority, the population and the FIGs linked to regime loyalists, remain happy. Nazarbayev needs to consider three crucial dilemmas when making public policy decisions. The first dilemma deals with the necessity of balancing private property rights against investment opportunities for loyalists. The second dilemma addresses the need to ensure the financial credibility of public investments with debt repayment. In other words, the regime had to ensure that if it decides to reward loyalists by distributing public assets, it also had to secure provisions for paying people's pensions when their time comes. The last dilemma deals with administrative discipline and information transparency, which are hard to ensure in neopatrimonial regimes. So Nazarbayev resorted to the rule by law, creating informal order and pressure on those who refuse to accept government decisions or attempt to subvert the policy.

By looking at the case study of pension reform in Kazakhstan, this chapter reviewed the decision-making logic. The reform solved the first dilemma by securing public money under government control, thereby guaranteeing the safety of retirement assets, while paying FIGs compensation for closing their pension funds and transferring money to the government. The second dilemma was resolved in a way that benefited FIGs, since Nazarbayev declared that the money will work for the benefit of local economy, that is it will end up supporting local businesses. In order to ensure that the population also benefits from their money as economic investments, Nazarbayev ordered the government to invest in infrastructure projects and to support small- and medium-sized businesses. Specifically, local entrepreneurs were promised better loans and debt restructuring. The money for the loans would be conveniently placed into the ten largest banks (i.e., those that belong to FIGs) due to their security and reliability. In order to resolve the third dilemma, Nazarbayev's regime had to acquire full control over information and asset distribution, while retaining the option to reverse decisions when necessary. In practice, it meant that the money that National Bank had the power to invest could only be spent after the approval of the Council for Management of Retirement Assets, an entity that is directly responsible to the president and whose members are personally appointed by him.

The crisis point formula provides us with an understanding that regime stability has its limits. Stability works while the regime has access to resources and is able to distribute them freely. If the resources run out, the predatory practices of FIGs and bureaucrats will tilt the balance into their favor and aggravate the population. Without resources, the regime might turn into a predatory state, when the "state preys on its citizenry, terrorizing them, despoiling their common patrimony, and providing little in the way of services in return."[70] Alternatively, in case of no resources, the population may yield control over political authority, creating a conflict similar to that which toppled the government in Kyrgyzstan in 2005. But as long as the regime has rents from natural resources, access to international credit, and a continued desire to avoid governance dilemmas, we should expect stability of the regime. Further comparative perspectives might be necessary to study the limits of this analytical framework.

NOTES

1. Richard Pomfret, "Kazakhstan's Economy since Independence: Does the Oil Boom Offer a Second Chance for Sustainable Development?" *Europe-Asia Studies*, 57, no. 6 (2005): 859–876; Anja Franke, Andrea Gawrich, and Gurban Alakbarov, "Kazakhstan and Azerbaijan as Post-Soviet Rentier States: Resource Incomes and Autocracy as a Double 'Curse' in Post-Soviet Regimes," *Europe-Asia Studies* 61, no. 1 (2009): 109–140.

2. Wojciech Ostrowski, *Politics and Oil in Kazakhstan* (New York: Routledge, 2010).

3. Joshua Kucera, "No One Rigs an Election Quite Like Kazakhstan," *The Atlantic*, April 5, 2011, accessed March 15, 2015, http://www.theatlantic.com/international/archive/2011/04/no-one-rigs-an-election-quite-like-kazakhstan/236817/.

4. Alternatively, scholars have used the terms "authoritarian persistence" and "authoritarian durability" to explain survival of the political regime. See Jason Brownlee, "Durable Authoritarianism in the Age of Democracy" (PhD diss., Princeton University, 2004); Oliver Schlumberger, *Debating Arab Authoritarianism: Dynamics and Durability in Nondemocratic Regimes* (Stanford, CA: Stanford University Press, 2007); Rex Brynen, Pete Moore, Bassel Salloukh, and Marie-Joelle Zahar, *Beyond the Arab Spring: Authoritarianism and Democratization in the Arab World* (Boulder, CO: Lynne Rienner, 2013); Michael Aleprete, "Authoritarian Persistence in History's Aftermath," in *International Dimensions of Authoritarian Persistence: Lessons from Post-Soviet States*, ed. Michael Aleprete and Rachel Vanderhill (Lanham, MD: Lexington Press, 2013), 1–10.

5. Alternatively, scholars have used the term "arbitrary rule." See Peter Evans, *Embedded Autonomy: States and Industrial Transformation* (Princeton, NJ: Princeton University Press, 1995); Vladimir Gel'man, "Post-Soviet Transitions and Democratization: Towards Theory-Building," *Democratization* 10, no. 2 (2003): 87–104.

6. David Levi-Faur, "The Regulatory State and the Developmental State: Towards Polymorphic Comparative Capitalism," in *The Rise of the Regulatory State of the South: Infrastructure and Development in Emerging Economies*, eds. Navroz Dubash and Bronwen Morgan (New York: Oxford University Press, 2013), 242.

7. Chalmers Johnson, *MITI and the Japanese Miracle: The Growth of Industrial Policy, 1925–1975* (Stanford, CA: Stanford University Press, 1982); Adrian Leftwich, "Bringing Politics Back in: Towards a Model of the Developmental State," *Journal of Development Studies* 31, no. 3 (1995): 400–427; Evans, *Embedded Autonomy.*

8. Evans, *Embedded Autonomy*; Nathan Jensen, "Economic Reform, State Capture and International Investment in Transition Economies," *Journal of International Development* 14, no. 7 (2002): 973–977; Anna Grzymala-Busse, "Beyond Clientelism: Incumbent State Capture and State Formation," *Comparative Political Studies* 41, no. 4/5 (2008): 638–673

9. Tom Ginsburg and Tamir Moustafa, *Rule by Law: The Politics of Courts in Authoritarian Regimes* (New York: Cambridge University Press, 2008).

10. Gerard Alexander, "Institutionalized Uncertainty, the Rule of Law and the Sources of Democratic Stability," *Comparative Political Studies* 35, no. 10 (2002): 1145–1170; Tamir Moustafa, *The Struggle for Constitutional Power: Law, Politics and Economic Development in Egypt* (New York: Cambridge University Press, 2007); Grzymala-Busse, "Beyond Clientelism"; Andreas Schedler, *The Politics of Uncertainty: Sustaining and Subverting Electoral Authoritarianism* (New York: Oxford University Press, 2013).

11. David Collier, *New Authoritarianism in Latin America* (Princeton, NJ: Princeton University Press, 1980); Anderson, "Institutionalized Uncertainty"; Matthijs Bogaards, "How to Classify Hybrid Regimes? Defective Democracy and Electoral Authoritarianism," *Democratization* 16, no. 2 (2009): 399–423.

12. Grzymala Busse, "Beyond Clientelism"; Neil Robinson, "Russian Patrimonial Capitalism and the International Financial Crisis," *Journal of Communist Studies and Transition Politics* 27, nos. 3/4 (2011): 434–455.

13. Neil Robinson, "Institutional Factors and Russian Political Parties: The Changing Need of Regime Consolidation in a Neo-patrimonial System," *East European Politics* 28, no. 3 (2012): 298–309.

14. Michael Ross, *The Oil Curse: How Petroleum Wealth Shapes the Development of Nations* (Princeton, NJ: Princeton University Press, 2013).

15. Ross, *The Oil Curse*.

16. Volker Perthes, *Arab Elites: Negotiating the Politics of Change* (Boulder, CO: Lynne Rienner Publishers, 2004); Alisher Ilkhamov, "Neopatrimonialism, Interest Groups and Patronage Networks: The Impasses of the Governance System in Uzbekistan," *Central Asian Survey* 26, no. 2 (2007): 65–84; Kevin Koehler, "Authoritarian Elections in Egypt: Formal Institutions and Informal Mechanisms of Rule," *Democratization* 15, no. 5 (2008): 974–990; Sebastian Schiek and Stephan Hansell, "Seeing Like a President: The Dilemma of Inclusion in Kazakhstan," in *Presidents, Oligarchs, and Bureaucrats: Forms of Rule in the Post-Soviet Space*, ed. Susan Steward, Margarete Klein, Andrea Schmitz, and Hans-Henning Schroder (Burlington, VT: Ashgate, 2012), 203–222.

17. Ilkhamov, "Neopatrimonialism, Interest Groups and Patronage Networks"; Schiek and Hansell, "Seeing Like a President."

18. This insight has been developed for the other parts of the world, but has not been systematically applied to Central Asia. See Perthes, *Arab Elites*, Koehler, "Authoritarian Elections in Egypt."

19. Laura Adams and Assel Rustemova, "Mass Spectacle and Styles of Governmentality in Kazakhstan and Uzbekistan," *Europe-Asia Studies* 61, no. 7 (2009): 1249–1276.

20. Neil Robinson, "Patrimonial Political Economy and the Global Economy" (paper presented at ISA/ABRI Conference, July 2009).

21. Robinson, "Patrimonial Political Economy and the Global Economy," 8.

22. *Otkat* is a form of predatory activity in which money from various formal enterprises is channeled to bureaucrats in exchange for the permission to function freely.

23. Ginsburg and Moustafa, *Rule by Law*, 308.

24. Ginsburg and Moustafa, *Rule by Law*, 312–314.

25. Kathleen Collins, *Clan Politics and Regime Transition in Central Asia* (New York: Cambridge University Press, 2006).

26. Sally Cummings, *Kazakhstan: Power and the Elite* (New York: Palgrave Macmillan, 2005); Ed Schatz, *Modern Clan Politics: The Power of "Blood" in Kazakhstan and Beyond* (Seattle: Washington University Press, 2004).

27. Dosym Satpayev, "An Analysis of the Internal Structure of Kazakhstan's Political Elite and an Assessment of Political Risk Levels," in *Empire, Islam and Politics in Central Asia* (Sapporo: Slavic Eurasian Research Center, 2007).

28. Louise Armistead, "SFO Launches Criminal Investigations into ENRC," *The Telegraph*, April 25, 2013, accessed May 7, 2013, http://www.telegraph.co.uk/finance/newsbysector/industry/mining/10017960/SFO-launches-criminal-investigation-into-ENRC.html; Simon Goodley and Mark Hollingsworth, "ENRC Chairman Quits amid Internal Inquiry into Corruption Allegations," *The Guardian*, April 23, 2013, accessed May 7, 2013, http://www.guardian.co.uk/business/2013/apr/23/enrc-chairman-quits-amid-corruption-inquiry.

29. Assel Rustemova, "Kazakhstan: March-April Report," *Central Asia Observatory*, May 2013, accessed March 12, 2015, http://www.asiacentral.es/uploads/kzmay13.pdf.

30. Wing Gar Cheng and Loretta Ng, "Chinese to Pay $4.2Bln for PetroKazakhstan," *Moscow Times*, August 23, 2005, accessed March 15, 2015, http://www.themoscowtimes.com/business/article/chinese-to-pay-42bln-for-petrokazakhstan/210434.html.

31. PetroKazakhstan, "Geological Exploration and Assessment," Areas of Activity, 2015, accessed March 12, 2015, http://www.petrokazakhstan.kz/eng/pages/geological_survey_and_estimation.html; PetroKazakhstan, "PetroKazakhstan is Ready to Build up its Resource Base," Addresses and Publications, 2009, accessed March 12, 2015, http://www.petrokazakhstan.kz/eng/news/public/43.

32. Bo Quilian, "Kazakhstan's Role in Energy Sector of China is Increasing," *Munaishy Magazine*, November 4, 2008, accessed March 12, 2015, http://www.petrokazakhstan.kz/eng/news/public/9.

33. Among them are: Samruk-Kazyna, TengizChevroil, ENRC, Karachaganak Petroleum Operating BV, CNPC, Mangystau MunaiGas, KazakhMys, KazZinc, KazgerMunai, Arcelor-Mittal, PetroKazakhstan. For the full list of the top 200 companies, please see Expert-Kazakhstan Rating Agency, "Reiting krupneishikh kompanii Kazakhstana po ob"emu realizatsii produktsii," Almaty, accessed March 12, 2015, http://www.raexpert.kz/rankingtable/?table_folder=/expert200/2013/main.

34. Andriy Osavolijk, "Workers' Strikes Have Become Ever More Frequent in Kazakh Enterprises," *Open Dialogue*, July 22, 2013, accessed March 15, 2015, http://odfoundation.eu/a/1213,workers-strikes-have-become-ever-more-frequent-in-kazakh-enterprises.

35. Joanna Lillis, "Kazakhstan: Landmark Eurasian Union Treaty Signed Amid Protests and Arrests," *Eurasianet.org*, May 29, 2014, accessed March 15, 2015, http://www.eurasianet.org/node/68416; "Police in Kazakhstan Detain Anti-Eurasian Union Activists," Radio Free Europe/Radio Liberty Kazakh Service, May 27, 2014, accessed March 15, 2015, http://www.rferl.org/content/police-in-kazakhstan-detain-anti-eurasian-union-activists/25400536.html.

36. Emily Andrews, "Kazakhstan: An Ambitious Pension Reform," Social Protection Discussion Paper No. SP 0104, Washington, DC: World Bank, 2001, accessed March 15, 2015, http://documents.worldbank.org/curated/en/2001/01/1620905/kazakhstan-ambitious-pension-reform.

37. Aigul Seitenova and Charles Becker, "Kazakhstan's Pension System: Pressures for Change and Dramatic Reforms," *Hitotsubashi Journal of Economics* 45, no. 2 (2004): 151–187, accessed March 12, 2015, https://hermes-ir.lib.hit-u.ac.jp/rs/bitstream/10086/7665/1/HJeco0450201510.pdf.

38. Seitenova and Becker, "Kazakhstan's Pension System."

39. Ostrowski, *Politics and Oil in Kazakhstan*; National Bank of Kazakhstan (2014). "Platezhnyi balans i vneshnii dolg Respubliki Kazakhstan za 1 polugodie 2014 goda," ed. D. Akishev, accessed March 12, 2015, http://www.google.com.tr/url?sa=t&rct=j&q=&esrc=s&source=web&cd=14&cad=rja&uact=8&ved=0CDIQFjADOAo&url=http%3A%2F%2Fwww.nationalbank.kz%2Fcont%2Fpublish475735_25583.pdf&ei=HRQYVerPLIbsaOHngUA&usg=AFQjCNEX1_YKV57-UJKae7bpwMIep37tdw&bvm=bv.89381419,d.d2s.

40. Institute of Political Decisions, "Pensionnaia Sistema Kazakhstana: Problemy, Perspektivy i Resheniia," Internet Association of Kazakhstan, 2012, accessed

March 18, 2016, http://www.iak.kz/ru/activity-iak/roundtables/ipr-pension-system/; Alexei Kolesnikov, "V Kazahstane Vremya Razbrasyvat Vznosy," Respublika, February 9, 2012, accessed March 16, 2016, http://www.respublika-kz.info/news/finance/20548/.

41. Single National Pension Fund, "Dokhodnost' pensionnykh fondov," Press Center, accessed March 12, 2015, http://www.enpf.kz/9179.

42. "Roundtable with the Representatives of Pension Funds," *Expert-Kazakhstan Magazine*, February 28, 2011, accessed March 15, 2015, http://www.enpf.kz/7409.

43. Zhanybek Aygazin, "Sistema pensionnogo maloobespecheniia," *Expert-Kazakhstan*, no. 6–7 (2012), accessed March 15, 2015, http://expert.ru/kazakhstan/2012/07/sistema-pensionnogo-maloobespecheniya/.

44. Andrey Efremov, "Vkladchikam pensionnykh fondov sdelaiut pereraschet," YK.kz, June 22, 2009, accessed March 12, 2015, http://www.yk.kz/news/show/3699; Kazakhstan Stock Exchange, "AFN okharakterizovalo nakopitel'nuiu pensionnuiu sistemu Kazakhstana po sostoianiiu na 01 Fevralia 2008 goda," *Irbis*, February 14, 2008, accessed March 12, 2015, http://www.kase.kz/news/show/1041816; Single National Pension Fund, "Dokhodnost' pensionnykh fondov."

45. According to Tashkinbayev, the money mostly probably belongs to citizens of who have left the country and did not take their pension funds. See Renat Tashkinbayev, "Proiskhozhdenie beskhoznykh pensionnykh schshetov poiasnila Duisenova," *Tengri News*, September 17, 2013, accessed March 12, 2015, http://tengrinews.kz/kazakhstan_news/proishojdenie-beshoznyih-pensionnyih-schetov-poyasnila-241812/.

46. "Glava Mintruda rasskazal ob ozhidaniiakh ot sozdaniia edinogo pensionnogo fonda," Tengri News, January 24, 2013, March 12, 2015, http://tengrinews.kz/kazakhstan_news/glava-mintruda-rasskazal-ojidaniyah-sozdaniya-edinogo-227267/.

47. Nariman Gizitdinov, "Samruk-Kazyna Won't Buy Pension Funds as Halyk Rejects BTA Deal," Bloomberg, November 19, 2013, accessed March 12, 2015, http://www.bloomberg.com/news/articles/2013-11-19/samruk-kazyna-won-t-buy-pension-funds-as-halyk-rejects-bta-deal.

48. Specifically, the reform cancelled indexation of welfare payments for mothers whose salaries were more than \$1,700 (as of February 2013) before pregnancies and proposed to index payments to minimum salary levels with the rest being covered by the employers. Nazarbayev's regime justified the proposed changes with the fact that the entity responsible for social payments, State Fund for Social Support, was bankrupt. The bankruptcy happened because the planners did not consider that many more women of reproductive age may make more than KZT300,000 a month (now about \$1,700), which made the fund pay the majority of its benefits to only 6,700 women out of 500,000 eligible participants. In addition, child support by the state was significantly reduced. Rather than indexing child support to the father's salary, the state proposed to pay minimum payment equally for all newborn kids. As a result, people began to feel restless and the number of protests across Kazakhstan began to increase. By May 2013, protests were registered in Almaty, Koshetau, Petropavlovsk, Pavlodar, and Semei. For more information, please see Rustemova, "Kazakhstan: March-April Report."

49. Daniyar Mukhtarov, "Kazakhstan Works on Unifying Pension Funds," Trend Agency, November 14, 2013, accessed March 12, 2015, http://en.trend.az/casia/kazakhstan/2211199.html.

50. "Marchenko: u pensionnykh fondov est' tri varianta," Tengri News, February 7, 2013, accessed March 12, 2015, http://tengrinews.kz/money/marchenko-u-pensionnyih-fondov-est-tri-varianta-228084/.

51. Clare Nutall and Ben Aris, "Kazakhstan Joins Growing List of State Pension Grabs," Stratfor, February 22, 2013, accessed March 12, 2015, http://www.stratfor.com/the-hub/kazakhstan-joins-growing-list-state-pension-grabs.

52. See Grigorii Marchenko, "Prikaz No. 356 ob utverzhdenii grafika priema—peredachi pensionnykh aktivov i obyazatel'st v nakopitel'nykh pensionnykh fondov po dogovoram o pensionnom obespechenii v edinyi nakopitel' pensionnyi fond," National Bank of the Republic of Kazakhstan, September 24, 2013, accessed March 15, 2015, http://www.afn.kz/attachments/9/22/publish22-1069604.pdf and http://base.spinform.ru/show_doc.fwx?rgn=63676.

53. Gizitdinov, "Samruk-Kazyna Won't Buy Pension Funds."

54. Halyk Bank, "Informatsiia o resheniiakh, priniatykh edinstvennym aktsionerom AO 'NPF Narodnogo Banka Kazakhstana,'" November 10, 2014, accessed March 15, 2015, http://www.halykfund.kz/ru/site/index/press/news/view:9827.

55. Department of Financial Oversight, "Reestr priostanovlennykh, libo prekrativshikh deistvie (lishennykh) litsenzii na osuchshestvlenie deiatel'nosti po privlecheniiu pensionnykh vznosov i osuchshestvleniiu pensionnykh v yplat po sostoianiiu na 01.02.2015g." National Bank of the Republic of Kazakhstan, Almaty, 2015, accessed March 22, 2015, http://www.afn.kz/index.cfm?docid=749.

56. Gizitdinov, "Samruk-Kazyna Won't Buy Pension Funds."

57. Tengri News, "Glava Mintruda rasskazal ob ozhidaniiakh ot sozdaniia edinogo pensionnogo fonda"; Anastasiya Kupriianova, "Pochemu na pensionnykh schetakh kazakhstantsev izchezaiut nakopleniia i kto na nikh polozhel glav?" YK-News.kz, February 2, 2015.

58. The National Fund accumulates revenues from oil and stores it by investing in foreign assets. It was designed as a cushion of cash in case international oil prices drop unexpectedly. The National Fund is managed by the National Banks.

59. Kuprianova, "Pochemu na pensionnykh schetakh kazakhstantsev."

60. Talgat Kamarov, "NPP: Osnovnaia tsel'—Sobliudenie interesov investorov i emitentov," *Exclusive Magazine*, November 21, 2013, accessed March 12, 2015, http://exclusive.kz/talgat-kamarov-npp-osnovnaya-tsel-soblyudenie-balansa-interesov-investorov-i-e-mitentov.html.

61. Kupriyanova, "Pochemu na pensionnykh schetakh kazakhstantsev."

62. Kupriyanova, "Pochemu na pensionnykh schetakh kazakhstantsev."

63. Alisher Akhmetov, "Bonds of 22 Companies Held by the Single Pension Fund of Kazakhstan Depreciate Four-fold," Tengrinews.kz, January 10, 2015, accessed March 12, 2015, http://en.tengrinews.kz/finance/Bonds-of-22-companies-held-by-Single-Pension-Fund-of-258014/.

64. Akhmetov, "Bonds of 22 Companies."

65. Akhmetov, "Bonds of 22 Companies."

66. Kupriyanova, "Pochemu na pensionnykh schetakh kazakhstantsev."

67. Talgat Mustafin, "ENPF: Sootvetstvie vyplat dokhodam," *Akmolinskaia pravda*, April 13, 2013, accessed March 12, 2015, http://apgazeta.kz/2013/04/13/enpf-sootvetstvie-vyplat-doxodam/.

68. Mustafin, "ENPF: Sootvetstvie vyplat dokhodam."

69. Kupriyanova, "Pochemu na pensionnykh schetakh kazakhstantsev."

70. Evans, *Embedded Autonomy*, 45.

Chapter 2

The Kazakh Neopatrimonial Regime

Balancing Uncertainties among the "Family," Oligarchs, and Technocrats

Sebastien Peyrouse

During the 1990s and early 2000s,[1] the academic literature devoted to the Central Asian political regimes, both Western and locally produced works, took the "clan" factor as one of its dominant interpretive prisms.[2] This approach assumed that regional or clan identities affected political life. This assumption, which had long been present in Soviet academic literature, emerged in the region's media with the great corruption scandals of the Brezhnev years at the beginning of the 1980s and was heatedly debated in the Soviet press at the onset of *perestroika*. Western researchers undertaking fieldwork in the 1990s reproduced this prism and contributed indirectly to validating it—the implicit idea was that so-called traditional or archaic elements were halting the birth of modern civic identities and classical political parties based on a shared ideology.

In the case of Kazakhstan, analysts argued that the three hordes (*juz*) that had historically constituted a supple system of tribal confederations assembled on the basis of a territorial principle,[3] determined the nature of the country's political life. During the Soviet period, the Great Horde, based in the Almaty region, was assumed to have largely controlled the apparatus of the Communist Party; the Small Horde, whose territory was situated in the west of the country, reportedly had symbolic control over the country's main oil wealth; whereas the Middle Horde, the most Russified, was well represented in intellectual circles and the administrative apparatus.[4] In the post-Soviet period, phenomena such as the high turnover of Kazakh senior officials and President Nursultan Nazarbayev's strategies for nominating cadres were interpreted as being the tip of the clan iceberg, indirectly revealing the precarious and continually renegotiated balance among the hordes.[5] If these solidarity strategies, which are far more pertinent in rural than urban milieus and were deeply transformed by the Soviet decades, have some social influence, in particular on marriage strategies and traditional exchanges of services, their role as drivers of political life has never be convincingly demonstrated.

In the second half of the 2000s, new works in political science set out to revamp the analysis of post-Soviet political transformations.[6] The notion of "patronal presidentialism," applied not only to Vladimir Putin's Russia but also to the Central Asian regimes, makes it possible to avoid the cultural pitfall linked to the supposed clan feature of the region.[7] The notion of neopatrimonialism, often used for the countries of sub-Saharan Africa and Latin America, is also relevant. Definitions of neopatrimonial regimes differ depending upon whether they emphasize political elements (patronage, paternalism, arbitrariness, weakness of institutions, and misuse of public office) or economic ones (endemic corruption, the kleptocracy of the established elite, management of national wealth as private property),[8] and whether they analyze the highest circles of the state (the presidents and their intimates), or more local mechanisms of the state apparatus. In this chapter, I work with the broad definition of neopatrimonial practices as blurring the boundaries between the political and the economic, the public and the private, the individual and the collective.[9]

The regime established since Kazakhstan's independence in late 1991 is intrinsically linked with strategies of economic development; it is often presented as an archetype of the rentier state.[10] The recentralization of oil and gas wealth; conflicts around the ownership of the mining sector and the banking industry; and success or failure in increasing living standards as promised by the president to his fellow citizens are key topics the Kazakhstani authorities use to assert their legitimacy.[11] Thanks to its economic success, the Kazakh regime has indeed managed to delegitimize its democratic liberal opposition and has established a paternalist state with weak institutions in which justice is not independent and the figure of the president—in power since 1989 and decreed by the parliament as "leader of the nation" in 2010[12]—dominates public life. Everyday corruption is endemic (the country is ranked 126th out of 175 by Transparency International[13]), the use of offshore and shell companies to facilitate capital flight is extensive,[14] and, despite large state subsidies, the implementation of decisions, especially the provision of public services like education and healthcare, remains inconsistent. The regime functions through a patronage system comprised of several concentric circles: the president and his intimates, often defined by local media and analysts as the "family"—a borrowing of the term used to designate the great Italian mafia families; the main oligarchs, whose relations with political authorities can be either harmonious or conflictual; the technocratic elite (key ministers, governors of capitals and regions, heads of the presidential administration, etc.); the regional elite; small- and medium-sized businessmen; and, at the outer-most level, the local administration.

This patronage system is founded on principles of loyalty to one's superior; that is, to the one who distributes administrative status and financial resources to his subordinates in accordance with his or her own strategies of promotion. Loyalty broadly prevails over competence, as it prevails over the criteria of clan belonging: established networks are essentially ones of personal loyalty and of belonging to a group that has the same economic interests, a shared past as university classmates, or workers who were employed as part of the same staff (*komanda*). References made to traditional solidarity criteria like regional or clan identities represent but one opportunity among many and are likely less influential the higher one rises through the echelons of power.[15] This neopatrimonial system is therefore at once fragile (its balance is precarious, and status and wealth are always liable to being challenged) and flexible (alliances and lines of rupture can rapidly recompose). The idea of an omniscient president who controls the entire hierarchical pyramid belongs to the realm of myth: Nazarbayev is as much master builder as a hostage to the system that he has created. His role as mediator between groups signifies that he is necessary to the equilibrium of the system, but it also indicates that his disappearance from the political scene will not necessarily lead to a fundamental change in the state's way of functioning.

This chapter is based on regular visits to Kazakhstan's two capitals, Almaty and Astana, as well as to provincial cities. The study revisits Western and local sources and relies on interviews with experts and local actors. It focuses mainly on the three innermost circles, that is the family, the oligarchs, and the technocrats, and leaves aside the more peripheral, but just as crucial, circles of the regional elite, small businessmen, and local administration. It argues that patronal practices linking political elites and business interests are key to interpreting the functioning of Kazakhstan's political system.

BUILDING A NEOPATRIMONIAL EMPIRE AND THE ROLE OF THE FAMILY

The 1990s: Privatization, Political Diversity, and a Multiplicity of Economic Actors

Kazakhstan was the last of the Soviet Union republics to proclaim its independence, which it did on December 16, 1991. President Nursultan Nazarbayev, in office since 1989, was quite unhappy to see the disappearance of Soviet institutions, particularly the ruble, which vanished in 1993.[16] At the time, the republic was considered one of the most fragile in Central Asia, both on the political level (with a small population distributed across an immense territory, a high risk of territorial fragmentation due to the large majority of Russian and Slav populations in the northern and western regions, the substantial

Uzbek minority in the south, and the capital's isolation from the rest of the country) and on the economic level (extreme dependency on Russia, brutal de-industrialization due to the collapse of the planned economy, and the vanishing trade links between the former Soviet republics). To guarantee both his political survival and that of the new state, Nazarbayev rapidly became what theoretician of neopatrimonialism Jean-François Médard has called a "politician entrepreneur," one who concurrently holds political and economic resources and successfully bases his power on symbolic and financial assets.[17]

Following the model established by Yeltsin's Russia, Nazarbayev opted for a shock therapy policy designed to accelerate the transition to a market economy. He privatized almost the entire service sector and industrial sphere, with the exception of agriculture, which remained collective or state property until the 2000s.[18] As in Russia, the first groups of wealthy businessmen or oligarchs formed shortly after the fall of the USSR by buying up industries in total collapse at low prices, in particular in the mining sector.[19] They prospered thanks to illegal trafficking, mainly by smuggling metal to China and by reselling basic goods imported from Turkey or Iran, and then later bought in Dubai or China. Kazakhstan also welcomed many foreign investors, in particular, in the largely privatized hydrocarbons sector: it was in this era that the largest contracts were signed, including those with Chevron and ExxonMobil to exploit the Tengiz deposit. The country's economy thus fell into the hands of a multitude of actors with divergent interests and political networks, the presidential family being merely one actor among several.

In the second half of the 1990s, the political system evolved: the second constitution, adopted in 1995, reduced political liberties; opposition parties, whether they were nationalist or pro-Russian, were liquidated; the decision-making autonomy of the parliament was restricted while parallel institutions such as the People's Assembly were created to strengthen the president's power to co-opt and weaken elected institutions.[20] Former prime minister Akezhan Kazhegeldin, whose National Republican Party had opposed Nazarbayev, was forced into exile. In parallel, the involvement of the presidential family in the country's most profitable economic sectors grew, particularly in the hydrocarbons and construction sectors.

In 1998, the so-called Kazakhgate scandal erupted, implicating in a series of financial misdeeds American operator James Giffen, a close friend of President Nazarbayev who had succeeded during the 1990s in becoming the gatekeeper of the country's oil wealth for the main foreign investors, in particular Chevron, via his company Mercator. According to U.S. prosecutors, Nazarbayev and two of his close senior officials allegedly received hidden payments of about US$80 million via an opaque system of offshore and shell companies, while Mercator allegedly laundered the money won from brokering international oil deals.[21] Concerned that the scandal would tarnish his international image, President Nazarbayev ultimately allowed the money discovered in his Swiss bank accounts to be spent on charitable works, while Giffen himself received only a minimal sentence and even was thanked for services rendered to U.S. interests in the region.[22] The transfer of the capital from Almaty to Astana in 1997 enabled the presidential family to reap substantial revenues in the construction sector.[23] Turkish and Russian firms invested in both residential and commercial buildings, as well as in building the government facilities for the new capital. The World Bank identified construction as a key sector for elite corruption in Central Asia, as elsewhere in the world: several construction projects with no commercial rationality won authorization with the presumed aim of obtaining kickbacks.[24] Nazarbayev's personal fortune remains a matter of conjecture since multiple frontmen and shell company networks conceal its real extent.

The growing role given to the president's daughters and sons-in-law strengthened the close interconnection between domestic political dominance and control over lucrative economic sectors in the second half of the 1990s. The president's youngest daughter, Aliya, was briefly married to Aydar Akayev, the son of the Kyrgyzstan's president, in 1998, in the hope of making more official the rapprochement between the two republics, but they later divorced and she married a Kazakh oligarch, Daniar Khasenov. The eldest daughter, Dariga, took over the leadership of the Khabar group, which owned more than 80 percent of the country's television and radio channels, as well as several newspapers,[25] while her spouse, Rakhat Aliyev, headed the financial police from 1997 to 1999 and invested in various sectors (including the leisure industry and a quasi-monopoly over sugar and vodka sales, among others). The control exerted by the couple was therefore political as much as commercial.[26]

The second daughter, Dinara, married one of the most famous oligarchs, Timur Kulibayev, whose father, Askar, had been regional secretary of the local Communist Party in Atyrau in the 1980s, before becoming governor of this Caspian region in the 1990s. Timur Kulibayev climbed the hierarchy and in 1990 became the director of the Fund for Cultural, Social and Sci-Tech Development of Kazakhstan, one of the organizations close to the government that trained the new elites. In 1992, he headed the Altyn-Alma group and, on the basis of this group, established the Almex holding. Three years later, he opened the ATF Bank SA, which manages the accounts of the Information Agency of Khabar. He also chaired the Supervisory Board of the Almaty Trade and Industry Bank prior to being appointed to the key post of head of the Directorate for Project Assessment and Negotiating under the Investment Committee of Kazakhstan, which gave him access to foreign investors. In 1997, he changed his focus to the oil sector and became deputy president of the national extraction company, KazakhOil.[27] Above all,

Kulibayev's success in advancing his own projects and getting rid of rivals was accomplished through becoming, in the same year, president of the Directorate for Project Assessment and Negotiating under the Investment Committee of Kazakhstan. In 1999, he joined the presidency of KazTransOil, a subsidiary of Kazakhoil, and from there took up the leadership or co-leadership of several companies: Munai-Impex, Transpetroleum, Kaspymunaibailanys, Bailanys, Aktyubneftesvyaz, Atyrau Zholdary, and KazTransGaz.

The 2000s: Centralization and the Nazarbayev Family as a Key Economic Actor

At the start of the 2000s, the country redefined the relationship between the political authorities and the economy, in a manner that was similar to Putin's "power vertical" in Russia. While the adoption of a market economy remained unchallenged, critics blasted the privatizations that took place immediately following the Soviet collapse. According to this new view of Kazakhstan's recent history, shock therapy weakened the authority of the state and its ability to command its own resources; stimulated political chaos by giving rise to a class of cosmopolitan oligarchs with nothing but contempt for national interests and ready to invest their fortunes in opposing the established authorities; and handing foreign investors overly favorable conditions, thus enabling "foreign interests" to influence local political life. This narrative about both state weakness and the collusion between internal and external enemies signaled Kazakhstan's entry into a phase that has often been qualified either as a return to "state capitalism" or as "resource nationalism."[28] The state dramatically changed its role in the hydrocarbons sector.[29] In 2001, it created a single company to transport hydrocarbons, Trans Neft i Gaz (TNG), itself the result of a merger between KazTransGaz and KazTransOil; in 2002, KazakhOil and TNG merged to give rise to the state-run company KazMunayGaz; and in 2004, the authorities asserted the right to preempt all oil and gas projects.[30] Today, shares of new consortiums must be 50 percent owned by KazMunayGaz, and the government regularly uses fiscal threats or alleged violations of environmental legislation to renegotiate better terms for existing contracts.[31]

The political will to re-nationalize and re-concentrate economic assets is intrinsically linked with the domestic political situation. While in Russia Putin used his first mandate to put recalcitrant oligarchs back in line, in Kazakhstan the sudden move into opposition by a part of the elite organized around the Democratic Choice of Kazakhstan party (DMK) surprised the authorities, who were used to fighting against opponents outside the elite, such as nationalists, Russians, and pro-Western liberal groups. Created at the end of 2001, DMK gathered members of the government, elected leaders, as well as businessmen concerned about Nazarbayev and his family's growing stranglehold on the country's wealth.[32] The movement was led by Pavlodar governor Galymjan Zhakyanov, Vice-Prime Minister Uraz Dzhandosov, and Temir Bank director and former minister of industry and commerce Mukhtar Ablyazov. In January 2002, Ablyazov and Zhakyanov were charged with a variety of crimes and imprisoned for a few months, though they were eventually released under international pressure and after publically apologizing.

After dealing with DMK, the authorities became aware that the oligarchs possess enough revenues to guarantee them political autonomy, which, a decade after independence, could be used against the president as the strong man of the country and against his family as an economic actor. The first decade of the 2000s was therefore marked by two interrelated phenomena: the control of all potential dissent from within the elite, and the reinforcement of the presidential family's stranglehold over the country's assets.

Several experiments were attempted. Like Yeltsin, Nazarbayev had not really invested any energy into constituting a presidential party, but, taking Putin's United Russia as a model, he understood the benefit of having a more stable political structure. Since then, the presidential party Nur Otan has represented the interests of "Ak-Orda," the presidential palace in Astana, a synonym for the presidential circles as a political actor.[33] As in Russia, the few attempts to constitute regime-friendly alternative liberal parties failed. The Asar Party, first created with the aim of rallying young elites loyal to the president under the leadership of his daughter Dariga,[34] was eventually forced to merge with Nur Otan. The effort to establish a democratic façade[35] while shoring up authoritarian practices resulted in Kazakhstan becoming a one-party regime; between 2007 and 2012 Nur Otan was the only party with parliamentary representation.[36] This situation harmed the democratic branding that Kazakhstan has tried to sell to the international community, in particular during its chairmanship of the Organisation for Security and Co-operation in Europe (OSCE) in 2010. This forced the government to water down legislation, to guarantee that the second-placed party would gain parliamentary seats irrespective of whether it cleared the 7 percent electoral threshold. With these new rules, two pseudo-opposition parties could gain seats in parliament during the 2012 elections.[37]

As in Russia, and following a long-standing Soviet tradition, control of both politics and the economy have been re-concentrated around the security services: Kazakhstan's National Security Committee (KNB), the Customs Committee, the fiscal police, border guards, the security service of the presidency, etc. The president's first son-in-law, Rakhat Aliyev, for instance, climbed the career ladder of the KNB and the presidential security service between 1999 and 2002. The presidential family's takeover of profitable economic sectors has also diversified and can be divided into four main sectors: energy, mining, finance and banking, and construction.

The most strategic sector remains the energy sector, in which Timur Kulibayev has invested most. In 2005, he created KazEnergy, becoming the director, a position he still retains. This company, which unites more than seventy major players in the oil, gas, and energy business—extracting, transporting, servicing, geophysical, uranium-producing, and other transnational companies, quickly became a Kazakhstan lobby group for procuring foreign investors. His wife Dinara is also significantly engaged in this sector: in 2001, she was elected president of the Administration Council of KazTransGaz. The mining sector, which has become more attractive in the 2000s thanks to the rise in world prices of minerals like cooper and zinc, has been re-appropriated by the presidential family via Nazarbayev's brother, Bolat. The family also entered the gold sector thanks to its close links with the Asaubayev family, which owned KazakhGold until 2009.

The family has made considerable moves into the financial and banking sectors. Bolat Nazarbayev, Nazarbayev's younger brother, is the owner of the financial and industrial holding BN Invest. The Almex holding, which he established with Timur Kulibayev and the latter's spouse, runs Kyrpso Holding and includes many subsidiaries, such as Iuzhny SENCRL, Atyraymunaionimderi, Continent Invest Group, and Munai Damu.[38] In 2001, Kulibayev bought Halyk Bank, then the country's third-largest bank. Through this holding, Kulibayev and his wife control the Cooperative Bank via Almex, as well as a number of shares of Almex Plus, Kipros, and the Mercury company.[39] Dariga Nazarbayeva was president of Nurbank between 2006 and 2010.

A large number of other sectors have been taken under the family's control, including agriculture, construction, tourism, and leisure. The family has for instance privatized part of the mountainous region of Almaty: Bolat Nazarbayev today owns and runs several sites such as Kaskelensk, or Uzun-Agach. The highest figures of state control sport clubs, which are important places for all sorts of trafficking and provide opportunities to monitor circles of young supporters. Kulibayev, for example, not only heads the Kazakhstan Boxing Federation, but is also a member of the Executive Committee of the National Olympic Council. The transport and communications sectors are highly coveted as well. In 2003, through legal decision, Kulibayev took control of the Kar-Tel company for the amount of $3,000, which he resold to Beeline for $350 million. In the education sector, Dinara Kulibayeva is president of the administrative council of the Kazakh-British Technical University and of the Kazakh University of International Relations and World Languages. She leads the Nursultan Nazarbayev National Education Foundation and was behind the creation of a private school, Miras, in Almaty.

Most of the family members involved in business have tried to diversify their investments in the largest possible number of sectors, at once commercial, but also political, in order to protect their commercial interests. Bolat Nazarbayev's son, Nurbol, owns the water services of Pavlodar and of Atyrbalyk, and was the prosecutor of the town of Kapchagai. Aliya Nazarbayeva, Nazarbayev's younger daughter, is the owner of Elitstroy, one of the largest construction companies in Kazakhstan. She also owns mobile telephone companies such as Dalacom and Pathword, the Luxor health and fitness center, the jeweler Alsara (in cooperation with the Italian company Damiani). She is the general director of Caspian Industries, Ltd., which produces Vita water. In 2011, she opened a pharmacy chain called Almatypharm.[40] She is also an assistant director of Europe Plus radio, an intern in the legal department of TuranAlem Bank, a consultant in the general department of the president's administration, and director general of Caspian Industries, Ltd.

Investing in the media makes it possible to ensure control over public expression, to prevent acts of dissidence, and to mitigate any attempt to destabilize the regime that would undermine their economic gains. Kulibayev controls the media holding belonging to Gazprom (he was elected an independent member of Gazprom's administration council in June 2011) and which includes newspapers such as *Izvestiya-Kazakhstan*, *Komsomol'skaia pravda*, and *Argumenty i fakty*, as well as two television stations: NTV-Kazakhstan and TV Astana. Dariga Nazarbayeva controlled KTK, the newspapers *Novoe Pokolenie*, *Karavan*, and *Kazakhstan Today*, as well as the advertising agency TV Media and Russkoe radio. Lastly, Dariga's son, Nurali Aliyev, headed the "Sugar Center" joint-stock company when he was 19, and, 2 years later, the television station Hit TV. He was the principal deputy board chair of the Board Nurbank SA when he was 21, and served as the deputy chief executive officer of the Development Bank of Kazakhstan. From 2013 to 2014, he was the president of the board of TransTeleCom. He controls AO "Capital Holding," the poly-metallic deposit Zerteu Sh, Radio City (Hit FM), a hotel (Donatello), and many shares in several media companies such as Alma-TV and NTK.

This business milieu requires foreign contacts, especially as Kazakhstan seeks to invest beyond its borders, often by having a direct presence abroad or through intermediaries. Kulibayev's interests in Russia are protected by one of his right-hand men, Mirbulat Abuov. Lastly, the family's financial investments are developed and shored up through the interplay of matrimony. The younger son of Dariga Nazarbayeva, Aysultan, is an alumnus of the highly reputed British Royal Military Academy, Sandhurst, famed for educating blue-blooded offspring. Aysultan is to marry the daughter of another Kazakhstan oil tycoon, Kayrat Boranbayev, chief executive of KazRosGaz LLP. This company is controlled by KazMunayGaz on a parity basis with Russian giant Gazprom.

The Fall of the "First Son-in-Law," An Example of Uncertain Gains

The balance of power in Kazakhstan is largely based on the relationship between the presidential family and the oligarchic groups. But as shown by the president's two sons-in-law, there is little separation between these worlds. While Aliyev has become an oligarch mainly thanks to his marriage to the president's eldest daughter, Kulibayev's economic base, at least initially, was more autonomous from his presidential spouse, since it was built on his own family ties and solidly rooted in western Kazakhstan. Moreover, the presidential family does not necessarily constitute a united group that displays systematic solidarity against other politico-economic actors, and is not without internal divisions. If, for a time, Aliyev was presented as the businessman of the family, his fall left the way open for Dinara Nazarbayeva and her husband Timur Kulibayev. In 2010, *Forbes* reported that each had a net worth of more than $2 billion, mostly but not only through their joint control of the country's third-largest bank, Halyk Bank.[41]

In the first half of the 2000s, the Kazakh press regularly reported the growing rivalry between Aliyev and Kulibayev.[42] Whereas the latter acted discretely in public and tried not to appear as the president's heir apparent, the former did not hide his political ambitions and sought to control key positions within the administrative apparatus and media resources. Aliyev's fall from grace, one of the most widely covered and politically scandalous episodes in the history of independent Kazakhstan, resulted from the growing rivalry within the presidential family. For the first time, the Nazarbayev regime seemed to be imperiled and took seriously the risk represented by Aliyev's dissidence. The latter went through a period of disgrace in 2001, ending with his dismissal from the state security services and his subsequent nomination to head the Olympic Committee of Kazakhstan. In 2002, he managed to regain the spotlight as ambassador to Austria and Kazakhstan's representative at the OSCE, and then, in 2005, he rejoined the leading circle after becoming the vice-minister of foreign affairs.[43]

At the start of 2007, the first son-in-law underwent a fall both rapid and complete. Accused by Kazakhstan's Supreme Court of being involved in the assassination of three members of Nurbank, one of Kazakhstan's largest banks of which he was a principal shareholder, Aliyev was stripped of his diplomatic immunity. In order to dodge the international arrest warrant put out on him, he sought refuge in Vienna where the Austrian authorities refused to extradite him to Kazakhstan.[44] Several of his close associates, including the secretary of Kazakhstan's Security Council and the vice-minister of justice, were arrested; his wife divorced him; and he was accused of kidnapping, insider trading, money laundering, and murder, and sentenced in absentia to life in prison. His economic empire collapsed rapidly and was in large part carved up. During his Austrian exile, Aliyev tried, without much success, to influence Kazakh political life by threatening to reveal state secrets.[45] Accused of having had an opponent, Altynbek Sarsenbayev, assassinated in 2006, as well as two managers of Nurbank the following year, he was arrested in Austria in June 2014, but was found hanging in his cell in February 2015. Dariga and her son Nurali Aliyev officially lost their status as shareholders of Nurbank, and her fiefdom, the media holding Khabar, was renationalized in 2008. Aliyev's disgrace was confirmation that the gains he had made had not been guaranteed for life and were always subject to be renegotiated by force.[46]

The second son-in-law of the president, Timur Kulibayev, himself seen as impervious, also got caught up in the tempest. At the end of the 1990s, Kulibayev presided over Transport Nefti i Gaza, and then became vice-president of KazMunayGaz between 2002 and 2005. In 2008 he was named CEO and a member of the board of directors of Samruk-Kazyna; in 2009 he joined the Council of Directors of KazMunayGaz, Kazakhstan Temir Zholy, and Samruk-Energo, and assumed the presidency of KazEnergy, an association grouping together the major oil and gas companies that also serve as an interface to foreign companies such as Lukoil, TengizChevroil, and BP. At the end of 2011, after some months as chairman of the Samruk-Kazyna board of directors, the highest position of his career and a possible platform leading to the presidency, Kulibayev was forced to resign when oil sector workers rioted in Zhanaozen.[47] This purge was intended to demonstrate that there were no untouchables in the president's inner circle. Even the president came under threat abroad: in 2012, Swiss authorities opened an inquest into money laundering bribes and into the illegal sale of the oil and gas resources of the Kazakh state.[48] However, Kulibayev has continued on as chairman of the Kazakhstan National Committee of the World Petroleum Council, and his career is probably far from over, especially given the presidential family's control over the state holding.

Samruk-Kazyna and the State Capitalism Model

Kazakhstan has followed Russia's model of creating large state corporations for the purpose of regrouping sectorial assets and forcing private companies to sell some of their shares to the state in order to join these consortiums. In 2008, the government decided, upon presidential decree, to merge the country's two main investment funds, both created 2 years before: Samruk, which was modeled on Singapore's Temasek Holdings with the official aim of making the large state companies autonomous from the administrative apparatus and reducing corruption; and the Kazyna Sustainable Development Fund, created to implement industrial policy, rationalize the use of funds focused on economic diversification, finance infrastructure projects, and provide support for small and medium enterprises, and facilitate investments.[49] The acknowledged objective of this merger was to reinforce the role of the state in the economy by combining control over assets with more investment power. In 2015, the Samruk-Kazyna fund held full or partial ownership stakes in more than 450 subsidiary companies, national institutes, and legal entities, with a total value of $100 billion in assets, or more than 56 percent of Kazakhstan's GDP.[50]

The fund invests in nearly every key sector of the economy. It has a large stake in oil and gas, electric power, metals, mining, chemicals, communications, transportation, financial development, corporate banking, and real estate. It includes energy giant KazMunayGaz, uranium miner and nuclear agency Kazatomprom, the Kazakhstan Development Bank, the Kazakhstan Electricity Grid Operating Company (KEGOC), the national rail company Temir Zholy, the national air company Air Astana, the commercial fleet Kazmortransflot, the main thermohydraulic power station AES-Ekibastuz, the pharmaceutical holding SK-Pharmaceuticals, and so on.

In the context of the global financial crisis, the stabilization and recovery of the financial sector became a priority. In 2009, Samruk-Kazyna acted as a crisis manager on behalf of the government, implementing the anti-crisis program's joint action plans in order to mitigate the impact of the crisis.[51] Another core goal of the fund is to bolster investments. To turn it into an efficient portfolio manager, it has participated in the financing of 157 major industrial projects, such as the Atyrau oil refinery, the Balkhash power station, and the construction of the Zhertygen-Korgas railway to the border with China. The holding's 2009 investments represented $109 billion and, in 2010, Samruk-Kazyna made 93 percent of all investments in Kazakhstan's energy sector.[52] It is estimated that today the holding employs 350,000 persons and contributes $13.8 billion to the country's GDP. About one-quarter of all investments in Kazakhstan are made by subsidiaries of the holding.

The largest scandal to have emerged from the recentralization strategy orchestrated through Samruk-Kazyna involved the nuclear sector. Over the course of the 2000s, the national company Kazatomprom—involved in both the extraction of uranium and the development of Kazakhstan's civilian nuclear strategy—succeeded in becoming one of the most efficient enterprises in the country, with growing international visibility. In 2009, its director and the architect of its success, Mukhtar Dzhakishev, was suddenly arrested and accused of dispossessing the country of close to 60 percent of its uranium deposits via dubious contracts with several companies, both foreign and domestic.[53] However, it appears highly unlikely that Dzhakishev had been able to misappropriate such a massive amount of state goods without the go-ahead of higher-placed figures, as all the contracts signed by Kazatomprom were validated by his supervisory ministry and the presidential administration. According to numerous local experts, this arrest concealed financial malpractices that had occurred with the nod of the president or his close associates for a period of several years by using the former director of Kazatomprom as a scapegoat.[54] It also enabled Samruk-Kazyna to takeover Kazatomprom and therefore to reinforce presidential control over uranium, which has become an increasingly profitable market since Kazakhstan's evolution into the world's primary producer.[55]

The holding's negative image forced the government to commit to reforms at the end of 2014 in order to make a show of greater transparency in the eyes of the international community.[56] The holding's president, Umirzak Shukeyev, stated that he wanted to retire the state functionaries who sat on his board of directors, to reduce the number of companies held by the holding from 600 to 300, as well as the levels of management from nine to four, in order to limit the intermediaries and, as a result, the risk of distribution of bribes and commissions. Officially, this reorganization should enable the program to contribute to the modernization of the Kazakh economy and to generate an additional $11 billion between 2014 and 2020.[57] This decision, a most definitely profitable one for these banks, raises many questions: the reduction of intermediaries is grasped as a way for the family and the circles that gravitate around the president to increasingly control certain economic sectors. Regardless of the reforms enacted, Samruk-Kazyna remains a symbol of Kazakh state capitalism and is also the instrument ensuring the family's stranglehold over the country's economy.

With an aging president—Nazarbayev was born in 1940—the issue of succession shuffles the cards by triggering the emergence of new figures. This is the case, for example, with Kairat Satybaldy, who is not new on the Kazahkstani political and economic scene. He created his circle at the start of the 2000s. Son of Nazarbayev's youngest brother, he was raised by the Kazakh president after the brother's death in 1981. At 30 years of age, Satybaldy was appointed vice-*akim* of the city of Astana. He was subsequently integrated into the security services and attained the rank of general at 35 years of age. He also worked for state company Kazakhoil, and for the Kazakhstani transport company Temir Zholy, of which he became the vice president. In 2010, he became secretary of the presidential party Nur Otan, where he coordinates the party's activities on questions of the military and patriotic education for youth. Through his involvement in both the political and economic milieus, he is seen today as a frontrunner in the presidential succession. Nazarbayev's daugther, Dariga, and her son, Nurali Aliyev, are also considered possible eventual successors to the presidency. In December of 2014, Aliyev was appointed a deputy mayor of Astana, without any prior experience of holding an executive government position. He resigned from his position in March 2016 after the Panama papers revealed that he was hiding assets offshore: Nurali Aliyev owned two companies registered in the British Virgin Islands and used the offshores for operating a bank account.[58]

Following the parliamentary elections in March 2016, Dariga unexpectedly did not take a position in the legislature, which has led to speculation that she is aiming for a more influential position before the formal succession commences. However, rival political elites will likely use corruption charges provided by the Panama Papers against Aliyev or his mother.[59]

Negotiating Oligarchic Autonomies in the Face of Patronal Presidentialism

The relations between the presidential family and oligarchic groups are key elements of the patronal functioning of the regime in Kazakhstan. Local oligarchs made their fortunes during the cut-throat privatization of the early 1990s, when they managed the main privatization funds, or later with the emergence of new economic and financial riches, such as in the banking sector.[60] The oil sector largely returned to state control at the end of the 1990s–early 2000s, but, as in Russia, the mining industries remained in the hands of private actors. The banking sector constituted a second space of autonomy for oligarchs, but this was greatly reduced during the 2008 global economic crisis, which forced most of the large banks to request public funds. As in Russia, returning the mining sector to state control could constitute the last great act of the "patrimonialization" currently underway in Kazakhstan.

The oligarchs all have close relations with the decision-making circles and with the presidential family's intimates. They are unable to function without garnering support in the highest circles; however, they also play on specific strategies of cooperation and competition with the economic ambitions of the family, and they can rapidly lose control of this balancing act. Two periods of tension between the family and the oligarchs marred the last decade: the first one between 2002 and 2005, which followed the economic recentralization carried out by Nazarbayev, and the second during and after the 2008 economic crisis. Today, in addition to the fortunes belonging to members of the presidential family, three large autonomous oligarchic fortunes are listed in the *Forbes* ranking of billionaires: Vladimir Kim at Kazakhmys, Adilzhan Ibragimov at the Eurasian Natural Resources Corporation (ENRC), and Nurzhan Subkhanberdin at Kazkommertsbank. Some fortunes are not considered "Kazakh" if the nationality of their owner is not, as is the case with Alexander Mashkevich, also at ENRC.[61]

Successes and Failures of Oligarchic Dissidence: Subkhanberdin and Ablyazov

Mukhtar Ablyazov and Nurzhan Subkhanberdin provide two diverging examples of failure and success in competing with the presidential family.

At the end of the 1990s and beginning of the 2000s, some oligarchs progressively lost control of the oil and gas sectors in favor of state companies. They grew concerned with Nazarbayev's attempts to establish a Putin-style "power vertical" in the other profitable economic sectors, particularly in metallurgy, finance, and banking. Two groups of oligarchs contested this presidential takeover, but were dismantled between 2002 and 2005. The first oligarchic group, headed by Mukhtar Ablyazov, who controlled the transport, telecommunications, and mass consumption industries, was carved up during the campaign against Democratic Choice of Kazakhstan. After establishing Astana Holdings, involved in multiple sectors, in 1998 Ablyazov and a consortium of Kazakh investors acquired the TuranAlem Bank, which later became BTA. A former director of KEGOC, he was appointed minister for energy, industry, and commerce. As leader of Democratic Choice, he was sentenced to 6 years in prison in 2002 and reportedly suffered torture, beatings, and other ill-treatment in prison.[62] After his release from prison, Ablyazov reportedly spent millions of dollars funding opposition groups and independent media.[63] He moved first to Moscow to rebuild his business and in 2005 took the position of chairman of the board of directors of BTA Bank, on the condition, however, of renouncing his political career. The second group, led by Zamanbek Nurkadilov, who controlled the construction and agriculture sectors, also fell apart after its leader's mysterious assassination in 2005, a few weeks after he said he would speak publicly about high-level corruption by foreign oil companies during contract talks with Nazarbayev in the early 1990s.[64]

Among the examples of well-managed opposition, the case of Subkhanberdin is probably the most revealing. The main figure of the Kazakh banking oligarchy, he controlled Kazkommertsbank, Kazakhstan's largest private bank and the fourth-largest in the Commonwealth of Independent States in terms of assets after Sberbank, Gazprombank, and Vneshtorgbank. The bank became quickly involved in multiple profitable activities, such as pension funds, insurance companies, and investment companies, and it opened several branches in Kyrgyzstan and in Russia.[65] The career of Subkhanberdin, nicknamed the "Kazakh Khodorkovsky" by local media, nonetheless reveals how difficult it is to transform economic success into political gain.

In the 1990s Subkhanberdin allied with Timur Kulibayev to wrest control of national companies like KazakhOil, KazTransOil, Kazakhtelecom, Temir Zholy, and Air Kazakhstan. However, when Nazarbayev, worried by Kazhegeldin's powerful networks, decided to reassert control over a part of the economy, Kazkommertsbank was obliged to surrender several companies and the alliance between Subkhanberdin and Kulibayev ended. The former wanted to remain in the private sector by controlling the banking domain, whereas the latter sought a takeover of the oil sector, which meant remaining dependent on state interests and large public companies. In 2001, Subkhanberdin sided with Democratic Choice of Kazakhstan, but the ensuing political repression against the movement's leaders pushed him publicly to withdraw his support for the opposition and abandon all political ambitions. After these two defeats, the young banker lost influence within the presidential administration.

However, despite these difficulties, Subkhanberdin continues to enjoy support among the "president's men," his main supporter being Sauat Mynbaev, a financial specialist close to the state leader. Yet several local observers believe that the oligarch has been well aware of the precariousness of his own status, hence his commitment to the European Bank for Reconstruction and Development's having shares of Kazkommertsbank's capital, which in principle guarantees some protection for his financial empire.[66] In 2007, Subkhanberdin increased his shares in the capital of Kazkommertsbank by buying some of those owned by Central Asian Industrial Investments, an offshore company based in the Dutch Antilles that is controlled by several Kazakh bankers. His official renunciation of all political ambition has not prevented him from issuing a veiled denunciation of the economic recentralization of the 2000s and implying that it would serve the direct interests of some members of the presidential family (specifically Rakhat Aliyev).[67] He has complained about the declining domestic investment climate and pushed for more autonomy in the private sector and for reforms that would create a greater separation of powers. Subkhanberdin framed his complaints as ethnic discontent insofar as he denounced the rise to power of "non-Kazakh oligarchs," criticizing them for their alleged cosmopolitanism: presumably their non-Kazakh origins leave the door open for suspicions about their diverting funds via offshore companies, a practice obviously employed by all players that bears no relation whatsoever to ethnic issues.[68]

A second phase of competition between presidential circles and oligarchic groups opened with the 2008 economic and financial crisis. Between 2005 and 2008, the BTA bank grew rapidly, becoming one of the country's largest, though this growth was founded on hedge funds and risky credits. When it defaulted, owing more than $10 billion to the Royal Bank of Scotland, Barclays, and others, Ablyazov was accused of mismanagement and money laundering a total of about $4 billion.[69] He then sought exile in the United Kingdom on the grounds that he faced politically motivated charges and to avoid an embezzling conviction. In early 2009, Samruk-Kazyna was obliged to inject substantial funds into BTA and became its majority shareholder. Though the bank was in significant difficulty, its renationalization, as well as the partial one of Subkhanberdin's Kazkommertsbank and of Alliance Bank, has been the subject of many virulent debates, since it allowed the state to gain a stranglehold over a large part of the promising banking sector. The Ablyazov affair might have been merely an example of a Kazakhstani bank failing spectacularly, but it took a political turn not only because Ablyazov sought political exile in London, but also because the accusation against him in Kazakhstan portrayed him as having betrayed the president's trust for a second time.[70] Ablyazov has denied accusations that he embezzled billions from BTA in which he held a majority stake. BTA has filed eleven lawsuits against him in Britain to recover billions of dollars he is accused of embezzling from the bank's operations in Kazakhstan, Russia, and Ukraine. The British courts rejected Ablyazov's appeal, sentenced him in absentia for lying about his personal fortune, and issued an international warrant for his arrest at the start of 2012.[71] He subsequently was arrested in France and imprisoned in July 2013. In 2016 he is awaiting extradition from France to Russia in the embezzlement case there.

OLIGARCHIC CIRCLES IN PARTNERSHIP WITH THE PATRIMONIAL EMPIRE: KIM AND MASHKEVICH

The relationship between the presidential family and the oligarchic circles is not only one of confrontation; on the contrary, confrontation has hitherto been the exception. Two oligarchs symbolize this alliance of interests and the difficulty involved in assigning oligarchs an autonomous status from political power *per se*, whether in terms of politics or control over their commercial empires: Vladimir Kim and Alexander Mashkevich.

Kim is today considered Kazakhstan's leading and richest businessman. He controls close to half of the assets of Kazakhmys, Kazakhstan's main copper producer, the tenth largest in the world for the production of cathode copper and fifth for the production of silver. Since 2004, Bolat Nazarbayev, the brother of the president, has been on the company's board of directors. The copper holding is regularly criticized for its lack of transparency, even though it has been listed on the London Stock Exchange since 2005.[72] Kim is regarded as part of Nazarbayev's inner circle, and Kazakhmys' Board of Directors was chaired by Vladimir Ni, the most influential shadow politician who was often presented as the president's personal treasurer and one of his longest serving and most faithful secret advisors until his death in 2010. Kazakhmys allegedly reflects the interests of several members of the presidential family and finances a large share of Nur Otan's campaigns.[73] As of late 2015, Kim remained the majority shareholder of Kazakhmys. He helped restructure the company by buying its unprofitable mines and split the company in two: a private company, Kazakhmys Corporation, and a public company, KAZ Minerals PLC.

Mashkevich is also one of Kazakhstan's principal businessmen. He built his empire during the first privatizations with two close associates, Patokh

Chodiev, of Belgian nationality, and Alizhan Ibragimov, an Uzbek originally from Kyrgyzstan and citizen of Kazakhstan. The trio heads an industrial group commonly referred to as the Eurasian Group. The Eurasian National Resources Corporation (ENRC) controls about one-third of the Kazakh economy, and dominates many strategic sectors such as metallurgy, coal, mining, and the financial institutions grouped around Eurasian Bank. It gathers together the companies controlled by the three men, including Alferon Management, the Group's main company, based in London, which owns several mines in various countries around the world (sub-Saharan Africa, Indonesia, Kosovo, and Russia), as well as Kazchrome, Aluminium of Kazakhstan, the mining and industrial complexes Zhairem and Sokolov Sarbai Mining Production Association (SSGPO), Eurasian Energy Company, and ENRC Marketing.[74] Like Vladimir Kim, the Eurasian trio decided to avoid confrontation with the family by orienting their activities around specific sectors. Thus, during the re-concentration of the hydrocarbon sector around KazMunayGaz, Mashkevich gave up the shares in the gas sector that he had acquired in the early 1990s, including those in Intergas Central Asia in order not to compete with the presidential family. This refusal to directly confront the presidential family enabled him to rescue ENRC.

ENRC is one example of the presidential circle's direct intervention in the management and control of an organization and, as a result, of collusion between political and oligarchic circles. Placed on the London Stock Exchange in 2006, the firm was withdrawn in November 2013 following a corruption scandal, legal tussles, and tumbling share prices.[75] This scandal not only damaged the ENRC structure, but notably tarnished Kazakhstan's investment climate, as Astana itself was considerably involved in the company's property structure. It also showed the ability of the oligarchs to minimize the oversight a company faces, as well as the very strong relations between the oligarchs and the government. Three oligarchs, Mashkevitch, Chodiev, and Ibragimov, with support from Astana, placed the ENRC in private hands: the trio (who owned 55 percent of the shares versus the Kazakh government's 11 percent) together formed a consortium to purchase ENRC. They were supported, moreover, by another actor close to the government, Kazakhmys, which sold 26 percent of its shares in ENRC to the consortium at a hefty loss. ENRC's withdrawal from the London stock exchange was highly controversial, with minority stakeholders accusing the oligarchs of mounting a takeover bid and of having undervalued the company. In addition, an inquest was opened by the British Fraud Office into the operations of ENRC in Kazakhstan and in Africa (the company has interests in the Democratic Republic of the Congo, Zambia, Mozambique, and South Africa). The ENRC suffers the same problem as many Kazakhstani companies—they are "more

Soviet than City":[76] exhibiting poor governance, opaque, concentrated ownership and management structures.

One of the distinguishing features of the Kazakhmys' and the Eurasian group's oligarchs is that they are ethnic minorities. As non-Kazakhs, they cannot exhibit political ambitions to rival the established elite and cannot run for high elective offices. They have all played the internationalist card: Vladimir Kim, like Vladimir Ni, represents the Korean minority, whose cultural organizations they finance, whereas Alexander Mashkevich, who has Israeli nationality, serves as a central intermediary for business with Israel and also presided over the Eurasian Jewish Congress, one of the five branches of the World Jewish Congress.[77] Nazarbayev wields the brand of non-Kazakh oligarchs on the international scene as an example of the success of interethnic cohabitation in the country, and on the domestic scene as a counterweight to the other oligarchs who might be tempted to convert their financial wealth into political tools. The non-Kazakh origins of these oligarchs have thus attracted criticism from rival groups poised to play the national card. Nurzhan Subkhanberdin was one of the first to insist on the need to "Kazakhify" the country's economy and exclude from it businessmen belonging to the national minorities. The argument has little relationship with reality, since both Kazakhmys and the Eurasian Group also represent the interests of the Kazakh elite: Kazakhmys has support from elites in Dzhezkazgan, where the company is headquartered; whereas, Mashkevich has an important ethnically Kazakh support network within the presidential apparatus.[78]

The Technocratic Circles: Actors and Objects

The technocratic circles also constitute key actors of the patronal regime in Kazakhstan. Senior officials have direct access to the president, control the administrative cogs allotting public resources to various sectors, and manage the crucial function of nominating cadres and regulating the turnover of key positions, both in Astana and Almaty as well as in the regions. The oligarchic groups cannot function without support in the upper administration: their ability to maintain their commercial empires is directly linked with their fostering administrative networks to guarantee themselves access to the president or his intimates, and regulations that favor their businesses. In return, the senior officials enjoy financial privileges, both official (status as members of corporate boards) and unofficial (bribes, positions for spouses or children), and can obtain posts in the private sector when they are ready to leave public service. Some individuals, however, seem to maintain their legitimacy in the system without having overt connections with business circles. This is the case, for example, with Marat Tazhin, former vice-president of the presidential administration and minister of foreign affairs between 2007 and 2009. In September 2009 he was named an advisor to Nazarbayev and secretary of Kazakhstan's Security Council and, in 2013, was appointed Kazakhstan's Secretary of State. Since February 2014, he has been ambassador to Russia. Tazhin's influence is concentrated in the sector of foreign policy and ideology. Relations among the family, the oligarchs, and the technocrats can take diverse forms: a strategic alliance or a rivalry among competing interest groups.

The "Holy Alliance": The Kulibayev–Masimov–Marchenko Trio

Karim Masimov, Kazakhstan's longest serving prime minister to date (2007–2012 and 2014–), is the very embodiment of the alliance among the family, the oligarchs, and the technocrats. He enjoys President Nazarbayev's continually renewed support, since the president sees him as a competent, respected politician who has the advantage of not being able to compete with him on the symbolic level—Masimov is of Uyghur origin, and thus lacks legitimacy to aspire to the highest state office. Moreover, he has major networks focused on China; indeed, he speaks Chinese, has been the representative of the minister of foreign affairs in Urumqi, and headed a Kazakh commercial house in Hong Kong.[79] He played a key role in the recentralization of state-run corporations carried out under the leadership of Samruk-Kazyna and nominates officials faithful to the president's interests for key positions in the holding.

But Masimov's influence within the state apparatus is best explained by his closeness with Timur Kulibayev and his links with Grigori Marchenko, director of the National Bank of Kazakhstan from 1999 to 2013. Marchenko is a key technocratic figure in Kazakhstan, a symbol of balanced state budgets and the success of the national banking system. His position as the head of the National Bank offered opportunities for significant leverage in terms of financing large national companies. Moreover, he has been linked directly to the Russian and international banking communities on which Kazakhstan is heavily dependent. He also ensures that international financial standards are at least nominally followed. However, Marchenko was not an easily controllable figure. He has repeatedly stressed the need to diversify the Kazakh economy in order to avoid "Dutch disease" and has harshly condemned the corruption of senior legal officials.[80] He has criticized the lack of government reforms, claiming it has become increasingly difficult to implement them, and has stated that Kazakhstan needs to be more liberal than Russia in order to attract foreign investors who might first look toward Moscow. Moreover, he has been very critical of the Chinese presence in the national energy sector.[81] He quit his position in 2013, officially for family reasons, a move that many interpreted as a consequence of disagreements with Nazarbayev, in particular over the reform of the pension system. Despite Marchenko's removal from such politico-economic games in Kazakhstan, the so-called Masimov–Kulibayev–Marchenko troika has been able to control most of the country's key economic sectors, especially the large national companies, through their joint control of Samruk-Kazyna, but they face discrete rivalry from other technocratic groups that desire to prevent them from taking over all the various instruments of power—financial, administrative, and decision-making.

Oligarchs in the Top Administrative Echelons: Bulat Utemuratov and Nurtay Abykayev

Since the 1990s, two circles of senior officials have been in competition with one another as the representatives of differing, sometimes contradictory interests—the circle of Bulat Utemuratov and that of Nurtay Abykayev. Abykayev is one of the oldest (he was born in 1947) members of the high-level Kazakh technocratic circles, linked to Komsomol activity during the Soviet period. Considered the éminence grise of President Nazarbayev, for a long time he remained head of the presidential administration, that is, the "number two" of the state apparatus, since he was in charge of nominating cadres, and the composition of the president's cabinet, and enjoyed privileged relations with foreign investors. His resume also includes time as chairman of the Senate, Kazakhstan's ambassador to Russia, and deputy foreign minister. Since 2010, he has been the head of the National Security Committee. He is usually viewed as a representative of the "Russian lobby" thanks to his networks in the Kremlin, the Russian Federal Security Service (FSB), and the institutions of the Commonwealth of Independent States (CIS) and Eurasian Economic Community.[82] Today he is active in many political institutions and heads, among others, the parliamentary delegation, and is president of the Interparliamentary Assembly of the EEU.

Utemuratov is often described in some specialized media as "Nazarbayev's personal cashier." He is a seasoned businessman, who started his career at the end of *perestroika* before joining the Ministry of Foreign Economic Relations, a strategic location for meeting foreign investors. In 1993, he was vice-president of the Foreign Trade Ministry. In 1994, he became first vice minister of industry and trade of Kazakhstan and, in 1995, the Kazakh ambassador to Switzerland. In 1999, he was appointed presidential advisor on foreign economic relations. Utemuratov has steered the Commercial and Financial Bank of Kazakhstan since its founding. Over the space of a few years, he became one of the president's main advisors, the secretary of the Security Council of the Republic of Kazakhstan, and the president of the national commission on democratization and the question of civil society. He is involved in the operations of Glencore International, a mining and commodities firm.

He then invested in various investment funds, created Verny Capital in 2006, and became its principal shareholder. Verny Capital has shares in the gold extraction firm Altyntau Gold, and in Kazzinc, a major and fully integrated zinc producer with considerable copper, precious metals, and lead holdings. Verny Capital stands accused of having organized the transfer of Kazakh capital through the purchase, among other things, of hotels abroad, including the Ritz Carltons in Vienna and in Moscow.[83] It is said to have sold its shares in both companies to Glencore in 2012 for a total of about $5 billion.[84] Utemuratov avoided the media and publicity until he emerged as one of Kazakhstan's wealthiest men in 2008.[85] His group supervises a large part of JSC Kazphosphat, as well as the media holding 31 canal, *Megapolis* and *Vox Populi* magazine and the media group Tan (which has a television station, Internet company Icon, newspaper *Business & Power*, and *RBC-Central Asia* magazine). His family controls a telecommunications company (Kar-Tel) and invested in the gold sector through a company Vasilkovskoe Zoloto. In February 2015, three Utemuratov-controlled banks, Alians Bank, Temirbank, and ForteBank were merged into a financial institution called ForteBank. After buying Samruk Kazyna's ForteBank shares in March 2015, Utemuratov now owns three-quarters of this group.[86]

The competition between these two networks is structured around the mining sector. Utemuratov's relations in this sector rival those of Mashkevich, whose ENRC also works in African markets, Glencore's territory, as well as those of Kazakhmys, which competes with Kazzinc for zinc and copper production. In deliberately stoking this competition, Utemuratov played the Kazakh nationalism card and hoped to assemble under his leadership Kazakh oligarchs opposed to the rising influence of non-Kazakhs. This alliance included Mukhtar Ablyazov before he fell into disgrace—whereupon Utemuratov then snapped up his business and communication empire—and Nurzhan Subkhanberdin. Nurtay Abykayev, on the other hand, supports the activities of both Mashkevich at ENRC and of Kim at Kazakhmys, as well as the relations of both oligarchs with their counterparts in Russia.[87]

The Generational Change

These different constellations of technocratic power contributed to state stability, but also to political gridlock: the same persons have held sway over key positions since the end of the 1980s,[88] and they often have friendships or other intimate relations dating from Soviet times.[89] But those loyal to Nazarbayev since the *perestroika* era are about to exit the political scene and be replaced by the new generation trained since independence. Changes in the balance of power of the state apparatus and the birth of new technocratic cultures—helped by those who were trained abroad, for instance—may impact the larger political culture and ways of reacting to demands coming from society.[90]

Abykayev and Utemuratov represent the Soviet generation, as does Imangali Tasmagambetov, the former first secretary of the Atyrau Komsomol. Tasmagambetov has occupied many key positions, including prime minister in 2002, state secretary in 2003, head of the Presidential Administration, and since 2008 has run the Astana City Council, a central site of power.[91] In October 2014, he was appointed minister of defense. This is also the case with Adilbek Dzhaksybekov, who has often remained in the president's shadow, but has been considered one of his most loyal lieutenants since the 1990s, as he was mayor of Astana from the time it was made the capital in 1997, and thereafter headed the Presidential Administration. He was made vice-president of the presidential party Nur Otan prior to being named ambassador to Russia and then defense minister.[92] This generation thus commonly combines positions linked with Russia (the embassy or ministries linked to defense and to security), the function of *akim* (governor) of the country's two large cities, Almaty and Astana, and the management of cadres through the presidential administration.

A new generation of technocrats, less linked with the Soviet past, is today in the process of climbing the upper echelons of the administration. This is the case with Kayrat Kelimbetov, who was trained in Kazakhstan's most prominent post-independence institutions of higher learning, such as KIMEP (Kazakhstan Institute of Management, Economics and Strategic Research), and received his university degree from the Edmund A. Walsh School of Foreign Service at Georgetown University. Close to Abykayev, he made the error of giving his support to the opposition party Democratic Choice of Kazakhstan before retracting his endorsement. He has served as the minister of economic development and trade, the CEO of Samruk-Kazyna, head of the Presidential Administration, and was appointed deputy prime minister of the Republic of Kazakhstan at the start of 2012.[93] Kelimbetov is seen as a direct rival of the Kulibayev–Masimov–Marchenko trio, since he competes with the president's second son-in-law and the prime minister for control of Samruk-Kazyna on behalf of the president himself.[94]

Kelimbetov has also denounced the "non-patriotic" decisions of some Kazakh oligarchs who invest abroad, and he has renewed ties with the groups of so-called southerners.[95] The latter group unites Umirzak Shukeyev, the former mayor of Astana and then the vice-prime minister, Sarybay Kalmurzayev, who headed from 2005 to 2008 the financial police and thus was in charge of the fight against corruption; General Kozy-Korpesh Karbuzov, who led the Customs Committee from 2007 to 2011 and now chairs the Center for Military and Strategic Research; and Sat Tokpakbayev, the former director of the KNB and former minister of defense. He is today a deputy of the Mazhilis (the lower house of the Parliament) and remains a member of the KNB. Kelimbetov is also close to Nurlan Balgimbayev, one of Kazakhstan's "oil kings," a consultant for Chevron, director of KazakhOil, and prime minister from 1997 to 1999. In 2007 Balgimbayev was named presidential advisor for energy issues. Since 2009, he has been director-general for joint projects with the Italian company ENI, and presides over the energy construction projects of KazMunayGas, including the Karachaganak refinery, offshore Caspian projects, the modernization of the Pavlodar refinery, and the Uralsk gas station.[96] The balancing game between the Kulibayev–Masimov–Marchenko trio and its competitors is therefore cultivated and probably fuelled directly by President Nazarbayev himself.

Nazarbayev uses the new generation to show the old guard that he still has the ability to alter the existing balance of power among the elite. The most revealing example is that of Darkhan Kaletayev's dazzling career. Both young (born in 1972) and liberal, Kaletayev was first appointed to the vice-presidency of the Presidential Administration, then to that of the presidential party Nur-Otan, before he ended up assuming leadership of Samruk-Kazyna in 2009.[97] This generational change will probably become a key driver in renegotiating the patronal system in Kazakhstan in the years to come. Like the older generation, young technocrats will remain unavoidable "go-betweens" between private interests and the political leadership, and help to defuse potential clashes among the elite, but they will probably also try to take into consideration accountability demands coming from Kazakhstan's society.

As do the members of the family, technocrats and oligarchs alike are aware of the fragility of their position: sanctioned in instances of dispute, they are kept on or even promoted when they submit, despite their averred corruption. No government officials blamed for corruption and abuses have been imprisoned, and none of them was punished in the aftermath of the mishandled accident in Zhanaozen in 2011. Several figures dismissed from their positions after the unrest have since been reinstated: Akchulakov was subsequently appointed deputy minister for gas and oil, while Kusherbayev became Nazarbayev's advisor and then governor of the province of Kyzylorda in 2013.[98] On the other hand, several opposition members were legally prosecuted, most notably Ablyazov and Kazhegeldin. Accusations of corruption are a way of regulating and balancing political influence and economic power.

CONCLUSIONS

At the economic level, neopatrimonial practices do not necessarily work against the country's development, at least not against increases in citizens' living standards: in Ivory Coast, the massive enrichment of the ruling class in the 1970s occurred without impeding growth, just as has happened in Kazakhstan. However, economic growth and long-term development are not corollaries: an enduring reversal in raw material exports to the world market can engender an economic crisis with high political risks.[99] Indeed, neopatrimonialism gambles on the continued exploitation of resources for export, and therefore created an increased risk of Dutch disease[100] to the extent that the elite promote raw materials and neglect other domains, in particular those, more competitive, of innovation and cutting-edge technology, which require extensive infrastructure investments with no immediate return on investment. For two decades now, the Kazakh leadership has not taken up opportunities for economic reform unless they conform to its pre-established interests. Kazakhstan's successful economic path has "purchased" popular support for the regime, and we may seriously question whether patronal practices would have been able to secure political legitimacy in the absence of resource wealth.[101]

At the political level, the reinforcement of neopatrimonial mechanisms in Kazakhstan runs parallel to a rising authoritarianism. Like in Russia, Kazakhstan's population remained largely depoliticized. The leaders' kleptocracy has been the butt of disillusioned mockery, which reveals the very widespread notion that private greed obviously trumps public interests. Few people embrace the idea of a common public space—a *res publica*—for which one may justifiably fight and demand a better distribution of wealth, since the state is not considered an instrument of fair redistribution. In addition, apart from the small, and often discredited, opposition groups, the only visibility the "opposition" has had is that of groups like Democratic Choice of Kazakhstan, whose leaders seem to be more interested in asset redistribution than promoting democracy. However, as a hybrid regime, Kazakhstan's neopatrimonial system also allows for innovation: over the course of many years, the presidential party Nur Otan has become an important and noted place of passage for those looking for a technocratic career. This was not previously the case, and it seems to confirm the indirect institutionalization of parties as one of the centers of power.[102] Meanwhile, the products of the Nazarbayev regime, the new middle class of civil servants and private actors, tend to increasingly demand public accountability and good governance mechanisms from inside the system.

One of Kazakhstan's main issues for the decade ahead is therefore to manage the long-term sustainability of this neopatrimonial regime with an aging president whose legitimacy has become contestable. As in all regimes based on practices of monopolizing wealth, the degree of institutionalization is too weak to enable the regime's beneficiaries to consider their gains secured and legally protected. The prospect of a political succession at the highest levels of state, even if it could be managed without apparent conflict, as in Turkmenistan in 2006 upon the death of Saparmurat Niyazov, potentially opens the way to challenge the wealth distribution among competing groups. That challenge, even if it is only potential and may not materialize, may have implications for the whole decision-making chain, since all actors will take this risk into consideration in elaborating their strategies of political and material survival.

Patronal practices are a way of managing uncertainties in weakly institutionalized systems, and this uncertainty increases when the leader is obliged to leave the scene because of his age. However, Nazarbayev's exit from Kazakhstan's leadership does not mean that the regime will drastically evolve, even if the second president will have to build another type of legitimacy than that of the "father of independence." Some formal evolutions—growing mechanisms of institutionalization, the weight of the presidential administration and of the presidential party, and a more ideologically polarized young generation—signal potential room for changing informal behaviors. Moreover, the authorities have refined their persuasion strategies in a more proactive way, helping to ensure a greater regime survival.[103] But change can also come from external, society-based pressure. Social protests contesting working conditions (salaries, environmental risks, pensions) began in the mid-2000s, but the 2008 economic crisis and the media visibility accorded to the riots in Zhanaozen in December 2011 gave them a long-term impact on public opinion that has taken the political authorities by surprise. The 2016 protests linked to land reform confirmed a change of atmosphere among some parts of the population, and a higher level of disillusion toward the regime's promises. Some parts of the elite could, therefore, decide to base their career strategies on political change and hope to arouse new features of popular support that would challenge the current regime.

NOTES

1. A first version of this article "The Kazakh Neopatrimonial Regime: Balancing Uncertainties among the 'Family,' Oligarchs and Technocrats" was published in *Demokratizatsiya: The Journal of Post-Soviet Democratization* 20, no. 4 (2012): 345–370.

2. Kathleen Collins, *Clan Politics and Regime Transition in Central Asia* (New York: Cambridge University Press, 2006); Ed Schatz, *Modern Clan Politics: The Power of "Blood" in Kazakhstan and Beyond* (Seattle: University of Washington Press, 2004); Nursultan Masanov, "Kazakhskaia politicheskaia i intellektual'naia elita: klanovaia prinadlezhnost' i vnutrietnicheskoe sopernichestvo," in *Evraziia: liudi i mify*, ed. Sergei Panarin (Moscow: Natalis, 2003), 365–380; Vitalii

Khiupin, *Kazakhstanskaia politicheskaia elita: mezhdu modernizatsiei i traibalizmom. Doklad na 2-m vserossiiskom kongresse politologov, Moskva, MGIMO, 22 aprelya 2000g,* Mezhdunarodnyi evraziiskii institut, April 2000, http://www.iicas.org/page .php?id=105.

3. Schatz, *Modern Clan Politics*; Kathleen Collins, "The Logic of Clan Politics: Evidence from the Central Asian Trajectories," *World Politics* 56, no. 2 (2004): 224–261.

4. Masanov, "Kazakhskaia politicheskaia i intellektual'naia elita."

5. Richard L. Wolfel, "North to Astana: Nationalistic Motives for the Movement of the Kazakh(stani) Capital," *Nationalities Papers* 30, no. 3 (2002): 485–506; Jonathan Murphy, "Illusory Transition? Elite Reconstitution in Kazakhstan, 1989–2002," *Europe-Asia Studies* 58, no. 4 (2006): 523–554.

6. Sally N. Cummings, *Kazakhstan: Power and the Elite* (London: I.B. Tauris, 2005); Sally N. Cummings, ed. *Power and Chance in Central Asia* (London: Routledge, 2002); Pauline Jones Luong, ed., *The Transformation of Central Asia: States and Societies from Soviet Rule to Independence* (Ithaca, NY: Cornell University Press, 2003); Pauline Jones Luong, *Institutional Change and Political Continuity in Post-Soviet Central Asia: Power, Perceptions, and Pacts* (New York: Cambridge University Press, 2002).

7. Henry E. Hale, "Regime Cycles: Democracy, Autocracy, and Revolution in Post-Soviet Eurasia," *World Politics* 58, no. 1 (2005): 133–165.

8. Daniel C. Bach and Mamoudou Gazibo, eds., *Neopatrimonialism in Africa and Beyond* (New York: Routledge, 2012); Andre Bank and Thomas Richter, "Neopatrimonialism in the Middle East and North Africa: Overview, Critique and Alternative Conceptualization" (paper presented at the German Institute of Global and Area Studies workshop "Neopatrimonialism in Various World Regions," Hamburg, August 23, 2010).

9. Alice Sindzingre, *The Concept of Neopatrimonialism: Divergences and Convergences with Development Economics* (Hamburg: German Institute of Global and Area Studies, 2010).

10. Anja Franke, Andrea Gawrich, and Gurban Alakbarov, "Kazakhstan and Azerbaijan as Post-Soviet Rentier States: Resource Incomes and Autocracy as a Double 'Curse' in Post-Soviet Regimes," *Europe-Asia Studies* 61, no. 1 (2009): 109–140.

11. On the link between Kazakhstan's nation-branding and promoting its economic competitiveness, see Assel Rustemova, "Political Economy of Central Asia: Initial Reflections on the Need for a New Approach," *Journal of Eurasian Studies* 2, no. 1 (2011): 30–39; Erica Marat, "Nation Branding in Central Asia: A New Campaign to Present Ideas about the State and the Nation," *Europe-Asia Studies* 61, no. 7 (2009): 1123–1136.

12. Rico Isaacs, "Informal Politics and the Uncertain Context of Transition: Revisiting Early Stage Nondemocratic Development in Kazakhstan," *Democratization* 17, no. 1 (2010): 1–25; Rico Isaacs, "'Papa'– Nursultan Nazarbayev and the Discourse of Charismatic Leadership and Nation-Building in Post-Soviet Kazakhstan," *Studies in Ethnicity and Nationalism* 10, no. 3 (2010): 435–452.

13. See Transparency International, accessed July 20, 2015, https://www.transparency.org/country/#KAZ.

14. On offshore Central Asia, see the special issue of *Central Asian Survey* edited by John Heathershaw and Alexander Cooley, 34, no. 1 (2015): 1–147.

15. The same conclusions are drawn by Barbara Junisbai, "A Tale of Two Kazakhstans: Sources of Political Cleavage and Conflict in the Post-Soviet Period," *Europe-Asia Studies* 62, no. 2 (2010): 235–269.

16. Richard Pomfret, *The Economies of Central Asia* (Princeton, NJ: Princeton University Press, 1995); Richard Pomfret, *The Central Asian Economies Since Independence* (Princeton, NJ: Princeton University Press, 2006); Yelena Kalyuzhnova, *The Kazakhstani Economy: Independence and Transition* (Basingstoke, UK: Macmillan, 1998).

17. Jean-François Médard, "L'Etat patrimonialisé," *Politique Africaine*, no. 39 (1990): 31.

18. Pomfret, *The Central Asian Economies Since Independence*.

19. Anne E. Peck, *Economic Development in Kazakhstan: The Role of Large Enterprises and Foreign Investment* (Abingdon, UK: Routledge Curzon, 2004).

20. Martha Brill Olcott, *Kazakhstan: Unfulfilled Promise* (Washington, DC: Carnegie Endowment for International Peace, 2002); Marlene Laruelle and Sebastien Peyrouse, *Les Russes du Kazakhstan. Identité nationale et nouveaux Etats dans l'espace post-soviétique* (Paris: Maisonneuve et Larose, 2004).

21. Alex Cooley, *Great Games, Local Rules: The New Great Power Contest for Central Asia* (New York: Oxford University Press, 2012), 139–140.

22. Cooley, *Great Games, Local Rules*.

23. Natalie Koch, "The 'Heart' of Eurasia? Kazakhstan's Centrally Located Capital City," *Central Asian Survey* 32, no. 2 (2013): 134–147; Adrien Fauve, "Global Astana: Nation Branding as a Legitimization Tool for Authoritarian Regimes," *Central Asian Survey*, 34, no. 1 (2015), 110–124; V. Khliiupin, *"Bol'shaia sem'ia" Nursultana Nazarbaeva. Politicheskaia elita sovremennogo Kazakhstana* (Moscow: Institut aktual'nykh politicheskikh issledovanii, 1998).

24. See the Construction Sector Transparency Initiative, accessed August 20, 2012, http://www.constructiontransparency.org/the_initiative/the_challenge.cfm.

25. Although Nazarbayev's daughter keeps some control on Khabar, the group was taken over by the state on May 5, 2006, which now owns 50 percent plus one of its shares. Maulen Ashimbayev, deputy head of the President's administration, was named the new chairman.

26. D. Ashimbaev, *Kto est' kto v Kazakhstane. Biograficheskaia entsiklopediia* (Almaty: Credo, 2006).

27. Didar Kassyamova, Zhanat Kundakbayeva, and Ustina Markus, *Historical Dictionary of Kazakhstan* (Lanham, MD: Scarecrow Press, 2012), 164.

28. Paul Domjan and Matt Stone, "A Comparative Study of Resource Nationalism in Russia and Kazakhstan 2004–2008," *Europe-Asia Studies* 62, no. 1 (2010): 35–62; Ryan Kennedy and Adilzhan Nurmakov, "Resource Nationalism Trends in Kazakhstan, 2004–2009," *RUSSCASP*, April 2010; Pauline Jones Luong, "Beyond 'Resource Nationalism'? Implications of State Ownership in Kazakhstan's Petroleum Sector," *PONARS Eurasia Policy Memo,* no. 98 (2010).

29. Wojciech Ostrowski, *Politics and Oil in Kazakhstan* (London: Routledge, 2010), especially the chapter "Strengthening the Informal Ties: The Kazakhization of the Oil Industry," 61–80.

30. Martha Brill Olcott, "Kazmunaigaz: Kazakhstan's National Oil and Gas Company," *The James A. Baker III Institute for Public Policy Report*, 2007.

31. Pauline Jones Luong and Erika Weinthal, *Oil Is Not a Curse: Ownership Structure and Institutions in Soviet Successor States* (New York: Cambridge University Press, 2010).

32. Barbara Junisbai and Azamat Junisbai, "The Democratic Choice of Kazakhstan: A Case Study in Economic Liberalization, Intraelite Cleavage, and Political Opposition," *Demokratizatsiya* 13, no. 3 (2005): 373–392; Heidi Kjærnet, Dosym Satpaev, and Stina Torjesen, "Big Business and High-Level Politics in Kazakhstan: An Everlasting Symbiosis?" *The China and Eurasia Forum Quarterly* 6, no. 1 (2008): 95–107.

33. Anthony Clive Bowyer, *Parliament and Political Parties in Kazakhstan* (Washington DC: Central Asia-Caucasus Institute and Silk Road Studies Program, April 2008).

34. Bhavna Dave, "Kazakhstan's 2004 Parliamentary Elections: Managing Loyalty and Support for the Regime," *Problems of Post-Communism* 52, no. 1 (2005): 3–14.

35. Sean Roberts, "Doing the Democracy Dance in Kazakhstan: Democracy Development as Cultural Encounter," *Slavic Review* 71, no. 2 (2012): 308–330.

36. The president's party, Nur-Otan, received about 88 percent of the vote and won all of the available seats. None of the six other parties contesting the election reached the 7 percent threshold to win seats.

37. "OBSE: Vybory v Kazakhstane daleki ot demokratii," *BBC*, January 12, 2012, accessed August 20, 2012, http://www.bbc.co.uk/russian/international/2012/01/120116_kazakhstan_elections_osce.shtml; International Partnership for Human Rights, "A Sobering Reality: Fundamental Freedoms in Kazakhstan, Turkmenistan and Uzbekistan Twenty Years after the Soviet Collapse," *Brussels*, March 2012.

38. Anonymous informant, *Astana*, June 2015.

39. "Timur Kylibaev," *Forbes*, http://forbes.kz/ranking/object/40.

40. Joanna Lillis, "Kazakhstan: Nazarbayev Clan Set to Grow," Eurasianet.org, June 10, 2013, http://www.eurasianet.org/node/67097.

41. "The Billionaires Burned by WikiLeaks," *Forbes,* February 12, 2010, accessed August 20, 2012, http://www.forbes.com/sites/clareoconnor/2010/12/02/the-billionaires-burned-by-wikileaks/; "Za chto Kulibaev pereplatil printsu?" *Respublika*, February 15, 2010, accessed August 20, 2012, http://respublika-kz.info/news/society/7622/.

42. Olcott, *Unfulfilled Promise*, 228.

43. Ashimbaev, *Kto est' kto v Kazakhstane*.

44. Aliev, Rakhat, Lenta.ru, accessed August 20, 2012, http://lenta.ru/lib/14170921/full.htm; "Rakhat Aliyev Searching for Ways to Flee to United States," Tengri News, June 29, 2012, accessed August 20, 2012, http://en.tengrinews.kz/crime/11146/.

45. See his book, R. Aliyev, *The Godfather-in-Law: Eine Dokumentation* (Vienna: Ibera Verlag, 2009).

46. See the chapter on Kazakhstan in Susan Stewart, Margarete Klein, Andrea Schmitz, and Hans-Henning Schröder, eds., *Presidents, Oligarchs, and Bureaucrats: Forms of Rule in the Post-Soviet Space* (Farnham, UK: Ashgate, 2012).

47. "Nazarbaev uvolil ziatia iz-za pogromov v Zhanaozene," Lenta.ru, December 26, 2012, accessed August 20, 2012http://lenta.ru/news/2011/12/26/soninlaw/.

48. "Kazakh president accused of money laundering," Swissinfo.ch, February 13, 2012, accessed May 8, 2016, http://www.swissinfo.ch/eng/kazakh-president-accused-of-money-laundering/32117144.

49. David M. Kemme, "Sovereign Wealth Fund Issues and The National Fund(s) of Kazakhstan," University of Memphis, December 15, 2011, accessed August 20, 2012, https://umdrive.memphis.edu/g-fcbe/www/docs/faculty/Kemme%20NFs%20of%20KZ%20Edited%2012–15-2011.pdf.

50. "Country Report Kazakhstan," *Rabobank,* June 24, 2015, accessed May 8, 2016, https://economics.rabobank.com/publications/2015/june/country-report-kazakhstan/; B. Jardine, "Kazakhstan: Economic Crisis, State Companies, And The Nation's Image," May 13, 2015, accessed May 8, 2016, http://www.rferl.org/content/kazakhstan-economic-crisis/27125331.html

51. "Samruk-Kazyna: Reload," *Kazakhstan International Business Magazine*, June 2009, accessed August 20, 2012, http://www.investkz.com/en/journals/65/552.html.

52. "Kazakhstan Business Forum," accessed August 20, 2012, http://kbf.co/materials/kbf-2010/sponsors/about-samruk-kazyna/; "Gov't Reviews Annual Report by Samruk Kazyna National Welfare Fund," http://portal.mfa.kz/portal/page/ portal/mfa/resources/Pictures/Astana%20Calling%20PDF%202011/Astana%20Calling%20012511.pdf.

53. "Byvshii glava Kazatomproma Mukhtar Dzhakishev poluchil 14 let tiur'my," *CentrAsia,* March 12, 2010, accessed August 20, 2012, http://www.centrasia.ru/newsA.php?st=1268408100; Joanna Lillis. "Kazakhstan: Business Climate Grows Gloomy Amid Arbitrary Arrest Controversy," Eurasianet.org, June 9, 2009, accessed August 20, 2012, http://www.eurasianet.org/departments/insightb/articles/eav061009.shtml.

54. Anonymous interviews with Kazakh experts working in private expertise firms, Almaty September 29, 2010.

55. "Record Year for Kazakh Uranium," World Nuclear Association, February 1, 2011, accessed August 20, 2012, http://www.world-nuclear-news.org/C-Record_year_for_Kazakh_uranium-0102117.html.

56. Guy Chazan, "Kazakhstan Fund Chief Aims to Clean House," *Financial Times*, August 7, 2013, accessed August 20, 2012, http://www.ft.com/cms/s/0/3378da40-ee2f-11e2-a325-00144feabdc0.html#axzz3gSVYkopO; *Alisher Khamidov*, " Kazakhstan Grapples With Reform of Sovereign-Wealth Fund," Eurasianet.org, August 4, 2014, http://www.eurasianet.org/node/69336.

57. Danna Bupezhanova, "Officials Unveil Details of Samruk Kazyna Transformation," *Astana Times*, October 11, 2014, http://www.astanatimes.com/2014/10/officials-unveil-details-samruk-kazyna-transformation/.

58. Vlad Lavrov and Irene Velska "Kazakhstan: President's Grandson Hid Assets Offshore," *OCCRP,* April 4, 2016, accessed May 8, 2016, https://www.occrp.org/en/panamapapers/kazakh-presidents-grandson-offshores/

59. Stratfor, "Who is and who isn't touched by the Panama Papers," April 10, 2016, accessed May 8, 2016, http://www.thepanamanews.com/2016/04/who-is-and-who-isnt-touched-by-the-panama-papers/

60. Bhavna Dave, *Kazakhstan: Ethnicity, Language, and Power* (London: Routledge, 2007), 145.

61. See www.forbes.com/billionaires.

62. Tor Bukkvol, "Astana's Privatized Independence: Private and National Interests in the Foreign Policy of Nursultan Nazarbayev," *Nationalities Papers* 32, no. 3 (2004): 631–650; Kjærnet, Satpaev, and Torjesen, "Big Business and High-Level Politics in Kazakhstan."

63. Daisy Sindelar, "How Far Will Nazarbaev Go to Take Down Mukhtar Ablyazov?" RFE/RL, January 12, 2013, accessed May 8, 2016, http://www.rferl.org/content/kazakhstan-nazarbaev-ablyazov/25010488.html

64. "Mysterious Death of Zamanbek Nurkadilov, Ex-Official Who Ended up in the Opposition to President Nursultan Nazarbayev," Fergananews, November 14, 2011, accessed August 20, 2012, http://enews.fergananews.com/article.php?id=1133 (2); "Kazakhstan: Opposition Figure Murdered At Home," https://metaleaks.net/data/Wikileaks-cablegate/05ALMATY4144.pdf.

65. "Kazkommertsbank Builds Disaster Recovery Distributed IT-Infrastructure Based on IBM Power Systems," Kase.kz, April 20, 2011, accessed August 20, 2010, http://www.kase.kz/files/emitters/KKGB/kkgb_reliz_200411_e.pdf; also see the bank's official website: http://en.kkb.kz/.

66. "EBRR priobrel 15% golosuiushchikh aktsii Kazkommertsbanka," *Kazakhstan Today,* June 7, 2003, accessed August 20, 2010, http://news.gazeta.kz/art.asp?aid=170656. Author's anonymous interviews with Kazakh experts, Almaty, September 27, 2010.

67. Author's anonymous interviews with Kazakh experts, Almaty, September 27, 2010.

68. On this nationalist narrative, see N. Amrekulov, "Stepnoe gosudarstvo (chast' 1)," Zona.kz, no date, accessed August 20, 2011, http://www.zonakz.net/blogs/user/amrekulov_nurlan/10490.html?mode=reply.

69. "BTA Bank nachinaet protseduru privlecheniia k otvetstvennosti Mukhtara Abliazova v Vysokom Sude Anglii za neuvazhenie k sudu," Kase.kz, May 18, 2011, accessed August 20, 2010, http://www.kase.kz/files/emitters/BTAS/btas_reliz_180511.pdf; Erik Larson, "BTA Bank Can Continue $4 Billion Ablyazov Case, Judge Rules," Bloomberg, May 10, 2011, accessed August 20, 2010, http://www.bloomberg.com/news/2011-05-10/bta-bank-wins-u-k-dismissal-of-ablyazov-s-conspiracy-claims.html.

70. M. Assenova, "Ablyazov Sentenced to Prison in UK for Contempt of Court," *Eurasia Daily Monitor*, February 27, 2012; K. Dowell, "BTA v Ablyazov: The Secret Billionaire," *The Lawyer*, February 6, 2012, accessed August 20, 2010, http://www.thelawyer.com/bta-v-ablyazov-the-secret-billionaire/1011246.article; "The Case of Mukhtar Ablyazov: Changing the Status Quo," *The Kazakhstan Insider*, February 5, 2012, 5–6.

71. Rupert Neale, "Arrest warrant for Kazakh billionaire accused of one of world's biggest frauds," *The Guardian*, February 16, 2012, accessed August 20, 2010, http://www.guardian.co.uk/business/2012/feb/16/arrest-warrant-kazakh-billionaire-mukhtar-ablyazov.

72. Global Witness, *Risky Business, Kazakhstan, Kazakhmys Plc and the London Stock Exchange*, July 29, 2010.

73. Global Witness, *Risky Business*.

74. See the company's official website: http://www.enrc.com.

75. Jack Farchy, "Eurasian Resources Group seeks to draw a line under scandals," *FT.com*, November 1, 2015, accessed May 8, 2016, http://www.ft.com/intl/cms/s/0/0132c21e-7800-11e5-a95a-27d368e1ddf7.html#axzz485C0FHj0

76. Simon Goodley, "Two Former Colleagues at Mining Giant ENRC Found Dead in US Hotel," *The Guardian*, May 15, 2015, http://www.theguardian.com/business/2015/may/15/former-colleagues-mining-giant-enrc-found-dead-us-hotel-business.

77. L. Galili, "A Kazakh Oligarch Trying to be a Jewish Tycoon," *Haaretz*, October 28, 2002, accessed August 20, 2012, http://www.haaretz.com/print-edition/features/a-kazakh-oligarch-trying-to-be-a-jewish-tycoon-1.30063; *Euro-Asian Jewish Yearbook, 2008–2009,* Moscow, 2009, http://photo-en.eajc.org/data/image/books/18/0/180_d.pdf#page=8; "Billionaire Mashkevich Quits Euro-Asian Jewish Congress presidency," *The Jewish Telegraphic Agency*, June 27, 2011, http://www.jta.org/news/article/2011/06/27/3088321/billionaire-jewish-leader-resigns.

78. Anonymous interviews with Kazakh experts, Almaty, September 29, 2010.

79. See http://en.government.kz/structure/government.

80. Anonymous interviews with Kazakh experts, Almaty, September 26, 2010.

81. Nurakhmet Kenzheev, "Grigorii Marchenko nadeialsia na 2012 god," *Respublika*, June 10, 2011, accessed August 20, 2012, http://comment-respublika.info/comment/showtopic/9316.

82. Author's anonymous interviews with Kazakh experts, Almaty, September 26, 2010.

83. "Dlia kogo Utemuratov kupil otel' v Vene?" Abiev.kz, October 17, 2012.

84. Ken Silverstein, "A Giant Among Giants," *Foreign Policy* (May–June 2012), accessed August 20, 2012, http://www.foreignpolicy.com/articles/2012/04/23/a_giant_among_giants?page=0,5.

85. "Bulat Utemuratov stanet samym bogatym chelovekom Kazakhstana posle vykhoda na birzhu Glencore," Tengri News, May 11, 2011, accessed August 20, 2012, http://tengrinews.kz/private_finance/187294/.

86. "Samruk-Kazyna vyshel iz kapitala ForteBank," *Kapital.kz*, March 16, 2015 http://kapital.kz/finance/38661/samruk-kazyna-vyshel-iz-kapitala-fortebank.html; "Bulat Utemuratov," http://forbes.kz/ranking/object/41

87. Author's anonymous interviews with Kazakh experts, Almaty, September 26, 2010.

88. Joanna Lillis, "Kazakhstan: Corporate Retreat from LSE Raises Governance Questions," Eurasianet.org, December 4, 2013, http://www.eurasianet.org/node/67830.

89. "Gruppy vliania vo vlastno-politicheskoi sisteme Respublike Kazakhstan," APN, November 29, 2005, accessed August 20, 2012, http://www.apn.kz/publications/article80.htm.

90. On the relationship between elite structure and the concept of political transition, see Jonathan Murphy, "Illusory Transition? Elite Reconstitution in Kazakhstan, 1989–2002," *Europe-Asia Studies* 58, no. 4 (2006): 523–554.

91. Author's anonymous interviews with Kazakh experts, Almaty, September 26, 2010.

92. Author's anonymous interviews with Kazakh experts, Almaty, September 28, 2010.

93. Author's anonymous interviews with Kazakh experts, Almaty, September 26, 2010.

94. E. Mazhitova,"U sviazi Kulibaev - Masimov est' shansy," *Respublika,* November 27, 2009, http://www.respublika-kz.info/news/politics/6518/; A. Saparova, "Sliianie i sliv. Metod Kelimbetova," *CentrAsia,* September 1, 2010, accessed August 20, 2012, http://www.centrasia.ru/newsA.php?st=1283489700.

95. Author's anonymous interviews with Kazakh experts, Almaty, September 26, 2010.

96. Author's anonymous interviews with Kazakh experts, Almaty, September 26, 2010.

97. Author's anonymous interviews with Kazakh experts, Almaty, September 28, 2010.

98. Karina Fayzullina, "Kazakhstan: The House that Nazarbayev Built," *Al Jazeera,* July 24, 2013, http://studies.aljazeera.net/en/reports/2013/07/20137177424222l773.htm.

99. Richard Pomfret, "Kazakhstan's Economy since Independence: Does the Oil Boom Offer a Second Chance for Sustainable Development?" *Europe-Asia Studies* 57, no. 6 (2005): 859–876.

100. Balazs Égert and Carol S. Leonard, "Dutch Disease Scare in Kazakhstan: Is It Real?" *The Michigan University William Davidson Institute Working Paper*, no. 866, March 2007.

101. Andrea Kendall-Taylor, "Purchasing Power: Oil, Elections, and Regime Durability in Azerbaijan and Kazakhstan," *Europe-Asia Studies* 64, no. 4 (2012): 737–760.

102. See Erica Marat's article and the similar conclusions it draws on the situation in Kyrgyzstan: "Kyrgyzstan: A Parliamentary System Based on Inter-Elite Consensus," *Demokratizatsiya. The Journal of Post-Soviet Democratization,* 20, no. 4 (2012): 325–344.

103. Ed Schatz and Elena Maltseva, "Kazakhstan's Authoritarian 'Persuasion'" *Post-Soviet Affairs* 28, no. 1 (2012): 45–65.

Chapter 3

Shrek Meets the President

Magical Authoritarianism in a 'Fairy-Tale' City

Mateusz Laszczkowski

INTRODUCTION: AN UNEXPECTED ENCOUNTER

On a sunny summer afternoon, a merry crowd was abuzz at the feet of Bayterek, the most prominent monument in Kazakhstan's capital, Astana.[1] All around, people strolled, kids flew their kites, and pop tunes blasted from car stereos. Suddenly, I heard the drumming of about a dozen rubber-soled boots and gleeful cries, "Shrek, Shrek!" I raised my head from above the copybook where I was scribbling my field notes and saw a group of elderly Kazakh ladies. Wearing dark velvet vests, white headscarves, long skirts, and rubber boots, they were advancing hurriedly toward a figure of Shrek, the world-famous cartoon character, owned by a photographer working at Bayterek. It was a plastic statue of the seated ogre, about the height of a standing man, movable on armchair wheels. The photographer told me he'd paid roughly $2,000 for it, and expected to recoup his investment soon: everyone wanted a picture with Shrek, and he was charging 500 tenge—about $3 in 2008.

Astana had changed spectacularly since the early 2000s, after Kazakhstan's capital had been relocated there from Almaty in 1997. Within a decade, Astana's population increased nearly threefold through migration from across Kazakhstan.[2] An expansive new part was added to the city, with glass-and-steel skyscrapers, grandiose palaces of officialdom, modern residential estates, and glitzy shopping malls. The construction boom focused on previously undeveloped grounds on the outskirts of the late-Soviet apartment-block neighborhoods and, especially, across the River Ishim. The new development areas on either side of the river quickly became locally known as Astana's "Left Bank." The emergence of this new cityscape materialized an elite vision of Kazakhstan's future as a "modern" developing state.[3]

Bayterek, a hundred-meter tower of white metal topped with a golden glass orb (Figure 3.1), is a central symbol of that vision. The monument's name and shape refer to the Tree of Life from Turkic mythology, while its high-tech style points to the future. Moreover, Bayterek is also the focus of President Nursultan Nazarbayev's "personality cult by proxy."[4] At the viewing platform inside the glass orb, from where the surrounding landscape of oriental domes, glittering towers, and meticulous floral rugs can be beheld (Figure 3.2), there is a stone pulpit with the president's handprint cast in gold (Figure 3.3). Visitors stand upright and stretch their right arm to touch it, prompted by Bayterek's staff to think of a wish, so it may come true. While young people tend to go through this rite posing for photographs with a relaxed cool look, fathers of families and middle-aged matrons make their faces beam with pride and reverence for whatever high values are encapsulated in the presidential handprint. Elderly ladies, like those I saw so excited about Shrek, come to Bayterek dressed up in their golden-embroidered vests. After touching the gold they will typically drag their open hands vessel-like along their faces, replicating the Muslim gesture of concluding a prayer.

Several contributions to this volume work to locate political dynamics in Kazakhstan outside institutional frameworks or in the blurry border zones between the official and the mundane—in areas as diverse as entrepreneurship (Tutumlu), pop music (Rancier), religious practice (Schwab and Bigozhin), and Internet sociality (Laruelle). Likewise, in this chapter, I explore the encounters between individual citizens—residents or visitors to Astana—and various elements of the capital's cityscape, such as Bayterek, as interactive moments in which specific visions of the state, development, and the relationships linking citizens and the regime, are produced. In particular, I begin by wondering, if Shrek and the president share ground—in other words, if encounters with pop-cultural funfair, state symbolism, and quasi-religious charisma are parts of a single experience—how are we to make sense of this? Is it just a coincidence, or perhaps an indication of something larger, to do with the cultural logic of politics in Kazakhstan? What might be the political significance of the particular aesthetics of the Astana cityscape? What may this imply for our understanding of Central Asian politics, and perhaps also for political theory at large?

Taking inspiration from Russian novelist Viktor Erofeev's reflections on the role of magical imagination in modern state power, I suggest that encounters with the new cityscape in Astana foster a mode of domination that I label "magical authoritarianism."[5] This consists of framing the regime vision of development and the president's rule itself as matters of "miracle," "dream," and "beauty," beyond ordinary rationality and thus implicitly beyond public dispute.[6] In this sense, rule and development are "depoliticized"—removed from the scope of what can be sensibly contested, beyond the horizon of the

Figure 3.1 Bayterek. *Source*: Mateusz Laszczkowski.

Figure 3.2 A View to the Left Bank from Bayterek. *Source*: Mateusz Laszczkowski.

"political."[7] In terms borrowed from literary theorist Tzvetan Todorov, the working of "magical authoritarianism" involves the rendering of material reality, and the social and political relations that produce it, as "fantastic"; that is, exceeding common notions of the real.[8] Yet the crucial passage is that between the fantastic and what Todorov calls "the marvelous," when the extraordinary is affirmed as nonetheless empirically real, implying the creative agency of forces or actors that transcend the ordinary. In "magical authoritarianism," that demiurgic role is attributed to the ruler or the elite. Importantly, that attribution rarely takes the form of explicit claims in official discourse. Rather, "magical authoritarianism" as I mean it here operates through the germination of affects and fantasies among citizens.

I highlight ways in which "magical authoritarianism" works as an effect of multiple only loosely connected discourses and performances, rather than a centralized strategy. Its success crucially depends on citizens' imaginations, as they project fantasies in response to the material environment, and on their willful involvement in visits to Bayterek or mass spectacles. Therein lies the ambiguity of "magical authoritarianism." It requires that citizens "suspend disbelief" and find space to sustain the fantastic alongside critical judgment.[9] The new cityscape and public celebrations stimulate imagination and attract citizens who find them aesthetically pleasing. Yet, citizens often remain uncertain as to how to make sense of those forms and actions, or whether Astana is even real.[10] Indeed, as Todorov stresses, ambivalence belongs to

Figrue 3.3 President Nazarbayev's Golden Handprint at Bayterek. *Source*: Mateusz Laszczkowski.

the very nature of the fantastic, balancing precariously between marvelous reality and sheer illusion. Thus, fantasies about the president and about the development of the capital coexist—in tension—with other, more "rational," more reflexive, and more critical modalities of thought. But, as Yael Navaro shown, the force of fantasy in sustaining the mythologies of the state lies precisely in its capacity to withstand critique and to hold together contradictory data.[11]

THE MAGIC OF THE STATE AND ARCHITECTURE

With its five states having followed different trajectories of state formation, post-Soviet Central Asia presents a fascinating field for empirical and comparative political theory.[12] It offers novel possibilities to answer the kinds of questions about relationships between rulers and citizens that have also been asked for other parts of the world.[13] The legitimation of authoritarian regimes—just how do they manage to reproduce consent for their domination?—has been one of the most persistent puzzles in social science literature on Central Asia.[14] However, scholars to date have usually found the stability of (at least some) Central Asian regimes hard to explain. While the Central Asian states are "not very effective" and their leaders' attempts to build legitimating symbols are undermined by "popular attachment to symbols of Sovietism" and Islam, the regimes' legitimacy is "weak," analysts conclude, and relies on "popular apathy."[15]

I suggest that the conventional political science approach, focused on explicit official ideologies, misses the responsiveness and agency of ordinary citizens. Despite excellent studies of imaging the state officially, most scholars of Central Asian politics overlook the significance of citizens' imaginations and fantasies.[16] This is a dimension explored, in contrast, by a growing trend in political anthropology that highlights how "the magic of the state"[17] operates not only through rational discourse and official symbols, but also through other, more affective, expressive, sensuous, and imaginational registers.[18] Even when ostensibly non-political, the diffuse, silent, quotidian work of imagination produces political effects and can turn unlikely, mundane items, say a piece of pipe, a building, or a Shrek mannequin, into compelling epitomes of "the state."[19]

The scholarly literature on the uses of public space and architecture by nationalizing and modernizing regimes is abundant.[20] Regarding Astana, scholars note that regime legitimation in Kazakhstan hinges on a "pre-political consensus"[21] about "development" as materialized in the capital's cityscape.[22] The monumental materiality of Astana helps "depoliticize" development by imposing the regime's particular vision of modernity as an overwhelming fact.[23] As Natalie Koch puts it, "The futuristic portrayal of Kazakhstani modernity inscribed in the Left Bank both imagines a particular future and creates it in so doing—while effectively preempting alternative envisionings of the future."[24]

However, while most studies focus on planners' ideas and the buildings' intended symbolic meanings, I highlight the roles of affect and aesthetics in shaping public imaginaries and generating the political effects of the cityscape. In so doing, I draw on the Benjaminian sense of "aesthetics" as sensory perception and on an established tradition of critical thought emphasizing the enchanting effects of modern technologies, including architecture.[25] I also draw on current work in anthropology, geography, and neighboring disciplines, exploring the multiplicity of ways in which the sensory and affective qualities of particular buildings and spaces bear impact on how citizens feel, think, and act.[26] In the light of this literature, Astana's spectacular, whimsical cityscape offers a compelling site to study how the aesthetics of public space sustain fantasies about the state, development, and technological modernity.[27]

Koch makes the important argument that journalistic and scholarly discourses that portray Astana as "utopian" or "whimsical" help conceal the reality of politico-economic relations behind the development of the Kazakhstani capital.[28] She is certainly right, yet my point is that constructions of Astana as "fairy tale," "miraculous," and "fantastic" are themselves a consequential element of the political reality on the ground, producing power effects. As Bruce Grant puts it, writing of a comparable case of "fairy-tale" monuments in post-Soviet Moscow, "The task is not to see them as an opaque screen that hides politics, but to understand how this particular kind of masking clears space for . . . political practices."[29] Thus my objective in the ethnographic sections that follow is to explore how the aesthetics of new built forms in Astana, the fantasies and affects they stimulate, and certain discourses and performances that qualify and reaffirm those perceptions, might facilitate the reproduction of consent for the given configuration of power relations in Nazarbayev's Kazakhstan.

THE LEFT BANK AS PHANTASMAGORIA

The heart of Astana's Left Bank is Nurzhol Boulevard, a two-kilometer pedestrian promenade with meticulous grass lawns, flowerbeds, small sculptures, and fountains. At one end, it is enclosed by the immense House of Ministries, behind which looms the blue dome of the Presidential Palace. At the opposite end, Nurzhol reaches the gargantuan gate-shaped headquarters of the national oil-and-gas company KazMunayGaz and the copper-red skyscraper of the Communications Ministry. Midway along the boulevard stands Bayterek, its centrality emphasized by a radial arrangement of roadways and sidewalks. Stylistically, Left Bank buildings mix pseudo-classicism with super-modern high-tech and combine references to diverse architectural traditions, including vaguely Arabian domes and Chinese pagodas, with abstract geometrical forms such as a pair of office buildings in the form of golden cones (Figure 3.4). The façades are an extravaganza of color and light reflected in expanses of hued plate glass, shiny metallic tile, or polished stone.

Post-structuralist studies of architecture emphasize that the tangible, brick-and-mortar or glass-and-steel aspect of built space is enmeshed with another aspect—representational, hyper-real, or virtual.[30] The primacy of one over the other cannot be clearly established. Accordingly, the Left Bank's material body of concrete, steel, glass, and other building materials is fused with a tissue of images. Left Bank simulacra are widely present in printed and electronic media in Kazakhstan, found on everyday objects such as chocolate wrappers and banknotes, on roadside billboards, and on the television.[31] In effect, Astana emerges as a visual object, a public image of, literally, picture-perfect, hyper-real order.[32]

However, my focus in this section is on how the sensory experience of the built forms themselves fostered a sense of the Left Bank as a fantastic environment, exceeding the confines of the ordinarily "real." I suggest that the Left Bank belongs to the kind of built space that Walter Benjamin called "phantasmagorias"—engineered environments that are sensorily perceived as

Figure 3.4 The Left Bank Cityscape. *Source*: Mateusz Laszczkowski.

real, yet simultaneously appear fantastic, beyond ordinary reality.[33] Phantasmagorias are as if technology made fantasy come true. Yet to maintain this effect, the possible forms of social engagement with those kinds of spaces must be limited and strictly regulated. Benjamin's chief example of the spread of phantasmagorias into public space were nineteenth-century Parisian shopping arcades whose rows of shop windows were but a faint anticipation of the technical possibilities of construction today. Already in the nineteenth century some sites, such as the World Fairs, "expanded [the] phantasmagoric principle to areas the size of small cities."[34] Much as in the Left Bank, "The sense of sight was privileged in this phantasmagoric sensorium of modernity,"[35] though sight was not the only sense that was targeted. Importantly, phantasmagoric spaces are experienced collectively: "Everyone sees the same altered world, experiences the same total environment. As a result . . . the phantasmagoria assumes the position of objective fact."[36] Thus also in Astana the diversity and scale of the new architectural forms, and their unfamiliar materiality, created a sense of the Left Bank's fantastical character, while simultaneously the particular vision of development epitomized by the built environment became a material fact.

To Astana residents, the new part of the city was extraordinarily impressive, but simultaneously both real and not quite. Its uses remained limited. The Left Bank was primarily a place to show guests around, or go watch others strolling down Nurzhol Boulevard. Other than visual beholding, most citizens had little use for and few ways to engage with the new space. The following quotation from my conversation with two young women, natives to the city, offers a typical illustration:

> *ML:* How do you like the Left Bank?
>
> *Katya:*[37] It's kind of alien to me. . . . One only goes [to the Left Bank] when relatives visit from another city. . . . It's mostly a business quarter. . . . None of my friends or acquaintances live there.
>
> *Sonia:* But the architecture is interesting, sure!
>
> *K:* Oh yeah! The fountains, the buildings, such an interesting style. . .
>
> *S:* It's not like what we're used to in the old city: basically only five-storey buildings—the tallest buildings in the old days had nine floors.

Many other informants of various backgrounds—young urbanites, pensioners, native residents, and migrants with blue-collar and white-collar jobs—similarly emphasized their appreciation for the visual forms of the Left Bank, calling it "interesting," "beautiful," "out-of-this-world," and "modern-looking," but simultaneously expressed a sense of artificiality and estrangement stemming from the limited possible uses of the new space.

Even those who lived or worked in the Left Bank often complained about a sense of isolation in this "one-purpose" space dominated by business and officialdom.[38]

Many residential complexes in the Left Bank are "gated communities" with limited access for non-residents. In turn, the shopping-and-entertainment centers, which in theory anyone can visit, are arguably sites of primarily visual "consumption of space," as dazzling as they are exciting, overflowing with signifiers of capitalist modernity and global markets.[39] Tellingly, when I asked informants to draw maps of Astana from memory, the two most-visited shopping malls at the time of my research, Mega and Sary Arka, were often drawn centrally located, far away from the area marked as "Left Bank," despite their actual location near Nurzhol Boulevard. As one of the map-authors (a female Kazakh psychology graduate, native of Astana) commented, these sites, which residents used relatively frequently, were experienced as "not really parts of the Left Bank at all—they're more like a kind of city-center." Moreover, the maps revealed how few personal connections linked non-Left Bank residents to the Left Bank: while Soviet-era Right Bank neighborhoods were usually densely dotted for sites where the map-author's acquaintances lived, the Left Bank parts of the maps remained almost blank.

In addition to the limited social use of Left Bank spaces, the materials and technologies used in their construction were novel and unfamiliar to most residents. From there stemmed both the enchanting force and the estranging effects of the new architecture. The shiny, smooth, and colorful surfaces and diverse shapes of the new buildings contrasted vividly with the porous and generally gray concrete façades and rectangular forms of Soviet-era structures that still make up the bulk of Astana's cityscape. Katya and Sonia hinted at this "technoaesthetic" difference, noting the humble size and monotony of Soviet-era buildings compared to the Left Bank.[40] Moreover, informants often stressed how quickly the new part of the city developed, changing beyond recognition between their one visit and the next. The rapid pace of construction added to the sense of its fantastic character.

In sum, construction technology, aesthetics, social (dis)use, and limited access converged to produce the Left Bank as a phantasmagoric space. This was an ambivalent effect. The new cityscape left citizens suspended between admiration and estrangement. City residents often criticized the Left Bank, pointing out that it was "like a picture"—aesthetically pleasing, yet suited almost exclusively to visual reception. Other expressions that were frequently used to describe the Left Bank included "artificial," "unreal," and "like a movie set." As I explore elsewhere, that notion of artificiality might imply a critique of the politico-economic relations that produced the cityscape.[41] However, in what follows I focus on some ways in which the phantasmagoric effects of the Left Bank were qualified in discourse and performance to sustain the pre-political consensus on the regime and development.

CITY OF "FAIRY TALE"

A variety of local discourses drew on and reinterpreted the sense of the technologically produced fantastic that saturated the new development areas in Astana. In particular, official and unofficial discourses that referred to the Left Bank as "fairy tale" (*skazka*) further removed the perception of the cityscape from the ordinary and concealed its technological and political nature.[42] Although literary theorists insist that fairy tales express real-life conflicts in society, the way the term was used in Astana usually implied a contradiction-free realm of happy reverie and endless possibility.[43] For example, in my conversations with migrants to Astana, the Russian expression *v skazku popast'* (literally, to get into fairy tale) recurred as a shorthand for the hopes for a perfect life that had driven my interlocutors to move to the capital, or for what they claimed their relatives back home imagined about successful migrants' lives in Astana.[44]

The concept of Astana as a "fairy-tale city" was common in unofficial discourse. My informants often invoked it when asked for their thoughts about the recent construction. Sometimes, the notion of the Left Bank as "fairy tale" allowed conveying the ambiguities that stemmed, as we saw in the previous section, from the material, aesthetic qualities of the new built forms. This can be grasped from the following snippet of a conversation I had with a retired Russian teacher, Efrosiniya Stanislavovna:

> *ES:* The city is beautiful, sure—such a rejuvenation! . . . But it's a little bit like a city of glass [*stekliannyi gorod*] . . . This House of the Ministries, for example—like a castle or something . . . You know, there's this fairy tale about the city of glass? That's the impression: everything there is so cold, as if I got into the ice realm of the Snow Queen!
>
> *ML:* I don't think I know the city-of-glass fairy tale.
>
> *ES:* The city of glass, it's in *The Wizard of the Emerald City* by Volkov. Emeralds are glass too, aren't they?[45]

Efrosiniya Stanislavovna's impressions of the glass-like surfaces and unusual shapes of Left Bank buildings such as the monumental House of the Ministries (Figure 3.5), much like Katya and Sonia's above, were ambiguous. She found the new structures "beautiful" but also "cold" and "alien." Any critique, though, that that might imply remained unarticulated and implicit.

Figure 3.5 The House of the Ministries. *Source*: Mateusz Laszczkowski.

In contrast, diverse public discourses supplied clichés for interpreting the Astana development as "fairy tale" in the unambiguous sense of wondrous, happy reverie come true. Anniversary celebrations of the capital relocation generated particularly intensified public discourse about Astana. In speeches by emcees and government officials, references to the capital as a "miraculous" or "fairy-tale" city (*gorod-chudo*; *skazochnyi gorod*) were recurrent. An especially elaborate example was found in the rousing speech delivered by a young actress as the finale of an animatronics spectacle at the entertainment center Duman. Since Duman is a private enterprise, this example additionally points to the blurring of distinctions between the official and the unofficial.

The spectacle was specially scripted for the Astana anniversary, in lieu of Duman's regular animatronics shows. It featured a quest for the egg of a miraculous bird, stolen by a monster-serpent. The audience participated as Duman guides led them through artificial caves and jungles filled with roaring dinosaurs, Indiana Jones-style temples, giant frogs, apes, spiders, and the like. In the final scene, the egg was recaptured from the monster by a crew of dancers dressed up as "savage warriors" and jungle animals. A girl in an elegant red dress took center stage and gave a speech explaining the meaning of the performance. She spoke of Astana as "the fairy-tale city" that had "risen amid the steppe," "the miracle city of the Tree of Life—Bayterek." In this manner, she made explicit the connection between the spectacle and the official exegesis of Astana's centermost architectural symbol. As mentioned, the name

"Bayterek" refers to the tree of life in a Turkic myth: the bird Samruk lays its golden egg (the Sun, kernel of all life) atop the tree, but a monster-snake devours the egg. Finally, life is saved when the snake is slain by a hero. In Astana, the cosmic egg of golden-hued glass rests safely atop the metal "tree" at the center of the Left Bank. Thus, the cityscape of Astana is not only called "miraculous" but also, implicitly, linked to a narrative that explains the present shape of the world by the feats of a supernatural hero.[46]

Commonly, residents and visitors alike expressed their apperceptions of the Astana development in terms of the "fairy tale"—fantastic, surpassing the ordinary. The Left Bank, in part because of the aesthetics of the built environment and in part due to circulating discursive clichés, was perceived as a wondrous space where development had become a "fairy-tale" fact. The emic notion of "fairy tale" usually implied happiness and the state of hardships overcome, as in the story of the golden egg. I now turn to official celebrations of Astana to examine how public spectacles and visual propaganda contributed to smooth over contradictions, thus further removing rule and development from the political realm of actual or potential contestation.

CELEBRATING ASTANA

The greatest official holiday in recent years in Kazakhstan was the tenth anniversary of the capital relocation, celebrated in 2008. For weeks, the streets of Astana were flooded with holiday visuals and the event was constantly on the news. The central celebrations took a full nine days, culminating on July 6 (which also happens to be President Nazarbayev's birthday), with dozens of concerts, exhibitions, street fairs, and the official opening of new squares, parks, and fountains. The air of the holiday period was one of joy and optimism. Even the weather helped: Astana was enjoying a beautiful summer. Lavish and stunningly colorful flowerbeds had been planted wherever there was an available patch of soil along all main streets. My local research assistant commented that, had I not asked her, she would have never paid attention to the contents of the visuals. But driving home past colorful flags on every lamppost she could feel a holiday atmosphere—and she found that an uplifting feeling.

Scholars have analyzed mass spectacles organized to celebrate official holidays in Kazakhstan, such as the spring holiday Nauryz, May 1, or Astana Day, as the government's means to monopolize the discourse on development, national and civic identities, and economic policy.[47] However, my focus is not so much on the explicit messages, but rather on the aesthetics of celebration. As Paul Connerton argues, the form of a public ceremony often matters more for ideological effects than the textual message purportedly conveyed.[48] The celebrations in Astana saturated public space with particular feelings and enhanced the public perception of the city as a "fairy-tale" space of reverie, obfuscating the political dimension of development.[49] Moreover, the celebrations helped construct an imaginary persona of the president in corresponding emotional terms.

Astana Day visuals (billboards, flags, posters of all sizes) featured watercolor images of selected parts of the new cityscape and citizens enjoying it: a little girl with a bunch of balloons; a smiling elderly war veteran; a young man, his gaze cast in the sky; a couple of romantic lovers. Other pictures showed hot-air balloons and sailboats parading past Astana's waterfront. The images were awash with warm shades of pink, orange, yellow, and green, as if to warm up whatever "cold" the Left Bank buildings might emanate (as the retired teacher above put it). The accompanying slogans emphasized emotions like joy, hope, and love with phrases such as "Space for endless opportunity," "The energy of hopes come true," and "My beloved city." The leitmotif was "Astana—my heart," allegedly the joyous words of President Nazarbayev. Another prominent slogan, also attributed to Nazarbayev, ran "*S liuboviu, Astana!*"—which, on many visuals, was also rendered in English as "From Astana with Love!"[50] This was reproduced in the president's handwriting on posters, in television videos, and in the nightly laser shows where images were projected on a screen of jet-sprinkled water while the audience watched from the riverbank. Many visuals carried no figurative images or verbal messages at all, just a background of colorful stripes and the holiday logo: an abstract composition of curves that could be read as a flower or, equally well, the silhouette of Bayterek.

Holiday spectacles matched this optimistic, carefree style. Each of the multiple shows was a several-hour sequence of blasting pop songs, classical orchestras, dancing ensembles, and colorful "ethnic" acts. Visually and aurally, the mix was dazzling. The lyrics of most songs were simple, about love and Astana, best exemplified by the hit chorus: *Zdravstvuy stolitsa, ty vol'naya ptitsa! Eto—Astana!* (Hello, capital, you're a free bird! This is Astana!). In addition to promoting interpretations of development in Astana as "fairy tale" and "miraculous," the celebratory discourse emphasized aesthetic and emotional qualities attributed to the new cityscape. Astana was referred to as "beautiful" (*krasivaya*) and "remarkable" (*zamechatel'naya*), the "face" (*litso*) or "business-card" (*visitka*) of the country. Speeches by the emcees, invariably dressed up in gala suits or flouncy ball dresses, tirelessly reiterated a limited range of clichés such as *krasavitsa—stolitsa* ("the beauty capital-city") or "the new capital raised from steppe soil like hope for a happy future," interspersed with invocations to the "beloved president."

Within the constraints of this chapter, I cannot elaborate on the reception of these shows by their audiences. Suffice it to say that while many Astana residents, especially members of the Russian minority and long-standing urbanites who felt "besieged" by rural migrants, avoided the celebrations, the concerts and street fairs were nonetheless well-attended.[51] Spectators appreciated the joyous atmosphere, colorful decorations, technological marvels, and pop star performances (while admission to Whitney Houston's show on Astana Day 2008 was strictly limited, shows by Kazakh stars such as Roza Rymbayeva attracted audiences of thousands or tens of thousands). The testimony of a migrant girl, a recent university graduate, who participated in a holiday parade dressed up as a butterfly gives a sense of that atmosphere:

> I enjoyed taking part in this. I liked the costumes—so funny and simple. But the costumes are not the point—the point is to participate. I'm such an artistic person, I liked it, and I called all my friends to come along. I invited people to dance and enjoy themselves. I enjoyed performing, I liked it very much.

According to Milan Kundera, official celebrations in communist Czechoslovakia demanded that citizens express not their approval of communism—an explicitly political position—but of life in general. Similarly, I suggest, the holidays in Astana evoked what Kundera calls the "aesthetic ideal of categorical agreement with being."[52] Through their aesthetic forms, the Astana celebrations construed the new capital as a space filled with "joy," "love," and "optimism." Smoothing over the contradictions of everyday social life, they framed the current political order in terms of feelings that could be approved by anyone and refuted by few. Little if any room was left for contestation.[53] Moreover, the figure of President Nazarbayev was situated in this aestheticized and depoliticized context: he was represented not only as an efficient leader, but as a miracle-worker, the creator of the miracle-city, and the source and object of "love."

VISITING BAYTEREK: SHREK MEETS THE PRESIDENT

The image of Nazarbayev as the architect of miracles is made explicit in a sculpture exhibited at the Presidential Cultural Center—a museum displaying the culture and history of Kazakhstan, with special focus on Astana and the country's development since independence. The sculpture features the president unfolding a spreadsheet with a project map of the new capital. As if on a magic carpet, miniature copies of the principal buildings, including Bayterek, rise from the spreadsheet (Figure 3.6). But the discussion above helps also to contextualize and better understand the curious encounter between Shrek and the president at Bayterek, with which this chapter began. The encounter took place within a material and symbolic space of

Figure 3.6 Nazarbayev as the Architect of Miracles. *Source*: Mateusz Laszczkowski.

"fairy-tale" reverie, constructed through architectural form, discourse, and public celebratory performance. Now it is time to return to Bayterek for a closer look at what goes on in there when citizens visit, and how the threads explored above connect.

Upon arriving at Bayterek, visitors enter a small round hall with a ticket booth and a souvenir kiosk. Built into the wall is a large aquarium with about a dozen goldfish, catfish, and algae-eaters. A fast elevator goes straight to the top floor. Awaiting visitors here are panoramic views of the city and the steppe beyond. As staff members inform the visitors, the platform is situated at the exact height of 97 meters above the ground—after 1997, the year of the capital relocation. Visitors find themselves inside a bubble, elevated high above the ground and insulated from outside sensory inputs: no sounds come in, wind and outside temperature cannot be felt, and even the views are not only extraordinary by virtue of the high vantage point, but additionally modified in color by the golden-hued glass. A short flight of stairs with a chrome-coated railing leads up to a round marble pulpit decorated with golden zoo- and anthropomorphic ornaments imitating the style of Scythian archaeological treasures. On that pulpit lies the golden triangle with Nazarbayev's handprint. Visitors crowd together, awaiting their turn to approach the artifact. When their turn finally comes, they stand upright, stretch out their right arm, and rest their hand into the hollow in the golden triangle. Then they have a picture taken. While immensely popular with casual visitors, this little ritual is a must for newlyweds, who are granted privileged access to the handprint. The groom and the bride put their right hands on it together, the man's palm resting atop his new wife's (Figure 3.7).

Visitors to Bayterek interact with a simulacrum of the president. Much as in the propaganda campaigns above, this simulacrum is disassociated from the political and instead shrouded in vague notions of extraordinariness, sublimity, and "beauty." That effect is produced through the technological engineering of aesthetics. If Astana's new cityscape in general is a Benjaminian phantasmagoria—a technologically manufactured version of reality that impacts the senses—then this applies to Bayterek in particular. The décor materials used (gold, marble, chrome, plate glass), the way they shine, the golden-hued surrounding vistas, and the sensory insulation from the outside environment, add up to create a corporeal sense of Bayterek as an extraordinary site. Moreover, Bayterek is in the center of the Left Bank "fairy-tale" landscape—here spread out before the visitors. Within this marvelous, phantasmagoric space, even the idea of making a wish while touching the presidential handprint may make some kind of sense. When I asked my Astana acquaintances about their wishes at Bayterek, most responses revealed an ambivalent attitude. While some informants called the rite "childish" or laughed at their own naiveté in reiterating it, most reported considerably

Figure 3.7 Newlyweds at Bayterek. *Source*: Mateusz Laszczkowski.

serious wishes: finding a job, an apartment, successful graduation, or even development for Kazakhstan and peace for the world.

The extraordinariness of Bayterek and the surrounding cityscape is associated with the imagined figure of Nazarbayev. Consider the following testimony by a middle-aged Kazakh visitor, who said she always thought Bayterek was on a par with Kazakhstan's most sacred Islamic pilgrimage-site, the Yasawi Mausoleum at Turkestan. "It's beyond ordinary people . . . Great people built it," the woman said, referring as much to the Turkestan Mausoleum as to Bayterek. She continued:

> The president thought of it, how it [Bayterek] would do—well, if not in five hundred years [a reference to the age of the Yasawi Mausoleum, dating back to around C.E. 1400], than in a hundred or two hundred years. . . . It took great people to build the Pyramids [in Egypt]. . . . The same thing here, each time I'm visiting Bayterek I think of it.

In semiotics, Alfred Gell explains, the term "abduction" refers to a kind of relation between a sign and its hypothetical origin.[54] When guesswork as to how the sign has come about and what it represents leads to a supposition of the kind "it must have been such-and-such who caused this," then this, in Gell's terms, is a case of "abduction of agency." The lady just quoted thus "abducts" the agency of "great people," Nazarbayev a case of that genus: since no "ordinary people" could have managed to create Bayterek, it must be the brainchild of the president. Implicitly, the president is posited as a figure endowed with extraordinary powers. In Todorov's terms, both Bayterek and its creator Nazarbayev are instances of "the marvelous"—real but surpassing ordinary reality.[55] Moreover, as Gell stresses, the relative impossibility to comprehend the technology behind a given artifact—how was it made?—strengthens its "enchanting" force.[56] Bayterek displays numerous products of superb technology, from golden carvings and marble pulpits to bird's-eye vistas filtered through golden-hued glass. As some visitors remembered, in the initial period after Bayterek was first opened, yet another technological marvel used to be in operation: when a visitor touched the presidential handprint, the golden orb filled with the sounds of the national anthem. The mastery of all that marvelous technology is attributed to Nazarbayev (via his artisans). To make sure visitors are sufficiently impressed, numbers such as the tower's height (105 meters), the golden ball's diameter (22 meters), its weight (70 tons), and surface area (1,553 square meters) are recited as proofs of technological excellence. Following Todorov, we might speak here of "instrumental" as well as "hyperbolic marvelous"—the former referring to extraordinary devices (akin to the flying carpet), the latter to phenomena that are extraordinary "by virtue of their dimensions."[57]

In a nutshell, it might be said that technology and aesthetics are employed at Bayterek (and, by extension, throughout the hyper-real Left Bank cityscape) to endow President Nazarbayev with charisma, in Max Weber's classic sense.[58] But charisma is not all there is to Nazarbayev's magical-authoritarian aura. As scenes such as the one opening this chapter make evident, with the constant snap-shooting and child-like excitements to which even the most mature visitors succumb, the experience of visiting Bayterek is not exclusively saturated with reverence and sublimity, but also much entertainment and carelessness. The president is encountered (metonymically, via his handprint) as a "great person," but it is equally relevant, I argue, that at Bayterek he shares ground with Shrek. The ogre's presence seems almost plausible amid the "fairy-tale" landscape where certain artifacts are said to make wishes come true. Shrek represents a pop-cultural fairy-tale imaginary conducive to a "categorical agreement with being," to invoke Kundera's words once more, and patently non-political. The fairy-tale imaginary is also congruent with the framing of the president's figure and of the development in Astana that he personifies in feel-good platitudes through official celebrations, as discussed earlier. Additionally, Shrek is foreign, cosmopolitan, and "modern"—coming from a recent, world-famous American cartoon—all of which makes him at home in the Left Bank. On the one hand, then, Shrek's presence appears only natural in Astana, while on the other it enhances President Nazarbayev's positioning as a fantastic figure—or rather, in Todorov's precise terms, a marvelous one: a ruler who surpasses ordinary reality and belongs to the world of "fairy tale" come true.

CONCLUSION

The route taken in this chapter, through the aesthetics of the built environment in Astana's Left Bank, public discourses, holiday celebrations, and finally back to where it started, to Bayterek, helps understand the president's unexpected encounter with Shrek. The spell of "magical authoritarianism" consists in creating a material-and-symbolic space of marvelous "fairy tale" where rule and development are framed as matters of "miracle," "beauty," "joy," and sources of "love." This is allowed, fundamentally, by construction technology that enables the creation of phantasmagoric milieus where visitors' sensory experience reaffirms that what seems a fantasy, beyond the ordinary real, is actually material and true. That experience is additionally articulated through multiple official and unofficial, quotidian and holiday discourses. The creative agency behind the marvelous reality is attributed to the president, and fantasies about his extraordinary, perhaps even supernatural powers, such us the power encapsulated in the president's golden handprint to make wishes come true, are encouraged. In effect, the president's rule and the regime's agenda of development are depoliticized—removed from the scope of what can be sensibly subject to public contestation. In conclusion, it seems in order to highlight the limits of the "magical authoritarianism" hypothesis and provisionally indicate some of its broader implications.

The interpretation offered above diverges from and complements available analyses of legitimation in contemporary Kazakhstan. While most scholarship focuses on explicit official ideologies and symbols, including the meanings inscribed in the architectural forms of Astana, I have highlighted the aesthetics of direct encounters with the constructed environment as important loci where the political and the non-political is defined. I have underscored the importance of subjective and often vague fantasies fostered by those encounters for the reproduction of "the magic of the state." But "magical authoritarianism," of course, is not the ultimate solution to the puzzle of consent for domination, in general, or in Kazakhstan, in particular. No doubt, it is just one of multiple factors in play—one that has largely been unglossed in the "regime legitimation" scholarship, I presume due to the implicit and ostensibly "innocent," "apolitical" character of its forms and mechanisms. The major challenge to this mode of reproducing consent is that it depends on citizens' readiness to suspend their critical judgment. In the ethnography above, that fragility of "magical authoritarianism" repeatedly became palpable, as when my informants expressed their uncertainty about what to make of the Left Bank cityscape or of the "rite" of the presidential handprint.

Furthermore, despite the image emerging from official and unofficial discourses in Kazakhstan of Nazarbayev as the mastermind behind pretty much everything to do with the public life of the country, "magical authoritarianism" turns out a contingent product of multiple subjective contributions. The supplying of images and discursive clichés through official propaganda is only one aspect of this dynamic. Both the force and the limitations of "magical authoritarianism" stem from the fact that it relies on citizens' subjective fantasies and their willingness to participate in performances. Scholars have approached the problem of popular involvement in the reproduction of domination and consent under authoritarian regimes in a diversity of ways. Lisa Wedeen, for instance, analyzes the "cult" of President Hafiz al-Asad in late-twentieth-century Syria. According to her, the compliance of Syrian citizens was underpinned with their "cynical apathy"[59]—an unenthusiastic realization that reproducing outward signs of submission, against better knowledge, allowed one to survive day-to-day with relative ease under what was otherwise a violently oppressive regime. In contrast, I argue that the reproduction of consent in Astana was based in a different "structure of feeling": hope, marvel, and enchantment, produced (even if ambiguously or ephemerally) by architectural phantasmagorias.[60] That is the difference, I suggest, between "phony," to use Wedeen's term, and "fairy tale."

Finally, the "magical authoritarianism" hypothesis presented here suggests revisiting the relationship between technological development and nondemocratic state power. Anthropologists have studied how discourses of modernization and development have the effect of preempting democratic control over government by positing it as an "objective," technical apparatus of "rational" improvement—a dynamics that James Ferguson has famously dubbed the "anti-politics machine."[61] Ethnographic focus on Astana complements the critique of such "anti-political" effects of technological development by emphasizing how technology becomes the source of fantasies and enchantments. Entanglements of technology, imagination, and aesthetics can frame domination not, or not only, as technical-rational, but also as "fairy tale." Indeed, as in all phantasmagorias, the technical is a crucial part of the "magic" in Kazakhstan's "magical authoritarianism." In Astana, construction technology has made the marvelous "fairy-tale" future tangible, despite all inherent ambiguity.

NOTES

1. This research was made possible by SocAnth—Marie Curie Early Stage Training network, MEST-CT-2005–020702 and hosted by the Max Planck Institute for Social Anthropology, Halle. I wish to particularly thank Svetlana Jacquesson for her support during my work on the larger project from which this chapter is drawn. I also wish to thank Judith Beyer, Alima Bissenova, Sally Cummings, Natalie Koch, Gabriel McGuire, Madeleine Reeves, Tommaso Trevisani, and Bea Vidacs for comments on earlier versions of the manuscript.

2. The population grew from about 275,000 in 1998 to approximately 700,000 in 2009.

3. Victor Buchli, "Astana: Materiality and the City," in *Urban Life in Post-Soviet Asia*, ed. Catherine Alexander, Victor Buchli, and Caroline Humphrey (London: University College Press, 2007), 40–69; Natalie Koch, "The Monumental and the Miniature: Imagining 'Modernity' in Astana," *Social and Cultural Geography* 11, no. 8 (2010): 769–787; Mateusz Laszczkowski, "Building the Future: Construction, Temporality, and Politics in Astana," *Focaal: Journal of Global and Historical Anthropology* 60 (2011): 77–92; Mateusz Laszczkowski, "State Building(s): Built Forms, Materiality, and the State in Astana," in *Ethnographies of the State in Central Asia: Performing Politics*, ed. Madeleine Reeves, Johan Rasanayagam, and Judith Beyer, (Bloomington: Indiana University Press, 2014), 149–172.

4. Laura Adams and Assel Rustemova, "Mass Spectacle and Styles of Governmentality in Kazakhstan and Uzbekistan," *Europe-Asia Studies* 61, no. 7 (2009): 1249–1272.

5. Erofeev speaks of "magical totalitarianism" to describe the kind of power that Stalin, according to the author, exerted upon Russian imagination. Viktor Erofeev, *Khoroshii Stalin: Roman* [The Good Stalin: A Novel] (Moscow: ZebraE, 2004), 133.

6. cf. Fernando Coronil, *The Magical State: Nature, Money, and Modernity in Venezuela* (Chicago: University of Chicago Press, 1997).

7. cf. James Ferguson, *The Anti-Politics Machine: "Development," Depoliticization, and Bureaucratic Power in Lesotho* (Minneapolis: University of Minnesota Press, 1994); Chantal Mouffe, *On the Political* (London: Routledge, 2005); Jacques Rancière, *The Politics of Aesthetics*, Gabriel Rockhill, trans. (London: Bloomsbury, 2004).

8. Tzvetan Todorov, *The Fantastic: A Structural Approach to a Literary Genre*, Richard Howard, trans. (Ithaca, NY: Cornell University Press, 1975).

9. Samuel T. Coleridge, *Biographia Literaria*, vol. 1 (1817; repr., Oxford: Oxford University Press, 1969)

10. cf. Mateusz Laszczkowski, "'Demo-Version of a City': Buildings, Affects, and the State in Astana," *Journal of the Royal Anthropological Institute* 22, no. 1 (2016): 148–165.

11. Yael Navaro-Yashin, *Faces of the State: Secularism and Public Life in Turkey* (Princeton, NJ: Princeton University Press, 2002). Also see Begoña Aretxaga, "Maddening States," *Annual Review of Anthropology* 32 (2003): 393–410.

12. Pauline Jones Luong, ed. *The Transformation of Central Asia: States and Societies from Soviet Rule to Independence* (Ithaca, NY: Cornell University Press, 2004); Madeleine Reeves, Johan Rasanayagam, and Judith Beyer, eds. *Ethnographies of the State in Central Asia: Performing Politics* (Bloomington: Indiana University Press, 2014).

13. For example Achille Mbembe, "Provisional Notes on the Postcolony," *Africa* 62, no. 1 (1992): 3–37; Lisa Wedeen, *Ambiguities of Domination: Politics, Rhetoric, and Symbols in Contemporary Syria* (Chicago: University of Chicago Press, 1999).

14. Andrew March, "From Leninism to Karimovism: Hegemony, Ideology, and Authoritarian Legitimation," *Post-Soviet Affairs* 19, no. 4 (2003): 307–336; Sally N. Cummings, *Kazakhstan: Power and the Elite* (London: I.B. Tauris, 2005); Anna Matveeva, "Legitimising Central Asian Authoritarianism: Political Manipulation and Symbolic Power," *Europe-Asia Studies* 61, no. 7 (2009): 1095–1121; Asel Murzakulova and John Schoeberlein, "The Invention of Legitimacy: Struggles in Kyrgyzstan to Craft an Effective Nation-State Ideology," *Europe-Asia Studies* 61, no. 7 (2009): 1229–1248; Edward Schatz, "The Soft Authoritarian Tool Kit: Agenda-Setting Power in Kazakhstan and Kyrgyzstan," *Comparative Politics* 41, no. 2 (2009): 203–222; Alima Bissenova, "Post-Socialist Dreamworlds: Housing Boom and Urban Development in Kazakhstan" (PhD diss., Cornell University, 2012).

15. Matveeva, "Legitimising Central Asian Authoritarianism," 1100.

16. cf. Laura Adams, *The Spectacular State: Culture and National Identity in Uzbekistan* (Durham, NC: Duke University Press, 2010); Sally N. Cummings, ed. *Symbolism and Power in Central Asia: Politics of the Spectacular* (London: Routledge, 2010).

17. Michael Taussig, *The Magic of the State* (New York: Routledge, 1997).

18. Aretxaga, Begoña. "A Fictional Reality: Paramilitary Death Squads and the Construction of State Terror in Spain." In Death Squad: The Anthropology of State Terror, edited by Jeffrey A. Sluka, 46–69. Philadelphia: University of Pennsylvania Press, 2000; Aretxaga, "Maddening States"; Uli Linke, "Contact Zones: Rethinking the Sensual Life of the State," *Anthropological Theory* 6, no. 2 (2006): 205–225; Navaro-Yashin, *Faces of the State*; Yael Navaro-Yashin, *The Make-Believe Space: Affective Geography in a Post-War Polity* (Durham, NC: Duke University Press, 2012); Mateusz Laszczkowski and Madeleine Reeves, "Introduction: Affective States—Entanglements, Suspensions, Suspicions," *Social Analysis* 59, no. 4 (2015): 1–14; Jonathan Spencer, *Anthropology, Politics, and the State: Democracy and Violence in South Asia* (Cambridge: Cambridge University Press, 2007).

19. Madeleine Reeves, "Materialising State Space: 'Creeping Migration' and Territorial Integrity in Southern Kyrgyzstan," *Europe-Asia Studies* 61, no. 7 (2009): 1277–1313.

20. See, for instance, John Agnew, "The Impossible Capital: Monumental Rome under Liberal and Fascist Regimes, 1870–1943," *Geografiska Annaler* 80B, no. 4 (1998): 229–240; Sibel Bozdoğan, *Modernism and Nation Building: Turkish Architectural Culture in the Early Republic* (Seattle: University of Washington Press, 2001); David Crowley and Susan E. Reid, eds. *Socialist Spaces: Sites of Everyday Life in the Eastern Bloc* (Oxford: Berg, 2002); Michael Denison, "The Art of the Impossible: Political Symbolism, and the Creation of National Identity and Collective Memory in Post-Soviet Turkmenistan," *Europe-Asia Studies* 61, no. 7 (2009): 1167–1187; James Holston, *The Modernist City: An Anthropological Critique of Brasilia* (Chicago: University of Chicago Press, 1989); Paul Rabinow, *French Modern: Norms and Forms of the Social Environment* (Chicago: University of Chicago Press, 1989); Lawrence J. Vale, *Architecture, Power, and National Identity* 2nd ed. (London: Routledge, 2008); Gwendolyn Wright, *The Politics of Design in French Colonial Urbanism* (Chicago: University of Chicago Press, 1991).

21. March, "From Leninism to Karimovism."

22. Adams and Rustemova, "Mass Spectacle and Styles of Governmentality in Kazakhstan and Uzbekistan"; Shonin Anacker, "Geographies of Power in Nazarbayev's Astana," *Eurasian Geography and Economics* 45, no. 7 (2004): 515–533; Richard L. Wolfel, "North to Astana: Nationalistic Motives for the Movement of the Kazakh(stani) Capital," *Nationalities Papers* 30, no. 3 (2002): 485–506.

23. Ferguson, *The Anti-Politics Machine*.

24. Koch, "The Monumental and the Miniature," 776.

25. Susan Buck-Morss, "Aesthetics and Anaesthetics: Walter Benjamin's Artwork Essay Reconsidered," *October* 62 (1992): 3–41; Walter Benjamin, "Paris, Capital of the Nineteenth Century," in *The Arcades Project*, Howard Eiland and Kevin McLaughlin, trans. (1939; Cambridge, MA: Harvard University Press, 1999), 14–26; Jane Bennett, *The Enchantment of Modern Life: Attachments, Crossings, and Ethics* (Princeton, NJ: Princeton University Press, 2001); Alfred Gell, "The Technology of Enchantment and the Enchantment of Technology," in *The Art of Anthropology: Essays and Diagrams*, ed. Eric Hirsch (London: Athlone Press, 1999), 159–186.

26. Navaro-Yashin, *The Make-Believe Space*; Nigel Thrift, *Non-Representational Theory: Space, Politics, Affect* (London: Routledge, 2008); Kathleen Stewart,

"Atmospheric Attunements," *Environment and Planning D: Society and Space* 29, (2011): 445–453.

27. Laszczkowski, "Demo-Version of a City."

28. Natalie Koch, "Urban 'Utopias': The Disney Stigma and Discourses of 'False Modernity'" *Environment and Planning A* 44, (2012): 2445–2462.

29. Bruce Grant, "New Moscow Monuments, or, States of Innocence," *American Ethnologist* 28, no. 2 (2001): 337.

30. M. Christine Boyer, *The City of Collective Memory: Its Historical Imagery and Architectural Entertainments* (Cambridge, MA: MIT Press, 1994); Michel Foucault, "Of Other Spaces," *Diacritics* 16, no. 1 (1986): 22–27; Fredric Jameson, *Postmodernism, Or the Cultural Logic of Late Capitalism* (Durham, NC: Duke University Press, 1991); Edward W. Soja, *Thirdspace: Journeys to Los Angeles and Other Real-and-Imagined Places* (Cambridge, MA: Blackwell, 1996).

31. cf. Jean Baudrillard, *Simulacra and Simulation* (Ann Arbor: University of Michigan Press, 1994).

32. Laszczkowski, "Building the Future," 84–90.

33. Benjamin, "Paris, Capital of the Nineteenth Century"; Margaret Cohen, "Walter Benjamin's Phantasmagoria," *New German Critique* 48 (1989): 87–107.

34. Buck-Morss, "Aesthetics and Anaesthetics," 22.

35. Buck-Morss, "Aesthetics and Anaesthetics," 24.

36. Buck-Morss, "Aesthetics and Anaesthetics," 23.

37. The names and nicknames of all informants appearing in this chapter have been changed.

38. This chapter draws on fieldwork conducted mainly in 2008–2009. By 2012, when I returned to Astana, the social uses of space in the Left Bank had become more frequent, inclusive, and diversified. Yet the perceptions to which I refer had not entirely vanished.

39. Jon Goss, "The 'Magic of the Mall': An Analysis of Form, Function, and Meaning in Contemporary Retail Built Environment," *Annals of the Association of American Geographers* 83, no. 1 (1993): 18–47; Mateusz Laszczkowski, "Superplace: Global Connections and Local Politics at the Mega Mall, Astana," *Etnofoor* 23, no. 1 (2011): 85–104; Mark Gottdiener, "The Consumption of Space and the Spaces of Consumption," in *New Forms of Consumption: Consumers, Culture, and Commodification*, ed. Mark Gottdiener (Oxford: Rowman and Littlefield, 2000) 265–285.

40. Buck-Morss, "Aesthetics and Anaesthetics," 22.

41. Laszczkowski, "Demo-Version of a City."

42. See Koch, "Urban 'Utopias.'"

43. cf. Jack Zipes, "Breaking the Magic Spell: Politics and the Fairy Tale," *New German Critique* 6 (1975): 116–135.

44. Laszczkowski, "Building the Future"; Mateusz Laszczkowski, *"City of the Future": Built Space, Modernity and Urban Change in Astana* (New York: Berghahn Books, 2016).

45. The Snow Queen refers to the internationally known tale by Hans Christian Andersen. *The Wizard of the Emerald City* by Alexander Melentyevich Volkov, in turn, draws on Frank Baum's *The Wonderful Wizard of Oz* and is familiar to generations of Russophone readers.

46. Other examples of explicitly fairy-tale elements in the cityscape can be quoted. In Nurzhol Boulevard, several enormous rings are scattered, as if dropped from the fingers of giants. Several architects and sculptors whose works adorn Astana emphasized in interviews that Kazakh folk tales and legends were a source from which they amply drew.

47. Adams and Rustemova, "Mass Spectacle and Styles of Governmentality in Kazakhstan and Uzbekistan."

48. Paul Connerton, *How Societies Remember* (Cambridge: Cambridge University Press, 1989), 41–71.

49. Sara Ahmed, *The Cultural Politics of Emotion* (Edinburgh: Edinburgh University Press, 2004).

50. This slogan was used interchangeably in Russian, Kazakh, and English. The English version is not quite true to the Russian original. The Russian phrase can be understood in the vocative: "[To you,] Astana, with love!"

51. Laszczkowski, *"City of the Future."*

52. Milan Kundera, *The Unbearable Lightness of Being*, Michael H. Heim, trans. (New York: Harper and Row, 1984), 248.

53. One of my local friends, Bella, at that time an economics undergraduate, argued that it was solely due to my own peculiar bias that I could see anything "political" about Astana Day at all. She thought Kazakhstan would be much better off if the government put forth an explicit "ideology" and tried to engage the citizens in "political" activism (cf. Murzakulova and Schoeberlein, "The Invention of Legitimacy"). Bella's words highlight the extent to which the political character of the Astana celebrations was successfully obfuscated.

54. Alfred Gell, *Art and Agency: An Anthropological Theory* (Oxford: Clarendon Press, 1998), 14–16.

55. Todorov, *The Fantastic.*

56. Alfred Gell, "The Technology of Enchantment and the Enchantment of Technology," in *The Art of Anthropology: Essays and Diagrams*, ed. Eric Hirsch (London: Athlone Press, 1999), 159–186.

57. Todorov, *The Fantastic*, 54–56.

58. Weber's definition of charisma might be worth recalling: "a certain quality of an individual personality by virtue of which he [*sic*] is considered extraordinary and treated as endowed with supernatural, superhuman, or at least specifically exceptional powers or qualities . . . and on the basis of them the individual concerned is treated as a 'leader.'" Max Weber, "The Types of Legitimate Domination," in *Economy and Society: An Outline of Interpretive Sociology*, 1922, ed. Guenther Roth and Claus Wittich, Ephraim Fischoff et al., trans. 212–301. (Berkeley: University of California Press, 1978), 241.

59. Weeden, *Ambiguities of Domination*, 147. Note the similarity of this phrase to Matveeva's "popular apathy," cited above in the introduction; Matveeva, "Legitimising Central Asian Authoritarianism."

60. Raymond Williams, *Marxism and Literature* (Oxford: Oxford University Press, 1977).

61. Ferguson, *The Anti-Politics Machine.* For Kazakhstan, see Koch, "The Monumental and the Miniature."

Chapter 4

Shrines and Neopatrimonialism in Southern Kazakhstan

Wendell Schwab and Ulan Bigozhin

INTERPRETATIONS OF SHRINE-BASED ISLAMIC PRACTICE IN CENTRAL ASIA

Shrines are important places of Islamic practice in Central Asia.[1] Central Asians go to shrines seeking luck, cures for illnesses, and knowledge about Islam and history. Some shrines are located on busy city streets, such as the shrine of Raiymbek Batyr in Almaty, where cab drivers silently ask for blessings as they speed by the shrine. Other shrines are found in the countryside; pilgrims must drive through the southern Kazakhstani desert to reach the shrine of Ukasha Ata. This chapter explores shrine-based Islamic practices in Qalakent, a small city in southern Kazakhstan near Taraz. Specifically, we link these practices to neopatrimonialism by examining two narratives describing the discovery of a shrine in the city.[2]

Other scholars have examined shrine-based religious practice in Kazakhstan. Bruce Privratsky, for example, argues that the persistence of shrine-based pilgrimage practices in Kazakhstan is the result of Soviet bureaucrats' incompetence in stamping out religion.[3] In his words, these practices survived in the "collective memory" of Kazakhs. In this view, Soviets attacked mosques, imams, sacred lineages such as Qozhas, and Islamic publishing. They were successful in creating a new, secular public sphere. However, Soviet bureaucrats ignored the domestic rituals and pilgrimages that sustained an Islamic ethos among many Kazakhs. Moreover, Soviet bureaucrats ignored the Islamic practices of pensioners and retirees. This created a flexible piety differentiated by age. Young men and women most involved with the Soviet state could participate in life-cycle rituals such as funerary feasts but otherwise be publicly secular. Kazakhs could become more publicly religious as they aged, if they desired. Domestic practices and shrine pilgrimage dominated religious life in Kazakhstan in the 1990s when Privratsky did his work, and this legacy continues to be important today.[4] Pavel Jessa similarly argues that the shrine-based practices of a particular Islamic movement, Aq Zhol, are a "rediscovered tradition."[5] This "rediscovered tradition" adds new-age ideas such as "bioenergy" to past practices while operating in a post-Soviet social environment that includes non-Muslims, such as Russians and other "Europeans." For Jessa and Privratsky, shrine-based Islamic practice has remained popular because it was historically important in Kazakhstan and survived the Soviet Union's assault on Islam.

Elsewhere in Central Asia, Maria Louw argues that Uzbekistani shrines are places for "moralities in the making."[6] For Louw, Uzbeks go to shrines to find meaning in the face of life crises or moral confusion. The expansion of shrine-based Islamic practice correlates with the anomie of post-Soviet Uzbekistan, as well as newfound state support for shrines. Johan Rasanayagam discusses shrine-based pilgrimage in terms of the debate between Muslims on how to perform pilgrimage and the intelligibility of pilgrimage to Uzbeks who have different theological interpretations of pilgrimage.[7] Krisztina Kehl-Bodrogi examines Uzbekistani pilgrimage in light of the changing state support for pilgrimage and shrines, and bureaucratic attempts to control Islamic practice at shrines.[8]

We want to add to this literature by suggesting that shrine-based practice is not only a continuation of Islamic practices that have endured in the Soviet era or a way to make meaning in the anomie of the post-Soviet world, although we find these two interpretations helpful.[9] We argue that shrine-based practices resonate with post-Soviet neopatrimonial politics because shrine-based practices resemble everyday action within a neopatrimonial political economy. This is not to say that neopatrimonial politics cause shrine-based practice or vice versa. Rather, they resonate with each other, increasing one another's potency.[10]

WEBER'S TYPOLOGIES OF RELIGION, RATIONALIZATION, AND DOMINATION

Weber argues that religions can be conceived of as one of two ideal types: "traditional," in which loosely ordered religious actions achieve concrete, often ad hoc, goals and "rationalized," in which coherently bundled religious actions achieve abstracted goals.[11] Examples help illustrate the concept: a Norse pagan may have performed a ritual to ask a spirit to ensure a good harvest; a Protestant reads scripture and compares methods of moral training in order to find the best method to get to Heaven. Weber further argues that rationalization is a process tied to modernity and the modernization of the world. The world becomes disenchanted as sacredness moves from commonplace objects such as trees and graves to intangible notions and realms such as God and Heaven Universal rules replace local routines. As Geertz remarks, even if these categories are overgeneralizations, they are a useful starting point to discuss religious change.[12]

In Kazakhstan, it would be easy to label scripturalist Muslims as "rational" Muslims.[13] They seek to understand the universe at large and formulate an internally coherent account of the universe and morality. Pilgrims or others involved in shrine-based Islamic practice could be seen as observing a "traditional" form of Islam. They seek answers to concerns of health and wealth, and their answers to particular events are tied not to grand theories but to fragmentary, local explanations. Scripturalist Muslims, following Weber, would be the future of Islam in Kazakhstan, while shrine-based Islamic practice would belong to the past. It is precisely this point that we want to challenge. Ethnographically, in the post-Soviet era, we have not seen a decrease in shrine-based Islamic practice. Part of the reason that "traditional" shrine-based practices are not disappearing is because shrine-based Islamic practices resonate with neopatrimonialism.

Neopatrimonialism is a concept built on Weber's work on patrimonial domination.[14] Patrimonial domination refers, in part, to ruling with an administrative staff that is related to the ruler through ties of loyalty and whose duty is to manage property or subjects for the ruler. For example, a king may recruit his staff from kinsmen, friends, or economic clients. Patrimonial positions lack "the bureaucratic distinction between the private and the official spheres."[15] In the ideal patrimonial government, who gets what, where, and when is based on personal relationships rather than bureaucratic rules. Neopatrimonialism is a hybrid political economy; legal-bureaucratic domination exists alongside patrimonial domination. State officials use laws and bureaucratic procedures to exploit state property for their own profit and to recruit others into a web of patron-client relationships. Bureaucrats' rule of law exists side-by-side with patrons' rule by law. Profits from state resources are often reinvested in other enterprises, such as commercial real estate, international mutual funds, or private manufacturing firms. Involvement in international flows of capital increases patrons' political and economic power, which reinforces the system.

NEOPATRIMONIALISM IN QALAKENT

Governance in Qalakent follows a roughly neopatrimonial pattern.[16] Officials in Qalakent use their offices in the city bureaucracy to extract personal gain from state resources. For example, the city administrator (*akim*) gave the directorship of the most selective lyceum in the city to one of his friends.

The lyceum director was able to amass financial capital by accepting bribes to admit particular students and to raise the grades of wealthy students;[17] in other words, the lyceum director used state property for personal gain. In return, the lyceum director gives gifts to the city administrator and politically supports him; put differently, the lyceum director became a client of the city administrator. This is not a relationship of strict *quid pro quo*. The city administrator never asks for a specific amount of money from the lyceum director or requires him to say, "The city administrator has done a great job" at wedding feasts. Rather, there is a patron-client relationship in which both men benefit by supporting each other in their use of state resources for private gain. Moreover, they are close friends. They visit each other for tea, gossip, and laugh, and play with each other's children and grandchildren. These patron-client relationships are not based on bribes. A motorist bribes a police officer whom he does not know; a lyceum director gives gifts to a city administrator at his daughter's wedding and vice versa.[18] Patron-client relationships are long-term.

These patron-client relationships are not only between two people, but they are networks that facilitate action and competition throughout a community. For example, a school director in Qalakent was investigated by members of a "commission" from Astana consisting of state security service members and a bureaucrat in the Ministry of Education who forced the school director to give them $5,000 a year. However, in return, the security services protected the school director when the lyceum director mentioned above attempted to have him replaced. After becoming a client—although this word was never used—of the Ministry of Education bureaucrat in Astana, the school director used his contact to secure a scholarship for his daughter at a prestigious university in Astana. He also continued to pay $5,000 a year to the "commission" and used his influence in Astana to secure resources for teachers at his school, such as additional English textbooks. What had started as a shakedown of a school director became a patron-client relationship that ultimately benefited teachers and students.

Sean Roberts argues that getting something done in Kazakhstan "is a matter of knowing people who can help facilitate action through mutually beneficial exchanges of favor."[19] What we hope to add to this insight is that those in position to do favors are also often models for behavior. The school director mentioned above was admired by his teachers as an educator. Teachers spoke of his dedication to students and ability to manage a classroom of young students. He was a moral model. He was also someone who could acquire resources. For example, one man discussed his recent unemployment—he had lost his job with the railroad—with a teacher at the school, who introduced him to the school director, who gave him a temporary part-time job as a history teacher. The school director did not need another history teacher, but felt responsible for his employees and his community, and therefore he used state resources to provide for them. He was solving a problem for members of his community, who looked up to him and supported him in turn. In short, he is a good man and has some powerful connections. The school director is not a simple altruist, and there is no doubt he will ask for a favor from the teacher later. Our point is that these mutually beneficial exchanges of favor within patron-client networks are often accompanied by genuine feelings of friendship, kinship, admiration, and paternalistic responsibility.

MOR ATA'S FOUNDING, VERSION 1: THE SHRINE CARETAKER'S STORY

Patron-client relationships are also the foundation of action in shrine pilgrimages. The way that Baidibek, the shrine caretaker of Mor Ata, relates to saints is indicative of the resonance between neopatrimonial governance and shrine-based Islamic practices. As will be seen later, his ties to a political patron were instrumental in his acquisition of the land for the shrine, and his narrative about founding the shrine emphasizes spiritual patronage.

Baidibek was born in Qalakent about 45 years before our interview, and he previously worked as a mechanic at a collective farm. On a scorching summer day, mitigated only by a very dusty wind, Baidibek told Schwab the following narrative while they ate greasy noodles and drank hot tea in the shade of an outdoor cooking area in the shrine complex of Mor Ata.

> In 1992, my stomach began to hurt, I think as the result of drinking alcohol and smoking cigarettes. I could not hold down food or even water. The doctors told me that they could do a very complicated operation, but they could not guarantee its success. I decided not to have the operation, and so I went to Taraz to be blessed by a healer.
>
> The healer told me, "Long ago, one of your ancestors received a spiritual gift from Baba Tukti Shashty Aziz. If you go to Baba Tukti Shashty Aziz, you will find a cure for your illness. You should live a pious life and recite the daily prayers and the Qur'an. You live on saintly ground (*aruaqty zherde otyrasyz*). Your star will be bright."
>
> I then went to the shrine of Baba Tukti Shashty Aziz with the healer and recited the Qur'an for our ancestors (*aruaqtargha quran baghushtadyq*). You should see the power of God. At that time, I could not drink any water, but I drank the water of the spring inside the shrine of the saint. I was very happy. We spent the night at the house of the shrine caretaker. I woke up the next morning very thirsty, and I went to the shrine again. I drank another bowl of water.

The ancestors gave [the healer] a revelatory dream (*ayan*) and told her that I should go to Baba Tukti Shashty Aziz's shrine seven times, and only then would I be fully cured. And truthfully, after I went to Baba Tukti Shashty Aziz's shrine seven more times, I was cured. After that, I started praying every day, stopped drinking, and placed myself on the path that God had set out for me.

The last time I went to Baba Tukti Shashty Aziz's shrine, in the spring of 1994, the saint gave me a revelatory dream, in which he said, "My dearest, my child, you have a relative, an uncle named Askerbek, and in his house there is a very valuable piece of jewelry. On its underside, there is writing in Arabic, and on its top it looks like a spearhead. This is your inheritance, and you must take it."

That day I went to my relative's house in [a nearby village] and told them about my dream. My aunt asked me, "Which saint's shrine were you at? How many times had you been there?" I told her I had gone to Baba Tukti Shashty Aziz's shrine seven times.[20] My aunt then got a signet ring (*mor*) that she had wrapped in a white cloth and showed it to me, saying, "This, my child, is what the saint was talking about in your dream."

After I found the signet ring, I hid it in a safe place. I went to [the shrine of] Arystan Bab, and begged him [for direction]. While at Arystan Bab, I received a revelatory dream in which a man with a white beard came to me and said, "I am Mor Ata. There is a saint right under your feet. Five or six steps from where you live is my grave." I did not receive this dream just once, but several times. I dug near my house and found his grave.

Afterward, all sorts of miracles happened. When we got enough money for the dome of the shrine, I asked the masons and other construction workers to build a simple dome. But when it was finished, it looked like the top of the Mor Ata's signet ring.

But we have also had a lot of conflict. The imam of the [smaller Qalakent] mosque, Alibek, has blackened our name and written in [the local newspaper] about us. There are some people who support Alibek too. Once, the Iranian mullah came with twelve of his followers and started to kick the ground and step on the saint's grave. What kind of Muslim would do that? Where is his Muslimness (*musylmanshylyq*)?

Others have criticized us as well. Last September, in [a large regional newsweekly], a man placed many obstacles in our path. The writer came here and then wrote: "In Qalakent, along a road where yurts are set up, a place is now considered holy (*ol zher alsatte kieli sanalyp ketti*). Mor Ata came to the dreams of a local citizen, who became the shrine caretaker. It is well-known that religious animosity has existed in our history. But these missionaries lead us away from Islam, and I would be surprised if there is much support for them among our relatives (*qandastar*)."

But I wonder what that writer would say if he knew what we have done here. For example, a Russian woman from Taraz came to Mor Ata and had me recite the Qur'an for her. She said, "I don't have to tell you that I am from a different nation and a different religion. Before this, I was very sick. I looked for a cure but could not find one. There was no place I had not searched. I had gone to well-known doctors and found no cure. So, I went to folk healers and in the end, *surahs* from the respected Qur'an were the reason I was healed of my illness." This woman then accepted Islam and changed her name to Umit (Hope). God's power is so great that afterward, Umit was blessed with the power to heal, and she has cured many people since then.

Or what would the writer say to the fact that two residents of Qalakent, a husband and wife, had been married for many years without having children. The wife had not had children for twenty-four years. She came to Mor Ata, stayed the night, and after revering the saint (*tau etuden keiin*), she now has a child named Ramadan. We have a lot of women come here. For example, there are people who don't have children for five or even seven years, but twenty-four years? This woman had three husbands before her current husband, all of whom divorced her because she could not have children. Only when she came here with her fourth husband to stay the night did she have a child. This is not in our hands. It is in God's hands. Because these saintly people served God, His divine light touched these people (*Bul aulie kisiler Allagha qyzmet etkennen keiin, osy kisiler shapaghaty tiedi*). People come here and then stop drinking alcohol or doing drugs. Or their children stop drinking alcohol.

The mosque-goers (*meshittegiler*) don't understand. They say, "Don't popularize saints and don't worship saints." The imams say, "Only worship God." They don't understand. We must respect saints. Our forefathers lie here. We remember them and recite the Qur'an. The mosque-goers say, "Don't go there" and bad-mouth us. I used to go to the mosque and participate in Friday prayers, and my son went as well. But now we don't go. I have to stay here in case people come on Friday.

A lot of people come on Friday and ask to pray with us. All sorts of people come here. Turks, Iranians, Uzbeks. [The road the shrine is on] is an international road [connecting Kazakhstan, Uzbekistan, and Kyrgyzstan]. We have Kurds and Azerbaijanis come here. Even sick Russians and Germans come here. Our well has healing water and they come here to drink it. People on the way to Turkistan come here, people come here before circumcisions, and people come here to give Islamic names to children. Converts to Islam come here.

And what would the people at the mosque say to this? One day, the head imam of [the oblast center] was driving on this road in a foreign car with two of his colleagues.[21] They said, "What kind of saint would be here?" They stopped and when they asked this, a young man on a bike came along and hit their car. The car's owner was angry and went to the bicyclist to curse him out. The imam said, "Are you drunk?" The young man was sober, but to our surprise, he said he had not seen the car. He said, "Older brothers, I lost the ability to see the car!" The imam said, "We have been to the mosque in Qalakent, we have been to the smaller mosque in Qalakent, and we have not seen such blessed land. How could a healthy young man lose the ability to see a car that is standing still? This is not just some [random] land, but land where we must remember our saints and ancestors, and say 'support us, ancestors.'"

Much like the unemployed railroad worker who contacted his friend in order to speak with the school director to ask for work, which he received in the form of an appointment to a part-time history post, Baidibek went to a healer who referred him to a spiritual patron who could cure his stomach. This brought Baidibek into a network of patrons and clients. Baidibek was cured by the blessed water at Baba Tukti Shashty Aziz's shrine, but a saint in the spiritual network of Baba Tukti asked Baidibek for a favor: he must uncover and honor the grave of Mor Ata. Favors beget favors. Some Kazakhs see spiritual patronage as a *quid pro quo* one of our interlocutors who sacrificed a sheep at Mor Ata explicitly stated that he expected to be cured of a disease because he had honored Mor Ata, who "owed" him. More often, favors are part of a network of distributed reciprocity, authority, and emotion. Baidibek did not directly do Baba Tukti a favor, but was rather expected to do a favor for Mor Ata, who Baidibek thought was somehow connected to Baba Tukti. He was grateful for the help of these saints, wanted to help and honor them in turn, and marveled at their exemplary past lives and current spiritual power. Shrines bring people into an Islamic community in which saints and ancestors who are closer to God intercede on pilgrims' behalf; pilgrims accept saints and ancestors as role models and provide spiritual nourishment through Qur'anic recitation. Emulating saints and ancestors puts pilgrims in a chain of learning and possibly divine contact with the prophets and God. Mor Ata, for example, was reputed to be a Companion of the Prophet Muhammad. Modeling one's comportment after Mor Ata means modeling one's life after a person who has learned directly from the Prophet in the past and who is currently closer to God in the afterlife. In short, Mor Ata was a good man and has some powerful connections.

Baidibek justifies the presence of Mor Ata's shrine by its influence on individuals. That is, the shrine is good and necessary because Mor Ata acts as a patron and moral benefactor. Baidibek wonders what his detractors would say if they only spoke to pilgrims who had come to the shrine and received the blessing of Mor Ata. Pilgrims have stopped drinking—that is become more moral—and been healed. Islamic law, citations of hadiths, and other trappings of the more scripturalist Islam of his detractors do not play a role in his justification. The experiences of clients of the shrine are proof of its holiness and importance. Establishing the shrine of Mor Ata was important because he is an excellent patron for the community, and in return, the community must honor him with a proper shrine, Qur'anic recitations, and changing their behavior.

Samuli Schielke persuasively argues that capitalist ethics and modes of thought have combined with particular types of Islamic ethics and ways of being to focus Egyptians on notions of religious reward and punishment in identifiably capitalist terms.[22] In his words, "When people who share the logic of profit, success, and consumption as metaphors of human relations and as modes of subjectivity come to act in religious terms, they bring their horizons of expectation and modes of action along. In short: religion, too, gains a flavor of capitalism."[23] We want to make two similar points. First, when people who share the logic of connections, patrons, and clients as metaphors of human relations come to act in religious terms, they bring their horizons of expectations and modes of action along. In short, religion gains a flavor of neopatrimonialism. If, for example, the best way to get a job in Qalakent is by using connections to find a patron, it is not hard to imagine that the best way to seek help from God is through an intermediary such as Baba Tukti Shashty Aziz or Mor Ata. Baidibek, for example, went to Baba Tukti Shashty Aziz because a healer referred him to the saint, who had also supported, one of his ancestors. It was important that he go to a saint to whom he had a personal connection. Second, our statement can function in reverse: when people who see religion partially in terms of patron-client relations, they bring these expectations along to human relations. Baidibek did not simply buy land to open a shrine. Rather, just as he sought out a saintly patron to cure his cancer, he sought out an economic patron—the city administrator of Qalakent, a man whose duties do not usually involve directly supervising land sales—to help him build a profitable shrine. The city administrator sold Baidibek public land on the main road in town, allegedly for a cut of the profits from the shrine, as will be seen below. This was prime real estate for a shrine, and Baidibek used the logic of patronage to acquire it. "Religious" action and "practical" action are not as separate or distinguishable as many scholars like to think. They commingle and resonate with each other, increasing one another's potency.

Patron saints are not a new phenomenon in Central Asia. DeWeese discusses saints' and prophets' patronage of Sayram, a small town in southern Kazakhstan.[24] In this article, DeWeese is primarily concerned with narrative and the sacralization of Sayram rather than religion's relationship to everyday politics. Sayram's fate was tied to the personal presence of prophets and saints. For example, Idris founded the city and governed in accordance with God's will; he left his shirt as a sacred object for the city's residents. When the city's residents used the shirt to intercede with God, they were successful in defeating invading infidel armies; when the city's residents could not find the shirt, they could not stop the progress of a plague. Other prophets, including Noah, Khizr, and Muhammad, played similar roles in Sayram's history. DeWeese argues, "The wars and sieges recounted in the sacred history [of Sayram], for example, are generic battles, set-pieces through which to evoke the protection of Sayram's saintly patrons."

The narratives of these generic battles, however, also reveal more than the identity of saintly patrons. They illustrate particular conceptions of political patronage. DeWeese relates the story of Mansur, a local ruler, who faced an immense infidel army.

> The story of his [Mansur's] tribulations begins with an attack on Sayram. An enemy army came and surrounded the city; the Prophet, in a dream, charged Mansur to drive them away, and the ruler went up to the top of the wall during the middle of the night to survey the enemy forces. There he found the Imam Ra'is al-Din, who as it turned out had had a similar dream, and who explained that Mansur had been honored with this dream for his justice, and he himself for his knowledge. The two men prayed together, prepared to go out against the foe, and saw that the enemy army stretched from Chumushlaghu to Chimkent. Mansur, trusting in God, took his sword and went out among them, and, finding that the enemy troops were asleep, he slew so many that their corpses formed heaps; when at last the enemy troops became aware of what was happening, in their confusion they killed one another, and the rest of them fled. One of them was captured and asked why they had fled; he explained that their attackers were seen to have lances 40 cubits long, which they simply could not withstand. Mansur then returned to the city and proclaimed that whoever wanted the spoils of war should go out and take what he could; and indeed the people of Sayram went out and took the defeated army's property, "and the poor people became wealthy."[25]

Here the historic and geographic sacralization of Sayram is connected to a particular type of patrimonialism. Who gets what, where, and how is decided by a single political patron, Mansur. Those who constructed and recorded this narrative clearly conceived of politics in terms of patron-client relations.

We do not connect our analysis to DeWeese's work to show that nothing has changed in Central Asia. Things have clearly changed. The paradigm of an economic patron distributing the spoils of holy war has given way to paradigms of patrons connected to multinational companies and offshore bank accounts. Saints are often imagined in newly nationalized ways or address more contemporary concerns, such as car crashes.[26] But the narrative provided by DeWeese and the narratives we provide above show the personalization of politics and religion and the necessity of building a community that follows the example of moral patrons, whether economic, political, religious, or all of the above.

To return to the Qalakent: Baidibek's notion of an Islamic community can be contrasted with that of the "Iranian" mullah, a Kazakh from Afghanistan who was labelled "Iranian" because of his knowledge of Persian. The "Iranian" mullah who physically attacked the shrine lived in a small farmhouse lit by a single bulb in a nearby village. Schwab once visited the Iranian mullah with Aqylbek, a 50-year-old local history teacher whose attempt to shut down the shrine we will discuss below. After giving Aqylbek a painstaking Arabic lesson focusing on translating hadiths from Nawawi's collection of forty hadiths, the Iranian mullah told Schwab about his disappointment in Kazakhs and Kazakhstan. He had come to Kazakhstan to be among his compatriots but instead found "Russians," faithless (*imansyz*) Kazakhs, and "charlatans" (Russian, *sharlatan*; this was the only Russian word the Iranian mullah used in our entire conversation) such as Baidibek. The Iranian mullah had attempted to give lessons at the local mosque, but the local imam had turned him away, fearful that the local government would see a learned Afghan as a "Wahhabi," despite the Iranian mullah's training in a Hanafi medressah.[27] His attack on the shrine was not sanctioned by the local imam, but he saw himself acting in lieu of the imams who could not afford to upset the city administration or jeopardize their precarious positions within the state.

For Baidibek, the behavior of the Iranian mullah was shocking. Baidibek sees himself as living a Muslim life in harmony with his neighbors by interacting with them in accordance with common standards of sociality. To him, Islam is, above all, how decent human beings—particularly decent human beings in Kazakhstan with Islamic ancestors and traditions—interact with each other. As related by many researchers of Islam in Central Asia, Central Asians often find more meaning in "Muslimness" (*musylmanshylyq*) as a moral communal experience than in a textually based intellectual tradition.[28] The physical conflict between Baidibek and the Iranian mullah is a distillation of the different understandings of Islam in Qalakent: one, more connected with shrines and appealing to communal life and tradition, and another focused on appeals to the authority of texts, which Schwab has called the "piety movement" in past publications.[29] Baidibek considers the well-being of a community—,determined in part by their relationship to spiritual patrons such as Mor Ata and the Prophet Muhammad—,to be the essence of Islam; for the Iranian mullah, the well-being of a community can only be guaranteed by the application of universal laws.

Baidibek points out that the "mosque-goers"—scripturalist Muslims in Qalakent—do not understand community and Islam: they ignore traditional authority, they do not respect the dead, they bad-mouth other members of the community, and disregard ritual uses of the Qur'an. Moreover, they do not properly draw the multi-ethnic community of Qalakent into its sacred landscape. Kazakhs make up about 60 percent of the city; Russians are at least 20 percent of the population. Muslim minorities make up the remainder of the population, including substantial Turkish (4 percent), Azerbaijani (3 percent), and Kurdish (3 percent) populations. These non-Kazakh populations were the result of Stalin-era deportations of most of the Muslim minorities and of employment-based Soviet migration of most of the Russians. Baidibek's shrine is visited by the minorities in the city, even Christians such as Russians and Germans. The notion of Muslimness is connected to living with non-Muslim "guests" in Kazakhstan, who are part of the extended community. Rather than creating a relatively exclusive Muslim community, as the mosque-goers do in his understanding, Baidibek sees himself as serving the community of Qalakent, which is located on sacred Muslim land. Through the blessing of Mor Ata, car crashes on the road have stopped, infertile women have become pregnant, and more people live in an Islamic fashion, whether through conversion to Islam or by stopping their alcohol abuse. The citizens of Qalakent are all clients of Mor Ata. His presence has blessed the city, and people in Qalakent should "respect" him. To quote Baidibek's recollection of the visiting imam's words, "This is not just some [random] land, but land where we must remember our saints and ancestors, and say 'support us, ancestors.'" The community must recognize its spiritual patron for his role in their continued moral and physical well-being.

MOR ATA'S FOUNDING, VERSION 2: THE SCRIPTURALIST'S STORY

Rationalization is not dominant in the economic or religious lives of many people in Qalakent. However, there is an undercurrent of rationalization, both in official government rhetoric on political economy and among Muslim scripturalists. For example, President Nazarbayev promotes economic reform and development in speeches, publications, and the development of infrastructure in particular parts of the country. This discourse excoriates the patron-client relationships characteristic of neopatrimonial governance and emphasizes the importance of rational bureaucracy. Note the importance of governmental efforts to "provide the conditions" for individual work in markets, rather than "manna" from a patron or the government, in a speech by Nazarbayev:

> The [2050] Strategy is a program of concrete practical actions, which on a daily basis will improve our country and the life of every citizen of Kazakhstan. However, everyone must understand that, in market conditions, we must work effectively, rather than wait for "manna from heaven." The government's task is to provide all conditions for this…
>
> The main benchmarks of the social sector development until 2050 are provided in concrete indicators. We should increase by 4.5 times our GDP per capita, from $13,000 to $60,000. Kazakhstan will become a country where the middle class makes up a predominant share of the population. Following the global trend, the share of our urban population will increase from the current 55 percent to roughly 70 percent. The cities and settlements of Kazakhstan will be linked by high-quality roads and high-speed transport…

> An important task is to create and implement the new anti-corruption strategy. Administrative reform should not turn into a cumbersome process of unnecessary paperwork and document circulation… It is necessary to keep on putting into practice the meritocracy principles in the management of human resources in state-owned enterprises, national companies, and state budget-financed organizations.[30]

Rather than the person-based action of patron-client ties, this discourse focuses on individual action in a meritocratic, rule-based system. Aqylbek, a 50-year-old local history teacher, loves this type of speech, even if he is very skeptical about the implementation of these programs. He praises the United States and Turkey for their "fair" economies based on meritocratic principles. He sent his daughter to the United States to study economics. He is also a member of the piety movement in Kazakhstan.

Members of the piety movement represent a more overtly rationalized form of Islam. They make sense of the world through a cultural complex emphasizing the ignorance of present-day Muslims, the authority of scripture and texts over communal norms and lived experience, and the importance of the unity of God (*tauhid*) and avoiding polytheism (*shirk*). The piety movement is led by imams and bureaucrats associated with the Kazakhstani Muftiate and Islamic educators, writers, television and media producers, and publishers. Generally, about 5–10 percent of the Kazakhstani population can be considered part of the piety movement. They cite hadiths in everyday life, women in the movement generally wear headscarves or hijabs, and they are more vocal about their beliefs in public, in print, and online.

Aqylbek tells a much different narrative than Baidibek, one which illustrates the piety movement's rationalized opposition to both shrine-based Islamic practice and neopatrimonialism. His upbringing emphasized advancing economically and socially in the Soviet Union, and he strives for a middle-class lifestyle now. His parents, despite being devout Muslims, did not relay much of their Islamic knowledge to him because they had barely survived Stalin's purges in the 1930s and World War II. However, when Aqylbek's father died in the mid-1990s, Aqylbek became an autodidact and began reading copious amounts of Islamic literature produced in Almaty. He began to pray five times a day shortly thereafter, and has become a leader in the piety movement in Qalakent, giving free lessons to young Muslims in his neighborhood. On a cool desert night over tea and dried fruit, Aqylbek told Schwab how he had tried to close the shrine of Mor Ata:

> One problem is that we have a lot of superstitions left over from the ignorant time before Islam (*zhihiliyattan qalghan nanym-senimder*) because we have too little religious propaganda (*nasikhat*) and because of the influence of the Soviet government. There are people with superstitions from the Soviet era,

innovations foreign to Islam (*islamgha zhat bidghattar*), like worshiping fire (*otqa tabunyshylyq*). We must purify these (*sodan da tazartu kerek*). Generally, one part of our nation is ignorant (*beikhabar*) of Islamic principles. Therefore, among our people there are all sorts of healers and fortune-tellers. Their main purpose is to find profit from our people's money.

We have these people in Qalakent too. One liar said that he found the grave of some Mor Ata, put up a shrine, and now is misleading people and taking their money. If we were a European nation and our people were literate, this would not be okay.[31] We must struggle for a pure Islam. We must get rid of beliefs foreign to Islam that are an obstacle to our people. You have been with me [over the last few weeks]. People read fantasy [*fantastika*] in magazines and think it is real.

Common Kazakhs (*qarapaiym qazaqtar*) will talk the main part of their monthly salary to go on a pilgrimage. They will say, "My daughter is sick. Her ears hurt. I must go on a pilgrimage" It would be better to go to a doctor.

I ran into Baidibek several times over the years. He is a former tractor driver and not very educated. At a feast to break the Ramadan fast (*auyz ashar*), Baidibek showed me his silver signet ring and said that it had come to him from God. He does not know anything about history. I told him that this was a ring from the nineteenth century and that the Arabic letters on it were just "alif-mim-ba" (*A-M-B*). Nothing special. Then I asked him why he thought he would get a ring from God when even the Prophet Muhammad only received words from God.

I told him there were several hadiths against building on graves. For example, in Tirmizi, there is a hadith that says, "Our Prophet (peace be upon him) said it is not permissible to build on graves, whitewash them, or write on them." Learned men know [these hadiths], but the ignorant don't.

But our learned men do not want to interfere. Our imam is patient and scared of the government. He has to kiss their asses. He was not going to do anything about the shrine. He preaches about daily prayer and fasting. He is a good man but scared of being dismissed from his position. So [because the imams would not act], I asked my wife [who was the director of the local hospital and on the city land commission] to speak with the city administrator about the Mor Ata shrine. The city administrator told her that she should not discuss this issue; the city administration had already sold them the land and their papers were in order. My wife knows that the city administrator got money out of the deal, but what can she do? I confronted Baidibek again, and he finally told me that the shrine was just a way to make money, but you know what Kazakhstan is like.

We want to point out three aspects of rationalization at play in Aqylbek's story. First, Aqylbek begins his narrative not with a personal biography like Baidibek, but with a general explanation of Kazakhstani society today and its ignorance of Islamic principles, scripture, and morals. Second, Aqylbek relies on the authority of his secular and Islamic education rather than personal connections. Finally, Aqylbek expects the imams, the bureaucrats in charge of Islam, to intervene and shut the shrine down.

Like most members of the piety movement, Aqylbek sees a lack of Islamic knowledge as the major problem facing Kazakhs today, an influence of the global Salafi movement and the emphasis on textual authority and education of the Soviet Muftiate and post-Soviet Kazakhstani Muftiate.[32] Aqylbek, like most members of the piety movement, thinks of himself as a Hanafi Muslim and denounces "extremists" like "Wahhabis." However, like many others in the piety movement, Aqylbek insists that all a Muslim needs to know is "the Qur'an and hadiths," and ignores centuries of Hanafi jurisprudence. For Aqylbek, an ignorance of Islamic scripture leads to un-Islamic "innovations."

Aqylbek's reference to fantasy was an allusion to a funerary feast (*toi, as*) that we had attended together a few weeks earlier. At this feast, a young man had said that he had read about the miracles of a different saint in a newspaper. Aqylbek immediately cut him off and said, "Newspapers, magazines, there is a lot of fantasy in them. If it is not in the Qur'n or the hadiths, you don't need it. The Qur'an, the hadiths, that's enough." Another man then argued with Aqylbek, saying that he had heard of a saint who was "pure" (*pak*, in this case meaning a man who had never sinned). Aqylbek then said, "No. This is a lie or a legend or a story (*bul otirik, angyz, angime*). No one except the Prophet has ever been pure. Even our Abu Hanifa has said that he would cry during the last prayer of the day because he knew he had sinned." These "fantastic" notions of religion—saints performing miracles, sinless men—were anathema for Aqylbek. People should stop looking for miracles and "go to a doctor." After the feast, Aqylbek sighed and told Schwab that those types of people think that he is a "Wahhabi" because he has a beard and knows something about Islam.

Aqylbek relies on two sources of authority in his arguments with Baidibek. First, he appeals to his secular authority as a history teacher. He knows history while Baidibek does not. He can read Arabic while Baidibek cannot.[33] Second, and unlike Baidibek, who appeals to the authority of lived experience, Aqylbek knows and can appeal to impersonal, scripturalist sources such as hadiths. Rather than the authority of a community in determining social mores and correct ritual, the community must look to the authority of scripture and discuss scripture's lessons for the community. Scripture is universal, and God is the patron of all communities; an individual community does not need anything but God and His scripture. This simplification of Islamic authority, of course, could be problematized. Baidibek sees hadiths as authoritative, but assumes that the saints and their descendants and followers—the Muslims in his area—have correctly incorporated scripture into their lifestyle. As Schwab details, many Kazakhs assume that the morality they have learned from their parents is a proper and Islamic morality, and that the rituals they have learned are proper and Islamic.[34] Aqylbek assumes that much of Kazakh Islamic culture was either lost during the Soviet era or corrupted by pre-Islamic rituals.

For Aqylbek, Baidibek is the personification of the general ignorance of Islam in post-Soviet Kazakhstan: he is a former tractor driver; he does not possess the knowledge of an imam or history teacher or other educated member of a profession; he claims that Mor Ata heals pilgrims, who would be better off going to a doctor; he is ignorant and anti-modern.

However, rationalized arguments could not change the political economy of Qalakent. Aqylbek alludes to the inability of the city's imams to stop the building of Mor Ata. The imam whom Aqylbek directly discusses, and the leader of the main mosque, is an ethnic Uzbek. The local community admires him for seeking permission from the Soviet authorities to build a mosque in Qalakent in the 1980s. However, as an Uzbek in Kazakhstan, he feels that his position is precarious, and that nationalist Kazakhs in the local city administration or in the Muftiate could find some pretense to fire him. He is a soft-spoken man who emphasizes communal harmony and basic ritual practice in his Friday sermons and in the short pamphlets published by the mosque. As Aqylbek indicates, this imam was unwilling to take direct action against the shrine despite his condemnation of the shrine in small study groups.

Alibek, a young ethnic Kazakh, is the imam of the second mosque in Qalakent. He is the imam, alluded to by Baidibek, who strenuously argued against the legitimacy of the shrine, following the general lead of the head Mufti of Kazakhstan and the long-established anti-shrine rhetoric of the Soviet Muftiate in Central Asia.[35] Alibek wrote a letter to the local newspaper railing against the establishment of the Mor Ata Shrine. In this letter, Alibek made a scripturally informed argument that while going to a grave to think about one's own mortality was acceptable, it was not acceptable to go to a grave and expect miraculous healing or other divine intervention. Alibek also gave sermons attacking the shrine, in which he argued that he had not ever heard of a companion of the Prophet called Mor Ata, despite his education at an official Islamic institution. However, this article and Alibek's preaching failed to change the minds of city officials, and, in fact, Alibek soon turned to other topics in his sermons. Some of his students told us that city officials asked him to stop preaching about the shrine, and said that these officials had been corrupted by the money that Baidibek had given to the city administration.

Aqylbek believed that the imams and Kazakhstani Muftiate should be in charge of all Islamic institutions, and thus should be able to shut down the shrine of Mor Ata. However, the shrine is officially registered as a charitable organization with the city administration, and thus the imams have no legal jurisdiction. Given the lack of influence of the imams, Aqylbek attempted to disrupt the patron-client relationship between the city administrator and Baidibek. His wife, also a client of the city administrator who supported his policies, attempted to leverage her influence to deregister the shrine. The city administrator denied her request, and the matter was settled. No amount of preaching or letter-writing would shut down the shrine as long as the city administrator supported it. Here is the crux of the issue for Aqylbek: despite his expertise in Islam and local history, which he used to preach in the community and directly to Baidibek, and the scripturally informed arguments of a local imam to the community and the local officials, neopatrimonial ties at the local level won the day for the shrine.

CONCLUSION: NEOPATRIMONIALISM AND ISLAM IN KAZAKHSTAN

In a previous article, Schwab detailed how an Islamic scripturalist press was only able to succeed after finding a patron.[36] This, and the attempt of Aqylbek to use his connection to the city administrator, may cast doubt on our argument that neopatrimonialism and shrine-based Islamic practice in particular resonate with each other. However, our claim is not that scripturalist Muslims do not have patrons while other Muslims do. Rather, our argument is that Kazakhs like Baidibek see political, economic, and spiritual patronage as the way of the world, and an often beneficial aspect of their lives, while Kazakhs like Aqylbek find patronage to be generally harmful and something that should be changed. Baidibek, when confronted with an illness, sought out a spiritual patron. When confronted with an economic problem, such as getting land for Mor Ata's Shrine complex, he sought out an economic patron. These were normal and good things to do. Kazakhs like Aqylbek understand the effectiveness of patronage, but seek to act in accordance with systematic rules, whether religious, political, or economic. They have thought about political and spiritual patronage, compared them with their systematized view of the world, and found them objectionable. Aqylbek sent his children abroad to gain knowledge and hopefully participate in a meritocratic economy with identifiable rules, laws, and property rights. Similarly, he hoped the arguments based on Islamic texts made by learned scholars would prevent the construction of the shrine of Mor Ata. Aqylbek was disappointed that he had to resort to using his connection to the city administrator; an Islamic argument made by scholars and based on canonic texts should have been enough. Similarly, the owner and editor of the Islamic press that Schwab discusses hoped that he would have enough of an audience to support his press.[37] He was disappointed that he had to find a sponsor for his magazine and hoped to create an audience that would consider their resources and the importance of Islam to them, and then appropriately devote money to Islamic magazines and books.

Although this chapter focuses on local politics and religion in Qalakent, the pattern described here is applicable in much of Kazakhstan. The central state plays large patrimonial and legal-bureaucratic roles in politics, economics, and religion. The state promotes rational market-oriented political economic ideology in official speeches, and scripturalist Islam through the Muftiyat.[38] These legal-bureaucratic cultural formations resonate with each other. However, neopatrimonial politics dominate Kazakhstani politics, and the national government also protects and promotes particular shrines through the Ministry of Culture, which controls shrines in places like Turkistan and Sayram. Moreover, wealthy and powerful individual patrons, including high-level officials in Astana and at the oblast level, also establish or support shrines in their home villages and regions. Clearly, there are (at least) two conflicting visions of political economy and Islam in Kazakhstan. It is our contention that these visions of political economy and Islam resonate with each other. In regards to shrine-based Islamic practices: shrines are not simply survivals of the past but resonate with neopatrimonial politics, increasing the potency of both neopatrimonialism and shrine-based Islamic practices.

NOTES

1. We would like to thank Jessica Carr and Devin DeWeese for reading drafts of this chapter, as well of the comments of our fellow participants in the conference "Kazakhstan beyond Economic Success."
2. All names, including the name "Qalakent," are pseudonyms.
3. Bruce Privratsky, *Muslim Turkistan: Kazak Religion and Collective Memory* (Richmond, UK: Curzon, 2001).
4. Wendell Schwab, "Traditions and Texts: How Two Young Women Learned to Interpret the Qur'an and Hadiths in Kazakhstan," *Contemporary Islam* 6, no. 2 (2012): 173–197.
5. Pawel Jessa, "Aq Jol Soul Healers: Religious Pluralism and a Contemporary Muslim Movement in Kazakhstan," *Central Asian Survey* 25, no. 3 (2006): 366–369.
6. Maria Louw, *Everyday Islam in Post-Soviet Central Asia* (London: Routledge, 2007).
7. Johan Rasanayagam, *Islam in Post-Soviet Uzbekistan: The Morality of Experience* (Cambridge: Cambridge University Press, 2011).
8. Krisztina Kehl-Bodrogi, "Who Owns the Shrine? Competing Meanings and Authorities at a Pilgrimage Site in Khorezm," *Central Asian Survey* 25, no. 3 (2006): 235–250; Krisztina Kehl-Bodrogi, *Religion Is Not So Strong Here: Muslim Religious Life in Khorezm after Socialism* (Berlin: LIT Verlag, 2008).
9. Schwab, "Traditions and Texts."
10. The notion of resonance is borrowed from William Connolly, *Capitalism and Christianity, American Style* (Durham, NC: Duke University Press, 2008).
11. Max Weber, *The Protestant Ethic and the "Spirit" of Capitalism and Other Writings* (New York: Penguin, 2002). Geertz's descriptions of traditional and rationalized religions are perhaps more evocative than Weber's original summaries.

See Clifford Geertz, "'Internal Conversion' in Contemporary Bali," in *The Interpretation of Cultures: Selected Essays* (New York: Basic Books, 1973), 171.

> Traditional religions ... meet the perennial concerns of religion, what Weber called the "problems of meaning"—evil, suffering, frustration, bafflement, and so on—piecemeal. They attack them opportunistically as they arise in each particular instance—each death, each crop failure, each untoward natural or social occurrence—employing one or another weapon chosen, on grounds of symbolic appropriateness, from their cluttered arsenal of myth and magic. (With respect to the less defensive activities of religion—the celebration of human continuity, prosperity, and solidarity—the same strategy is employed.) As the approach to fundamental spiritual issues which traditional religions take is discrete and irregular, so also is their characteristic form.
>
> Rationalized religions, on the other hand, are more abstract, more logically coherent, and more generally phrased. The problems of meaning, which in traditional systems are expressed only implicitly and fragmentarily, here get inclusive formulations and evoke comprehensive attitudes. They become conceptualized as universal and inherent qualities of human existence as such, rather than being seen as inseparable aspects of this or that specific event. The question is no longer put merely in such terms as, to use a classic example from the British anthropologist Evans-Pritchard..." By what means can I discover who practiced witchcraft against my brother, thereby causing the granary to fall on him?" but, "How can one know the truth?"

12. Geertz, "Internal Conversion," 171.

13. Clifford Geertz, *Islam Observed: Religious Development in Morocco and Indonesia* (Chicago: University of Chicago Press, 1971).

14. Max Weber, *Economy and Society: An Outline of Interpretive Sociology* (Berkeley: University of California Press, 1978). For a critical discussion of neopatrimonialism, see Gero Erdmann and Ulf Engel, *Neopatrimonialism Revisited: Beyond a Catch-all Concept*. Hamburg: GIGA Working Papers, 2006.

15. Weber, *Economy and Society*, 284.

16. Neopatrimonialism at the national level has been discussed in the following: Barbara Junisbai, "A Tale of Two Kazakhstans: Sources of Political Cleavage and Conflict in the Post-Soviet Period," *Europe-Asia Studies* 62, no. 2 (2010): 235–269; Rico Isaacs, *Party System Formation in Kazakhstan: Between Formal and Informal Politics* (London: Routledge, 2011); Paul Georg Geiss, "Central Asia: Changing Political Systems and Regime Types: In Between the Neopatrimonial and Bureaucratic-Developmental State in Central Asia," in *Presidents, Oligarchs, and Bureaucrats: Forms of Rule in the Post-Soviet Space*, ed. Susan Stewart, Margarete Klein, and Andrea Schmitz (Farnham, Surrey, UK: Ashgate, 2012), 187–202; Sebastian Schiek and Stephan Hensell, "Seeing Like a President: The Dilemma of Inclusion in Kazakhstan," in *Presidents, Oligarchs, and Bureaucrats: Forms of Rule in the Post-Soviet Space*, ed. Susan Stewart, Margarete Klein, and Andrea Schmitz (Farnham, Surrey, UK: Ashgate, 2012), 20–22.

17. For more detailed stories of corruption in higher education in Kazakhstan, see Stephen Heyneman, "Three Universities in Georgia, Kazakhstan, and Kyrgyzstan: The Struggle against Corruption and for Social Cohesion," *UNESCO Prospects* 3 (2007): 305–318. For details on how corruption in higher education has become a "habit" for professors, see Nataliya Rumyantseva and Timothy Caboni, "Are

Academics in Kazakhstan Capable of Self-regulation? A Study of Faculty's Normative Structure in the Midst of Higher Education Decentralization Reforms," *Tertiary Education and Management* 18, no. 1 (2012): 1–16. Finally, for a general examination of "corruption" in Kazakhstan, see Natsuko Oka, "Everyday Corruption in Kazakhstan: An Ethnographic Analysis of Informal Practices," Interim Report for *Exploring Informal Networks in Kazakhstan: A Multi-Dimensional Approach.* IDE-JETRO, 2013.

18. Werner discusses how "bribe" and "gift" are difficult to disentangle in Kazakhstan. See Cynthia Werner, "Gifts, Bribes, and Development in Post-Soviet Kazakhstan," *Human Organization* 59, no. 1 (2000): 11–22.

19. Sean Roberts, "Doing the Democracy Dance in Kazakhstan: Democracy Development as Cultural Encounter." *Slavic Review* 71, no. 2 (2012): 317.

20. This is an inconsistency in Baidibek's story: if he first went to Baba Tukti's shrine on his way to Turkistan and subsequently went seven more times, then he would have gone to the shrine eight times in total. It is unclear if Baidibek thought he had only gone to Baba Tukti Aziz seven times or if the number seven had important connotations and therefore he chose to use it.

21. This part of the story may be an exaggeration or fabrication. Schwab has spoken with the head imam of the main mosque in the oblast center, and this imam spoke strongly against the type of shrine-based activities that Baidibek endorses.

22. Samuli Schielke, "Capitalist Ethics and the Spirit of Islamization in Egypt," in *Ordinary Lives and Grand Schemes: An Anthropology of Everyday Religion*, ed. Samuli Schielke and Liza Debevec (Oxford: Berghahn, 2012), 131–145.

23. Schielke, "Capitalist Ethics and the Spirit of Islamization in Egypt," 140.

24. Devin DeWeese, "Sacred History for a Central Asian Town: Saints, Shrines, and Legends of Origin in Histories of Sayrām, 18th–19th Centuries," *Revue des Mondes Musulmans et de la Méditerranée* 8 (2000): 24–95.

25. DeWeese, "Sacred History for a Central Asian Town."

26. Louw, *Everyday Islam in Post-Soviet Central Asia.*

27. For an extended meditation on the pejorative definition of "Wahhabi" in Central Asia, see Johan Rasanayagam, "'I Am Not a Wahhabi': State Power and Muslim Orthodoxy in Uzbekistan," in *The Postsocialist Religious Question: Faith and Power in Central Asia and East-Central Europe,* ed. by Chris Hann (Berlin: LIT Verlag, 2006), 99–124.

28. Privratksy, *Muslim Turkistan*; Louw, *Everyday Islam in Post-Soviet Central Asia*; Kehl-Bodrogi, *Religion Is Not So Strong Here*; Rasanayagam, *Islam in Post-Soviet Uzbekistan.*

29. Wendell Schwab, "Establishing an Islamic Niche in Kazakhstan: Musylman Publishing House and Its Publications," *Central Asian Survey* 30, no. 2 (2011): 22–42; Schwab, "Traditions and Texts"; Wendell Schwab, "How to Pray in Kazakhstan: The Fortress of the Muslim and Its Readers," *Anthropology of East Europe Review* 32, no. 1 (2014): 22–42; Wendell Schwab, "Islam, Fun, and Social Capital in Kazakhstan," *Central Asian Affairs* 2, no. 1 (2015): 51–70.

30. Nursultan Nazarbayev, "Address of the President of the Republic of Kazakhstan N. Nazarbayev to the Nation, January 17, 2014," accessed June 29, 2014,

http://www.akorda.kz/en/page/page_215839_address-of-the-president-of-the-republic-of-kazakhstan-n-nazarbayev-to-the-nation-january-17-2014#page.

31. It may be worthwhile to mention that Kazakhstan, like all post-Soviet countries, has an extremely high literacy rate. Aqylbek's connection of literacy with Europe parallels Jadidist discourse from the late nineteenth and early twentieth centuries. See Adeeb Khalid, *The Politics of Muslim Cultural Reform: Jadidism in Central Asia* (Berkeley: University of California Press, 1998). We are grateful to Devin DeWeese for pointing this parallel out.

32. Schwab, "Traditions and Texts."

33. For more on the Soviet Islamic education system's emphasis on secular history, mastery of Arabic, and the science of hadith, see Eren Tasar, "The Official Madrasas of Soviet Uzbekistan," *Journal of the Economic and Social History of the Orient* 59, no. 1/2 (2016): 265–302.

34. Schwab, "Traditions and Texts."

35. For fatwas on shrine-based Islamic practice and pilgrimages from the Kazakhstani Muftiyat, see: Absattar Qazhy Derbisali and Mukhammed Hussien Qazhy Alsabekov, *Qazaqstan Musylmandary Dini Basqarmasynyng 2000 Zhyldan Bastap Shyqqan Patualary Zhiyntyghynyng Bir Boligi* (Almaty: Kokzhiek, 2008), 69; Spiritual Administration of the Muslims of Kazakhstan, *Qabirstandy Ziyarat Etu Ukimi*, 2013, accessed June 29, 2014, http://muftyat.kz/kz/fatwa/view?id=7; Spiritual Administration of the Muslims of Kazakhstan, *Qabirde Otyru, Uiyqtau, Qabirge Daretke Otyru, zhane Onyng Ustimen Zhuru Ukimi*, 2013, accessed June 29, 2014, http://muftyat.kz/kz/fatwa/view?id=710. For the official treatment of shrine-based Islamic practice in the Soviet era, see Eren Tasar, "Soviet and Muslim: The Institutionalization of Islam in Central Asia, 1943–1991" (PhD diss., Harvard University, 2010).

36. Schwab, "Establishing an Islamic Niche in Kazakhstan."

37. Schwab, "Establishing an Islamic Niche in Kazakhstan."

38. Pawel Jessa, "Religious Renewal in Kazakhstan: Redefining 'Unofficial' Islam," in *The Postsocialist Religious Question: Faith and Power in Central Asia and East-Central Europe*, ed. Chris Hann, (Berlin: LIT Verlag, 2006), 169–190; Schwab, "Traditions and Texts"; Schwab, "How to Pray in Kazakhstan."

Part II

THE NATION: CONFLICTING LEGITIMACIES AND REPERTOIRES

Chapter 5

Nationalizing Elites and Regimes

Nation-building in Post-Soviet Authoritarian and Democratic Contexts

Diana T. Kudaibergenova

The puzzle over post-Soviet nationalizing nationalisms remains unresolved as questions such as why some states nationalize more than the others remain open and require a detailed historical study and empirical approach. Why do some democratic states nationalize more than authoritarian states given similar ethno-demographic contexts, Soviet legacy experiences, and more or less similar ethno-lingual divides and challenges? This study focuses on elites—political, cultural, and economic. These powerful men—and, more rarely, women—control decisions about the nationalizing discourses and projects in the post-Soviet states. I contend that an analysis of the motivations, interests, and processes used by power elites to construct and influence the nation-building processes will shed light on how and why post-Soviet states undertake nationalization. The interplay of different elites' power over decision-making, the outcomes of elite competition, the historical and political contexts under which such decisions are made, as well as the final outcome of these motivations are termed here as a *nationalizing regime*. It is both an analytical tool through which we can piece together different processes and contexts of the nation-building development as well as a concept under which the process of power relations in the nationalizing context occurs. By applying this framework to post-Soviet "democracy" and "authoritarian" political scenarios, I aim to demonstrate the complexity of the processes involved in nationalization and to analyze how different political regimes influence nation-building.

The question I pose in this chapter is very specific to the chosen cases of post-Soviet Latvia and Kazakhstan—the two post-Soviet countries with the largest Russian-speaking minorities, as a percentage of total population, outside Russia. The voluntary, coerced, and/or planned migration of ethnic Russians and other Slavic groups that are identified in the political and theoretical discourses as "Russian-speaking minority groups" has resulted in significant demographic shifts and challenges for nation-builders in Kazakhstan and Latvia.[1] In 1989 these were the only two countries in the Soviet Union where the cumulative percentage of minority groups was almost as high as the titular group (the Russian-speaking minority in Latvia comprised 40 percent of the total population compared with 54 percent of Latvians) or even higher than the titular group (39 percent of Kazakhs and more than 40 percent of Russian-speaking minority[2]) See Tables 5.1–5.3 for comparisons of ethnic composition.

In Latvia, the processes of political competition were traditionally structured within the ethnic Latvian democracy—the idea of re-established pre-1941 Latvian independence and Citizenship Law which circumscribed Soviet-era Russian-speaking migrants from the political competition; and Russo-Latvian political competition. This led to the consolidation of the Latvianized nationalizing regime and the marginalization of the diffuse alternative (centrist and non-Latvian) parties and groups. The wider elite consensus

Table 5.1 Ethnic Composition in Kazakhstan, 1897–1979

	1897	*1926*	*1939*	*1959*	*1970*	*1979*
Total	5,136,300	6,197,900	6,151,10	9,294,700	13,013,000	14,688,300
Kazakhs	71.1%	58.5%	37.8%	30.0%	32.6%	36.0%
Russians	10.5%	20.6%	39.9%	42.7%	42.4%	40.8%
Germans	0.1%	0.8%	1.5%	7.1%	6.6%	6.1%
Ukrainians	1.8%	13.9%	10.7%	8.2%	7.2%	6.1%
Tatars	1.1%	1.3%	1.8%	2.1%	2.2%	2.1%

Source: Based on *Itogi perepisi naseleniia Rossiiskoi imperii* (1897), *Itogi Vsesoiuznoi perepisi naseleniia* (1926 and 1939); *Itogi Vsesoiuznoi perepisi naseleniia* (1959, 1970, 1979); A.N. Alekseenko, A. N. (2001) "Respublika Kazakhstan v zerkale perepisei naseleneiia," *Informatsionnyi b'ulleten Tsentra demografii i ekologii cheloveka Instituta narodnokhozaistvennogo prognozirovania RAN*, no. 47 (2000).

Table 5.2 Ethnic Composition of Population of the Republic of Kazakhstan 1989–2009

	1989	*1990*	*1994*	*1999*	*2009*
Total	16,464.4	16,451.7	16,870.6	14,953.1	16,442.0
Kazakhs	39.7%	40.3%	44.3%	53.4%	63.1%
Russians	37.8%	37.6%	35.8%	30%	23.7%
Germans	5.8%	5.5%	3.6%	2.4%	1.1%
Ukrainians	5.4%	5.4%	5.1%	3.6%	2.1%
Tatars	2%	2%	2%	1.7%	1.3%

Source: Based on *Kratkie itogi Vsesoiuznoi perepisi naseleniia 1989 goda po Kazakhskoi SSR* (Alma-Ata, 1990), 7–9; "Predvaritel'nie itogi perepisi naseleniia 1999 goda v Respublike Kazakhstan Almaty, 2000," in *Dinamika chislennosti i sostava naseleniia Kazakhstana vo vtoroi polovine XX veka*, ed. E. Zimovina (2003); *Results of the 2009 National Population Census of the Republic of Kazakhstan*, ed. A.A. Smailov (Astana: Kazakhstan Statistical Agency, 2011), 19.

Table 5.3 Ethnic Composition of Population in Latvia, 1920–2011

	1920	*1935*	*1959*	*1989*	*2011*
Total (million)	1.86	1.91	2.08	2.67	2.06
Latvians	72.6%	75.5%	62.0%	52.0%	62.1%
Russians	5.7%	10.6%	26.6%	34.0%	26.9%
Byelorussians	4.1%	1.4%	2.9%	4.5%	3.3%
Ukrainians	0.0%	0.1%	1.4%	3.5%	2.21%
Germans	3.6%	3.2%	0.1%	0.1%	0.1%
Jews	5.0%	4.8%	1.7%	0.9%	0.3%
Poles	3.3%	2.5%	2.9%	2.3%	2.3%
Lithuanians	4.0%	1.2%	1.5%	1.3%	2.7%

Source: Latvijas Statistikas – Latvian Statistics Agency.

is solidified and focused on the guardianship of the Latvian nation, language, and heritage as well as democracy. This leads to the marginalization and radicalization of the Russian-speaking parties and movements that focus on the provision of Russian-speaking minority rights in the socio-cultural sphere. However, because the rules of the nationalizing regime in Latvia are so consolidated by the support of the major political players, even centrist parties such as Harmony have to incorporate some components of the Latvian regime's nationalizing rhetoric.

In Kazakhstan, the regime is dependent on the discourses of interethnic stability, harmony, and the active role of President Nursultan Nazarbayev as the main elite, ideology-consolidating actor, and guarantor of stability and prosperity. The Nazarbayev regime also seeks legitimacy by providing stability among the elite groups. Discourses on nation-building are strategically ambiguous and context-dependent, while radicalization in party rhetoric toward a national identity project is controlled and marginalized. Thus, the neopatrimonial system in Kazakhstan that dominates the political field simultaneously controls the overspill of nationalist ideas and creates a heterogeneous mix of discourses and perceptions about the nation. However, growing discontent among a new generation of Kazakh nationalists may pose a threat to this fragile status quo.

COMPARING REGIMES IN LATVIA AND KAZAKHSTAN

A democratic regime "requires open contestation over the right to win control of the government, and this in turn requires free competitive elections, the results of which determine who governs."[3] Authoritarian regimes are defined by the lack of political pluralism or by limited political pluralism and "are based on political apathy and demobilization of the population or limited and controlled mobilizations."[4]

Latvian democratic development is ensured by the elite consensus on open, competitive elections and the legal continuity of the interwar independence that preceded Latvia's incorporation into the Soviet Union in 1941–1945. This legal continuity of the main state documents also retained the 1938 Citizenship Law and its postulates. The first post-Soviet Latvian Parliament (*Saeima*) passed the current Citizenship Law in 1994 after very turbulent discussions and disputes; it immediately divided the country into citizens and non-citizens. Under this Law only descendants of pre-1941 Latvian citizens received automatic citizenship; more than one-quarter of the country's population was relegated to non-citizen status. The majority of these people were Soviet-era migrants who were now "citizens without a country."[5] The non-citizen status allows for permanent residency but provides no political rights and very limited economic rights. According to the same 1994 Citizenship Law, non-citizens had the right to apply for naturalization according to age-based quotas. However, this type of naturalization was a tremendous failure, as only a very few young people were motivated to naturalize under such seemingly "unfair" conditions.

By 1998 and with extensive involvement by the OSCE High Commissioner on National Minority, the *Saeima* dropped the quota-based system and naturalization rates tripled in the first months after the amendments. According to the latest statistics, currently almost 300,000 people—14 percent of the total Latvian population—still remain non-citizens.[6] Unable to run for office even in their municipality or to vote in any elections and referendums, the majority of non-citizens are Russian-speakers who live in the fully Latvianized society. Russian-speaking elites have rare political victories,[7] although the country saw the recent emergence of the centrist party Harmony that, despite electoral victories, has been marginalized as an "artificial opposition" by the ruling coalition of Latvianized parties (conservatives and nationalists).

The situation in Kazakhstan is characterized by soft authoritarianism—the "elite's ability to frame political debate, thereby defining the political agenda and channeling political outcomes" by framing the political opposition, Kazakh nationalists, and other counter-elites as unable to provide vital stability and prosperity in this multi-ethnic country.[8] Kazakhstan's system is identified in the literature as patrimonial,[9] noting the personalized regime of President Nazarbayev. A neopatrimonial regime is defined here by the president's full ability to "maintain authority through personal authority, and informal power networks" that "are mobilized to capture the state (or state assets) in the interests of their members."[10]

The Nazarbayev regime's legitimacy rests on the overall societal and neopatrimonial system's stability. While elites are under the control of personalized rule, society is governed by multiple discourses of semi-civic or Kazakhified nation-building that are used by the regime interchangeably, depending on the specific moment or crisis. The discourse of stability and the marginalization of undesirable radicalization in any sphere of socio-political or economic life guides not only nation-building, but also other important policies and discourses facilitated by the regime. In particular, foreign policy is guided by similar principles of peace-building and harmonious coexistence.

The variations among the post-Soviet elites and regimes guide the development of nation-building policies and discourses via the specific framework of the nationalizing regime and elites' motivations and interests. I contend that elites and the ideological regimes they form serve as the main legitimating bodies and decision-making agents within and outside the state. Elites and elitist regimes, which are defined as discursive structures and agents who produce and control a specific hegemonic idea of the nation and national identity, construct and control the outcomes of "legitimizing identities" and projects to legitimate their interests and motivations.[11]

TOWARD THE NATIONALIZING REGIME

To date, studies of post-Soviet nationalism focused attention on rather ambiguous definitions of the state. Rogers Brubaker's famous concept of the nationalizing state, for example, never provided a clear definition and contextualization of different state-types in the post-Soviet space.[12] Brubaker asserts that the state is distinct from society and understood more or less as a country—both an agent of nationalization and something that undergoes it. The state has been marginalized as an ambiguously defined decision-maker, while recent studies in Eurasian political science demonstrate that it is elites and elitist regimes that have the real decision-making powers in the post-Soviet nation- and state-building context.[13] In my interviews with elites in Latvia and Kazakhstan, opinions vary from vaguely defined but nevertheless equally legitimate concepts of a nation-state assumed to be fully formed in Latvia and partially or completely unfinished in Kazakhstan, and what can be vaguely identified as the political nation.

Empirically and contextually, a nation-state in these cases is defined as having nationalizing nationalism, but the political and discursive field of its production is almost entirely appropriated by the elites. In this manner it is different from the nationalizing state approach. Indeed, the state as an overarching powerful entity and category occupies a stable position in the eyes of the regimes—ruling elites and coalitions in Latvia or the personalized regime of Nazarbayev in Kazakhstan. However, the position and perception of the "state" category among the citizens of these countries is rather blurred. Recent expert opinion polls in Kazakhstan, for example, noted that the population has long marginalized the state aspect of state institutions[14] or to a failing and quite ambiguous connection between the nation and the state in Latvia.[15] My analysis of elite interviews, speeches, and discourses shows how the state is imagined as a "provider" of fundamental socio-political values—from welfare, law and order, to ideology and stability. However, in return, what defines these projects and discourses are the power elites and the nationalizing regimes that they constitute, re-constitute, and define throughout not only their term in office, but from pre-independence by generating pre-political consensuses.[16]

A nationalizing regime is a specific political decision-making framework that is governed by specific interests of the elite groups. Derived from comparative politics where regimes are referred to as "the formal and informal structure and nature of political power in the country, including the method of determining office holders and the relations between the office holders and the society at large,"[17] the concept of nationalizing regimes is introduced here to uncover and analyze nation-building through the internal networks and interests of those who govern such policies—elites. Why do elites matter and how are they defined in the post-Soviet context? Without question, elites—a "tiny but powerful minorities" that are "made up of autonomous social and political actors who are interested primarily in maintaining and enhancing their power, so that their power struggles are not reducible to classes or other collectivities"[18] play a crucial and dominant role in major decision-making on the political and economic levels in post-Soviet states as well as many other modern states. The elite paradigm that puts elite competition at the center of the processes that shape and define "political and to some extent wider social orders, format political and many social divisions and enflame or contain major conflicts"[19] is the most viable paradigm for analysis of any political, social, and economic transformations in modern societies, including those of nation-building.

Why is it important to analyze processes, policies, and discourses in these post-Soviet states through the lens of nationalizing states? Because my major concern was to focus on the decision-makers. Elites have the resources to define, shape, and change the main power discourse at a given time. With a more powerful and concentrated elitist agency, for example, in the form of an authoritarian leadership or the hegemony of an elite group with strong and similar interests, discourses become either more powerful and difficult to change (Latvia) or set in a specific framework defined by the regime for its own legitimation (Kazakhstan).

The role of the elites as decision-makers is not new to political science or to social science in general. Some of the recent studies of Catalonian nationalism, for example, have pioneered in providing the other side of these processes. By analyzing discourses and popular responses to these discourses, along with elite interviews and polls, Jeffrey Thomas Miley concluded that nationalist movements are elite-led projects that may not even be supported by the majority of the population.[20] The gradual defeat of radical nationalist groups and political parties in the Basque Country of Spain also demonstrates the same trend.[21] Finally, the growing homogenization, feelings of abandonment, and distrust of the state as a whole that has generated out-migration in Latvia,[22] fueled by a more intensively nationalizing policy from above, also demonstrate this trend.

Elites, attitudes, rhetoric, and contextualization of the nation-building process were further shaped by socio-political pressures. Studies of contemporary nation-building in these states must also take account intra-elite competition and the ongoing need to legitimize their approach to the population.[23] Political elites are the representatives of the people's will, assuming that the government in power was popularly elected. In the case of a nondemocratic regime, elites are co-opted and selected by an authoritarian ruler or a group of authoritarian elites, thus decision-making rarely reflects the will of the people. However, elites may also be co-opted and pre-selected in democratic regimes through the system of party co-optations and coalitions of post-Soviet elites will demonstrate in the Latvian 1990s political scene.

Elites in power regarded nationalism as the strongest tool to legitimize the nation's right to dominate the state as well as to establish their rights to control which framework of the nation and the state-building would be used.

> Nationalism would not be the troublesome force it is today were it not for the fact that efforts to define the boundedness of political communities engender controversy and evoke challenge. As Ernst Gellner recognized, nationalism revolves around attempts to convert the intrinsically ambiguous and controversial into the conventional and seemingly natural, to impose a normalized order on a much more complex cultural reality. In this sense, nationalism is not simply about imagined communities; it is much more fundamentally about a struggle for control over defining communities, and in particular, of control over the imagination about the community.[24]

The desire to convert the ambiguous and controversial ideas about the nation and nationhood in the post-Soviet region went hand-in-hand with the interests that political elites in power had to represent at each social and historical context.

REGIME DICHOTOMY

There are several similarities that drive both Kazakh and Latvian elites in their nationalization processes. I define these structures as legitimacy (both for the masses and within the elites' field) and competition (mostly among the elites).

Legitimacy here is understood not only as a concept of "shared-meaning" construction or value systems, like the belief in newly built democracy, but also as a concept of normalizing conditions.[25] The rule and the framework—in this case, the framework of nationalist ideology legitimation and national revival—are represented by both Latvian and Kazakh elites as a return to the normal and usual development of the nation. Such a normalizing framework stands in opposition to unusual developments like those that happened during Soviet rule. Defined as occupational and colonial rule, the Soviet regime is represented in the official newspaper and political discourses as illegitimate and wrong. The Soviet regime's policies (including those regarding nation-building) were perceived and presented by the "new" (i.e., post-Soviet) elites (many of whom were simultaneously "old" elites—communists-turned-nationalists) as wrongdoings and harmful actions against the real, authentic nation that now needed remedial action for its "normal" development.[26]

The problems of the nation and how to enhance its weak position became the central point for elites, legitimation and competition in both Latvia and Kazakhstan. Elites used nationalization via nation-building as a tool for building legitimacy both within the population and among the elites. In the key early independence years the elite struggled to convince its own members of their legitimacy, much less the general population and the outside world.[27]

The first years of independence brought challenges in these new states with a vast ethnic minority group whose language and culture is quite distinct from the indigenous Baltic or Kazakh core that the elites in both cases tried to promote as a new strong identity for state- and nation-building. The Russian-speaking minority has continued to influence the internal politics of constructing the nation in both states. Latvian dominant elites still face competition from the more adept Russian-speaking elites who were able to gain access to political rights and legitimacy by mastering the official language and gaining citizenship despite restrictive citizenship law. In Kazakhstan, the regime neutralized any opposition to the dominant ideology by co-opting the Russian elites and providing them with symbolic capital within the internal political system and by marginalizing those Kazakh nationalists who decided not to co-opt to the regime's framework.

Another challenge was the self-identification of elites. The new elites that eventually came to power in both states had to legitimize their right to rule within their own political field, or, put simply, they had to reassert their rights and ability for the benefit of those with whom they were sharing power.[28] New elites were recruited in two ways—either through fair democratic elections (in Latvia) or through informal networks based on the Bourdieuan symbolic and cultural capital, cadre capabilities, and their importance for the country's development. Thus, new elites were also chosen through the existing networks within power sharing arrangements both in Latvia and Kazakhstan.

The divide between nationalizing and nationalist elites is very clear. Nationalizing elites use national rhetoric for self and regime legitimation, while nationalist elites truly believe in such ideas. That is one of the biggest differences in elite composition in Kazakhstan (nationalizing elites) and Latvia (nationalist elites). Throughout my interviews with key politicians in both regimes and with members of marginalized elites[29] (e.g., marginalized Russian minority groups in opposition both to the leading pro-Latvian parties and to the Harmony Center or marginalized Kazakh nationalist groups in Kazakhstan) and through the existing elite surveys, I was able to conclude the following aspects of elite composition.[30]

In Kazakhstan most members of power elites (those in the president's administration and other high positions) tend to be more cosmopolitan and open-minded about ethnic issues. As noted by one of my respondents, a former advisor to President Nazarbayev, right after independence, "There were not many hot-hearted Kazakh nationalists [among the power elites], it was simply dangerous to allow them into the circle [of high decision-making]."[31] During the turbulence of 1994, various organizations led by ethnic Russian discourses and ideas, for example Lad, were actively engaged in political activities promoting secessionist or separatist ideas within the republic based on the ethno-demographic regional representations of the population. The official press became involved in framing the discourse of planned (strategic) stability needed in the country:

> Since the beginning [of independence] it was clear that it would be hard to keep the sovereignty of the republic and not only due to economic reasons. There were great hopes associated with the [following internal and external aspects]: (a) that we would be able to create a state-power [*gosudarstvenno-vlastnyi*] mechanism with the president atop that would be able to regulate the society and to organize it in the new conditions; (b) that Russia, with which Kazakhstan is in very close relations, would be able to become a real democracy and by overcoming the pro-imperial and pro-chauvinistic tendencies inside it, would lend its hand with helpful and unselfish support and help for Kazakh republic; (c) that Kazakhstan with its multinational population that was known before as a republic of "peoples' friendship" would become a country of international stability and Kazakhstani patriotism. Along with that a lot of hope was associated with the role of the Russian nation that constitutes one-third of the population. All of these forces that constitute the spine of stateness and democratic development of Kazakhstan have shown serious cracks [recently].[32]

Despite the fact that there was a need to legitimize elites to the growing majority of ethnic Kazakhs through the gradual nationalization of ideology and space, the Kazakh elites were far less nationalizing than other elites in the former Soviet Union. There are several explanations for that phenomenon.

First, elites in Kazakhstan were challenged by the biggest Russian-speaking minority and their proximity to their external homeland as well as rather friendly relations with Russia. Yet this situation did not allow Kazakh elites to choose the Baltic scenario, nor was it technically possible as Kazakhstan lacked the initial legitimacy or "national authenticity" available to Latvia by 1990.

Second, legitimation was based on several layers of sometimes conflicting narratives. For example, as noted by many researchers in the field, the Kazakh state uses a set of both civic and ethnic narratives in its nation-building efforts.[33] This legitimation technique is not unique for Kazakhstan or Uzbekistan,[34] Ukraine, and Estonia.[35] By linking separate narratives to different socio-political and socio-ethnic audiences, among both the masses and the elites, the ruling elites try to legitimize their ability and their right to rule both over the Kazakh ethnic majority as well as over the multiethnic society. The third layer of legitimacy is external—for its international legitimacy in the eyes of the closest kin-state (Russia) or the wider international community that accepts the civic rights of minorities.[36]

Third, many of the current Kazakh elites were politically informed and educated during the Soviet period. Their mindset (*myshlenie*) was formed during that particular regime where some elites were far more ideologically tainted than any mass supporters of the regime. Even though 20 years of independence has changed both the initial socio-political contexts in the country and elites' perceptions, the old elites in Kazakhstan still use the rhetoric and forms of address typical for Soviet ideological constructions, for example, people's friendship (*druzhba narodov*) or universal labor values (a narrative that appeared in Nazarbayev's speech in summer 2012, several months after the Zhanaozen uprisings in December 2011). This particular way of approaching nation-building content from afar (that contributes to its lack of national authenticity) specifies the peculiar elite behavior and orientation toward nationalizing on the surface but not within their core values. This fact differentiates Kazakh elites from their Latvian counterparts although both have a common feature of authoritative protection of defined frameworks of legitimation and national imagination—both used for the legitimation of the state and elites' rule.

Latvian elite development after independence underwent severe structural changes and this might explain its differentiation from the Kazakh elites' behavior and attitudes. In Latvia, independence brought a tightening of nationalist ideology and exclusion of non-Latvian symbolism from the ideological content and the exclusion of non-Latvians from the political field. This happened through the series of laws (starting with the 1989 Language Law, adaptation of the old Constitution in 1990, the 1994 Citizenship Law, and, finally, Educational Reform of 2004) that first excluded any non-Latvian speakers from the official public sphere by making Latvian the only official language.[37]

Finally, the 1994 Citizenship Law established highly restrictive procedures (a quota system, for example) and legal hurdles for acquiring citizenship that excluded all non-Latvian migrants who moved to the country after 1940 (and thus in line with the discourse known in Latvia as the Soviet occupation). Some of the most restrictive discourses of Right movements like TB-LNNK (Tēvzemei un Brīvībai-LNNK—For Fatherland and Freedom-LNNK) proposed that those groups of people who were not able to secure Latvian citizenship after independence were expected to leave Latvia and come back to their ethnic homelands (e.g., Russia, Belarus, or Ukraine). Other groups and parties on the spectrum have supported the proposal to allow the most loyal non-Latvian residents to naturalize through the highly bureaucratic process. Until amendments to the law in 1998, the process had included a quota of about 10 percent of naturalized citizens out of the non-citizen population per year (in the early 1990s not more than 100 people a year naturalized due to the window system (age-based quota system) problem. This also included an advanced Latvian language proficiency test that many Russians were not able to master at the time. Special restrictions were applied against former communists and, later, members of the Soviet militia—they were not allowed to run for any office and, in some cases, were not allowed to naturalize. Latvia also introduced a special blacklist for the former communists propaganda and KGB workers who were accused of crimes against the Latvian nation.[38] These developments largely contributed to the elite structures right after independence that saw the decline of the number of Russophone elites[39] (even those who had supported Latvian independence and were active members of the Popular Front). A few former ethnic Latvian communists remained in power. Among them was Ivars Godmanis, one of the key power elites in the 1990s (and prime minister twice: 1990–1993 and 2007–2009) and the architect of Latvian privatization. Politicians like Godmanis were part of the nationalizing elites—those communists-turned-nationalists—but they were a minority in the Latvian political sphere because the political dynamics changed fast and new elites who entered the field were genuinely nationalist and did not have a communist past.

The post-1993 elections dealt the biggest political loss to the Latvian Popular Front, while strengthening ethnic democratic institutions (those favoring ethnic Latvians in official positions but otherwise following democratic standards and frameworks). It also saw the development and the return of the Western Latvian diaspora—those elites and ethnic Latvians who spent the Soviet occupation in exile and upon their return to their homeland turned into proper authentic nationalist elites pushing for exclusionist ideologies and national identity projects. Until mid-2000s the elitist field in Latvia was mostly represented by pro-Latvian elites except for the Russian party ZaPHCEL (*Za Prava Cheloveka v Latvii*—For the Human Rights in Latvia) that was highly marginalized. Harmony Center actually declared itself to be a centrist party—a very unusual development in Latvia's political life where the ideological distinctions existed only on the basis of ethnic division and elites' orientation toward inclusion or exclusion of a particular ethnic theme.

Elites in Latvia and Kazakhstan underwent quite different dynamics throughout the years of independence. There are several important distinctions that shape the outcomes of elites' fields and their decision-making. There is a strong presence of the dominant discourse about nation-building—either clearly formulated around the boundaries of ethno-historical and ethno-nationalist approach of the dominant titular group (Latvia) or several dichotomous narratives deliberately constructed by elites to legitimize themselves to different audiences (Kazakhstan). Despite the regime differences, both the Kazakh and Latvian cases are ruled by the power elites—the top group of decision-makers whose official position may not always correspond to the actual power they have. These top elites have enough power to define the frameworks of nation-building as well as the framework of the political field in the national imagination. They construct boundaries and restrictions against deviations within the framework. One of the examples of such open resistance to deviation in the nationalist framework was the parliamentary discussions (led by the leading pro-Latvian party, Unity) and elaborations on the law that would prohibit usage of any Soviet symbolism in Latvia. The discussions commenced few weeks before May 9th in 2013—Victory Day for the USSR in World War II, a very pro-Russian event among Russophone minority groups who use Soviet symbolism (e.g., St. George's ribbon or even Soviet and Russian flags) to represent their past identities. The desire of power elites in Latvia to define and restrict national symbolic frames so meticulously is very similar to the same restrictive frameworks in Kazakhstan. The regime difference does inform different techniques of such frames and the behavior of elites. However, the difference of the regime cannot always predict the outcomes it may have on the nation-building. Thus, elites inform the framework of nation-building as well as change and influence variations of the regime in the former Soviet region.

CONCLUSION

Post-Soviet nation-building is constructed and shaped by the structures of the elitist regimes and their powers, which I identified here[40] as nationalizing regimes. These regimes have the biggest impact on the formation and re-formation of specific nationalizing policies in similar ethnic divisions but very distinct political conditions. The motivations and insecurities of the ruling elites influence the outcome of the nationalization, sometimes regardless of the political regime. I argued that nationalist elites in Latvia aimed to marginalize non-Latvian parties and discourses from the dominant national discourses and that this ideological consolidation of the ruling elites solidified the discursive power of the nationalizing regime. In democratic Latvia, with its changing electoral cycles, the nation-building policy is more stable and even rigid compared with the Kazakh case. In the less democratic Kazakh system, the neopatrimonial personalistic regime relies on interethnic and elite stability and thus avoids radicalization of national discourses. Elites in Kazakhstan are nationalizing, meaning the nationalizing agenda is used for legitimacy-building rather than purely personal motivations like in Latvia. Elite competition under a neopatrimonial system is restricted, and all deviant national discourses that do not fit within the regime's strategically ambiguous approach to nation-building are framed as dangerous and unfavorable.

In a nationalizing regime, elite competition strongly influences regime dynamics. Loyal to the president, elites in the Kazakhstani regime are unable to compete against each other on the so-called Kazakhified field, proposing alternatives to the official, wobbly nation-building policy. Moreover, among the power elites in Kazakhstan there are not many actors who could successfully pursue such alternative paths as many of the power elites are cosmopolitan state-builders. In Latvia, the political defeat of non-Latvian parties, coupled with their leaders' inability to exercise political rights after independence, meant that many "Soviet-era migrants" were cut-off from Latvian citizenship for years. Even after the abandonment of naturalization quotas, many leaders of the Russian Union still cannot apply for citizenship under the "communist" lustration of Article 15 of the Citizenship Law. Pro-Russian parties are also marginalized as their electorate is only slowly growing and country's potential Russian-sympathetic electorate still remains confined to the 14 percent non-citizen populace.

The processes of oppositional "framing" and their marginalization from the dominant political arena in both Latvia and Kazakhstan are similar and usually fall under the national categories. The Latvian political field is long divided into Latvianized parties and minority parties. The national ideology in Latvia is guided by the sacral values of national guardianship that narrows the non-Latvian demands in ethnopolitics. In Kazakhstan, the only remaining opposition to the regime is the ideological opposition of the Kazakh national-patriots who are seen as "firebrands" and "destabilizing elements." This is partially a stereotypical approach to the growing movement of Kazakh national supporters and positions them negatively in the non-Kazakh speaking field and facilitates further dichotomy between the regime's ambiguous nation-building discourses and Kazakhified opposition parts, which are in danger of further radicalization.

It is important to tackle these macro- and microprocesses in comparative perspective to shed more light on the post-Soviet variations and progress in the nationalizing processes. The myopic approach of the nationalizing state as an overarching, yet very vague, framework for the study of political processes on the ground is no longer viable. It fails to acknowledge how and under which conditions nationalization is reshaped and who are the main driving forces behind these processes. I have argued that the state approach is important though problematic in the post-Soviet context and needs further re-conceptualization, whereas nationalizing regimes instead of nationalizing states appear to be the main actors in the ongoing political developments and decisions on nation-building in very different post-Soviet states.

NOTES

1. David Laitin, *Identity in Formation: The Russian-Speaking Populations in the New Abroad* (Ithaca, NY and London: Cornell University Press, 1998); Charles King and Neil Melvin, *Nations Abroad. Diaspora Politics and International Relations in the Former Soviet Union* (Boulder, CO: Westview Press, 1998); Marlene Laruelle and Sebastien Peyrouse, *Les Russes du Kazakhstan. Identites nationales et nouveaux Etats dans l'espace post-sovietique* (Paris: Maisonneuvre, and Larose: IFEAC, 2004.)

2. David Laitin (*Identity in Formation*, 1998) famously identified the Russian-speaking minority as the "conglomerate identity" that "includes [ethnic] Russians, Belarusans, Ukrainians, Poles, and Jews, all of whom speak Russian as their first language in republics outside their putative homelands." This conglomerate identity does not include other ethnic groups who are highly Russified, for example, Germans and Kazakhs and also a substantial part of ethnic Latvians who are fluent in Russian. In my investigations I deliberately separate "Russian-speaking" conglomerate identity in Laitin's classic terms to define non-titular "Russian" minority as it is presented in Latvia (Russian-speakers) from the "Russian-speaking" populations, many of whom are ethnic Kazakhs who speak mostly/or only Russian but do not consider themselves as "Russian-speaking" minority group in their own homeland, for example, Kazakhstan. The ethno-lingual situation is Kazakhstan is rather complex, and minority groups of "Russian-speakers" (ethnic Slavs and other non-titular, traditionally non-Central Asian groups) are not defined as clearly as minority in Latvia. President Nazarbayev's official rhetoric simultaneously draws boundaries of ethno-cultural communities within Assembly of the People of Kazakhstan (formerly Assembly of the Peoples of Kazakhstan), for example, but also blurs the line in terms of language use and identity. Kazakh nationalist groups and informal movements dispute this position by separating ethnic Russians, Kazakh-speaking (*nagyz Qazaq*) and Russian-speaking (*shala Qazaq*) ethnic Kazakhs.

3. Juan Linz and Alfred Stepan, *Problems of Democratic Transition and Consolidation: Southern Europe, South America, and Post-Communist Europe* (Baltimore, MD and London: The John Hopkins University Press, 1996), 3.

4. Juan Linz, *Totalitarian and Authoritarian Regimes* (Boulder, CO and London: Lynne Rienner, 2000), 54.

5. Laitin, *Identity in Formation.*

6. Data from the Latvian Statistics Agency 2014.

7. PCTLV (currently Russian Union of Latvia) was one of the most successful "Russian" parties in Latvia and was led by Tatiana Zhdanoka, perhaps the most famous pro-Russian activist from Latvia in Europe. The party first ran for elections following the 1998 (post-quota) amendments. In their first elections PCTLV (then known as "For Human Rights in United Latvia") secured 14 percent of votes and 16 seats out of 100 in the parliament. They advocated zero-option citizenship for all remaining non-citizens. Members and leaders of PCTLV actively supported minority Russian schools, Russian language status, and other sensitive issues regarding Russian-speaking minority rights. However, the diverse movement was competitive and fractured into several parties and single leaderships. By 2005 a new union of leftist and centrist parties called Harmony was formed. Under the charismatic leadership of the former Russian-Latvian TV presenter Nils Ushakovs (currently mayor of Riga), the party became the only viable political and ideological opposition to the highly Latvianized spectrum of political parties in Latvia. *Harmony* won majority of seats in the 2011 and 2014 elections and succeeded in municipal elections. However, party's position in interethnic and nation-building policies is centrist for the provision of civic and multilingual harmony. In the contemporary Latvian party field, Harmony is considered to be the "Russian" party by the ruling right coalition of Latvian conservatives and nationalists but a "traitor" party by the radical Russian parties and movements, especially by the marginal ZARYA (For the Mother Tongue) movement.

8. Edward Schatz, "The Soft Authoritarian Tool Kit: Agenda-Setting Power in Kazakhstan and Kyrgyzstan," *Comparative Politics* 41, no. 2 (2009): 203.

9. Ed Schatz, *Modern Clan Politics: The Power of "Blood" in Kazakhstan and Beyond* (Seattle and London: Washington University Press, 2004); Rico Isaacs, *Party System Formation in Kazakhstan: Between Formal and Informal Politics* (London: Routledge, 2011); Eric McGlinchey, *Chaos, Violence, Dynasty: Politics and Islam in Central Asia* (Pittsburgh, PA: University of Pittsburgh Press, 2011); Kathleen Collins, "Economic and Security Regionalism and Patrimonial Authoritarian Regimes: The Case of Central Asia," *Europe-Asia Studies* 61, no. 2 (2009): 24–81.

10. Isaacs, *Party System Formation in Kazakhstan*, 10; see also Alisher Ilkhamov, "Neopatrimonialism, Interest Groups, and Patronage Networks: The Impasses of the Governance System in Uzbekistan," *Central Asian Survey* 26, no. 1 (2007): 65–84; McGlinchey, *Chaos, Violence, Dynasty.*

11. Manuel Castells, *Communication Power* (Oxford: Oxford University Press, 2009); Anton Steen, "Elite and Mass Confidence in New Democracies—Towards Congruence? The Baltic States 1992–2007," *Historical Social Research* 37, no. 3 (2012): 12–47.

12. Rogers Brubaker, "Nationhood and the National Question in the Soviet Union and Post-Soviet Eurasia: An Institutionalist Account," *Theory and Society* 21, no. 1 (1994): 4–8; Rogers Brubaker, "Nationalizing States Revisited: Projects and Processes of Nationalization in Post-Soviet States," *Ethnic and Racial Studies* 34 (2011): 1785–1814.

13. Schatz, "The Soft Authoritarian Tool Kit"; McGlinchey, *Chaos, Violence, Dynasty*; Sally Cummings, "Legitimation and Identification in Kazakhstan," *Nationalism and Ethnic Politics* 12, no. 2 (2006): 177–204; Isaacs, *Party System Formation in Kazakhstan*.

14. Strategiya 2007 Sociological Reports, May and March 2007.

15. Brigita Zepa et al. *National Identity in Latvia Report* (Riga: University of Latvia and Chicago: University of Chicago Press, 2011).

16. Andrew F. March, "State Ideology and the Legitimation of Authoritarianism: The Case of Post-Soviet Uzbekistan," *Journal of Political Ideologies* 8, no. 2 (2003): 209–232; Cummings, "Legitimation and Identification in Kazakhstan."

17. Bernard Badie et al. (2011) *International Encyclopedia of Political Science*.

18. John Highley and Jan Pakulski. "Elite Theory versus Marxism: The Twentieth Century's Verdict," *Historical Social Research* 37, no. 1 (2000): 320–332 and in Higley, J. and Lengyel, G. *Elites After State Socialism: Theories and Analysis* (Rowman and Littlefield Publishers, 2000), 229.

19. Ibid.

20. Thomas J. Miley, "The Politics of Language and Nation: The Case of Catalans in Contemporary Spain." PhD diss., Yale University, 2004.

21. Fernando Molina, "The Historical Dynamics of Ethnic Conflicts: Confrontational Nationalism, Democracy, and the Basques in Contemporary Spain," *Nations and Nationalism* 16, no. 2 (2010): 240–260; Enric Martinez-Herrera and Thomas J. Miley, "The Constitution and the Politics of National Identity in Spain," *Nations and Nationalism* 16, no. 2 (2010): 6–30.

22. Recent studies show that those out-migrating are mostly Latvian citizens with migration at 56 percent in the period of 2000–2010. See, for example Zepa et al., *National Identity in Latvia Report.*

23. Sally Cummings, "The Central Asian Economies since Independence," *Slavic Review* 66 (2007): 75–56; Rodney Barker, *Legitimating Identities: The Self-Presentation of Rulers and Subjects* (Cambridge: Cambridge University Press, 2001).

24. Mark Beissinger, *Nationalist Mobilization and the Collapse of the Soviet Union* (Cambridge: Cambridge University Press, 2002), 18.

25. Castells, *Communication Power*, 12.

26. Diana T. Kudaibergenova, "Use and Abuse of Postcolonial Discourses in Post-Independent Kazakhstan," *Europe-Asia Studies*, 68, no. 5 (2016): 917–935.

27. Cummings, "Legitimation and Identification in Kazakhstan," *Nationalism and Ethnic Politics* 12 (2006): 178.

28. Barker, *Legitimating Identities*; Cummings 2006 "Legitimation and Identification in Kazakhstan."

29. A total of more than 150 interviews were collected in Kazakhstan and Latvia during the eighteen months of subsequent fieldwork trips to these two regions from 2011 to 2013. The sample included mostly members of the political elite, members of cultural elites, opposition politicians, marginalized Russian politicians in Latvia and Kazakhstan, as well as marginalized Kazakh nationalists in Kazakhstan. An additional sample was drawn from regional elites and intellectuals. A separate sample was also made with Russophone non-citizens in Latvia and Latvians who supported nationalist programs.

30. Steen, "Elite and Mass Confidence in New Democracies"; S. Zhusupov, "Dinamika Sociological Data 1999–2002," in *Politicheskaia analitika issledovaniia* (Almaty: "Arna-b." 1998–2001).

31. Author's interview #45, August 2012, Almaty.

32. Salyq Zimanov, chairman of the Committee for Constitutional law-making and human rights of the Verkhovnogo Soveta of the Republic of Kazakhstan "Ne nado rasshativat' godusarstvennye ustoi," *Kazakhstanskaia pravda,* January 21, 1995, 3.

33. Bhave Dave, *Kazakhstan: Ethnicity and Power* (London: Routledge, 2007); Cummings 2006; and most recently Donnacha Ó Beacháin and Rob Kevlihan, "Threading the Needle: Kazakhstan Between Civic an Ethno-Nationalist State-Building," *Nations and Nationalism* 19, no. 2 (2013): 337–356.

34. Laura Adams, *The Spectacular State: Culture and National Identity in Uzbekistan* (Durham, NC and London: Duke University Press, 2010).

35. Brubaker, "Nationalizing States Revisited."

36. Erica Marat, "Nation Branding in Central Asia: A New Campaign to Present Ideas about the State and the Nation," *Europe-Asia Studies* 61, no. 7 (2009): 1123–1136; Magdalena Solska, "Citizenship, Collective Identity, and the International Impact on Integration Policy in Estonia, Latvia, and Lithuania," *Europe-Asia Studies* 63, no. 6 (2011): 1089–1108.

37. Shortly after independence Latvian officials introduced language tests for employees of any official office (including the airports), and anyone who did not pass the language test was dismissed from their job. This was followed by the regular language check-ups by language officials and fines for any inability to communicate in Latvian when the customers desired to do so. Testimonials from non-citizens that I've collected during my fieldwork in Latvia proved that language check-ups are still a regular feature of daily life and the main reason that non-Latvian speakers or those who did not master Latvian seek jobs outside city center (where the parliament and most ministries are situated) and work in special Russian-speaking urban enclaves like Kengaraks or Maskavas iela in Riga. See Pal Kolstoe et al., *Nation-Building and Ethnic Integration in Post-Soviet Societies: An Investigation of Latvia and Kazakhstan* (Boulder, CO: Westview, 1998).

38. Citizenship Law 1994, Article 14, Paragraphs 1, 3, 4, 5.

39. From the first official elections to the fifth parliament (renewed structure from 1937) in 1993 to till more recent victories by Harmony Centre in mid-2000s, there were about 12 representatives of Russian elites (out of 100 representatives in total) in the Latvian Parliament *Saeima* (Rosenvalds 2013).

40. Diana T. Kudaibergenova, "The Archaeology of Nationalizing Regimes," *Problems of post-communism,* 2016 forthcoming.

Chapter 6

Imagining Kazakhstani-stan

Negotiations of Homeland and Titular-Nationality

Alexander C. Diener

"God grant that no one should stir up Kazakhstan on ethnic grounds. It would be far worse than Yugoslavia."

—Nursultan Nazarbayev[1]

"...the Kazakh people, having given their proud name to the country, have the responsibility of an historical mission to become the consolidating center of unity for the Nation" (*konsolidiruiushchii tsentr ob'edineniia Natsii*)

—Doctrine of National Unity of Kazakhstan[2]

In February 2014, Kazakhstan's President Nursultan Nazarbayev prompted controversy by suggesting that his state might benefit from a name change.[3] He advocated using the Kazakh-language word for country (*yeli*) in place of the current *-stan* ending, thereby altering the state name from *Kazakhstan* ("land of the Kazakhs") to *Kazakh Yeli* (Kazakh state). Nazarbayev's motive was to distance Kazakhstan from other "stans" (e.g., Pakistan, Afghanistan, Turkmenistan, Uzbekistan) whose capacity for global integration is limited by poor human rights records, blatant autocratic political structures, and unfriendly investment climates. Though the idea was soon abandoned, it reflects the Astana government's desire to advance Kazakhstan's geopolitical and geo-economic image as a "bridging state" between Europe and Asia.[4] Paralleling this unique international positionality are Kazakhstan's domestic efforts to reconcile civic, ethnic, and transnational dynamics of identity formation. The result is a questionably sustainable, multinationalistic, quasi-patriotic hybrid.

Possessing popular sanction for soft-authoritarian leadership, Kazakhstan's government promotes a transnational "Eurasian" cultural identity in conjunction with a "Kazakhstani" civic identity, while simultaneously reifying the "Kazakh" ethno-nation. Such an approach may be considered a shrewd deportment with regard to global norms, a judicious geopolitical stance in relation to regional neighbors, and, given Kazakhstan's ethno-demographic, cultural, and linguistic conditions, an expedient internal political strategy. In essence, this multipronged identity project continues the Soviet "friendship of peoples" rhetoric that promoted multinational patriotism, based less on democratic ideals than attachment to place, a robust economy, and a globally aspirational, future-oriented state ideology.

THE CRISIS OF THE HYPHEN AMID MODERNIST STATE IDEALS

The ambiguous approach to nationalization embraced by the Nazarbayev regime reflects a broader "crisis of the hyphen" in the contemporary international system.[5] As discussed by Marco Antonsich, the spatial congruence between nation and state is being eroded by global financial flows, devolution of powers to sub- and supranational institutions, mounting voter apathy, tensions between secular and religious allegiances, and changing ethno-demographic compositions resulting from corporeal mobility.[6] For Jürgen Habermas, this attests to a positive transition toward cosmopolitanism and an era of "post-nationality" that enables belonging within a given territory without restrictive claim to national membership.[7] Other scholars are more skeptical of "territory as a ground of loyalty and national affect … increasingly divorced from territory as the site of sovereignty and state control of civil society."[8] Benedict Anderson, for example, bemoans the "proliferating ethnic identities and portable nationality" cutting populations loose from "the structured accountability and the sacrifices that accompany old-fashioned citizenship."[9] Khachig Tololyan also warns against a "discursive complicity between diasporists and the transnational project" in which "re-articulating the nation-state seems also to require the option of disarticulating it."[10] The latter is obviously resisted by state elites.

Most governments view the de-coupling of "nation" and "state" as a challenge to their modernist conceptions of territory that developed around notions of sovereignty and the nation-state dating to the Peace of Westphalia.[11] The contemporary crisis of the hyphen therefore compels governments to either plow under identities that deviate from the nation-state ideal through ethno-nationalization (often involving dynamics of territorial cleansing) or some form of assimilationist nationalism that integrates the "other" into a titular state identity. This can take the form of inclusive ethno-nationalization (e.g., expanding the scope of the term *russkii* to include non-ethnic Russians—the former *rossiiskii*)[12] or making ethnicity addendus to a territorial or civic national identity (e.g., Russian-Kazakhstani). In terms of policy, the crisis of the hyphen triggers two interrelated responses.

First, some Western states have made efforts to "de-ethnicize" the nation and rewrite identity in civic terms. Such efforts seek to co-opt the principles of democracy in service of the territorial state (i.e., replace the *ethnos* with the *demos* by cultivating a new sense of "we" based on shared values and commitment to the politico-institutional bounded space). Second, states have attempted to enhance cultural compatibility between core ethno-national groups and immigrant newcomers and/or resident "others." At times enacted concomitantly with the first approach, the latter efforts retain a focus on the cultural-ethnic character of the state by implementing restrictive immigration/asylum laws, citizenship tests, and various symbols of titular-group primacy. The foremost symbol of such primacy is the ethnic state name.

While civic nations like the United States and Canada employ non-ethnic state names to facilitate common identification and advance territorialization for their diverse populations, they nevertheless struggle to form inclusive societies amid geographic, racial, ethnic, economic, and cultural boundaries.[13] This being said, it is fair to argue that states possessing ethnonyms (France, Germany, Japan, etc.) face an inherently more complex task of integrating peoples of different ethnic/national heritage. Will a fourth generation Turk in Germany call herself German, a second generation Algerian proclaim himself French, or a recent Korean immigrant in Japan refer to herself as Japanese? More to the point, would such self-identification be recognized by the society at large? This chapter joins a broader literature assessing how non-titular peoples reconcile their identities within a system still predicated on modernist state ideals and a doctrine of nationalism.[14] Such systemic ideals are evidenced by the fact that almost every post-Soviet government opted for an ethnic state name and thereby set the stage for the enactment of some form of titular nationalization.[15]

Rogers Brubaker's 2011 revisiting of "nationalizing states" offers a fruitful benchmark from which to consider Kazakhstan today. His assertion that "civic" and "ethnic" nations are ideal types refutes the traditional binary between the two.[16] Rather, these tropes are best employed for comparative purposes in measuring the disposition of various national ideologies and state-building projects. Given that ethnic and civic elements are perpetually negotiated into lived political reality, the process of nationalization and the commensurate crisis of the hyphen are never fixed or immutable, but constantly reimagined. Where Brubaker and other scholars[17] suggest that Kazakhstan's nationalization manifests "strong, quasi-racial, and inter-generationally persistent ethno-national boundaries," recent studies suggest that such an assessment unduly de-emphasizes the presence and affect of multinational and transnational ideals, along with their de-and re-territorializing effects.[18] I similarly suggest that a conception of homeland and an ideal of patriotism are developing across the ethnic spectrum and territory of Kazakhstan. This conception revolves around the persona of Nursultan Nazarbayev and is contingent on the prospects of continued economic well-being in the state.

Kazakhstan's efforts to combine *jus sanguinis* and *jus soli* begs the question, what effect does the ethnonym have on Kazakhstan's identity politics and status as a homeland for non-titular peoples? Moreover, does the ethnonym limit options for civil-society development by institutionalizing the subaltern status of post-Soviet minorities?

CONTEXTUALIZING TITULAR NATIONALISM AND KAZAKHSTAN'S IDENTITY POLITICS

The Nazarbayev regime has been characterized in recent literature as "threading the needle," engaging in "a balancing act," and intentionally pursuing a course of "strategic ambiguity" in identity politics.[19] While the coupling of multi/civic nationalization with de facto ethnic nationalization was prudent in order to preclude irredentist/secessionist movements and curb large-scale emigration when Kazakhs composed only 40 percent of the state's population in 1989 (see Table 6.1), the fact that this ambiguity remains in play 25 years later suggests that it is more than a post-Soviet transition strategy.[20] Rather, it may constitute a conscious integration of civic-, ethno-, and transnational elements.

Such a complex entwining of identities was presaged by the Soviet nationalities policy, which contained its own mix of ethno-, civic-, and transnationalism.[21] This mix may be characterized as "internationalism" or the multicultural rhetoric that pervaded much of Soviet nationality policy.[22] By the 1970s, Kazakhs were among the most thoroughly Sovietized peoples,[23] and the foremost political actor in Kazakhstan, Nursultan Nazarbayev, was himself raised in this "internationalist" context and ascended to power through the patronage of both ethnic Kazakhs and Russians.[24] Nazarbayev's quote in the opening epigraph speaks to his awareness of potential ethnic discord on his territory in 1991 and suggests that he valued a broadly inclusive national development strategy for the state. Despite this fact, "titular-nationalization" emerged alongside his administration's civic- and multinational rhetoric in the early stages of independence. Initiated by Kazakh elites within and outside the Nazarbayev regime,[25] an ethno-national movement legitimized by the state's ethnonym sought to redress historic

Table 6.1 National Composition of Kazakhstan 1989, 1999, 2009

	1989		*1999*		*2009*	
Nationalities	*Count*	*(%)*	*Count*	*(%)*	*Count*	*(%)*
Kazakhs	6534616	39.7	7985039	53.4	10096763	63.1
Russians	6227549	37.8	4479620	30.0	3793764	23.7
Ukrainians	896240	5.4	547054	3.7	333031	2.1
Germans	957518	5.8	353441	2.4	178409	1.1
Uzbeks	332017	2.0	370663	2.5	456997	2.9
Tatars	327982	2.0	248954	1.7	204229	1.3
Uighurs	185301	1.1	210365	1.4	224713	1.4
Belarusian's	182601	1.1	111927	0.7	66476	0.4
Koreans	103315	0.6	99665	0.7	100385	0.6
Others	717325	4.4	546398	3.7	544326	3.4
Total	16464464	100.0	14953126	100.0	16009597	100.0

Note: Changes in Kazakhstan's territorial administrative structure have altered some of the population data from 1989 to 1999.
Source: *Natsionalnyi Sostab Naselenia Respubliki Kazakhstana: Itogi Perepisi Naselenia 2009 v Respublike Kazakhstana*, V.1 pp. 6–8.

wrongs of Russian/Soviet colonization, as well as to cement their communal position in the social hierarchy.

Though conspicuous, efforts at "Kazakhization" were not overtly antagonistic,[26] and in the 1990s Kazakh ethno-nationalization was consistently, if awkwardly, coupled with inclusive rhetoric and policies.[27] Ascension of Kazakh primacy nevertheless combined with economic uncertainty during this period to catalyze considerable emigration among European ethnic groups (see Table 6.1).

With upward of 66 percent of Russian residents having been born in the Kazakh SSR as of 1989, and 37 percent of those born elsewhere having lived in the republic for over 20 years, the large-scale ethnic "un-mixing" of the 1990s meant that either those lacking the resources to migrate or those with the most ardent claims to territorial belonging remained.[28] Similar combinations of an inability to move and/or fervent attachment to place are evident among other ethnic communities that regard themselves as either "indigenous" or having created a homeland through multigenerational residence in the Kazakh SSR.[29] Given these circumstances, retention of the word "Kazakh" from the provincial toponym (i.e., Kazakh SSR) to the independent state name (Kazakhstan) was both a "logical" continuation of Soviet approaches to ethno-territoriality that were internalized by the new ruling elites (and indeed the people themselves) and a not-so-banal symbol of political primacy and the proprietary territorial claim of the titular group.[30]

During the early years of independence, irredentist claims made on portions of Kazakhstan's territory by various factions within neighboring states[31] generated concerns about the territorial integrity of the new state.[32]

Similar geopolitical anxieties existed within many former Soviet republics, providing the recently transitioned Soviet-to-national elite a rationale for the pervasive embrace of ethnonyms in support of self-determinative frames for state sovereignty.[33] In Kazakhstan, the use of an ethnic-place-name was therefore commonly regarded, not only as "logical," but indeed "natural" relative to popularized perspectives on territorial history (i.e., Kazakh autochthony)[34] and Moscow's institutionalization of "titular privilege" (see the policy of *korenizatsiia* or nativization).

The very phrase "titular nation" (*tituliarnaya natsiia*)—referring to ethnic groups for which Soviet Republics were, and now independent states, are named—has become such common vernacular in international relations writing pertaining to the post-Soviet realm that it manifests an all-to-often "taken-for-granted" social status.[35] Governments under the direction of titular elites are implicitly encouraged to embrace ethno-national state-building strategies as the most expedient path to legitimacy and sovereignty.[36]

NEGOTIATING KAZAKHIZATION AND KAZAKHSTANI-ZATION

While titular/ethno-nationalism undoubtedly exists in Kazakhstan, it is fair to suggest that civic-nationalism has been more prominent than in most post-independence states—particularly in Central Asia.[37] The state's "ambiguous," "dualistic," "ambivalent," "paradoxical," and "hybridized" nation-building process[38] derives, at least in part, from the Nazarbayev regime's desire to propel the state onto the global stage as a "respectable actor." This effort may be characterized as the "image project" (*imidzh proekt*).[39]

The centerpiece of this effort to "brand" the state for the global stage and reap the benefits of enhanced domestic legitimacy is Kazakhstan's new capital city of Astana. Nazarbayev uses "the city as a 'showpiece,' indicative of reforms and transformations in the entire country—it is to be the 'face of the country' (*litso strany*), figuratively speaking, its business card (*vizitnaia kartochka*)."[40] Alima Bissenova has suggested that the Astana project demonstrates the Nazarbayev regime's intense desire to find complementarities between nation-building and globalization by blending statist nationalism and neoliberal market ideology.[41] Moreover, in accordance with Nazarbayev's prescription for Kazakhstan to have a "Eurasian," transnational character,[42] the city has been constructed to be inclusive of cultural forms from Russia and broader Central Asia. Bissenova goes on to suggest that this mix of styles conveys a multicultural "brand" for Kazakhstan, in which the interplay of culture, ideas, and the spirit of creativity sets a trajectory for the state that will see it joining the global elite in short order.[43]

Akin to these efforts of architectural and urban design is the strategy of seeking prestige through sport. Over the last 20 years, Kazakhstan's elites and citizens have increasingly placed value on the international athletes and teams representing them in global competition. Tennis players, weightlifters, wrestlers, and especially the Astana cycling team have generated a new sense of collective pride. As noted by Natalie Koch,

> In Kazakhstan, like so many places around the world, sport does not just provide a repertoire of metaphors and images of international competition and difference, but it is an important venue for the performance of identities and differences, as well as for the inscription of a certain synecdochic imaginary in which the "team" stands for the "state" and the "nation," and the state and the nation stand for the team. This metaphor does not just establish a relation, it calls these very things into being.[44]

In playing to both domestic and international audiences, such efforts work to advance the national image and are overtly useful to the soft-authoritarianism of the Nazarbayev regime. The result of all this branding and state promotion appears to be an increased popular affinity for a uniquely conflated regime and state.

THE ASSEMBLY OF THE PEOPLE(S) OF KAZAKHSTAN AND THE DOCTRINE OF NATIONAL UNITY

Any discussion of nationalization in Kazakhstan and its unique conflation of regime and state requires consideration of the Assembly of the People(s) of Kazakhstan, as both a symbol of the Nazarbayev government's support of multicultural ideals and its efforts to manipulate identity politics. Launched in March of 1995 by a decree of the president of the Republic of Kazakhstan, the Assembly of the Peoples of Kazakhstan (APK—*Assembleia Narodov Kazakhstana*)[45] is a consultative body comprised of representatives of officially sanctioned ethnic associations. It is a "platform where representatives of different nationalities can meet, express their concerns, and propose ideas about how to manage ethnic diversity."[46] The stated goals of the Assembly are to:

1. promote stability of interethnic and inter-confessional consent in the society;
2. work out proposals for state policy promoting the development of friendly relations among representatives of nations living on the territory of Kazakhstan;

3. form a political culture of citizens, based on civilized and democratic norms; and
4. strive for a compromise in conditions of social contradiction.[47]

Nazarbayev is chairman of the APK for life and as such determines and directs its main activities. He also appoints two deputies and a staff from among the representatives of state bodies, national-cultural "houses" (organizations of non-titular peoples), and other social associations. At present the APK has 350 members and a Secretariat, which is part of the Presidential Administration. A 2007 amendment to the constitution specifies that representatives of the APK fill nine seats of the lower chamber of parliament; significantly, this amendment also changed the name to the Assembly of the *People* of Kazakhstan (*Assembleia Naroda Kazakhstana*),[48] signifying the state's desire for a cohesive state identity.

Yves-Marie Davenel suggests that the APK "mirrors and implements the government policy on nationalities. One of its first objectives was, and still is, the preservation of interethnic harmony and development of national culture and language."[49] Significantly, this is not conceived as "a" national culture and language but as a multicultural ideal that provides opportunities for all groups to "recover" their national heritage. "The strategy of the APK for the 2002–2011 period, adopted in April 2002, stated that these goals [i.e., recovery of national culture] had been reached. The new strategy placed an emphasis on 'the forging of a Kazakhstani identity,' that is, a 'civic Kazakhstani identity.'"[50] This is to be achieved through a variety of civic national institutions and programs supported by the government.[51]

These programs and policies constitute the basis for the government's renaming of the APK to reflect the singular national ideal of a "people" of Kazakhstan. APK Deputy Chairman Sergei Dyachenko has noted that since the APK was founded in 1995, "We have indeed transformed into the people of Kazakhstan."[52] While many consider the appointment of representatives to be part and parcel of presidential authoritarian control of the state, an infrastructure of civic ideology may nevertheless be argued to at least nominally exist within this body. Efforts to operationalize this civic ideology, however, have recently resulted in a heated debate pertaining to the trajectory of Kazakhstan's nation-building.[53]

In 2008 President Nazarbayev commissioned APK representatives to produce a Doctrine of National Unity intended to provide "a blueprint for strengthening the interethnic harmony of Kazakhstan for years to come in a country destined to maintain its multicultural character and consolidate around common values."[54] Soon after the presentation of an initial draft in 2009, leaders of Kazakh nationalist movements, such as Dos Koshim of *Ult Tagdyry* (Fate of the Nation) and Mukhtar Shakhanov of *Memlekettik*

Til (State Language), espoused vociferous opposition. Interpreting the draft doctrine as an attack on ethnic Kazakh identity, language, and culture, they went so far as to threaten hunger strikes should the APK-produced document be adopted. Kazakh nationalists were not alone in their protests. Opposition political parties, such as OSDP Azat and Ak Zhol (White Road), disavowed the draft and joined with nationalist groups to devise an alternative approach to the national identity question.[55]

Reflecting Brubaker's characterization of Kazakhstan as a "nationalizing state," the coalition's January 2010 National Unity Blueprint differed radically from the APK version by premising recognition of Kazakhs as Kazakhstan's core group. As argued in their letter to the president, unification of all the republic's citizens under the banner of the Kazakh nation would naturally entail "raising the level of the Kazakh language to the de facto state language and turning it into a factor uniting all ethnic groups."[56] The authors also called for altering the country's formal name from the Republic of Kazakhstan to the Kazakh Republic.[57] Leaders of the allied nationalist and oppositional groups contended that "the state's espousal of equality for all groups was coming at the expense of the ethnic Kazakhs' assertion of their identity."[58]

As anticipated by Brubaker, Kazakh nationalists cited Soviet-era Russification policies as a rationale for promoting Kazakh linguistic and cultural primacy. In his role as president of the Bolatkhan Tayzhan Foundation, Mukhtar Tayzhan told a February 2010 Institute of Political Solutions (IPS) roundtable in Almaty, "The emotions of the people cannot be disregarded, because ordinary (ethnic Kazakh) people understand the situation precisely in those terms."[59] With ethnic Russians currently composing roughly 24 percent of the population, and no other non-titular group comprising more than 3 percent of the population, Tayzhan and his compatriots oppose a "tail wagging the dog" situation, in which state policy skews toward minority rights at the expense of majority aspirations.[60]

In contrast, many of the state's intellectuals regard the "nationalists' approach" as discriminatory. In a March 20, 2010, article in the newspaper *Strana i mir*, the chairman of the Association of Germans of Kazakhstan, Aleksandr Dederer, accused some parties in the debate of "shaping their efforts in the form of proposals and initiatives that have nothing in common with the formation of national unity." He went on to state, "They propose a revisionist path—essentially a rollback from the level Kazakhstani society has grown to."[61]

A compromise in the state's approach to nationalization was achieved following the appointment of a working-group that included members of the APK, nationalist, and oppositional parties. Deputy chairman of the APK and Head of Secretariat Yeraly Tugzhanov led the group, which announced on April 29, 2010, that a new National Unity Document had been agreed upon and approved by President Nazarbayev.[62] Incorporating over 500 proposals from nationalist leaders, political parties, and academics, the document succeeded in placating most of the interested parties—though at some cost to the "Kazakhstani ideal" at the core of the original document.[63]

As noted by Nick Tyan of Eurasian National University, following the negotiated revisions "the word 'Kazakhstani' was totally eliminated from the Doctrine."[64] In the draft the word had appeared seventeen times.[65] The final version replaces the notion of strengthening "Kazakhstani identity" with "recognition by citizens of their deep connections with the Republic of Kazakhstan." Also eliminated were provisions for the recruitment of non-titular peoples into governmental posts and state funding of ethno-cultural associations. Efforts to assuage Kazakh nationalists' demands for titular-group primacy manifested in the phrasing "consolidation of all citizens of the Republic around the Kazakh ethnicity."[66]

Perhaps the most impactful change to the original draft is the "priority given to the development and diffusion of the state [Kazakh] language as the most important factor of strengthening national unity."[67] Where traditionally Kazakhstan's language policy documents have offered provisions for the role and significance of the Russian language in the state,[68] the final version of the Doctrine contains no such caveat. This bodes for potentially more aggressive Kazakhization in the future.

Only gestures toward civic nationalism and multiculturalism remain in the doctrine's final version. For example, the text acknowledges the "shared tragic and glorious histories of all peoples living there and those who made the country their home."[69] This notion of all peoples having claim to a "home" within its territory is a pale reflection of the state efforts toward inclusiveness so prevalent in the draft. Though the website of Kazakhstan's embassy to the United States suggests that the doctrine represents the "strategic priority for contemporary Kazakhstan in achieving a national unity based upon acknowledging a common system of values and principles for all citizens of the country," the principles of "one country—one fate," "different origin—equal opportunities" and "development of the national spirit,"[70] are largely lost in the document's identification of the titular group as the "consolidating center for unification of the nation." As anticipated by Brubaker, an ethno-national core for the state is embedded in claims that modern Kazakhstan is a logical continuation of a long tradition of statehood on its current territory.[71]

By linking the notion of contemporary statehood to an imagined ethno-historical territoriality, the document invokes the Westphalian principles of titular autochthony and perpetual sovereignty of a nation-state. As noted by Donnacha Ó Beacháin and Rob Kevlihan, "Kazakh claims to primordial autochthony in the national territory is the first principle of state policy in post-independence Kazakhstan. Kazakhstan means, after all, the 'Land of the Kazakhs.'"[72]

While not all non-titular peoples are equally conciliatory and willing to accede to Kazakh linguistic predominance, evidence from the last 20 years suggests that most non-titular populations have made concerted efforts to adapt to minority status within Kazakhstan. Some promote—usually passively but sometimes overtly—the irredentist claims of neighboring states;[73] some espouse a diasporic identity and court de-territorialized, transnational relations with their respective kin-states;[74] some emphasize their shared cultural heritage with the Kazakh-titular group in the interests of garnering domestic political leverage;[75] and some embrace a role of cross-border linkages that enhance both Kazakhstan's and neighboring states' economies.[76]

DATA ANALYSIS

While Kazakhstan's 25-year history has seen the Nazarbayev regime make at least nominal efforts to comply with Western advocacy for broad-based social inclusion, the state lacks well-developed democratic institutions that could counter the ethnic state name's palpable signification of a "rightful" politico-cultural primacy for Kazakhs. Though many "non-titular" peoples are relatively resigned to their "second among equals" status and applaud Nazarbayev's rejection of overtly assimilationist approaches to state-building, long-term sustainability and even sincere efforts at civic nationalization, democratization, and civil-society formation remain at least partially impeded.

The formation of a functional "Kazakhstani"—or, as has been recently suggested, "Kazakhi"—identity that legitimizes the Astana government while reinforcing social cohesion and broad-based belonging among the citizenry remains elusive. Author interviews in 2011–2012 support this point. The interviewees included twenty-five people between the ages of 18 and 72 with a roughly equal gender distribution. All were current residents of Almaty, though some had lived in other cities and villages during their lifetimes. The ethnic composition of this sample included: ten Kazakhs, six Russians, two Uyghurs, three Koreans, one Tatar, two Germans, and one Ukrainian.[77] The following questions proved most pertinent to the topic of this chapter: (1) Do you call yourself Kazakhstani? (2) Can you envision yourself or your children embracing this identity?

Murat (Tatar, Male, Retired Blue-Collar Worker, 60–70)

> No I do not use this word. Though there is something to it. Perhaps my grandchildren will see themselves in this light. Particularly if there is marriage between nationalities.

Aselya (Uyghur, Female, Blue-Collar Worker, 30–40)

> No. This is not a term I use about myself. I am Uyghur but I am from Kazakhstan—so, I may be Kazakhstani but I don't call myself this. My kids are Uyghur as well but are from here. Yes, I could see them using this term if there were talking to you in America but not here.

Tatiana (Russian Female, White-Collar Worker, 30–40)

> No. Ha! No one uses this word. I won't use it; I can't use it. What would it make me? No longer Russian ... Maybe I could say I am Russian Kazakhstani like your African American. Maybe this will come to be someday.

Anatoly (Russian, Male, Blue-Collar Worker 40–50)

> No. But I know what you are asking; and the answer is no... It [the identity] doesn't have history, so I don't think I will use it but I am from here and my kids are from here so maybe they can use it. But I think they will always say I am Russian.

Erkin (Kazakh, Male, White-Collar Worker, 20–30)

> No. I say I am Kazakh. I think this term will be useful for other groups in Kazakhstan though. They can say they are Kazakhstani and people will know them to be from our country. I am Kazakh, so I don't need to say this.

Danyar (Kazakh, Male, Blue-Collar Worker, 20–30)

> I said this once to a researcher from the UK. He was so excited to hear me say it. But I don't say to people everyday, "Hey I am Kazakhstani." I don't tell them I am Kazakh either. But only to a foreigner will I use this term, if ever.

Chimin (Korean, Female, White-Collar Worker, 40–50)

> I have not taken this term into my vocabulary but my daughter is marrying a Kazakh boy. I think there children may have this identity. Their child will be Korean and Kazakh –a Kor-zakh—and will see Kazakhstan as his homeland for sure.

While no respondents claim to use the term regularly, most suggest it has a place in the lexicon. Some project its growing popularity, but none seem willing to embrace it themselves. When asked why, non-titular peoples suggest that the word "Kazakh" was the stumbling block.

Anatoly (Russian, Male, Blue-Collar Worker 40–50)

> Kazakhs are a people with a history of their own. They have their own culture. To call a Russian a Kazakh or a Kazakhstani makes no sense. They don't have claim to this history or culture.

Murat (Tatar, Male, Retired Blue-Collar Worker, 60–70)

> Like I said, if there is a marriage between a Tatar and a Kazakh then all right. The child will be part Kazakh. But how can a Tatar or a German or Russian call themselves Kazakh?

Sattar (Kazakh, Male, White-Collar Worker, 20–30)

> If I moved to Russia, I would call myself a Kazakh not a Russian. After two or three generations maybe my grandchildren would have married Russians and they would say they are Russian.

Heinrik (German, Male, Blue-Collar Worker 30–40)

> I know you see it as a connection to the land, like Canada or America. You can say I am American, but do you notice people here ask what else you are? We see it differently than you. I am German that is my identity and I live here. That is my place of residence. If I moved to America, I would still be German. I don't think I would become American. Though I think my kids would be American if I moved there. They would forget the Russian language and would just be Americans.

Moderator: Can that happen here?

> No. We have too much history between our peoples. We cannot forget that history. It will stay with us and keep us distinct. Kazakhstan is our country but we are Germans, Russians, and so on living here. President Nazarbayev makes this a place for us, but he will not be here forever. So we shall see.

The acknowledgment of a possible civic identity among children in several of the quotes suggests that decades of socio-political stability, the "image project," and a recent economic boon benefiting the spectrum of ethnic groups within the state has produced a measure of patriotic loyalty, along with a tentative sense of homeland.[78] Surveys conducted by various independent research organizations and scholars in the mid-to-late 2000s support this conclusion but also reveal the lingering uncertainty and limited potential for civil unrest.[79]

For example, the Kazakhstan-based Institute for Political Solutions published results of polls of 2,301 people in sixteen towns cities conducted in February 2010 and May 2011. These polls showed 39 percent and 56.2 percent, respectively, characterizing relations between ethnic groups as "friendly—no problem at all." Though the number was higher in 2011, it remains lower than Astana anticipated and would like the global public to believe. The 2011 poll's 20.1 percent declaring that "no relationships and no common interests" exist between ethnic groups is particularly problematic. According to the 2011 survey, an aggregate share of respondents who deny the possibility of open interethnic conflict in Kazakhstan stands at 70.8 percent.[80] While this bespeaks a clear majority perception of social solidarity, the roughly 30 percent perception of some measure of social discord is troublesome.[81]

Data from the 2010 and 2011 surveys nevertheless remained supportive of civic or at least multinationalization with both polls purporting a popular rejection of the idea that ethnic Kazakhs should have a "special role." While in 2010 some 31 percent supported the concept of Kazakh socio-political primacy, a full 60 percent embraced the notion that all citizens should be thought of as "state-forming." Just one in five people supported changing the official name of the country to the Kazakh Republic as suggested by nationalists during the debate over the Doctrine of National Unity.[82]

CONCLUSION

Aptly characterized as a "crisis of the hyphen," global dynamics of state-building pulls Kazakhstan in two directions. In one sense, the Astana government is compelled to pursue the principles of modernist state-ism as a means of securing Kazakhstan's place on the world stage. From this perspective Kazakhstan must be confident of its sovereignty and the clarity and strength of its borders, as well as being assured of its national character. Given the mix of Russification and titular privilege manifest during the Soviet era, many Kazakh elites consider ethno-nationalization the most expedient strategy to ensure this goal. But global norms of human rights also resist assimilationist policies. Civic-national and democratic ideologies are Western standards and constitute at least nominal motifs for the group of states with which Kazakhstan wants very much to be associated. Nazarbayev's effort to "brand" Kazakhstan in this light has given rise to its concerted and expensive "image project," as well as an ambiguous national ideal.

Nazarbayev's consideration of a new state name, mentioned at the start of the chapter, reflects his understanding of a name's role in defining a state. This realization is echoed by nationalists who call for converting the state name to the "Kazakh Republic" as a means of trumping civic advances that threaten Kazakh primacy. What has not been suggested is a name change that would provide symbolic space for membership and belonging to all peoples within the state. As argued by the author in 2002,[83] an ethnically neutral name would better reflect the civic, multi-, and transnational ideals that have been so much a part of the state's rhetoric since its inception.

Nevertheless, an opportunity exists for nation-building within Kazakhstan, as homeland conceptions relating to places of residence (*malaia rodina*) and to some extent the state territory (*bol'shaia rodina*) have manifested across the ethnic spectrum. Identity parallels may be drawn to the increasingly common reference to ethnicity through the term "people" (*narod*), whereas the political nation (*natsiia*) is understood as being Kazakhstani—though, as noted above, this term is rarely wielded in daily discourse. Such dynamics speak to the prospect of social solidarity, loyalty, and belonging generating from the "prosaic act of living together within a politico-institutional bounded space."[84] But is such belonging sustainable in the absence of a state-level identity/moniker that accedes to modernist state ideals and the doctrine of nationalism?

The ambivalent nationalization process enacted in Kazakhstan over the last 25 years is integrally linked to the social stability afforded by the Nazarbayev regime's soft authoritarianism and the economic prosperity of the state. What happens when Nazarbayev is gone? What happens in a slowing economy? Will non-titular peoples embrace a national identity centered on a Kazakh cultural/linguistic core? Will interactive ethno-nationalization ignite as nationalists of various camps become more assertive?[85] Will civic ideals evaporate as Kazakh demographic predominance increases? Could democratization serve as the antidote to overt expressions of titular primacy and/or more-assertive minority political agendas?

While Nazarbayev's *Kazakhstan 2030* and *2050* development strategies detail advances in national security, material well-being, political stability, consolidation of the state, foreign investment, and expanding infrastructure, they give little direction for democratization.[86] The future of the state's identity politics therefore remains largely couched in the ambiguous mix of ethnic-, civic-, and transnationalism with social stability and limitation of extremes guaranteed by soft authoritarianism. To whatever extent Kazakhstan's efforts to align with Western liberal ideals can be seen as legitimate, they will nevertheless remain blunted by requirements of regional and domestic politics that reflect a modernist-statism rather than post-modernist cosmopolitanism. In short, the "crisis of the hyphen" continues.

NOTES

1. *Kazakhstanskaia pravda* (November 23, 1991): 1.
2. Doctrine of National Unity of Kazakhstan, Inform.kz, April 29, 2010, http://www.inform.kz/rus/article/2263364.
3. The Presidential website contains a report about the utterance dated February 6, 2014. See Nursultan Nazarbayev http://akorda.kz/ru/pa ge/page_215918_poseshchenie-intellektualnoi-shkoly-goroda-atyrau-i-vstrecha-s-pedstavitelyami-obshchestvennosti-oblasti.
4. Sally Cummings, "Eurasian Bridge or Murky Waters Between East and West? Ideas, Identity, and Output in Kazakhstan's Foreign Policy," *Journal of Communist Studies and Transition Politics* 19, no. 3 (2003): 139–155; Natalie Koch, "Why Not

a World City Astana and Ankara: Geopolitical Scripts in Urban Networks," *Urban Geography* 34, no. 1 (2013): 109–130; Marlene Laruelle and Sebastien Peyrouse, *Globalizing Central Asia* (Armonk, NY: M.E. Sharpe, 2013).

5. Arjun Appadurai, "Disjuncture and Difference in the Global Cultural Economy," *Public Culture* 2 (1990): 1–24.

6. Marco Antonsich, "On Territory, the Nation-State, and the Crisis of the Hyphen," *Progress in Human Geography* 33, no. 6 (2009): 791.

7. Jürgen Habermas, *The Inclusion of the Other: Studies in Political Theory* (Cambridge MA: MIT Press, 1998); Jürgen Habermas, *The Postnational Constellation: Political Essays* (Cambridge MA: MIT Press, 2001).

8. Arjun Appadurai, "Sovereignty Without Territoriality: Notes for a Post National Geography" in *The Geography of Identity*, ed. Patricia Yaeger (Ann Arbor: University of Michigan Press, 1996), 47.

9. Benedict Anderson, "Introduction," in *Mapping the Nation*, ed. Gopal Balakrishnan (New York: Verso, 1996), 8–9. See also Bruce Robbins, "Actually Existing Cosmopolitanism," in *Cosmopolitics: Thinking and Feeling Beyond the Nation*, ed. Pheng Cheah and Bruce Robbins (Minneapolis: University of Minnesota Press, 1998), 1–20.

10. Khachig Tololyan, "Rethinking Diaspora(s): Stateless Power in the Transnational Moment," *Diaspora* 5, no. 1 (1996): 3–36.

11. John Agnew, *Globalization and Sovereignty* (Lanham, MD: Rowman and Littlefield, 2009).

12. In Russia, *russkii* is tending to replace *rossiiskii* in a form open to interpretation in both ethnic and civic senses. This point was made by Marlene Laruelle at the conference "Beyond Economic Success. Exploring Social and Cultural Changes in Eurasia," Central Asia Program and the Uppsala Center for Russian and Eurasian Studies (UCRS), Uppsala University, Sweden, June 13–14, 2014.

13. Marco Antonsich, "On Territory, the Nation-State, and the Crisis of the Hyphen," *Progress in Human Geography* 33, no. 6 (2009): 789–806.

14. See Alexander Murphy, "Territory's Continuing Allure," *Annals of the Association of American Geographers* 103, no. 5 (2012): 1212–1226; Antonsich, "On Territory, the Nation-State, and the Crisis of the Hyphen"; Marco Antonsich, "Searching for Belonging: An Analytical Framework," *Geography Compass* 4, no. 6 (2010): 644–659; Anna Korteweg and Triadafilos Triadafilopoulos, "Is Multiculturalism Dead? Groups, Governments, and the 'Real Work of Integration,'" *Ethnic and Racial Studies* 38, no. 5 (2014): 663–680; Jean Beaman "Boundaries of Frenchness: Cultural Citizenship and France's Middle Class North African Second Generation," *Identities: Global Studies in Culture and Power* 22, no. 1 (2014): 36–52.

15. An exception to this would be Belarus' President Lukashenka's efforts to eschew Belarusian identity—See Grigory Ioffe. "Understanding Belarus: Belarusian Identity," *Europe Asia Studies* 55, no. 8 (2003): 1241-1272.

16. Rogers Brubaker, "Nationalizing States Revisited: Projects and Processes of Nationalization in Post Soviet States," *Ethnic and Racial Studies* 34, no. 11 (2011): 1785–1814.

17. Brubaker, "Nationalizing States Revisited." See also Ingvar Svanberg, "In Search of a Kazakhstani Identity," *Journal of Area Studies* 4 (1994): 112–123; Azamat Sarsembayev, "Imagined Communities: Kazak Nationalism and

Kazakification in the 1990s," *Central Asian Survey* 18, no. 3 (1999): 319–346; Martha Olcott *Kazakhstan Unfulfilled Promise* (Washington DC: Carnegie Endowment for International Peace, 2002); Sally Cummings, "Legitimation and Identification in Kazakhstan," *Nationalism and Ethnic Politics* 12 (2006): 177–204; Erlan Karin and A. Chebotarev, "The Policy of Kazakhization in State and Government Institutions in Kazakhstan" in *The Nationalities Question in Post-Soviet Kazakhstan*, ed. Natsuko Oka (Chiba: Institute of Developing Economies, 2000).

18. See Donnacha Ó Beacháin and Rob Kevlihan, "Threading the Needle: Kazakhstan Between Civic and Ethno-Nationalist State Building," *Nations and Nationalism* 19, no. 2 (2013): 337–356; Regina Faranda and David Nolle, "Boundaries of Ethnic Identity in Central Asia: Titular and Russian Perceptions of Ethnic Commonalities in Kazakhstan and Kyrgyzstan," *Ethnic and Racial Studies* 34, no. 4 (2011): 620–642; Scott Spehr and Nargis Kassenova, "Kazakhstan: Constructing Identity in Post-Soviet Society," *Asian Ethnicity* 13, no. 2 (2012): 135–151.

19. Ó Beacháin and Kevlihan, "Threading the Needle"; Spehr and Kassenova, "Kazakhstan"; Faranda and Nolle, "Boundaries of Ethnic Identity in Central Asia."

20. Alexander Diener, "Assessing Potential Russian Irredentism and Separatism in Kazakhstan's Northern Oblasts" *Eurasian Geography and Economics*, 56, no. 5 (2015): 469–492.

21. Robert Kaiser, *The Geography of Nationalism in Russia and the USSR* (Princeton, NJ: Princeton University Press, 1994); Francine Hirsch, *Empire of Nations* (Ithaca, NY: Cornell University Press, 2005).

22. "Internationalism" as applied in Soviet policy may also refer to a uniting of proletarian workers across international borders in the struggle against capitalism. Further discussion of impact of the Soviet legacy on post-Soviet identity politics may be found in Diana Kudaibegenova, "National Identity Formation in Post-Soviet Central Asia: The Soviet Legacy, Primordialism, and Patterns of Ideological Development since 1991," in *Social and Cultural Change in Central Asia: The Soviet Legacy*, eds. Sevket Akyldiz and Richard Carlson (New York: Routledge, 2014), 160–173; Nathan Paul Jones, "Assembling a Civic Nation in Kazakhstan: The Nation Building Role of the Assembly of the Peoples of Kazakhstan," *Caucasian Review of International Affairs* 2, no. 4 (2010): 159–168.

23. Shirin Akiner, *The Formation of Kazakh Identity: From Tribe to Nation-State* (London: Royal Institute of International Affairs, 1995).

24. Jonathan Aiken, *Nazarbayev and the Making of Modern Kazakhstan* (London: Bloomsbury Academic Press, 2009).

25. Following the model of Russian culture as a basis for a "friendship of nations" in the Soviet era, Kazakh ethno-nationalism was cultivated in presidential speeches during the 1990s. "The culture of the Kazakhs must be seriously assimilated by the representatives of the other *ethnoi*, just as the Kazakhs, in their own time, earnestly studied Russian culture." See, N.A. Nazarbaev, *V potoke istorii* (Almaty: Amatura, 1999), 124. Nazarbayev also suggested that the Republic "bears the responsibility of the Kazakh nation" and the "rebirth and development of a specific culture, of traditions, of the language, and the reinforcing of national pride of the Kazakh nation and the other nationalities living in Kazakhstan constitutes one of the main missions of the statehood of the republic of Kazakhstan." *O Deklaratsii o gosudarstvennom*

suverenitete Respubliki Kazakhstan. Postanovlenie Verkhovnogo Soveta Kazakhskoi SSR ot 25ogo oktiabria 1990, http://adilet.zan.kz/rus/docs/B900001700.

26. By contrast, both Estonia and Latvia enacted far harsher nationalization projects than did Kazakhstan, despite the presence of large numbers of ethnic Russians. See Brubaker, "Nationalizing States Revisited"; Diana Kudaibergenova, "Post Socialist Culture in Latvia and Kazakhstan: An Introduction to Reasons, Criticisms, and Perspectives," in *National Identity: Time, Place, and People* (Riga: University of Latvia, 2012), 40–51. It should nevertheless be noted that in 1989 Kazakhstan possessed the second largest number of Russians in the post-Soviet realm (Kazakhstan having 6 million, Ukraine having 11 million) but the largest in proportion to total population (37 percent). This number reduced rapidly after emigrations following the collapse of the USSR.

27. The 1993 Constitution offered guarantees of ethnic equality, thereby implicitly setting a goal of civic nation formation (Konstitutsiia Respubliki Kazakhstana, 1993 http://www.akorda.kz/en/category/konstituciya). An early 1990s literature/media campaign promoting multiculturalism included a revision of the 1995 Constitution—Article 1—which declares "Kazakhstani patriotism" to be one of the guiding principles of the Republic (Konstitutsiia Respubliki Kazakhstana 1995 http://www.akorda.kz/en/category/konstituciya).

28. Sebastien Peyrouse, "Nationhood and the Minority Question in Central Asia: The Russians in Kazakhstan," *Europe Asia Studies* 59, no. 3 (2007): 482; David Laitin, *Identity in Formation: The Russian-Speaking Populations in the near Abroad* (Ithaca, NY: Cornell University Press, 1998); Jeff Chinn and Robert Kaiser, *Russians as the New Minority* (Boulder, CO: Westview, 1996); Brubaker, "Nationalizing States Revisited," 1790–1792; Alexander C. Diener, "Transnationalism and Minority Territorialization in Kazakhstan," *International Journal of Central Asian Studies* 11 (2007): 86–102. Diener "Assessing Potential Russian Irredentism and Separatism."

29. See Natsuko Oka, "Neither Exit nor Voice: Loyalty as a Survival Strategy for the Uzbeks in Kazakhstan," Institute of Developing Economies Discussion Paper No. 286 (2011): 1–17; Yves-Marie Davenel, "Cultural Mobilization in Post-Soviet Kazakhstan: Views from the State and from the Non-Titular Nationalities Compared," *Central Asian Survey* 31, no. 1 (2012): 17–29; Alexander Diener, "Diasporic Stances: Comparing the Historical Geographic Antecedents of German and Korean Migration Decisions in Kazakhstan," *Geopolitics* 14, no. 3 (2009): 462–487.

30. This approach is reflected in much of the theoretical literature on nationalization. See Michael Billig, *Banal Nationalism* (London: Sage, 1995) and Anthony Smith, *Ethnic Origins of Nations* (New York: Wiley Blackwell, 1991); Benedict Anderson, *Imagined Communities* (London: Verso, 2006).

31. Rarely were these claims made directly by governments of neighboring states. Though both China and Uzbekistan have insisted on minor boundary adjustments—see Necati Polat, *Boundary Issues in Central Asia* (New York: Brill, 2002)—more commonly non-governmental group or individuals put forth irredentist claims. See Bhavna Dave, *Kazakhstan: Ethnicity, Language and Power* (New York: Routledge, 2007): 123–126.

32. Some suggest that the move of the capital from mostly Russian and southeasterly city of Almaty to the centrally located and predominantly Kazakh city of Astana

related to fears of a secession by the north of the country. See Richard L. Wolfel, "North to Astana: Nationalistic Motives for the Movement of the Kazakh(stani) Capital," *Nationalities Papers* 30, no. 3 (2002): 485–506.

33. As Brubaker suggests in Nationalizing States Revisited (1786), the process of ethno-nationalization was commonly rationalized in the former USSR by an alleged weakness or unhealthy condition in the core nation that required redress through the promotion of language, culture, economic conditions, and political power. Ultimately all of the Commonwealth of Independent States (CIS) countries converted their ethnic provincial toponyms to state names. Kazakhstan's 1993 Constitution makes specific reference to the state as a homeland for the "self-determined Kazakh nation" (Konstitutsiia Respubliki Kazakhstana, 1993).

34. There is a discursive history to such claims, as even Nazarbayev's *V potoke istorii* insists that "A legal, constitutional, and international foundation has been given to the fact that all Kazakhstan is the historico-genetic territory of the Kazakh nation" (195). Similar statements embedding the legitimacy of the Kazakh regime in historical territory may be found in 1995 Constitution's preamble maintaining that the people of Kazakhstan are *"united by a common historic fate, create a state on the indigenous Kazakh land"* (Konstitutsiia Respubliki Kazakhstana 1995).

35. Graham Smith, Vivian Law, Andrew Wilson, Annette Bohr, and Edward Allworth, *Nation-Building in the Post-Soviet Borderlands: The Politics of National Identities* (New York: Cambridge University Press, 1998), 131–154; James Hughes and Gwendolyn Sasse, *Ethnicity and Territory in the Former Soviet Union* (London: Frank Cass, 2002); Chinn and Kaiser, *Russians as the New Minority*.

36. Smith et al., *Nation-Building in the Post-Soviet Borderlands*, 139–166; Brubaker, "Nationalizing States Revisited"; Mohira Suyarkulova, "Reluctant Sovereigns? Central Asian States' Path to Independence," in *Sovereignty after Empire: Comparing the Middle East and Central Asia*, eds. Sally N. Cummings and Raymond Hinnsbusch (Edinburgh: Edinburgh University Press, 2011), 130.

37. William Fierman, "Kazakh Language and Prospects for Its Role in Kazakh "Groupness,"" *Ab Imperio* 2 (2005): 393–423; William Fierman, "Language and Education in Post-Soviet Kazakhstan: Kazakh-Medium Instruction in Urban Schools," *Russian Review* 65, no. 1 (2006): 98–116.

38. Brubaker, "Nationalizing States Revisited," 1800; Ó Beacháin and Kevlihan, "Threading the Needle," 340; Davenel, "Cultural Mobilization in Post-Soviet Kazakhstan," 19; Spehr and Kassenova, "Kazakhstan," 136; Peyrouse, "Nationhood and the Minority Question in Central Asia," 485; Faranda and Nolle, "Boundaries of Ethnic Identity in Central Asia," 624–626.

39. A "Great Power" brand of nationalism is expected in Kazakhstan and holds that the government is responsible for garnering *respect* on the global stage. After the public relations debacle relating to the film *Borat*, Kazakhstan invested heavily in internationally high profile projects that resound within the state and by consequence bolster the Nazarbayev regime's legitimacy. Recent scholarly work approaching Kazakhstan's image project (*imidzh proekt*) includes Robert A. Saunders, "In Defense of Kazakschilik: Kazakhstan's War on Sacha Baron Cohen," *Identities* 12, no. 3 (2007): 224–255; Robert A. Saunders, "Buying into Brand Borat: Kazakhstan's

Cautious Embrace of Its Unwanted Son," *Slavic Review* 67, no. 1 (2008): 63–80; Edward Schatz, "Transnational Image Making and Soft Authoritarian Kazakhstan," *Slavic Review* 67, no. 1 (2008): 50–62; Natalie Koch, "Sport and Soft Authoritarian Nation Building," *Political Geography* 32 (2013): 42–51; Natalie Koch, "The 'Heart' of Eurasia? Kazakhstan's Centrally Located Capital City," *Central Asian Survey* 32, no. 2 (2012): 134–147; Alima Bissenova, "The Master Plan of Astana: Between the Art of Government and the Art of Being Global," in *Ethnographies of the State in Central Asia: Performing Politics*, eds. Madeleine Reeves, Johan Rasanayagam, and Judith Beyer (Bloomington: Indiana University Press, 2014), 127–148; Rico Isaacs, "Nomads, Warriors, and Bureaucrats: Nation Building and Film in Post Soviet Kazakhstan," *Nationalities Papers* 43, no. 3 (2014) 1–18; Stephen Norris, "Nomadic Nationhood: Cinema and Remembrance in Post-Soviet Kazakhstan," *Ab Imperio* 13, no. 2 (2012): 378–402.

40. Koch, "Sport and Soft Authoritarian Nation Building," 46.

41. Bissenova, "The Master Plan of Astana," 130; see also Schatz, "Transnational Image Making and Soft Authoritarian Kazakhstan"; Sally N. Cummings, ed., *Symbolism and Power in Central Asia* (New York: Routledge, 2009); Koch, "Sport and Soft Authoritarian Nation Building."

42. According to Nazarbaev, "Kazakhstan is a unique state in Asia where European and Asian roots are intertwined. [...] The combination of different cultures and traditions allows us to absorb what is best in European and in Asian culture." N. Nazarbaev, *Evraziiskii soiuz: idei, praktika, perspektivy* (Moscow: Fond sodeistviia razvitiiu sotsial'nykh i politicheskikh nauk, 1997), 27.

43. Bissenova, "The Master Plan of Astana," 138.

44. Koch, "Sport and Soft Authoritarian Nation Building," 50.

45. See Article 44 of the Constitution of the Republic of Kazakhstan (Konstitutsiia Respubliki Kazakhstana 1995). See also Natsuko Oka, "Ethnicity and Elections under Authoritarianism: The Case of Kazakhstan," *IDE Discussion Paper* no. 194, 2009, for further description and discussion of the role of the APK.

46. Davenel, "Cultural Mobilization in Post-Soviet Kazakhstan," 20.

47. Embassy of the Kazakhstan, "Assembly of the People of Kazakhstan," http://www.kazakhstan.org.tr/index.asp?sayfa=144.

48. Oka, "Ethnicity and Elections under Authoritarianism," 23. The Law on the Assembly of the People of Kazakhstan October 2008 states: "The Assembly contributes to the realization of the government's policies regarding nationalities ...[and] to guaranteeing interethnic harmony in Kazakhstan within the process of forming a Kazakhstan state identity and nation ... in relation to the consolidating role of the Kazakh people." See Nursultan Nazarbayev "Ob Assemblee naroda Kazakhstana," *Kazakhstanskaia pravda*, October 21, 2008, 1.

49. Davenel, "Cultural Mobilization in Post-Soviet Kazakhstan," 20.

50. Davenel, "Cultural Mobilization in Post-Soviet Kazakhstan," 20. See also Nazarbayev's prominent use of the term "Kazakhstani" in a 1997 speech on the development strategy program for Kazakhstan entitled "Kazakhstan 2030." Here, he asked who Kazakhstanis were: "Today it is not everybody that can answer the seemingly simple question: Who are we—the Kazakhstanis?" (Nursultan Nazarbayev,

Kazakhstan 2030, http://www.akorda.kz/en/category/gos_programmi_razvitiya 1997, 52).

51. These institutions include more than 100 national and 170 weekend schools where 23 different languages are taught and to which the government allocates KZT 12 million in support. Additional, financial assistance is rendered from local budgets at the discretion of *akimats* (local governments—*akims* head the local governments and are appointed by the president). See Danevel, "Cultural Mobilization in Post-Soviet Kazakhstan"; and Oka, "Ethnicity and Elections under Authoritarianism" for insightful analyses of non-titular groups maneuvering within Kazakh-controlled governmental structures at both the local and national scales. Four republican and fifteen regional national-newspapers are published and six national theaters are currently active (Kazakh, Russian, German, Korean, Uzbek, Uyghur) in Kazakhstan. Public holidays of non-titular peoples such as *Nauruz* (Persian New Year/Spring Festival), *Maslenitsa* (Eastern Slavic Christian Folk Holiday) and *Rozhdestvo* (Christmas), among others, are traditionally celebrated throughout the country with the support of the government.

52. Cited in Oka, "Ethnicity and Elections under Authoritarianism," 23.

53. Aleksander Dederer, *Strana i Mir*, March 20, 2010; Joanna Lillis, "Kazakhstan Follows Thorny Path Toward National Unity" Eurasianet.org, April 29, 2010, accessed June 9, 2014, http://www.eurasianet.org/node/60952; Nick Tyan, "Kazakhstani Nation," http://www.academia.edu/3532663/Kazakhistani_nation2014.

54. Kazakhstan Embassy to the United States, "Statement on Doctrine of National Unity," 2014, http://www.kazakhembus.com/page/national-unity-doctrine.

55. "Protest protiv doktriny 'Kazakhstankaia natsiia,'" Turkistan.kz, no date, accessed June 1, 2014, http://turkistan.ru/kul-tura-i-traditscii/naselenie-kazahstana/protest-protiv-doktriny-kazahstanskaya-natsciya.html.

56. "Protest protiv doktriny 'Kazakhstankaia natsiia.'" See Lillis, "Kazakhstan Follows Thorny Path Toward National Unity"; and Tyan "Kazakhstani Nation," for analysis.

57. Kyrgyzstan's 1993 renaming to the Kyrgyz Republic provides an example of similar "titularization" of a state name in Central Asia.

58. Lillis, "Kazakhstan Follows Thorny Path Toward National Unity."

59. Parenthetical added—quoted in Lillis, "Kazakhstan Follows Thorny Path Toward National Unity." For further discussion of Tayzhan's position see Saule Isabayeva, "O kazakhom natsionalizme—na chistotu," *Central Asia Monitor* July 5, 2013, http://bit.ly/14ZFfVy.

60. The nationalists' case is best accessed through a series of commentaries published in various media outlets. For example, Roza Yessenkulova suggests that the idea of civic identity would lead to ignorance of Kazakh history and traditions (Roza Yessenkulova, "Kazakhstan skoro pridet k 'edinoi kazakhstanskoi natsii,'" Tengrinews.kz, accessed July 3, 2014, http://tengrinews.kz/kazakhstan_news/kazahstan-skoro-pridet-k-edinoy-kazahstanskoy-natsii-197473/). Yurii Kirinitsiianov suggests that Kazakhstan has "one nation - Kazakhs—all others are diasporas and have a homeland for their people" (Yurii Kirinitsiianov, "My kazakhi ili kazakhstantsy?" *Vechernii Almaty*, accessed July 3, 2014, http://vecher.kz/node/13466). A similar point is made in "Protest protiv doktriny 'Kazakhstankaia natsiia.'"

61. Dederer, *Strana i mir*.

62. See "Text of National Unity Doctrine Draft," Kazinform.kz, November 5, 2009, accessed June 9, 2014, http://www.inform.kz/rus/article/2210265

63. The head of the National Patriotic Movement of Kazakhstan, Dosmukhamet Nurakhmet, went so far as to express satisfaction that the nationalist viewpoint had been taken into account. See Lillis, "Kazakhstan Follows Thorny Path Toward National Unity."

64. Tyan, "Kazakhstani Nation."

65. "Text of National Unity Doctrine Draft."

66. "Text of National Unity Doctrine Draft."

67. "Text of National Unity Doctrine Draft."

68. In a 2007 Presidential address, Nazarbayev went so far as to suggest that every citizen of Kazakhstan should speak three languages—Kazakh as a state language, Russian as a language of interethnic communication, and English as a language of global economy. See Nazarbayev, *Kazakhstan 2030*. Opponents of the draft Doctrine's promotion of Russian and English claim that these languages are "Stronger and will destroy Kazakh." See Mukhtar Shakhanov, "Zaiavlenie o doktrine 'Natsional'nogo edinstva' ('Kazakhstanskaia natsiia') beushchei svoiu osnovu ot 'Amerikanskoi natsii,'" Zona.kz, November 26, 2009, accessed July 3, 2014, http://www.zonakz.net/articles/27350 .

69. "Text of National Unity Doctrine Draft."

70. "Text of National Unity Doctrine Draft."

71. Brubaker, "Nationalizing States Revisited," 1786.

72. Ó Beacháin and Kevlihan, "Threading the Needle," 342.

73. For example, Russians and Cossacks during the 1990s. See Peyrouse, "Nationhood and the Minority Question in Central Asia." Though Diener, "Assessing Potential Russian Irredentism and Separatism" suggests that this is less a threat to Kazakhstan's civil stability than portrayed by many pundits since Russia's invasion of Ukraine in 2014.

74. For example, Germans and Koreans. See Alexander Diener, *Homeland Conceptions and Ethnic Integration of Kazakhstan Germans and Koreans* (Lewiston, NY: Mellon Press, 2004).

75. For example, Tatars—see Danevel, "Cultural Mobilization in Post-Soviet Kazakhstan"; and Uzbeks—see Oka, "Ethnicity and Elections under Authoritarianism."

76. This dynamic is particularly evident in the Dungan community. See Marlene Laruelle, "Cross Border Minorities as Cultural and Economic Mediators Between China and Central Asia," *China and Eurasia Forum Quarterly* 7, no. 1 (2009): 93–119. The notion of some groups providing key economic contributors is also prevalent in reference to Germans, Russians, Koreans, and Ukrainians.

77. Interviews were conducted by the author in informants' homes with a research assistant from a local university present to assist with translation when needed. The interviews were semi-structured, touching upon key points relating to identity politics in Kazakhstan. The sample was gathered through the snowball technique.

78. It is commonly argued in recent studies of Kazakhstan's society that the economic boom of recent years benefits the vast majority of citizens. See Spehr and Kassenova "Kazakhstan," 139; Ó Beacháin and Kevlihan, "Threading the Needle," 346.

79. For example, the Asia Barometer Survey of 2005 found that 87 percent of Kazakhstan's citizens are "very proud" or "proud" of their citizenship (Asia Barometer https://www.asiabarometer.org/en/data); a Centre for Social and Political Research report characterizes interethnic relations in Kazakhstan to be "quiet and friendly" (Centre for Social and Political Research, *Specifics of Interethnic Conflicts in Kazakhstan: Report of a Mass Population Survey and Focus Group Research*, Almaty: Centre for Social and Political Research 2009, 3); I.M. Akylbayeva et al.'s 2010 research purports some 57 percent of respondents regard "interethnic tolerance" to be well formed within the state, with 18 percent contending this is not the case and 25 percent having no clear opinion (I.M. Akylbaeva, Z.B. Malgaraeva, and L.A. Umirzakova, *Ethnic Identity Condition and Tendency: Materials of the Republican Scientific Practical Conference and "The Independent Kazakhstan: History and Experience" Devoted to the 20th Anniversary of Kazakhstan Independence*, Astana 2011, 239); A Kazakhstan Institute of Social and Economic Information and Forecasting (KISEIP) survey in 2009 revealed a hierarchy of identity in which 53 percent preferred a civic identity, 26 percent ethnic identity, and only 10 percent a religious identity (cited in Spehr and Kassenova, "Kazakhstan," 142)

80. Though generally avoided in Russia-language media, Kazakh-language media mention scattered ethnic clashes and points of contention between ethnic communities. See Dinara Tussupova, "Mass Media and Ethnic Relations in Kazakhstan," *Problems in Post Communism* 57, no. 6 (2010): 32; Akylbayeva, Malgaraeva, and Umirzakova, *Ethnic Identity Condition and Tendency*, 720, also acknowledge a measure of ethnic strife. Much like in the United States, Russia, and Europe, illegal migrants are commonly cast as a deleterious element within society though fulfilling a needed role in the economy. They are an easy target for negative attention and face discrimination and occasional violence in Kazakhstan.

81. For discussion of the IPS Survey see Lillis, "Kazakhstan Follows Thorny Path toward National Unity"; see also Özecan Kesici, "The Dilemma in the Nation-Building Process: the Kazakh or Kazakhstani Nation?," *Journal of Ethnopolitics and Minority Issues in Europe* 10, no. 1 (2011): 1–58.

82. "Interethnic Relations Survey, May 2011," TengriNews, June 13, 2011, accessed July 10, 2014, http://en.tengrinews.kz/opinion/79/.

83. Alexander Diener, "National Territory and the Reconstruction of History in Kazakhstan," *Eurasian Geography and Economics* 43, no. 8 (2002): 632–647.

84. Antonsich, "On Territory, the Nation-State, and the Crisis of the Hyphen," 797.

85. Shantha Hennayake, "Interactive Ethnonationalism: An Alternative Explanation of Minority Ethnonationalism," *Political Geography* 11, no. 6 (1992): 526–549.

86. "The Strategy for Development of the Republic of Kazakhstan until the Year 2030," Akorda.kz, 1997, http://www.akorda.kz/en/category/gos_programmi_razvitiya. See the website devoted to the Kazakhstan 2050 strategy at http://strategy2050.kz/en/.

Chapter 7

Which Future for National-Patriots? The Landscape of Kazakh Nationalism

Marlene Laruelle

Kazakhstan offers a multifaceted state narrative about the nation's identity. Officially, the Kazakhstani state is a multinational one, celebrating the diversity of ethnic groups living on its territory, while at the same time insisting on the *primus inter pares* role of ethnic Kazakhs in creating the state, its legitimacy, and its cultural symbols and values. This ambiguity is not specific to the country and in many ways resembles the narrative used in Russia to bridge the civic nature of the Russian state (*rossiiskii*) and the role of ethnic Russians (*russkie*) in it.

As I have discussed in other works,[1] Kazakhstan elaborated a three-level discursive paradigm or repertoire about its state identity. The first one is that of *Kazakhness*, which has been concretized through state-run narratives about the country's identity, policies of ethnic repatriation, and promotion of the titular language. *Kazakhstanness*, the second paradigm of state identity, emerged at the country's independence with the idea of maintaining the difference, inherited from Soviet nationalities policy, between citizenship and nationality/ethnic identification. This paradigm is deployed as much on the domestic scene as on the international arena around the theme of Kazakhstan as the harmonious homeland of various ethnic groups and religions. It is elaborated in parallel with the notion of Eurasianism, which makes it possible to smoothly articulate foreign policy and domestic policy. A third paradigm became Kazakhstan's main discursive currency in the 2000s, especially in the second half of the decade, boosted by the financial manna flowing from oil redistribution. This third paradigm can be defined as *transnationalism*, i.e., the idea that interconnectivity and globalization alter the nation-state and facilitate its integration into the world community. This paradigm, elaborated for both domestic and international audiences, is intrinsically linked to the regime's legitimacy and purposely conflates the state and the regime through sophisticated branding strategies.

In this chapter, I set aside in the state narrative on Kazakhness and focus on groups of activists who put forward an alternative discourse that argues that state policies lack Kazakhness and therefore need more openly pro-Kazakh policies. They can be defined as nationalists or national-patriots. During *perestroika*, Kazakh nationalist motifs flourished within specific intellectual circles before attaining a more political inflection at the start of the 1990s thanks to the Azat and Alash movements, which were quickly liquidated by the authorities. Nationalist dissidence has since vanished from the political scene, yet remains visible but discrete in the academic world, especially around the promotion of Kazakh literature and the production of a national history alternative to the state-sponsored one. Since the late 2000s and early 2010s, Kazakh nationalism has reemerged on a different social basis, with a younger generation that interacts mostly on social media.

This chapter offers a comprehensive overview of this emerging Kazakh national-patriotic landscape. It first analyzes the main groups and networks and their sociological profile, then explores the shared themes and lines of differentiation, and eventually addresses the potential of national-patriotism for broader social mobilization. This article is based on printed and Internet sources in Russian, as well as on semi-structured interviews conducted with Aldan Aimbetov, the chief editor of *Kazakhskaia pravda*, in May 2002, March 2003, and June 2004, and with five leading activists: Zhanbolat Mamay, Mukhtar Taizhan, Aidos Sarym, Dauren Babamuratov and Valikhan Tuleshov in June 2015 in Almaty and in January 2016 in Washington DC.[2]

The fact that I did not access texts in Kazakh obviously limits the reach of my analysis. Kazakhstan today is home to a whole Kazakh-speaking Internet landscape that still awaits scholarly study. So far, very few scholars have tapped into it, with the notable exception of Diana T. Kudaibergenova and Serik Beysembayev.[3] However, and this is a recurring paradox of Kazakh "national-patriotism," many of these nationalist texts, publications, interview transcripts, and social media are available in Russian. With this restriction in mind, this study hopes to partially fill in the gap in our knowledge of this growing social trend and offers a first mapping of the landscape of Kazakh nationalism.[4]

TERMINOLOGICAL ISSUES

In the Soviet tradition, nationalism (*natsionalizm*) is defined as a negative feature typical of pre-socialist societies and/or a "remnant" (*perezhitki*) noticeable among Soviet people that should be eradicated. Patriotism and internationalism are presented as the genuine way of expressing feelings of belonging to a national community. In the post-Soviet world, the terminological load of "nationalism" is still very present and broadly shared by the populations, but multiple borrowings from Western literature and changes in mindset have also questioned it. In Kazakhstan, some groups define themselves as nationalist and claim for themselves this terminology. However, in the Kazakh language "nationalism" can be translated in two ways: *ultzhandylyq* and *ultshyldyq*. The first translation carries positive connotations, while the second is more ambiguous; sometimes it is negative, sometimes positive.

"Nationalism" in the sense of *ultzhandylyq* can be considered as emic: the subject actually uses the term, it is not merely a perspective applied by outside observers. During the *perestroika* years, the three main movements representing this trend, Alash, Azat, and Zheltoksan (see below), defined themselves as "national-democrats" (*natsional-demokraty* in Russian, *ultshyl-demokratialyk* in Kazakh), a terminology common among those calling for the Soviet regime to democratize politically and for the Soviet nationalities policy to give more autonomy to national cultures. In the second half of the 1990s the terminology evolved, with groups identifying themselves as "national-patriots" (*natsional-patrioty* in Russian, *ult-patriottary* in Kazakh), a term that was also, simultaneously, widespread in Russia to identify opponents of the Yeltsin regime. This term stays in use in Kazakhstan, and a whole group of *natspat*, or national-patriots, emerged.

In today's Kazakhstan, the Soviet-era distinction between "good" patriotism and "bad" nationalism is still used by state organs, and therefore all those who add "national" to their definition of patriotism position themselves in opposition to the state on matters of national identity. However, terminological debates among Kazakh nationalists themselves are numerous. The majority believes that patriotism only refers to state loyalty, while nationalism refers to the ethnic nation and should be promoted among ethnic Kazakhs. Some, such as Dos Koshim (see below) self-identify as nationalists (*ultshyl*), not as national-patriots. According to him, "the so-called Kazakh nationalists are in fact Kazakh patriots. Without these 'nationalists' it is possible that Kazakhstan as a state wouldn't even exist."[5] As noted by Diana Kudaibergenova, Kazakh national-patriots have not been able to develop a coherent theoretical and terminological framework for the use of *ultshyldyq*.[6]

There also are a handful of radical groups who want to combine nationalism with socialism. For example, former Alash leader Aron Atabek insists on the need to create a national state for Kazakhs with a strong socialist component. "National-Socialism is not fascism of Mussolini or Hitler!" he writes. "National-Socialism is a political and economic term which founds scientifically the state construction with, at its core, the interest of the Nation and of Social Justice."[7]

The process of self-definition of this Kazakh nationalist trend is not, as we have seen, specific to Kazakhstan: they refer to terms that are widespread all over the world, especially Europe. However, part of the debate is also specifically rooted in intra-Kazakh debates about the supposed loss of Kazakh identity by Sovietization/Russification. The use of the adjective *nagyz* ("real" Kazakhs) to define Kazakhs who have well preserved their identity, and *shala* Kazakhs for those who have "lost" it, has deteriorated into mutual accusations and a way to privilege certain categories of citizens. Shala Kazakh literarily means "half-Kazakh" and is used to target Russophone and urban Kazakhs, who are considered detached from their Kazakhophone and rural roots.[8] This dissociation is based on the notion that Kazakhs have been colonized by Russians and should now "decolonize" their national conscience, a topic that was indirectly already formulated in the word *mankurt*, an old Turkic term updated by Chingiz Aitmatov (1928–2008) in *The Day Lasts More Than a Hundred Years* (1980), who described a people enslaved and deprived of memory and therefore of identity. The term got a huge resonance in Kazakh and Kyrgyz society at a time of criticizing the Soviet regime for its nationalities policy.

A large number of *publitsitika*—popular essays—have been published in Kazakhstan on the issue of nationalism, but they often read more like a nationalist manifesto or at least an engaged discussion on the topic. This is the case, for instance, for the *Kazakhskaia missiia* (Almaty: Daik-Press, 2007) edited volume coordinated by Berik Abdylgaliuly, a member of the Kazakhstan Institute for Strategic Studies (KISI) and a nationalist theoretician of nationalism, or in the second category, *Kazakhstan: Natsional'naia ideia i traditsii* (Almaty: Aspandau, 2011) by Kanat Nurov, president of the Aspandau Fund, an organization that acts as a consulting firm on questions of communication and education, a publishing house, and a think tank, and that has the support of some important political figures.[9]

MAPPING THE NATIONAL-PATRIOTIC LANDSCAPE IN KAZAKHSTAN

The national-patriotic landscape in Kazakhstan is not unified, either politically or ideologically. Several generations, social networks, and ideological orientations compete with each other. But even if any effort to create a typology is by definition schematizing, it is still meaningful to sketch the main groups. I identify four of them: the first historical parties of the *perestroika* years, Zheltoksan, Alash and Azat, the intellectual figures at the forefront of the language and culture struggle, the more politically oriented figures who try to capitalize on so-called patriotic values; and the younger, social-media-oriented generation.

The Founding Fathers

During the last years of *perestroika*, three Kazakh nationalist movements emerged, each exhibiting differing degrees of radicalism.[10] Chronologically, the first one, Zheltoksan (December), was established in 1988 to request the liberation of prisoners arrested after the anti-Soviet/anti-Russian riots of December 1986.[11] Led by an anti-communist activist, Khasen Kozhakhmetov (1949–), and poet-activist Aron Atabek (1953–), who had founded the national-patriotic society Zheruyuk in August 1989, the movement was officially registered in March 1990 after Moscow authorized a multiparty political system in the Soviet Union. Zheltoksan demanded that the government revisit its interpretation of the anti-Soviet riots of December 1986, exhibited special concern for Kazakhs abroad, and called for Islam to be a central political and ideological factor of the new Kazakh society. It adamantly opposed the possible privatization of the country's land or natural resources. It did not call for Russians to be expelled en masse but urged their voluntary migration and demanded that Cossack activities be restricted. Zheltoksan attempted to present itself as an alternative to President Nursultan Nazarbayev at the 1993 elections and was supported by some members of the two other parties.

More virulent was Alash, a political party established in April 1990. It took its name from the historical Alash-Orda Movement of 1915–1920, and hoped to play on this strong symbolic link to obtain recognition as the major representative of national interests. Alash's followers rallied around the slogan "Islam, Turkism, and Democracy": the party wanted to create an independent Islamic state, the Greater Turkestan, which would have included all the Turkic peoples of the Commonwealth of Independent States, and expelled all Slavs from Kazakhstan.[12] After the mufti of Kazakhstan, Ryspek Nysambayev, was attacked in December 1991 by some Alash members, charges were brought against the party and it was prohibited.[13] Its main leader, Aron Atabek went into exile in Moscow, but was arrested by the Russian Security Services, on behalf of Kazakhstan, after having published the newspaper *Khak*, which disseminated a virulent anti-Nazarbayev article written by the dissident Karishal Asanov.[14] Atabek then fled to Baku, Azerbaijan, where he ardently defended the Azeri view of the Nagorno-Karabakh conflict. He became a well-known pan-Turkist activist as part of the Turkestan Committee, which sought to rally opposition groups from all four Turkophone countries of Central Asia. He returned to Kazakhstan in 1996, published some poetry inspired by Abai, and joined the self-defense militias operating in certain districts of Almaty. In 2009 he was convicted of hostage taking and killing a policeman in a riot in the Shanyrak *mikroraion* and sentenced to 18 years in prison.[15] Still incarcerated as of mid-2016, he is considered a political prisoner by such organizations as Pen International.[16]

The most imposing political organization, however, was the Azat (Freedom) Movement, founded in July 1990 by former foreign minister Mikhail Isinaliev, Dos Koshim, and historian Sabetkazy Akatai (1938–2003). Very active during *perestroika* in demanding the independence of Kazakhstan, Azat was weakened after its core demands were met with the Soviet collapse and accession to independence. In contrast with the other two parties, Azat stood firmly opposed to violent interethnic relations and recruited members from among Slavs and other ethnic groups. It called for the formation of a democratic Kazakhstani patriotism that would nonetheless give priority to the eponymous population and the Kazakh language.[17] Historical Azat should not be confused with an opposition party of the same name, Azat, created by Bolat Abilov in 2005.

In 1992, segments of each of these three parties decided to establish a coalition with a less virulent ideology. They gathered together as part of the Republican Party of Kazakhstan (*Respublikanskaia partiia Kazakhstana*), led by Sabetkazy Akatay. Although the new party toned down its rhetoric in order to obtain registration, it refused to use the term "Kazakhstani" and endorsed the systematic usage of "Kazakh" when speaking of the new state. On May 16, 1994, a group of eleven nationalists organized a hunger strike in front of the parliament building in Almaty and demanded the resignation of the established political authorities.[18] Instead, the militants were arrested and imprisoned, leading the various nationalist parties to abandon their plans for national large-scale demonstrations directly targeting the authorities for several years. In 1999, Alash, still led by Sabetkazy Akatay, was the only nationalist party that succeeded in getting re-registered, now under the name of the National Party of Kazakhstan—Alash (*Natsional'naia partiia Kazakhstana—Alash*). It received 2.76 percent of the votes in the legislative elections, lost its registration in 2003 and disappeared from political life.[19]

The Intellectual Circles

Several intellectual figures representing academic and artistic circles have become the standard-bearers of the national struggle to preserve and promote the Kazakh language and culture. Many of them come from the fields of history, literature, and linguistics, which were already the most Kazakhified sectors of academic life during Soviet time, for obvious reasons linked to the need to master the national language and access local sources. Many of these figures have been molded by the *Zhas tulpar* Movement, a Kazakh student organization active in Moscow and Leningrad in the 1960s promoting Kazakh culture and accused by the KGB of "bourgeois nationalism."[20]

Even if some became involved in politics, such as the above-mentioned Sabetkazy Akatay, most of these intellectual figures tried to remain above political divisions and interests and were therefore able to craft a consensus with the Nazarbayev regime and navigated the gray zone between official institutions and the opposition. The face of this group is probably the writer and poet Mukhtar Shakhanov (1942–) a lawmaker, former ambassador to Kyrgyzstan, member of the parliament, as well as editor-in-chief of the cultural and literary journal *Zhalyn*, which is being published since 1969.[21] Shakhanov actively participated in ecological groups asking for Aral Sea protection and led the state commission investigating the 1986 Zheltoksan events.[22]

In the same groups one can add the linguist and historian of Kazakh literature Tursynbek Kakishev (1927–2015), professor at the Al-Farabi National University and one of the authors of a multi-volume work on the *History of Kazakh Literature*;[23] another prominent Kazakh writer, Qabdesh Zhumadilov (1936), born in Xinjiang in a Kazakh family who emigrated to the Soviet Union during the period of the USSR-Communist China honeymoon of the 1950s, or Sofy Smataev and Mukhtar Magauin. Like Shakhanov, Akatay, Kakishev, and Zhumadilov were known for their defense of Kazakh culture already in Soviet times and did not share the same agenda as the famous Zhas tulpar Movement, which united mostly Russian-speaking Kazakh writers such as Olzhas Suleymenov, Murat Auezov, and Satimzhan Sanbayev.[24]

Many figures of this generation have been feeding the Mother Tongue Society (*Ana tili Qogami*) and the Kazakh State Language movement (*Memlekettik Til*), constituting the core of Kazakh cultural activism during the *perestroika* years. They contributed to the creation of the *Qazaq Tili* (Kazakh Language), registered as an association and a journal of the same name in early 1990 with the goal of ensuring the promotion of Kazakh language as the republic's state language.[25] Another important figure, the journalist Aldan Aimbetov (1931–2006), belonged to this generation but chose another fate for himself. Professor at the State Medical University, he launched in 1993 the journal *Kazakhskaia pravda*,[26] and published it until his death with his budget and force, making it, for years, the only Kazakh national-patriot journal publishing entirely in Russian.[27] It has been complemented by *SolDat*, and more recently *Tribuna (Ashyq Alan)*, two other Russian-speaking newspapers pushing for a national-patriotic agenda.[28]

A younger generation of activists emerged from foundations and associations promoting Kazakh history and educational issues. The leading one is probably the Alash-Orda Fund, which collects works about the Alash-Orda founding fathers as well as about Kazakh historians who worked on the topic during Soviet times.[29] One of its main figures today, Sultan Khan Akkuly (1962–), trained at the Mukhtar Auezov Institute for Literature and Art and after working for years at the Radio Free Europe/Radio Liberty offices, joined the Lev Gumilev Eurasian National University to lead a small foundation on Alash. Sultan Khan Akkuly has been visible in the media in recent years on the issue of identifying the skull of Kenesary Kassymov, the last Kazakh military leader to fight against Russia, with the hope of repatriating it to his homeland.[30]

The Conservative Patriots

A third group offers a more political reading of national-patriotism and tries to capitalize on its potential outreach in order to build a political career. This is the case, for instance, for the *Ult tagdyry* (Fate of the Nation) group that emerged in 2005 under the leadership of Dos Koshim (1955), focusing mostly on language issues,[31] and inviting Russians to "take the opportunity" of Russian President Vladimir Putin's repatriation policy launched in 2006.[32] Unhappy with the lack of a national holiday that celebrates Kazakh history, Ult tagdyry also lobbied, without success, for making either the 1916 uprising or the 1986 Zheltoksan events a national holiday.[33] Dos Koshim has a long career of political activism, which began during the *perestroika* years with the fight to recognize Kazakh as the republic's official language. In the 1990s, he worked closely with the social-democratic party Azat, part of a network that included former prime minister Akezhan Kazhegueldin, Evgeni Zhotvis, and Sergey Duvanov. Loyal to his friends, Dos Koshim supported the trajectory of Zhotvis and Duvanov as human right activists despite their obvious disagreements on the national identity issue. Dos Koshim continues to participate in the public debate about issues such as the Kazakh language and history, Oralmans, and the need for public policies in favor of the rural population today.[34]

At its launch in 2005, Ult tagdyry was briefly in competition with another movement of the same name, which then changed to *Khalyk dabyly* (the tocsin of the nation), led by Bolatkhan Taizhan (who passed away in 2007) and Sabyrzhan Makhmet.[35] Another small political party, *Ruhaniyat* (Spiritual Strength), tried without success to register to participate in the 2011 elections with a combined agenda of nationalism and environmental concerns. Its leader, Serikzhan Mambetalin, was put on trial in 2015 for "inciting interethnic hate" after having published on his Facebook page excerpts from the latest book by Murat Telibekov, the leader of the nongovernmental organization Union of Kazakhstan's Muslims, known for his provocative anti-Kazakh statements.[36] However, the rising star of this patriotic trend is Bekbolat Tleukhan, an MP and singer of classic Kazakh music, who calls for a nationalist agenda with assumed conservative values, shaped by Islam.

Some of these patriotic groups are focused on empowering youth, also with an agenda based on conservative values. This is the case for the Almaty-based *Bolashaq* (Future) youth movement—not to be confused with the state-funded fellowship program of the same name. Its leader, Dauren Babamurat (1984–), has been working with rural youth and with Oralmans since the mid-2000s, especially bringing books to rural libraries and screening films in order to increase national pride.[37] The Bolashaq movement is known for its strong opposition to Western values: in 2013 its members burned symbols of Valentine's Day, seen as a decadent Western tradition forcing young girls into early sex, and promoting in response a more national commemoration, that of the legendary Kazakh couple Bayan sulu and Kozy Korpesh, to be celebrated on April 15.[38] Bolashaq was one of the most visible street movements supporting the introduction—which failed—in Kazakhstan of a copy of the Russian law against so-called homosexual propaganda. As Babamurat stated,

> We have stooped so low that LGBTs no longer hide their orientation. One can see a lot of people in the city's malls and other public places—these are young people in colored pants. This means they no longer hide their [sexual] orientation. I think it is very easy to identify a gay person by his or her DNA. A blood test can show the presence of degeneratism in a person.[39]

Another youth movement is *Alash kyzdary* (or *Alash arulary*), which seems to have emerged in 2009 as the female counterpart of Bolashaq. As the latter, it defends the same conservative values: its young leader, Sandugash Dzhumagulova, wants to fight against "American ideology [which pushes for] girls to smoke, drink alcohol, use slang, and have sex with almost unknown men."[40] The group, which claimed about 1,500 activists, organized anti-abortion campaigns and "raids" to confiscate Kazakh porn videos.

The Social Media Activists

A fourth group is comprised of younger people who use new tools such as social media to reach their potential audience. Among them, the most famous is probably Zhanbolat Mamay, who began his career as a very popular journalist for the Kazakh-language *Zhas Alash* newspaper and is now the editor of *Tribuna/Ashyq Alan*. He leads the *Rukh pen Til* (Spirit and Language) youth movement, a small structure officially devoted to promoting Kazakh language, but which has emerged rapidly, as early as 2011, as a political platform for this new generation of national-patriots.[41] Mamay has been one of the most active social media critics of the Eurasian Union project and of Kazakhstan's entry into the Customs Union and then the Eurasian Economic Union. The feeling that Nazarbayev's era is coming to an end and that the Eurasian Economic Union was a strategic mistake perpetrated by an aging leadership, gave national-patriots their largest public platform to date. They organized an "anti-Eurasian Forum" that was tacitly allowed by the authorities, as they were authorized to meet publicly, and garnered support from recognized intellectual and literature figures such as poet and writer Kabdesh Zhumadilov (1936–), Sofy Smataev (1941–), and Temirkhan Medetbek (1945–).[42] They also tried to organize a referendum on the Eurasian Union[43] and then staged several digital actions, for instance inviting people to wear medical masks against Russia's "imperial virus."[44]

The attitude of the authorities toward this new generation of national-patriots is ambiguous: they are both marginalized and sometimes repressed, while at the same time not totally silenced. In early 2012 Mamay was charged with inciting social discord during the Zhanaozen workers riots,[45] a charge carrying a jail sentence of up to 12 years, but was then quickly released.[46] Mamay was back in court a few years later on trumped up charges. In May 2014, as tensions around the Donbass War peaked, the Kazakhstani authorities arrested Mamay and Russian "white power" nationalist Alexander Belov-Potkin, the Moscow-based former leader of the powerful Movement Against Illegal Immigration (DPNI), for inciting interethnic hate.[47] Belov-Potkin allegedly organized a training camp for young members of the Kazakh nationalist group *Ult-Azattygy*, including Mamay. This story around Belov-Potkin and Mamay shares many features of the conspiracy theories and counter-messaging that shapes the post-Soviet information space. The Kazakhstani authorities opened the case at a highly opportune moment, allowing them to kill two birds with one stone: they signaled to Russia that they were taking the risk of destabilization seriously, and they neutralized the most visible Kazakh nationalist activist at a time of growing popular resentment against Kazakhstan's entry into the Eurasian Economic Union. The allegation that Russian and Kazakh nationalists were working hand-in-hand to destabilize Kazakhstan does not look plausible, even if Belov-Potkin has been later accused of receiving funds from the opposition oligarch Mukhtar Ablyazov.

Several other social media activists can be mentioned here. Mukhtar Tayzhan, an economist who has been very active in drawing attention to the negative impact of the Customs Union with Russia for Kazakhstan's economy, leads the small foundation named after his father, Bolatkhan Taizhan, a Zhas tulpar member during the Soviet era. Maksat Il'yasuly, one of the leaders of the Antigeptil group, that objects to Russia using the Baikonur cosmodrome,[48] became very visible during the spring 2016 protests against land reform. Aidos Sarym, a historian and archivist by training, now coordinates the online Kazakh cultural project Abai.kz and heads the Altynbek Sarsenbayuly Foundation. He held a number of leading positions in the Ministry of Information of Kazakhstan as well as at the Office of the President of Kazakhstan in the early 2000s. He edited *National Tragedy of February 11, 2006*, about Sarsenbayev's political assassination, and *Zheltoksan*, a collection of documents and materials in ten volumes

(Almaty, 2011). Valikhan Tuleshov, a philosopher by training and founder and coordinator of the European Club of Kazakhstan Public Fund, worked for several years at the Institute of World Economy and Politics under the Fund of the First President, and he later led the School of State and Public Policy at Almaty Management University. To this list can be added political scientist Serikzhan Mambetalin; social activist Rasul Zhumaly; renowned essayist Azimbai Gali; Makhambet Abzhan, the head of the Shanyrak public association, former leader of the Union of Patriotic Youth, and also close to the Kazakhstani Communist Party;[49] and Rysbek Sansenbayuli, brother of the assassinated oppositioner Sarsenbayev, and chief editor of the popular newspaper *Zhas Alash*.[50]

This group does not share entirely similar worldviews, but they all are united by a strong anti-Russian narrative that does not rely only on linguistic issues or historical memories. Instead, they argue that a pro-Russian position favors authoritarianism in Kazakhstan and calls for a more democratic regime. One of the main products of this new social media activism is the Facebook page Qazaqskaia Orda, which has about 25,000 likes.[51] The page fights for what it calls Kazakhstan's decolonization, proposing multiple anti-Russian news articles, graphs, and memes. Qazaqskaia Orda was particularly active during the Ukrainian crisis, republishing pro-Ukrainian, including pro-Bandera, flyers and memes, anti-Putin caricatures and jokes, making the parallel between Putin and Hitler ("Putler"), between Kazakh and Ukrainian genocides, and developing posters about Kazakh history, symbols, and right to independence.

SHARED WORLDVIEWS AND LINES OF DIVIDE

The groups that self-identify as national-patriots are heterogeneous; if they share a similar broad agenda of promoting the Kazakhness of Kazakhstan, they may advance different viewpoints on several important questions. Consensus exists on some issues, but lines of divide are also critical. This long quote from *Kazakhskaia pravda* gives a good and concise insight into the national-patriotic perceptions of current Kazakhstan:

> One can say Kazakhs have almost negated themselves. Which people among all civilized people, having officialized its national language, speak in a foreign language? Which people had to leave the soil of its ancestors, on a territory that occupies the ninth place in the world, while having one of the lowest population density in the world? Why every three Kazakh today lives abroad, while their place is occupied by 129 diasporic nationalities? Which native people on the authentic soil of its ancestors—with the exception of American natives—lives

> in reserves, having given its best territories to a non-native population? Which people do not have the right to create a national-patriotic party or at least a movement? What else [do] Kazakhs have to give up, in the second decade of their independence, to trample drawn their language, culture, and mentality?[52]

The most widely shared topic is obviously the saving and promoting of the Kazakh language. This language-centric agenda has its roots in the Soviet period, when fighting for the right to speak and be taught in the titular language constituted the cornerstone of nationalities policy. As Kazakhs were among the federal titular nationalities with the smallest share of national language fluency and the highest level of Russian use, during the *perestroika* years it was crucial to fight to protect the Kazakh language from near-certain extinction.[53] After independence, state authorities put promoting Kazakh at the forefront of their Kazakhization policy, with limited success.[54] All national-patriots believe the Kazakh language should be given priority and be the only state-recognized language, with Russian losing its status as a "language of interethnic communication," a policy interpreted as a way to protect Russian and avoid learning Kazakh.[55] "The language of each people, with the physical appearance of its representatives, is the foundation, the particularity, the shield of each nation. If the language were to disappear, the people would disappear as well."[56] The majority of national-patriots favor the shift to Latin script, an old debate that regularly re-emerges on the Kazakhstani public scene. According to them, Latin script is the symbol of modernity and of a pan-Turkic identity—with Kemalist Turkey as a beacon showing the path—and a symbolic way to confirm the end of the Russian colonial era.[57] Some have been calling for shifting to Arabic: this was proposed during *perestroika*, in 1989, when the journal of the young communists, *Pioner*, launched a project to teach Arabic script[58]—but today this claim sounds too "Islamic" to get broad support.

National-patriots all position themselves in opposition to the state-backed notion of a Kazakhstani nation that celebrates the coutry's multiethnicity similar to the Soviet-era notion of "friendship between peoples." According to them, this Kazakhstani nation is an illusion created by the Nazarbayev regime in order to avoid confronting Russia and Russians, and because the elites currently in power are themselves a pure product of the Soviet regime and its ideology. This Kazakhstani nation would negate the right of Kazakhs to claim their own nation-state and therefore the linguistic and cultural primacy they deserve. Many national-patriots openly refer to European nation-states as a model: an authentic civic nation should emerge as an historical process from the merging of all ethnic or regional groups into one nation shaped by the language and culture of the majority. All citizens of Kazakhstan should therefore be called Kazakhs, the same way all citizens of France are called

Frenchmen, whatever their original ethnicity may be. Dos Koshim asked, for instance, for "The Republic of Kazakhstan" to be renamed "Kazakh State" or "Kazakh Republic."[59]

Once that declaration of intent has been made, many national-patriots disagree about what kind of relationship to build with the Russian and Slavic minorities. Very few promote a pure "Kazakhstan for Kazakhs" or call for expelling non-Kazakhs. Among this minority was the *Kazakhskaia pravda* editorial board, who, in the early 2000s, was calling for expelling Russians in the name of the need for jobs and housing.[60] Today the majority of national-patriots claims that minorities are welcome to stay, but they should speak Kazakh and share Kazakh values and traditions and integrate into the nation. The Assembly of the People, which recognizes cultural rights for minority associations, should be abolished. All national-patriots are enthusiastic proponents of repatriation of ethnic Kazakhs from abroad: Oralmans have been rescued from Russification and Sovietization and will contribute to the re-Kazakhification of Kazakhs, inculcating traditions long lost by their modernized brethren in the homeland.[61]

National-patriots share a similar reading of Kazakh history, especially since the nineteenth century. They believe the Tsarist empire played one Kazakh *juz* (tribal confederation) against the other, whipped up fear of the Dzhungars conquering the Kazakh territory, and planned the agricultural and demographic colonization of the steppes by Russian peasants. They see Soviet history as the direct continuation of Russian colonial policy, with an assumed agenda of demographic domination. Their narrative of victimization is built on two foundations. This first one is the memory of the political repression of Alash-Orda historical leaders (Alikhan Bokeikhanov, etc.) and the mass repressions of the 1937–1938 purges (about 100,000 people arrested, 25,000 executed for the Kazakh SSR). Small groups of activists commemorate these tragic events every May 31, the day of victims of political repressions.[62] For them, the December 1986 riots were another episode in the Russian/Soviet policy of repressing everything Kazakh. The second strand is the bloody sedentarization and collectivization of the early 1930s that killed about one-third of the traditionally nomadic Kazakh population and pushed another third to emigrate. National-patriots progressively borrowed from the Ukrainian construction of a Holodomor narrative and created a Kazakh term to express the famine, *Asharshylyka*, asking for the same status as victims of genocide, and hoping for similar international recognition.[63] At least two documentary films are available online in Kazakh, based on archival documents, to describe the events, a short one from 1992 by Kalila Umarov and based on Valerii Mikhailov's book *The Chronicle of the Great Dzhut* (*Khronika Velikogo Dzhuta*),[64] and a longer one from 2013.[65]

The national-patriotic worldview is largely based on a shared culture of alternate history and a romanticized past. It finds inspiration in multiple sources, including: nineteenth-century Orientalist fascination for the supposed authenticity of the cultures of the steppes, Olzhas Suleymenov's grand vision of the unity of the steppes and its critical role in founding ancient cultures of the Mediterranean world,[66] Lev Gumilev's rehabilitation of Turkic ethnic groups in the history of the Russian state,[67] and Murad Adzhi's folk history of the 1990s around the notion that Turks are at the origins of all main civilizations and human inventions. This alternate culture is shaped both by the legacy of the cultural underground of the Soviet era, and by the contemporary popularity of folk history and conspiracy theories.

All national-patriots, at different levels, call for reviving the Turkic roots of Kazakhness, although with varying levels of pan-Turkism. Some give preference to an assumed pan-Turkic ideology relatively similar to the one in place in Turkey and in early twentieth century Jadid circles, therefore also linked to Islam. Others shift it to a more Kazakh-centric pan-Turkism, detached from Turkey, and which is often combined with Aryan motives, such as the theory of Kazakho-aryanism of Aron Atabek.[68] For all of them, the historical continuum among the peoples of the steppes is critical, even if all recognize the Kazakh Khanate of the fifteenth century as the birth of a first Kazakh state. They also cultivate romanticized motives about the freedom of nomadic culture and the figure of the *batyr,* the noble knight.

On more contemporary issues, national-patriots also present a relatively unified front. They consider Kazakhstan to still be a colony of Russia and denounce what they see as Nazarbayev's submission to the Kremlin. They ask for the closing of all Russian military bases on Kazakhstani territory, including of the Baikonur cosmodrome, and violently reacted to the rapprochement with Russia signified by the Customs Union in 2010 and then the Eurasian Economic Union in 2015. On the latter question, national-patriots were able, for the first time in years, to get some visible popular support. They were also the ones initiating a counter-narrative to the state-backed version on the 2014 Ukrainian crisis, offering striking support for Ukrainians against Moscow. Dos Koshim and other leaders shared with some Western observers the parallel made between Putin and Hitler and identified Kazakhstan with Ukraine.[69] In 2014, the Kazakh-language journal, *Zhuldyzdar otbarsy-Anyz Adam* (The Celebrity Family–The Most Famous Man), known for popularizing world history, came under the media spotlight for publishing an issue devoted to Adolf Hitler and *Mein Kampf.*[70] A Russia-based veterans' group accused the journal of propagating interethnic hate, while the chief editor, Zharylkap Kalybay, defended himself by saying the journal had merely explained who Hitler was to the wider public, without supporting Nazi ideology.[71] The Kazakhstani justice system ordered him to pay a significant fine to the veterans' group, but this scandal resonated among Kazakh nationalists who tried to use the case to demonstrate the subordination of Kazakhstani institutions to Russian public opinion and its obsession for fighting "Fascism."[72]

On the relationship with China, national-patriots have not forgiven Nazarbayev for abandoning some disputed border territories to Beijing in 1996, and they criticize China's exploitation of Kazakhstani raw resources. Like many nationalist groups in the post-Soviet space, Kazakh national-patriots share strong environmental concerns—a legacy of the Soviet ecological movement of the 1960s—and this provides another reason to denounce China's exploitation of both environmental norms and workers' rights. They also warn the country of becoming a Chinese agricultural colony and vocally participated in the 2009 protests against the presumed transfer of over 1 million hectares of arable land to Chinese farmers. These protests forced the government to retract its plans, as it officially recognized the impossibility of transferring land to foreign nationals.[73] In spring 2016, the protests against land reforms and the ability of foreigners to rent lands for 25 years increased the public visibility of the national-patriots, especially in some provincial cities.

But beyond this consensual façade, national-patriots are divided on many other important questions. Some, such as Murat Taizhan, Aidos Sarym, and Valikhan Tuleshov, call for classic liberal values and a European model of development, nonetheless they do not stand for a pro-US foreign policy and many of them are proponents of a kind of pan-Turkic identity.[74] Some others are much more critical of the West both in terms of foreign policy—denouncing, for example, U.S. firms operating in the Caspian Sea, which help consolidate the Nazarbayev regime without enriching the country—and in terms of values. Indeed, many who call for conservative values are careful to differentiate the liberal West from the conservative West. They support the rise of far-right parties in Europe, the shared agenda of a strong nation-state sovereignty, their refusal to accept any supranational construction, and the promotion of so-called traditional family values. To a lesser extent, national-patriots are also divided in seeing Russia or China as Kazakhstan's main enemy, depending if they look back toward recent history and in a medium-term future—in that case, Russia is the problem neighbor—or, if they look back to ancient history and the long-term future—in that case priority is given to China.

Another dividing question relates to the nature of national identity. All believe in the permanence of the nation and its primordial nature, but some add a racialist tone that the others deny. For instance, Dos Koshim states that "Turkic unity, it seems to me, is in the blood."[75] Similarly, some consider Kazakh society should value the *juz*/clan difference as a constitutive element of the national identity, while others see it as a "backward" element cultivated by Russians and Soviets and that should be bypassed to access a unified modern nation-state.

However, the main disagreement relates to religion. Here at least three schools can be identified: those who promote liberal values and a secular state; those who call for rehabilitating Tengrism, the pre-Islamic religion of Turkic-Mongolian peoples based on the divinity of the sky and of nature;[76] and those who link Kazakh national identity to Islam. In the early 1990s Alash was calling for a theocratic regime but has rapidly shifted toward a more secular narrative.[77] One of its historical leaders, Aron Atabek, has since then became a fervent proponent of Tengrism. He considers Islam to be a universalistic religion that negates the specific national features of each nation and denounces Wahhabism as a new internationalism, with an underlining conspiracy subtext regarding the links between Islam and "Masonic" culture, an indirect way to consider Arabs and Jews under the unified category of Semites.[78] However, it seems a growing trend among national-patriots to link national and religious identity as, for instance, Bekbolat Tleukhan, who calls for Kazakhs to adhere strictly to Hanafi traditions.[79]

WHICH POTENTIAL FOR SOCIAL MOBILIZATION?

What will happen if this national-patriotism is fully mobilized? What audience supports it, and what topics may crystallize public opinion in favor of national-patriots? Where do they lack credibility?

The first priority for national-patriots is to secure their political legitimacy in front of a regime which has successfully captured the narrative on the nation. The Kazakhization, both ethnically and linguistically, of the state administration has been underway since the mid-1990s, and the regime has—at least so far—been a source of upward social mobility for many of the young generations of Kazakhs. National-patriots may claim that the Nazarbayev regime is a-national or anti-national (it is supposed to be dominated by ethnic minority oligarchs, to sell its resources to foreign firms, etc.) but this discourse is too radical to get broad public support. Or they have to recognize the success of the regime in nationalizing Kazakhstan, and therefore work in its shadow. Many *natspat* recognize that they are both repressed and used by the regime against Moscow, and therefore involuntarily play a role of "useful idiots" or puppets for the president administration, Akorda, even if that does not undermine their ability to act autonomously. One good example of being used by Akorda has been the case of Askar Nursha, a young scholar who was fired from the very official Kazakhstan Institute for Strategic Studies under the president after expressing too openly concerns about the benefits of the Eurasian Economic Union, but who quickly found a new niche at the no-less official Institute for World Economy and Politics under the Fund of the First President.[80]

National-patriots themselves diverge on the political nature of their movements. Some see it uniquely as an intellectual trend that will progressively become mainstream with the rise of a post-Nazarbayev generation, while others would like to be engaged politically immediately, but denounce the repression they are facing from the authorities. Any attempt to organize national-patriotism as a political force has failed so far. Any mention, for instance, of the need to give preference to ethnic Kazakh oligarchs versus non-Kazakh ones such as Alexander Mashkevich and Vladimir Kim, which was discretely mentioned by businessmen Nurzhan Subkhanberdin and Mukhtar Ablyazov at the peak of their influence, were considered as a direct attack against Nazarbayev's legitimacy.[81] Aidos Sarym summarizes this dual strategy:

> First possibility. The political landscape will soon be nationalized and all parties will then speak in the state language and define their ideology based on Kazakh culture, traditions, and historical background. In that case the creation of a Kazakh political party is not necessary. Why create a Kazakh party if all other parties are Kazakh by spirit and essence? Second possibility. The political system will not modernize and will stay the same. In that case, for sure, the question of creating such a party will emerge. But in that case the debate should be not about creating a party that will advance some questions and topics, but a party that will ask for structural changes in the whole political landscape of Kazakhstan.[82]

Second, national-patriots have not been able to bridge the gap between rural and urban populations, a schism that remains the main social and cultural divide in the country. A large part of their "natural" audience could be rural Kazakhs, but *natspats* are themselves educated urbanites shaped in the late Soviet and early post-Soviet mold, whose life is largely disconnected from the countryside. National-patriotic literature reproduces the classic topics of romantic national awakening of the nineteenth century in Europe and Russia: it mourns the lost "authenticity" of Kazakh culture, exalts the Kazakh *aul* (village), tries to recreate genuine national values from scratch, and complains about the degenerated and russified "asphalt Kazakhs," but this does not automatically create an audience. Moreover, in order to mobilize rural youth, the issue of Islam and its place in national identity would have to be addressed openly.

Third, national-patriotism is still very much centered on the language issue. Yet, as shown by the last 25 years of independence, many of the laws promoting Kazakh have not succeeded in changing the linguistic practices of many citizens. Indeed, in order to successfully implement Kazakh as an effective national language, the issue of human capital should have been addressed first. The Kazakh educational system still lags behind the one in Russian, and pupils cannot speak Kazakh well even after the full 12 years of school. If the Kazakh language is increasingly used in public spaces, it is through natural, demographic processes, not political decree. Moreover, once the language is rescued from disappearing, which is the case now, its symbolic defense is not enough to become a political project per se. This is the conclusion raised by a group of young activists, the WikiBilim group, which wants to develop educational online content in the Kazakh language. Registered in 2011, WikiBilim develops Kazakh content for Wikipedia, in order to show the potential of an audience not only consuming Kazakh-language content but also capable of producing it. Thanks to them, the Kazakh part of Wikipedia, simultaneously in three alphabets, Cyrillic, Latin, and Arabic, has soared from about 8,000 articles to 207,000 articles, jumping from 125th place to 31st in only a few years.[83]

Aside from these weaknesses, national-patriotism can rely on several strengths. The first relates to demographics and the ongoing generational shift.[84] The demographic gap between Kazakhs and non-Kazakhs is widening fast. In 2015, the natural growth rate of the Kazakh population was 2.3 percent (2.6 percent for the Uzbek minority), while that of Russians was negative, at –0.51 percent (–1.96 percent for the Ukrainians).[85] This impacts the average age of each group. In 2013, the average age of Kazakhs was 28.9 (26 for the Uzbek minority), compared with 38.5 for Russians and 43 for Ukrainians.[86] This gap of about a decade means that the aging of Russian and Slavic minorities will accelerate—the majority of them are already past reproductive age. In 20–30 years, the number of Russians will decline abruptly because of natural factors; the northern regions will be largely populated by pensioners. This already unbalanced equation tilts further in favor of Kazakhs with Astana's repatriation policy: more than one million Kazakhs from neighboring states—Uzbekistan, China, Mongolia, Afghanistan—have settled in the country.[87]

In the forthcoming two decades, Kazakhstan will demographically "Kazakhify" quickly. New generations, especially new middle classes and provincial notables, will probably be the ones bearing the flag of Kazakh nationalism. A more nationalist policy will then become a niche to capture for new politicians. Already today, among the current elites, some do not hide their support for a more pro-Kazakh policy in terms of language, culture, and memory: Imangali Tasmagambetov, former mayor of Almaty, Astana, and now defense minister; Marat Tazhin, former foreign affairs minister, secretary of the National Security Committee, secretary of Kazakhstan's Security Council, now ambassador to Russia; Akhmetzhan Yessimov, former mayor of Almaty; Mukhtar Kul Mukhammed, former minister of culture; and Berik Abdylgaliuly, who worked as *akim* (governor) or deputy *akim* in Kostanay and Karaganda. To this list could potentially be added, even if their positions toward national-patriotism are less straightforward, Oraz Zhandosov, former deputy prime minister, former minister of finance and of economy, now director of the Rakurs Center for Economic Analysis; or Bulat Utemuratov, who occupies several positions in the presidential administration and served as the president's special advisor on several issues. Moreover, a younger generation—sometimes sponsored by the state-funded Bolashak program—is already involved in the presidential party Nur-Otan and the presidential administration, and pushes for a more assertive policy in terms of national identity.

The *natspat* movement is therefore becoming increasingly visible. In 2009–2010, it was mostly intellectual figures led by Mukhtar Shakhanov protesting against the Doctrine of National Unity and its mention of a Kazakhstani nation. This issue reached a happy end for the protesters: the adjective "Kazakhstani" disappeared from the document, which now speaks only about a Kazakh nation.[88] In 2011, 138 public figures addressed an open letter to President Nazarbayev, the prime minister, and the heads of the two chambers of parliament, asking them to strip the Russian language of its special status granted by the constitution.[89] After 2010, the topic of the relationship with Russia became the main channel for *natspats* to reach a broader public. It began with public protests outside Russia's embassy and consulates in Astana, Almaty, and Uralsk, demanding the suspension of Russian rocket launches from Baikonur after a Proton rocket crashed in Kyzylorda province in 2013. The same year, some 500 people gathered in Almaty to protest against the decision to join the Eurasian Economic Union and asked for a referendum on the matter.

One of the probable, but still to be explored, strengths of national-patriotism in Kazakhstan would be its ability to capture the current wave of "conservative values" that is noticeable all over the post-Soviet space as well as in Europe. Sociological surveys conducted by the Almaty-based Strategy Center for Social and Political Research reveals that only 18 percent of respondents consider Western countries to be a good model of development (13 percent for European countries, 5 percent for the United States). Russia collects 22 percent of the preferences, probably mostly among Russians and Russia-oriented populations, while the notion that Kazakhstan should build its own path was selected by 43 percent of the respondents.[90] Another survey of 2014 shows that only 17 percent of respondents believe that Western values are becoming more and more prevalent in society, while 69 percent agree that the culture of Kazakhstan should stay distinctive and resist outside influences and intrusions. One-third suggest that further cultural developments should be based on Kazakh national customs, values, and traditions.[91]

CONCLUSIONS

The landscape of Kazakh nationalism or national-patriotism remains only loosely structured. Compared to those existing in Russia, Ukraine, the Baltic states, or Georgia, it seems to be still in its infancy. But compared with the neighboring Central Asian states, this national-patriotic trend can be considered an active part of the society, in a relatively similar manner as its Kyrgyz neighbor, but with a huge and meaningful difference: Kazakhstan has been able to avoid mass interethnic riots—skirmishes between ethnic groups happen regularly but on a very localized base, in rural areas, mostly Kazakhs versus Uzbeks, Dungans, Uyghurs, Chechens or Turks—while Kyrgyzstan's political life has been partly shaped by the tensions between the Kyrgyz majority and the Uzbek minority.

Like many nationalist groups, Kazakh national-patriots occupy small niches: they dominate some cultural institutions, often state-sponsored but with a limited outreach, and use the Internet to spread their message without having to build popular support. Many of them recognize that before even trying a Gramsci-style strategy of penetrating the state and energizing the official political and intellectual life, national-patriots should focus on cultural enlightenment (*prosveshchenie*) to raise awareness about what they consider to be critical issues for the future of the nation.

Kazakh national-patriots display classic identity anxieties and post-colonial narratives that are typical of many so-called young nation-states. They feel alienated in their own country and have difficulties molding an autonomous space for expression: they find themselves either co-opted by the authorities if they agree to rally official institutions that promote Kazakh language and culture, or marginalized and sometimes penalized by a heavily developed red tape system. But their main difficulty is more structural: given the success of the Nazarbayev regime in capturing the national identity narrative, the national-patriots have little maneuvering room to attract an audience. However, the aging president and the ongoing adjustment of the elites in preparation for a post-Nazarbayev era will probably re-open the domestic landscape for *natspats*. But they will have to demonstrate that they have a structured political project to offer: fighting for the symbols of the nation does not say anything about the nature of the regime to come—democratic, hybrid, authoritarian—about its values and ideological orientations—pro-Western or not, with Islam as one of its main values, or not—and its economic orientations. How can the relationship with Russia be rebuilt without breaking up with Moscow? How to build the democratic regime many of them call for, without alienating the ethnic minorities?

National-patriots will also have to prove that a cosmopolitan nationalist elite can legitimately represent a rural Kazakh society, which is mostly interested in upward social mobility and economic prospects. Valuing the *aul* as the place of authenticity of Kazakh values does not offer any clear economic development strategy. Integrating the Oralmans in post-Soviet conditions has shown obvious limits, and an anti-Oralman xenophobia developed among ethnic Kazakhs themselves. To the despair of national-patriots, many ordinary Kazakhs find it easier to coexist with Russians than with Oralmans: Soviet and post-Soviet shared values remain a more efficient "glue" for building a civic identity than a reconstructed and artificial pan-Kazakh identity, unifying Soviet Kazakhs and Oralmans. Feelings of belonging are much more embedded in "banal nationalism" than in the existence of a theoretical nation: to be successful, national-patriots will have to come to terms with the Russian and Soviet past of the Kazakh nation and integrate it in a more positive way into their ideological construct.

NOTES

1. Marlene Laruelle, "The Three Discursive Paradigms of State Identity in Kazakhstan: Kazakhness, Kazakhstanness, and Transnationalism," in *Nationalism and Identity Construction in Central Asia: Dimensions, Dynamics and Directions*, ed. Mariya Omelicheva (Lanham, MD: Lexington Books, 2014), 1–20.

2. To protect them, I will not attribute any of the references to any of them individually.

3. See, by Serik Beysembayev, *Fenomen kazakhskogo natsionalizma v kontektste segodniashnei politiki: ot otritsaniia k ponimaiiu* (Almaty: Open Society Public Policy Program 2015), http://caa-network.org/cassions/wp-content/uploads/2015/07/nationalism_final.pdf.

4. I am very grateful to Diana Kudaibergenova, Serik Beysembayev, and Aitolkyn Kourmanova for their help on this article and for introducing me to many new figures of the Kazakh-speaking landscape. All mistakes remain mine.

5. Dos Koshim, "Kazakhskii natsionalizm—positivnyi natsionalizm," *Altyn-Orda*, January 27, 2015, http://www.altyn-orda.kz/dos-koshim-kazaxskij-nacionalizm-pozitivnyj-nacionalizm/. See also Dos Koshim, "Natsional'nye problemy nevozmozhno reshit' bez politicheskikh reform," October 10, 2014, https://www.youtube.com/watch?v=zTvm19_OPyw.

6. Diana Kudaibergenova, "O natsii i ee nositeliakh," *Ekspert Kazakhstan*, August 5, 2013, http://expertonline.kz/a11460/.

7. Aron Atabek, "Odin bog, odna religiia, odna ideologiia, odin narod," Atabek's website, June 26, 2006, http://aronatabek.com/odin-bog-odna-religiya-odna-ideologiya-odin-narod.html.

8. See, for instance, the book by Zhumabay Zhakupov, *Shala Kazakh*, and the discussion it generated, September 25, 2009, at http://ia-centr.ru/expert/5914/.

9. See their website http://www.aspandau.kz/.

10. See B.G. Ayaganov, *Politicheskie partii i obshchestvennye dvizheniia sovremennogo Kazakhstana* (Almaty: Ministerstvo pechati i massovoi informatsii respubliki Kazahstan, 1994), 62–66, 77–80.

11. During the *Zheltoksan* (December in Kazakh) riots in Almaty, the student crowds protested against the nomination of a Russian in a position that had been

traditionally given to a Kazakh, seeing this as an unacceptable act of humiliation on Moscow's part. Taras Kuzio, "Nationalist riots in Kazakhstan," *Central Asian Survey* 7, no. 4 (1988): 79–100. See also for later events, Yacoov Ro'i, "Central Asian Riots and Disturbances, 1989–1990: Causes and Context," *Central Asian Survey* 10, no. 3 (1991): 21–54.

12. K.E. Kusherbaev, *Etnopolitika Kazakhstana: sostoianie i perspektivy* (Almaty, 1996), 130.

13. "Oppozitsionnaia partiia obviniatsia v izbienii muftiia," *Kommersant*, December 23, 1991, http://www.kommersant.ru/doc/2072.

14. "Oskorbili prezidenta Kazakhstana," *Kommersant*, no. 35, November 14, 1992, http://www.kommersant.ru/doc/29998.

15. Sultan-Khan Akkuly, "Kogda kazakhskii dissident saditsia v tiur'mu, eto vygliadit ego lichnoi problemoi," *Azattyq*, December 17, 2009, http://rus.azattyq.org/content/aron_atabek/1905440.html.

16. "Take Action for Aron Atabek," Pen International, http://www.pen-international.org/take-action-for-aron-atabek/.

17. Consulter *Programma grazhdanskogo dvizheniia Azat* (Alma-Ata, 1992).

18. On the general political situation of Kazakhstan in the 1990s, see Martha Brill Olcott, *Kazakhstan: Unfulfilled Promise* (Washington, DC: Carnegie Endowment for International Peace, 2002). On the hunger strike, see Boris Kagarlitski, "Kazakhstan's parliament is dissolved," Greenleft.org, April 12, 1995, https://www.greenleft.org.au/node/9524.

19. On these three parties see Vladimir Babak, Demian Vaisman, and Aryeh Wasserman (eds.), *Political Organization in Central Asia and Azerbaijan* (London: Frank Cass, 2004), 99–104, 107–113, and 175–178.

20. Diana Kudaibergenova, *Re-writing the Nation: Elites, Networks and Narratives in Modern Kazakh Literature* (Lanham, MD: Lexington, 2017).

21. Recent issues can be found at http://adebiportal.kz/FlippingBooks/Zhalyn/3-2011/index.html#14.

22. Mukhtar Shakhanov, "A Report on Commission Proceedings and on Further Clarification of the Circumstances of the December 1986 Events in Alma-Ata," in Helsinki Watch, *Conflict in the Soviet Union: The Untold Story of the Clashes in Kazakhstan* (New York: Helsinki Watch, 1990), Appendix A.

23. "Honored figure of Kazakhstan, Doctor of Philology Tursynbek Kakishev passed away at the age of 88," *Inform.kz*, September 7, 2015, http://www.inform.kz/eng/article/2815227.

24. See Kudaibergenova, *Re-writing the Nation: Elites, Networks and Narratives in Modern Kazakh Literature*.

25. Jacob M. Landau, Barbara Kellner-Heinkele, *Politics of Language in the Ex-Soviet Muslim States* (London: Hurst and Company, 2001), 87.

26. Not to be confused with the official *Kazakhstanskaia pravda*.

27. "Umer Aldan Aimbetov," *Zonakz.net*, April 21, 2006, http://zonakz.net/articles/15338.

28. See, respectively, Vladislav Yuritsyn, "'Taszhardan' ('Dat') okonchil desiatiletku," *Zonakz.net*, April 15, 2008, http://zonakz.net/articles/21669; and, from the

same author, "Ezhenedel'nik 'Ashyq Alan' ('Tribuna')—novoe nezavisimoe izdanie," *Zonakz.net*, September 10, 2012, http://zonakz.net/articles/54339?mode=reply.

29. See the website http://rus.alash-orda.kz/.

30. "Gde nakhoditsia cherep poslednego kazakhskogo khana Kenesary?" Kaztube.kz, November 3, 2014, https://kaztube.kz/video/154957. See also Sultan Khan Akkuly, "Bez golovy Kenesary khana prazdnovanie 550-letiia Kazakhskogo khanstva budet nepolnym," 7news.kz, May 15, 2015, http://7news.kz/politika/sultan-han-akkuly-prazdnovanie-550-letiya-kazahskogo-hanstva-budet-nepolnym-bez-golovy.

31. "Dvizhenie Ult tagdyry predstavilo svoi proekt zakona o gosudarstvennom iazyke," Kt.kz, July 4, 2006, http://www.kt.kz/rus/society/dvizhenie_ult_tagdiri_predstavilo_svoj_proekt_zakona_o_gosudarstvennom_jazike_1152012520.html.

32. "Kazakh National Patriots Urge Ethnic Russians to Go Home," Zonakz.net, August 16, 2006, http://enews.fergananews.com/articles/1555.

33. Dilbegim Mavlonii, "V Kazakhstane xotiat prazdnovat' Nauryz v tri raza dolshe, nesmotrya na krizis," *Azattyq*, March 12, 2009, http://rus.azattyq.mobi/a/1508127.html.

34. "Novye trebovaniia registratsii protivorechat Konstitutsii i ne reshaiut problem—Dos Koshim," 365info.kz, February 4, 2015, http://365info.kz/2015/02/novye-trebovaniya-registracii-protivorechat-konstitucii-i-ne-reshayut-problem-dos-koshim/.

35. "Dvizhenie Ult Tagdyry-el tagdyry pereimenovalo's' v Khalyk dabyly," Zonakz.net, November 25, 2005, https://zonakz.net:8443/articles/10250?mode=reply.

36. "Kazakhstan: Two Activists Detained. Vague Criminal Charge Used to Target Critics," Human Rights Watch, October 16, 2015, https://www.hrw.org/news/2015/10/16/kazakhstan-two-activists-detained.

37. Author's interview with Dauren Babamuratov, Almaty, June 20, 2015. See also "Dauren Babamuratov, rukovoditel' molodezhnogo dvizheniia Bolashaq," YouTube, November 5, 2014, https://www.youtube.com/watch?v=k07Z5HCVWjU.

38. Vitalii Kovalev, "V Kazakhstane Den' Koza Korpesh i Bayan-Suly pochti nikto ne prazdnuet," KTK, April 15, 2013, http://www.ktk.kz/ru/news/video/2013/4/15/22144.

39. "Kazakhstan Looks to Ban Gay 'Propaganda' and Identify Gays by Searching for Degeneratism in Their DNA," Tengrinews.kz, September 13, 2014, https://en.tengrinews.kz/laws_initiatives/Kazakhstan-looks-to-ban-gay-propaganda-and-identify-gays-by-256105/. See also Dauren Babamuratov, "Ia solidaren s Al-Farabi," *Tribuna Kommunist Kazakhstana*, October 14, 2014, http://vmeste.com.kz/?p=2654.

40. Tat'iana Alad'ina, "Destvennitsy atakuiut," Express.kz, November 13, 2009, http://old.express-k.kz/show_article.php?art_id=34526&start=20.

41. See, already in 2011, the very critical article by Elmira Sagatova, "Novaia politicheskaia zvezda Kazakhstana, ili Mal'chik dlia provokatsii Zhanbolat Mamay?" CentrAsia, June 19, 2011, http://www.centrasia.ru/newsA.php?st=1308464520.

42. Asylkhan Mamashuly, "Protivniki soiuza govoriat o roli Nazarbaeva," Azattyq, May 22, 2014, http://rus.azattyq.org/content/antievraziyskiye-slushaniya-v-almaty/25394060.html.

43. "Aktivisty boiatsia 'evraziiskogo razmyvaniia RK,'" Azattyq, January 17, 2014, http://rus.azattyq.org/content/article/1180775.html.

44. "V Kazakhstane protivniki sozdaniia soiuza s Rossiei nadeli meditsinskie maski," Uralskweek.kz, May 29, 2014, http://www.uralskweek.kz/2014/05/29/v-kazaxstane-protivniki-sozdaniya-soyuza-s-rossiej-nadevayut-medicinskie-maski/.

45. On the riots, see Dossym Satpayev and Tolganay Umbetaliyeva, "The Protests in Zhanaozen and the Kazakh Oil Sector: Conflicting Interests in a Rentier State," *Journal of Eurasian Studies* 6, no. 2 (2015): 122–129.

46. "Zhanbolat Mamay released from arrest," Open Dialogue Foundation, July 13, 2012, http://en.odfoundation.eu/a/793,zhanbolat-mamay-released-from-arrest.

47. "V RK rassleduiut delo po faktu razzhiganiia mezhnatsional'noi rozni," Zakon.kz, May 21, 2014, http://www.zakon.kz/4625687-v-rk-rassledujut-delo-po-faktu.html.

48. See https://www.facebook.com/Antigeptil/.

49. "Prigovo molodomu oppozitsioneru Makhambetu Abzhanu ostalsia bez izmenenii," Azattyq, February 10, 2007, http://rus.azattyq.org/a/1180775.html.

50. http://zhasalash.kz/.

51. https://www.facebook.com/QazaqOrda.

52. "Kazakhskaia Pravda vykhodit na tropu voiny?" Zonakz.net, February 19, 2003, https://zonakz.net:8443/articles/2663.

53. See William Fierman, ed., "Implementing Language Laws: Perestroika and Its Legacy in Five Republics," *Nationalities Papers* 23, no. 3 (1995): 505–659.

54. Bhavna Dave, *Kazakhstan. Ethnicity, Language and Power* (London: Routledge, 2007). See also William Fierman, "Language and Identity in Kazakhstan: Formulations in Policy Documents, 1987–1997," *Communist and Post-Communist Studies* 30, no. 2 (1998): 171–186.

55. "Dvizhenie Ult tagdyry predstavilo svoi proekt zakona o gosudarstvennom iazyke," Kt.kz, July 4, 2006, http://www.kt.kz/rus/society/dvizhenie_ult_tagdiri_predstavilo_svoj_proekt_zakona_o_gosudarstvennom_jazike_1152012520.html.

56. *Kazakhskaia pravda*, no. 6, 1999, 4.

57. Author's interviews with young nationalist activists, Almaty, June 2015.

58. Ingvar Svanberg, "Kazakhs," in *The Nationalities Question in the Soviet Union*, ed. Graham Smith (London: Longman, 1990), 318–330.

59. "Dos Koshim. 'Za kazakhov ia umru. Ia natsionalist,' Zonakz.net, January 31, 2008, https://zonakz.net:8443/articles/20831.

60. Author's interview with Aldan Aimbetov, Almaty, March 2002.

61. Author's interviews with young nationalist activists, Almaty, June 2015.

62. "V Kazakhstane otmechaiut den' just a pamiati zhertv politicheskikh repressii," Tengrinews.kz, May 31, 2014, https://tengrinews.kz/kazakhstan_news/kazahstane-otmechayut-den-pamyati-jertv-politicheskih-256238/.

63. "Genotsid kazakhov (Makash Tatimov, chast' 1)," YouTube, 2008, https://www.youtube.com/watch?v=SdpePACdkpY&nohtml5=False.

64. *Asharshylyq*, by Kalila Umarov, https://www.youtube.com/watch?v=Ag6PalmQ7g4&nohtml5=False.

65. *Asharshylyq (Famine of 1920–1930s)*, 2013, https://www.youtube.com/watch?v=JtyiiQ9j9Wc&nohtml5=False.

66. On Suleymenov, see Harsha Ram, "Imagining Eurasia: The Poetics and Ideology of Olzhas Suleimenov's *AZ i IA*," *Slavic Review* 60, no. 2 (2001): 289–311;

F. Diat, "Olzhas Sulejmenov: *Az i Ya*," *Central Asian Survey* 1 (1984): 101–210; Marlene Laruelle, "Olzhas Suleimenov," in *Russia's People of Empire: Lives Stories from Eurasia, 1500 to the Present,* eds. S. Norris, and W. Sunderland (Bloomington: Indiana University Press, 2012), 319–325.

67. See Mark Bassin, *The Gumilev Mystique: Biopolitics, Eurasianism, and the Construction of Community in Modern Russia* (Ithaca: Cornell University Press, 2016).

68. Aron Atabek, "Serdtse Evrazii ili Velikii Ariiskii Kaganat Altyn-Orda," Atabek's website, November 2012, http://www.aronatabek.ru/.

69. Dos Koshim, "Natsional'nye problem nevozmozhno reshit' bez politicheskikh reform."

70. "Znaete, kakim on parnem byl? V Kazakhstane vyshel zhurnal posviashchennyi 125-letiiu Adolfa Gitlera," Russiankz.info, April 18, 2014, http://www.russianskz.info/society/5568-znaete-kakim-on-parnem-byl-v-kazahstane-vyshel-zhurnal-posvyaschennyy-125-letiyu-adolfa-gitlera.html.

71. "Zharylkap Kalybay: Propaganda Giltera ne bylo, vy xotia by prochitaite!" Tengrisnews.kz, April 21, 2014, https://tengrinews.kz/tv/novosti/obschestvo/1533/.

72. "Zharylkap Kaylbay: ia ne opravdyvaiu fashizm," *YouTube*, July 9, 2014, https://www.youtube.com/watch?v=S0nCEOddlZQ.

73. Joanna Lillis, "Kazakhstan: China Looking to Lease Land for Agricultural Purposes," Eurasianet, February 3, 2010, http://www.eurasianet.org/departments/insight/articles/eav020410.shtml.

74. Aidos Sarym, "Kazakhstan vybyraet tiurko-evropeiskii vektor," Kazakhi Rossii, no date, http://kazakh.orgfree.com/index.php?dn=article&to=art&id=230&p=2.

75. "Dos Koshim. 'Za kazakhov ia umru. Ia natsionalist.'"

76. Marlene Laruelle, "Religious Revival, Nationalism, and the 'Invention of Tradition': Political Tengrism in Central Asia and Tatarstan," *Central Asian Survey* 26, no. 2 (2007): 203–216.

77. Kusherbaev, *Etnopolitika Kazakhstana: sostoianie i perspektivy*, 130.

78. Atabek, "Odin bog, odna religiia, odna ideologiia, odin narod."

79. "Deputat Bekbolat Tleukhan proshel proverku na detektore lzhi," Tengrisnews.kz, October 16, 2011, https://tengrinews.kz/kazakhstan_news/deputat-bekbolat-tleuhan-proshel-proverku-na-detektore-lji-199283/.

80. He signed a collective petition against Kazakhstan's entry into the Union. See "Kazakhstanskie politologi protiv vkhozhdeniia Kazakhstana v Evraziiskii soiuz," Nur.kz, May 9, 2012, https://www.nur.kz/217304-kazahstanskie-politologi-protiv-vhozhdeniya-kazahstana-v-evrazijskij-soyuz.html.

81. See Sebastien Peyrouse's chapter in this volume.

82. Aidos Sarym, "Edinym kazakhskim frontom. V prodolzhenii diskussii o natsionalizme," MGU Laboratory of the political and social development of near-abroad countries, July 13, 2013, http://ia-centr.ru/expert/16138/.

83. Interviews with Rauan Kenzhekhanuly at the International Conference, "Youth in Kazakhstan: Societal Changes, Challenges and Opportunities" (Washington, DC, George Washington University), April 21, 2014.

84. On youth, see Azamat Junisbai, "Are the Young Truly Different? Youth Opinion about Selected Social and Political Issues in Kazakhstan," presentation

at the international conference "Youth in Kazakhstan: Societal Changes, Challenges and Opportunities." George Washington University Central Asia Program, April 21, 2014. See also Serik Beysembayev, "Tendentsii sotsial'no-demograficheskogo razvitiia kazakhstanskogo obshchestva (na baze sotsiologicheskikh issledovanii)," *Tsentral'naia Aziia i Kavkaz* 14, no. 2 (2011): 83–100. See also *Molodezh Kazakhstana 2014* (Astana: Council for Youth Policy under the President of the Republic of Kazakhstan, 2014).

85 *Etnodemograficheskii ezhegodnik Kazakhstana* (Astana: Kazakhstan State Agency of Statistics, 2013), http://stat.gov.kz/getImg?id=ESTAT074326. I thank Aitolkyn Kourmanova for providing me with these figures.

86. Ibid.

87. On the Oralman issue, see Sally Cummings, "The Kazakhs: Demographics, Diasporas, and 'Return,' in *Nations Abroad: Diaspora Politics and International Relations in the Former Soviet Union*, ed. Charles King and Neil Melvin (Boulder: Westview Press, 1998), 137–154; Alexander Diener, "Kazakhstan's Kin-State Diaspora: Settlement Planning and the Oralman Dilemma," *Europe Asia Studies* 57, no. 2 (2005): 327–348; Michelle Witte, "Proposed Changes to Oralman Legislation to Relax Some Settlement Rules," *Astana Times*, July 28, 2014, http://www.astanatimes.com/2014/07/proposed-changes-oralman-legislation-relax-settlement-rules/.

88. See Alexander Diener's chapter in the same volume.

89. "Pis'mo 138-mi: vzryvoopasnoe obrashchenie i kto stoit za nim?" *Altyn-Orda*, October 28, 2011, http://www.altyn-orda.kz/pismo-138-mi-vzryvoopasnoe-obrashhenie-i-kto-stoit-za-nim/.

90. Beysembayev, "Tendentsii sotsial'no-demograficheskogo razvitiia kazakhstanskogo obshchestva." See also *Molodezh Kazakhstana 2014*.

91. Institute of Eurasian Integration, *Sovremennoe sostoianie i tendentsii vsekazakhstanskoi kultury*, October 2014. See also, even if from 2009, *Ideologicheskie ustanovski i osobennosti identifikatsii naseleniia RK* (Almaty: Strategiia, 2009).

Chapter 8

Cowboys, Gangsters, and Rural Bumpkins

Constructing the "Other" in Kazakhstan's "Texas"

Natalie R. Koch and Kristopher D. White

"*Shymkent—eto nash Texas*," we have been told countless times over the years in Kazakhstan. "Shymkent is our Texas."[1] The idea of Shymkent—if not the entire South Kazakhstan *oblast'* (region)—being equated with Texas is a cultural trope that is typically repeated without thinking. A prime example of "substituting cliché for thought,"[2] most Kazakhstanis express a degree of surprise and inarticulateness when they are asked "Why?" This chapter analyzes their struggle to produce an answer to our—perhaps impertinent—question. Some suggest that the label comes from the region's southern location within Kazakhstan, along the border with Uzbekistan, comparable to Texas' southern location in the United States, along the border with Mexico. Others suggest that it is because both places are hot, that the landscape is similar, or that the shape of South Kazakhstan *oblast'* looks a bit like the shape of Texas. While all this may have a degree of truth, the trope primarily operates in the cultural landscape of contemporary Kazakhstan as a means of describing—and specifically *stigmatizing*—a certain kind of person coming from the south, coding them as "criminals," "bumpkins," and variously "foxy" or "cunning" (*khidryye*) characters. This dominant use of the metaphor to insult southerners is by no means undisputed. As we show in this chapter, explaining why South Kazakhstan is called "Texas" is a political process, whereby ordinary Kazakhstanis create and contest their situated geographical imaginaries about the independent state and its socio-cultural divides.

Scholars of contemporary Kazakhstani politics have long considered ethnic divisions within the country and, in particular, the political and social implications of independence for the so-called "beached diaspora" of ethnic Russians.[3] Often locally termed the "Russian question," the shifting status of

Kazakhstan's Russian minority has been a major point of scholarly interest.[4] However, this fixation with Kazakhstan's interethnic borders has resulted in a systematic failure to analyze certain divisions among ethnic Kazakhs themselves. Where scholars have considered intra-ethnic divisions, their work has focused on clan politics and tribal affinities.[5] Although they note that many of these divisions map onto regional divides, they do not attempt to account for regional identities per se. This is the task taken up in this chapter. We argue that analyzing regional identity construction is a productive alternative to illustrating how *difference* is performed in contemporary Kazakhstan—moving beyond both essentialized ethnic divides (Russian vs. Kazakh) and tribal affinities (Great/Middle/Junior *zhuz*). In particular, we focus on just one of Kazakhstan's many regional imaginaries—that of "the south"—to raise broader questions about intersecting affinities, stigmas, inequalities, and territorial imaginaries. We thus begin by outlining some of the scholarly work on regionalism and "internal othering" and sketch some general characteristics of Kazakhstan's regional divisions before then moving on to the case study.

LITERATURE REVIEW

Regionalism and "Internal Othering"

Political geographers and nationalism scholars have amply illustrated that national identities are usually constructed through articulating a national "self" in opposition to a foreign "other."[6] But as David Jansson underscores, while it is true that these foreign others are essentialized, they are also connected with constructing an essentialized self.[7] Curiously, few scholars have considered how national identity construction unfolds through processes of othering groups *internal* to the national body. So even though it is acknowledged that a coherent national "we" must be constructed—out of a presumably heterogeneous population—few have actually considered how the hegemonic "we" can also take shape through this very heterogeneity. This is an especially important project for those who adopt a constructivist approach to nationalism and consider it to be "a social process by which certain historically contingent forms of territorial identities, symbols, and ideologies are instilled into the social and individual consciousness. Through this process individual experiences are colonized by collective ones to join them in the communal story."[8] But, Anssi Paasi asks, how do "individual life-histories become involved with more general socio-spatial processes in various social practices in concrete time-space-specific contexts"?[9] And what happens to those alternative narratives that are deemed unworthy or discordant with the hegemonic nationalist vision?

The most common academic approach to analyzing diversity internal to the "nation" itself is to focus on ethnic, racial, and religious divisions. When some groups are seen as representing norms antithetical to prevailing nationalist ideals, they can be subject to a practice of "internal othering."[10] However, national groups and territories are often divided regionally and frequently on the basis of stark internal inequalities. A smaller set of studies have thus considered these regional divisions, which give rise to place-based identities of groups that are (a) *not* separatist and (b) *unquestionably understood to be part of that national group*. That is, they are not irredentist "others" with inclinations toward an alternate ethno-territorial structure. They are simply understood as somehow different from the dominant national "we." Previous studies on such "internal others" have only considered a handful of contexts, ranging from Europe[11] to the U.S. South[12] and China.[13] In these studies, the region that is being othered is always positioned as an exception to the national norm and frequently evincing values and behaviors that are deemed antithetical to dominant understandings of nationhood.[14] Because othering, as a set of practices, implies variously scaled power differentials, the group or place considered exceptional is most typically stigmatized for their otherness. That is, their difference is denigrated rather than celebrated.[15]

In the case of Kazakhstan, this stigmatization does not necessarily lead to or result from economic and political subordination. More accurately, the various rhetorical practices of stigmatizing the "other" are a reflection of *contest* over power differentials. Indeed, what makes Kazakhstan so instructive is that in the years since gaining independence, the relative power balance between the North and South, the city and the village, and the Russified Kazakhs and the non-Russified Kazakhs has been undergoing rapid transformation.[16] We thus agree with Johnson and Coleman's point that "the economic and cultural marginalization of a seemingly subordinate region are contemporaneous and dialectical processes."[17] Power relations are necessarily at the heart of any study of regionalism for, as Paasi has argued, regions are "social constructs that do not rise in a vacuum," but "are made in broader social practice—regions are hence contested results of power relations." The very act of defining a region "is an act of power."[18]

Regionalism in Kazakhstan

The fact that Kazakhstan is said to have "its own" Texas is not unique. Internationally, the moniker is somewhat popular (at least among the media): Nigeria has been called the "Texas of Africa,"[19] Alberta is commonly known as the "Texas of Canada,"[20] and Mongolia has been dubbed the "Texas of Asia."[21] Although the metaphor is deployed for various reasons in all these cases, in Kazakhstan, it is bound up with the same civilizational metaphors explored in the studies of internal othering noted above. That is, the dominant use of the Texas label is one of dividing Kazakhstan's territory in spaces of modernity, order, and civilization and spaces of backwardness, lawlessness, and tradition—a division that is then mapped onto the people from those different regions. The country's urbanites and northerners are generally coded as more modern and civilized, typically evidenced by their urban way of life and their cultural and linguistic Russification, and supported by their comparable political and economic privilege. By contrast, rural and Southern places and people have conventionally been framed as traditional, uncivilized, and culturally and linguistically Kazakh.[22]

Although these binaries are rooted in Soviet and pre-Soviet identity projects, they acquired new significance upon the collapse of the Soviet Union in 1991.[23] As Michael Billig has noted, "Sudden crises can produce quickly sharpened stereotypes [that] will build upon older cultural myths."[24] With the loosening of residency controls after independence, large numbers of southerners and rural migrants moved to the city, while many ethnic Russians and other non-Kazakhs left the country. The result was a dramatically altered social fabric in Kazakhstan's urban centers, as well as a heightened visibility and awareness of social disparities. President Nursultan Nazarbayev even acknowledged as much in the country's development agenda, *Strategy 2030*:

> Today we witness new poles of confrontation: between the poor and the wealthy, the rulers and the ruled, the countryside and the city. Polarization acquired a geographic manifestation in the relations established between the city and the countryside. In both cases we witness a global process of social differentiation with the gap there between growing steadily. Within the nearest decade the countryside must become a priority area from the point of view of giving an additional impetus to market transformations, to emphatic settlement of social problems and development of infrastructure. We are to expect considerable rejection of a free labor force in the countryside, significant migration to the city from the countryside and ever developing processes of urbanization.[25]

In a truly Soviet fashion, Nazarbayev here names urban-rural disparities as a problem, and one that needs to be addressed, lest it impede the country's future development.[26] But the development of infrastructure and economic opportunities in Kazakhstan's hinterlands today has so far been insufficient to remedy these disparities and to keep rural and southern migrants in place.

In moving to the city, rural migrants are understood to bring the village with them—identified through various physical attributes, dress, manners, and use of the Kazakh language.[27] Catherine Alexander explains: "There was huge resentment from longstanding citizens against these incomers. Sometimes this was expressed as more competition for few jobs, but very often a whole raft of anxieties crystallized around these rural migrants."[28] In the

1990s, these new arrivals were the subject of extensive fear-mongering and rumor-mills, accused of bringing disorder, crime, and backwardness from the village to the city.[29] As Nazpary argues, "The urban population lumped street traders and hooligans together as southern Kazakhs (*iuzhnye Kazakhi*) or *aul* Kazakhs (*aul'nye Kazakhi*), whom they blamed for crimes."[30]

Based on this association of southerners with criminality and social disorder in the 1990s, it is easy to see how Kazakhstanis came to narrate parallels with the "wild west" image of Texas cowboys and lawlessness. It is impossible to say precisely where and how this metaphor originated, as it has taken on a life of its own in the past decades. Yet our data amply demonstrate that people pick up on a diverse range of similarities between South Kazakhstan and the U.S. state. Metaphors are not simply a matter of language, as Lakoff and Johnson have famously argued: "They also govern our everyday functioning, … structure what we perceive, how we get around in the world, and how we relate to other people."[31] If the function of metaphor is to allow us to comprehend one aspect of a concept in terms of another, this requires that the metaphor "highlight some features of reality and hide others …, which forces us to focus *only* on those aspects of our experience that it highlights."[32]

Looking at the different ways that Kazakhstanis articulate the Texas–South Kazakhstan comparison, we can gain insight into how the metaphor both structures thought and practice in contemporary understandings of space, place, and identity in Kazakhstan. Importantly, this approach also allows us to explore how the othered individuals—the South Kazakhstanis themselves—interact with the trope. This is important because, as Jansson has noted, "internal orientalism" is significantly more complex than Orientalism as elaborated by Said because those in the othered region "have more of a voice in the national discourse than the Orient had in the discourse of the Occident."[33] Although more research is needed to adequately capture the voice of those from South Kazakhstan, our data do indicate an effort by the small number of respondents from South Kazakhstan to push back against the hegemonic script and articulate a more positive image of the region.

METHODS AND RESULTS

Methodology

The data for this project comes from four sources:

1. focus groups conducted in October 2010 (n = 36 individuals, 5 groups total);
2. a countrywide survey conducted in September and October 2010 (n = 1233);

3. ethnographic methods, including informal interviews and participant observation, conducted from 2005–2014; and
4. a mini-survey conducted with students at KIMEP University in Almaty between 2010 and 2013 (n = 406).

A detailed description of the methods and sampling procedures for the first two sources is available elsewhere,[34] but we should note that for the purposes of this chapter, we only use a few questions from the survey and responses from only one of the focus group "trigger images," which is shown in Figure 8.1. In the groups, which were conducted at Kazakhstan National University, participants were shown approximately eight images, to which they were asked to respond freely. When necessary, the moderator (a Kazakh woman in her 50s) asked a pre-defined set of questions to stimulate discussion about the images. The image in Figure 8.1 was specifically designed to get participants talking about the South Kazakhstan–Texas metaphor, as a means to explore popular imaginaries of place and regional identity within Kazakhstan. Lastly, the mini-survey consisted of five questions, which were listed in English, Russian, and Kazakh; and students answered in any of these three languages. The results were transcribed into a digital database by a Syracuse University student research assistant who identified as Azerbaijani, but had family ties in Kazakhstan. Fluent in Russian, Azeri, and English, she translated all results into English. Where Kazakh was used, she used her Azeri skills or when this was insufficient, she consulted with her Kazakh-speaking relatives to secure the best English translation possible.

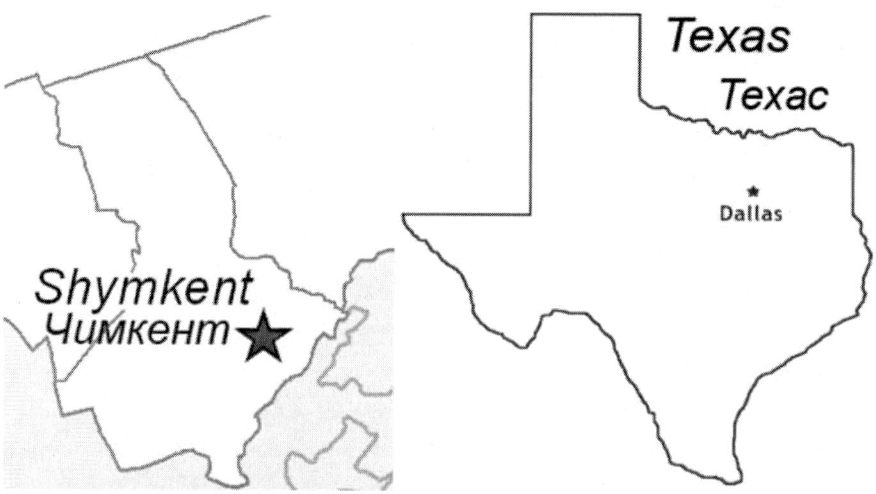

Figure 8.1 Trigger Image for Focus Groups: Map of South Kazakhstan Oblast′ and Map of Texas. *Source*: Natalie R. Koch.

General Attitudes Toward Regional Differences in Kazakhstan

In the large, countrywide survey, there were several questions pertaining to regional disparities that sought to address citizens' perceptions of divisions within Kazakhstan. One question asked respondents to consider whether regional inequalities actually existed in Kazakhstan. Some 72 percent (888) of the respondents replied in the affirmative, with the remaining 28 percent (345) claiming that there are no inequalities on the basis of territorial location. For those answering in the affirmative, they were asked a further question of how they viewed these inequalities on a positive/negative scale (n = 888). As Figure 8.2 illustrates, 72 percent of respondents saw this as either "negative" or "somewhat negative," whereas 10 percent viewed it as "positive" or "somewhat positive," and the remaining 18 percent were neutral.

The next questions pertaining to regional differences asked respondents to consider the most and least desirable places to reside in Kazakhstan. To better contextualize these responses, they were asked how they judged what made locations of residence desirable. The answers, which included the possibility for ranking the top three rationales, are found in Figure 8.3. Economic opportunity is a clear first choice for most participants, with proximity to family and other ancestral ties to the locale appearing to be the second-most common rationale. The natural environment, location, and cultural activities were ranked as somewhat less important factors determining whether some place is deemed a desirable place of residence. Figure 8.4 illustrates the response to the question about the most and least desirable places in Kazakhstan. They show a clear identification of Kazakhstan's southern and western provinces as being least desirable, whereas Astana and the Almaty regions (both the cities themselves, which have a special administrative

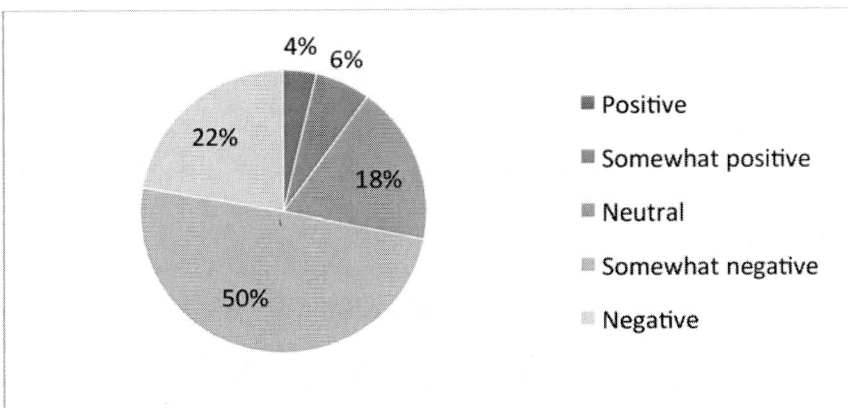

Figure 8.2 Attitude toward regional inequalities. *Source*: Natalie R. Koch.

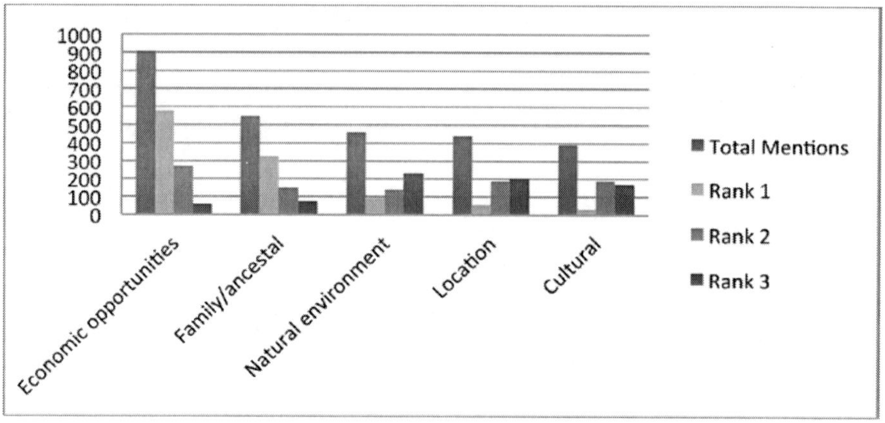

Figure 8.3 What Makes a Place Desirable to Live in? *Source*: Natalie R. Koch.

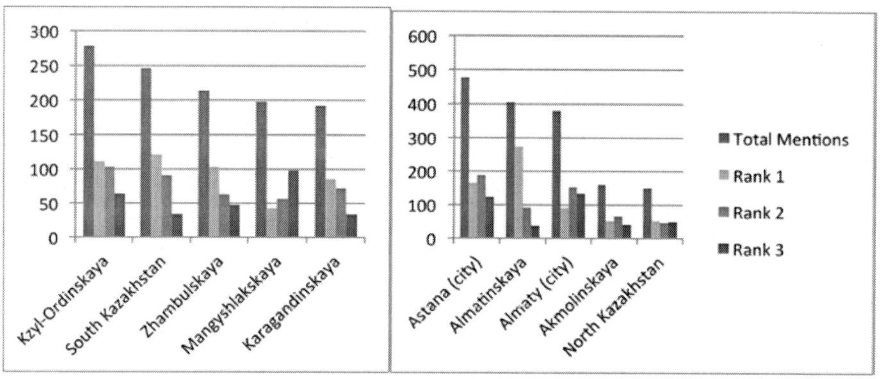

Figure 8.4 Least Desirable (left) and Most Desirable (right) Places of Residence. *Source*: Natalie R. Koch.

status, as well as the regions in which they are situated) come out clearly as the most-favored regions, while North Kazakhstan also ranked among the top five places mentioned.

The last question about state-scale regional differences asked respondents whether there are certain areas of Kazakhstan that they consider unsafe. Only 9.5 percent of the total sample (n = 1233) answered in the affirmative, and those who did were asked to specify where. The top seven responses are shown in Figure 8.5 (n = 117). This question was actually asked out of anticipation that Southern Kazakhstan might surface as a perceived site of danger, but as the graph shows, Semipalatinsk, near the Soviet-era nuclear weapons testing site that still suffers from extensive nuclear contamination, was identified most frequently. Almaty, Kazakhstan's largest city, comes in

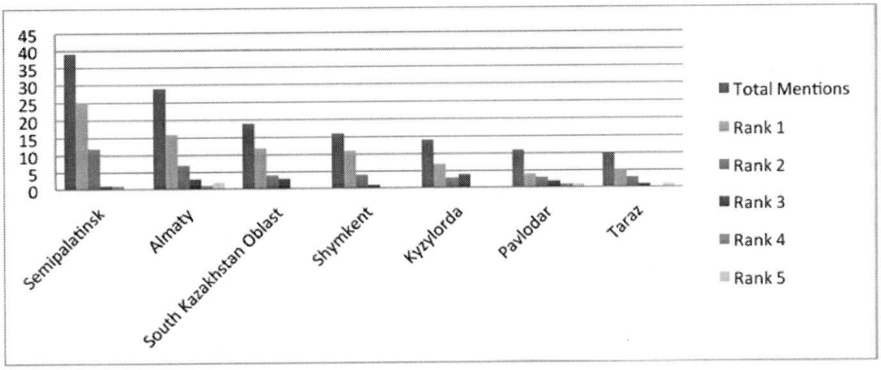

Figure 8.5 Which Parts of Kazakhstan Are Unsafe? *Source*: Natalie R. Koch.

second, only then followed by southern places, including South Kazakhstan *oblast*', Shymkent, Kyzylorda, and Taraz. Besides Semipalatinsk, Pavlodar is the only northern location that was mentioned as a dangerous place (presumably because of its proximity to Semipalatinsk, although this is uncertain).

Interpreting Kazakhstan's "Texas"

Drawing from our ethnographic experiences, focus groups, and the mini-survey, this section introduces some of the common themes in narratives about South Kazakhstan, used by Kazakhstanis of diverse backgrounds. The vast majority of our interlocutors did not come from the region; for example, only 40 of the 406 survey respondents (9.9 percent) were from southern *oblasts* (Kyzylorda, South Kazakhstan, or Zhambul) and of those, seventeen (4.2 percent of the total sample) were from Shymkent. As such, the narratives explored here are predominantly *about* the region, rather than *from* the region. More often than not, our respondents had no direct experience of traveling in South Kazakhstan. Since stereotypes are often *not* based on contact with the group or place being labeled, exploring the narratives of "outsiders" is perhaps the most appropriate method for understanding how region-making is at work in Kazakhstan today.

Like myth and rumor, stereotypes do not operate through rationalist measures of "truth" and "fiction," but rather circulate as second-hand *information*, about which "there is a sort of lethargic indifference, or at least hesitation, about truth and fiction."[35] This indifference is captured succinctly by one focus group participant, who remarked on the credibility of stereotypes about South Kazakhstan with the aphorism: "There's no smoke without a fire" (FG4P5). For this respondent, and many others who were not conflicted by claiming hearsay as actuality, even if unverifiable, the very fact that such stereotypes circulate so widely is deemed proof that they must have some grounding.

In the mini-survey, the first question asked was: "Where are you from? (country, city/town)." As noted above, 9.9 percent came from southern *oblasts*, while 10.8 percent were from western *oblasts* (West Kazakhstan, Atyrau, Aktobe, Magystau), 51 percent from Eastern *oblasts* (East Kazakhstan, Almaty), 10.8 percent from north and central Kazakhstan (North Kazakhstan, Kostanai, Karaganda, Pavlodar, Akmola), 3.4 percent from unspecified regions of Kazakhstan, and 14 percent from abroad. The responses for international respondents were eliminated from the analysis for this section, as our interest lies in how *Kazakhstanis* perceive and articulate regional identities and traits in their homeland. The second question asked: "Do you know about a region here in Kazakhstan known as 'Texas'?" Of all the students surveyed, 90.6 percent affirmed that they did. Question 4 asked: "Which cities/towns are included in 'Texas'?" The answers to this question are mapped in Figure 8.6, showing a clear association with South Kazakhstan, although not exclusively. Beyond this *oblast*', some respondents named other places in the south more generally and, occasionally, Kazakhstan's western regions.

Figure 8.6 Map of Places Mentioned in Response to Question, "Which Cities/Towns Are Included in 'Texas'?" The circular symbol is proportional to the number of mentions. 91.5 percent of the named locations were geo-coded and mapped, 4.5 percent of the named locations were regions (not locales) and not depicted on this map, and the remainder were not locatable. *Source*: Natalie R. Koch.

The remainder of this section considers the answers to Questions 3 and 5, which were related and thus analyzed together: (3) "Why, in your opinion, is this region called 'Texas'?" and (5) "Please describe any cultural attributes/characteristics unique to 'Texas'?" The short answer responses to these questions were coded for common themes, and Table 8.1 indicates the number of times one particular code appeared in any answer. Some single answers might have covered five or six different thematic codes, whereas others might have addressed only one. The table thus indicates the total times a theme was mentioned by all respondents.

Behavior and Mentality

The study participants most frequently emphasized that people from South Kazakhstan have a unique mode of comporting themselves and possess a particular southern "mentality" (*mentalitet*). Respondents would frequently just mention that they have their "own" mentality and behave differently, without specifying what they meant by "different." When respondents were more specific, the most common adjectives included some combination of the following: aggressive, angry, bad-mannered, cheeky, confident, conservative, crazy, dishonest, family-oriented, foxy/cunning/clever (*khidryi*),[36] impudent, impulsive, patriotic, pushy, rude, spirited, talkative, rough, uncivilized, uncultured, unintelligent, violent, and wild. Common nouns included: bumpkins, cowboys, rednecks, *membets*,[37] "cool guys" (*krutye*), and show-offs (*ponty*). For example, one respondent explained that the region is called

Table 8.1 Themes Mentioned by Individual Respondents

Theme	*Count*
Behavior / mentality	169
Culture / traditions / religion	131
Climate	113
Language / dialect	110
"Wild" / crime / gambling	94
Location (South / West)	91
Cars / driving	43
Agriculture / livestock	24
Family / gender / patriarchy	23
Uzbekistan / Uzbek culture	23
Physical appearance / dress	18
Oil / gas	14
Shape of the territory	14
Bride kidnapping	13
Development status	12
Population size (large)	7

Texas "because there are a lot of people who are still living like in villages. As I know, Texas in USA is also the place full of undeveloped personalities (bumpkins)" (student from Almaty). Another illustrated their supposed rudeness through the following example: "They use very unpleasant swearing words like humiliating your mother" (student from Zharkent), or another simply noted: "Abuse of swearing words, especially mother related" (student from Almaty). Indeed, the southern use of foul language was mentioned frequently in the survey, and the region's unique repertoire of curse words is well known around the country.

South Kazakhstanis were also frequently described as being highly entrepreneurial or enterprising, but typically in a bad way. For example, one respondent explained that "they always seek to gain benefit from any relationship (use people in their own interest)" (student from Almaty), while another argued: "People mostly look for profit in anything: it is because of [the] lack of money there" (student from Kazakhstan, unspecified). Or in the words of another:

> People from Shymkent are foxy, they always try to benefit from others. They do "bastard" things very often, especially on the roads. But if they are sitting in governmental organizations, you are really unlucky, because Shymkent people always wish some bribes. (student from Almaty)

The issue of official corruption is discussed below, but this example points to how people from "Kazakhstan's Texas" are often said to be so single-minded in their enterprising spirit, that their behavior becomes downright unsociable and unscrupulous.

While the survey responses coded under the behavior theme were predominantly negative, there were fifteen individual mentions (of 169 total) of regional hospitality and locals' kindness. Oftentimes this was attributed to being an element of traditional Kazakh mores, which is discussed in the following section. Sometimes this more positive stereotyping originated with those from the region, as in the case of one respondent from Shymkent, who wrote, "People in South Kazakhstan are very kind, many of them are religious, students are clever." But this was not always the case, as those offering praise actually came from all over the country—Almaty, Astana, Mangystau, etc. The following survey response is also typical of our ethnographic observations, whereby people explaining the stereotype would first list the negatives and then qualify this with another list of positives: "[They are] impudent, confident, but for some reason they live in good conditions. But I can also mention good parts; they are kind and generous. Actually, it all depends on the person, so we cannot generalize everyone. Some are very, very good" (student from Almaty). Similarly, in one author's interviews in

Astana, a young Kazakh woman in her 20s, Dinara, explained of the stereotypes: "in the South, they are very kind, generous, helpful, open, but they will sell you out for money or any other immediate benefit."

In a few cases, though, respondents were less circumlocutory in the way they sought to temper the negative stereotypes. For example, Dinara's cousin, also a 20-something living in Astana, rejected the negatives by arguing that the stereotype about South Kazakhstan being like Texas "is really just about the people who left [the region] and came to the cities—not about the people living there now. All the people from Shymkent that I know are very nice, but actually, I know some very bad people, who are from Almaty and Astana." For her, being "bad" is not a fair character judgment for people from this region, but can be applied to individuals from all over the country. In other cases, some respondents outrightly refused to speak about the issue, rejecting it as utter nonsense, as in the case of one survey respondent who simply wrote: "It is pure marginalism covered by stupid stereotypes" (student from Karaganda) or another who explained that the region was called Texas "because some stupid guys labeled it so" (student from Almaty).

In one of the focus groups, a young man from Shymkent, who had been highly vocal throughout the discussion, clammed up when the Texas slide was shown. He got visibly agitated and, waving his arms, exclaimed in English, "No comment!" He did interject at a few points, though, to insist that the region's criminal reputation lacks validity and is only a stereotype, and to argue that the Kazakh nation does not have regional differences: "Kazakhstan is altogether Kazakh—all of it, not piece by piece" (FG4P9). Although few of our interlocutors actively negated the stereotype—in no small part, but not entirely, due to the study's methodology—some did seek to present a more positive image of people from "Kazakhstan's Texas." This ambivalence is also reflected in the second and fourth most frequently mentioned themes, culture/religion and language/dialect, which are analyzed together in the following section.

Culture and Language

As noted above, South Kazakhstan is popularly understood to be a bastion of Kazakh tradition, where locals "consider themselves the keepers of Kazakh culture" (student from Almaty). Within this set of narratives, the speaker's positionality is essential to determining whether this was deemed as positive or negative—although our respondents were mostly in accord that this characterization was correct. Some, for example, were clearly not in favor of the southern affinity for Kazakh traditions, evident, for example, in the way that the following respondent codes it as extreme: "People are more concerned with culture [and] traditions in this region and I think that it is even radical" (student from Almaty). On the other hand, some were more clear about their respect for their values: "People there speak only in Kazakh language (I respect them for it)" (student from Almaty). Indeed, in discussing the locals' traditional values, many respondents explicitly framed this in terms of "honoring" or "respecting" traditions and Kazakh culture:

> Shymkent is known as the city where traditions of Kazakh people are *honored* by many people. (student from Shymkent)

> People from Shymkent are very hospitable, they *respect* Kazakh culture more than other Kazakhs in other regions. (student from Astana)

> They *respect* old traditions. (student from Shymkent)

> For me, in Texas live patriots of Kazakhstan, they all *respect* all Kazakh tradition[s]. They really love speaking in Kazakh. (student from Almaty)

Another mode of framing this was to say that people "saved" (*sokhronili*) Kazakh traditions in the face of Russian influence, as in the following set of survey answers:

> It is usually considered that people in Shymkent are different from other region's population in terms of culture. We can say that our history began in this region and of course people in Shymkent are more patriotic and *saved* all the customs and traditions of Kazakhs, and *saved* its cultural identity. (student from Almaty)

> Southern people try to *save* Kazakh culture and language. [This region] differs from others, where Russian language and culture dominate. (student from Shymkent)

> I strongly believe that this region was not under big influence of Russian Empire and USSR. I can say that they tried to *save* almost all traditions and cultural peculiarities. (student from Kazakhstan, unspecified)

> People from south Kazakhstan are more likely to speak Kazakh in contrast with northern Kazakhs. Also, southern people try to know all traditions and customs more than northern [people]. There is no domination of Russians. (student from Kyzylorda)

> We are real Kazakh people. This is [a place of] real and ancient culture of Kazakh people [who] *saved* Turkistan. (student from Shymkent)

Numerous other respondents mentioned the region's many historical buildings and religious/pilgrimage sites, such as the mausoleum of Khoja Ahmed Yasawi in Turkistan, noted in the last quote. These narratives are interesting for the way that they reflect a spatial imaginary about the extension of

Russian colonial power prior to and during Soviet times. As becomes apparent in these quotes, respondents often framed this in terms of the "reach" of Soviet or Russian power. In the case of one focus group discussion, when the moderator asked why South Kazakhstan is commonly said to be more traditional, one participant twice answered: "Because Russia simply didn't reach it (*ne doshla prosto*)" (FG2P9).

Another important element of these narratives is that they tap into ideas about what it means to be a "real Kazakh." Though rarely articulated as explicitly opposed to Russian influence, the "real Kazakh" trope depends precisely on this binary: that there was some more essential Kazakh identity that predated Russian influence. The participants were rarely overly specific about what it meant for those from South Kazakhstan to hold onto "real Kazakh" culture, often stating that they are simply "conservative" or something like the following: "I think people from Texas really keep or try to keep all traditions, our culture and language, compar[ed] to those who live in Astana for example" (student from Almaty). That said, when they did give examples, the most frequently mentioned elements were dress, the prioritization of family, food (especially *shashlik*), holiday celebrations, hospitality, language, patriarchy, and respecting elders.

Figure 8.7 Actors at the Celebration of Nomadic Civilizations in 2011. *Source*: Natalie R. Koch.

The "real Kazakh" narrative also operates on the basis of an urban/rural binary, in that rural areas are understood to be the home of traditional culture. As Natalie was told by her Russian host family in Almaty, who had never traveled to the villages, "You've been to the village, where the 'real' Kazakhs are."[38] This sort of romanticization or exoticization of the rural is pervasive of nationalist imaginaries the world over and is enacted through a wide range of cultural festivities in Kazakhstan.[39] The distinctly rural nationalist "we" is both essentialized and written into the country's urban landscapes through objects such as yurts, which are erected during various national holidays, like Astana Day. Figure 8.7 illustrates this at work in Astana during the "Nomadic Civilizations" celebration during Astana Day 2011. The actors at this event were simply walking around the complex assembled near the Khan Shatyr, to be photographed like the fairy-tale characters roaming about Disneyland—but functioning as exotic symbols of "traditional" Kazakh culture rather than Walt Disney's figures of fantasy.

As orientalist discourses do anywhere, romanticizing Kazakh traditions and culture frequently obscures deeper stigmas and marginalization. This ambivalence is again apparent in how language was discussed in the survey responses. Many simply noted the prevalence of Kazakh language use, which does not come across as an overt critique when it stands alone. However, as

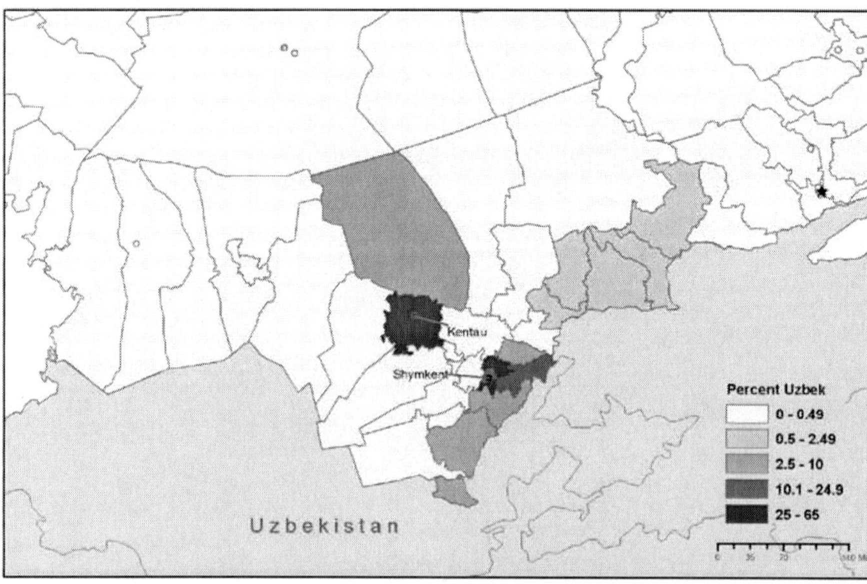

Figure 8.8 Uzbeks as a Percent of Total Raion Population. 2010 census data from the Agency for Statistics of the Republic of Kazakhstan (ASRK 2010). *Source*: Natalie R. Koch.

Nazpary has discussed, speaking Kazakh in the cities in the 1990s was highly stigmatized, since during Soviet times, "Russian language was associated with civilisation, progress and urbanisation and Kazakh was depicted as a backward tribal language (*ne razvityi kochevoi iazyk*)."[40] Although Kazakh language use is far less stigmatized today than it was 20 years ago, it remains a political issue, around which citizens variably articulate their own affinities and claims to modernity. Yet, having an accent from South Kazakhstan is still stigmatized, and numerous respondents remarked upon locals' "unique phrases" (student from Aktan), as well as their unusual pronunciation, slang, and overall dialect. For many, this was seen as a product of Uzbek influence—with the language said to be mixed or in one case, "deformed" (student from Semipalatinsk)—due to the proximity with the Uzbekistan border and the large Uzbek minority there (see Figure 8.8).

Gender relations—particularly *patriarchal* family relations—were noted by various respondents, as well as the practice of bride kidnapping (mentioned by thirteen respondents total), which was suggested to persist in this region alone. Most of these characterizations were negative and coded as signs of regional backwardness. Some examples illustrate this:

> [The] man is domineering in Shymkent families. (student from Shymkent)
>
> Boys [are] not democratic with girls (after marriage, wife should stay at home). (student from Almaty)
>
> They all marry virgins only. All Kazakhs are like this, but sometimes non-virgins are acceptable. But in Shymkent it is shame. (student from Almaty)
>
> Women and men are not treated equally in this area. Men run this area. There is one tradition, which is seen [as] most likely [to occur] in this area, called "abduction of women," where men can steal a woman and make her marry him without her agreement. (student from Almaty)
>
> My mother told me to never marry a guy from Shymkent. The daughter-in-law is not equal to everyone else. If I married [someone from there], I would [be] wearing slippers and serving everyone. (student from Almaty)

These quotes reflect a wide range of anxieties, from gender to class and beyond, but it is interesting to point out that, even though did not collect data about the gender of the respondents, it was clear that women had been warned about the supposed dangers of marrying a man from South Kazakhstan (and more generally any man from the village). Some respondents, though, did mention that "Texas girls are good wives" (student from Almaty), and that a local woman "can be a great house wife, she knows how to cook, very good" (student from Karasai). We cannot say with certainty, but it is likely that these respondents were men, who had been socialized in quite a different manner than their female classmates, who were threatened with loss of status and liberty if they married a "Texas guy."

Lawlessness, Hooligans, and Corruption

In addition to the first theme about South Kazakhstanis' "unique" behavior and mentality, many respondents explicitly referenced the region's "high criminal rate" and the fact that it is heavily populated with "cowboys," "as in Texas's movies, *Wild Wild West!*" (student from Pavlodar). When they specified the shape of local criminality, respondents would mention theft, murder, gun violence, fighting, bribery and official corruption, driving violations, drug use, gambling, and the prevalence of "gangsters." This was also observed in the other methods we employed, including our informal interviews and the focus groups. For example, when asked about negative stereotypes of Shymkent, one focus group discussion proceeded as follows:

> *FG3P6:* Lawlessness!
>
> *FG3P2:* [It is a] dangerous region, criminal region.
>
> *FG3P1:* Yes, very dangerous.
>
> *FG3P4:* Why do they call it Texas?
>
> *FG3P3:* Because there are gangsters there.
>
> *FG3P9:* Gangsters have been preserved in Texas like a tradition.

In addition to simple attributions of South Kazakhstan being "the most dangerous state in the country" and characterized by "lawlessness" (*bespredel*), some would describe how laws are simply not respected or circumvented, as in the following example:

> They have "cool grass" [weed] and there it's like characters of westerns: power dominates law, not the civil law. This may be some informal truth… In "Texas": (1) If something is "not allowed" (for example after the restaurant closes, to go inside and have dinner), but [if] "you really want to" then you can. (2) Law functions through "fairness" according to the situation. (student from Almaty)

Other respondents noted the use—or abuse—of family connections to secure one's desired ends, such as getting a government job. Similar to John Agnew's description of the Northern Italian conflation of Sicilians and *Mafiosi*, there is a sense in these narratives about other parts of Kazakhstan experiencing "a veritable invasion of criminal elements whose presence

Figure 8.9 Drawing of One Survey Respondent, Depicting a Man from "Kazakhstan's Texas" and His Car. *Source*: Kristopher White.

corrupts the local fibers of what is left of a healthy body politic."[41] This sense of "contamination" is a longstanding point of concern for the former Russified elites of Kazakhstan since independence, and it is often narrated through the alleged "takeover" of government positions by southerners.[42] This was apparent in a few responses in this study, however the corruption of order on Kazakhstan's *roads* was discussed far more by our respondents. Students—mostly those from Almaty as in the following examples—consistently emphasized that "people from Shymkent [. . .] don't know how to drive a car. On the road they are really ill-bred." They were also said to "drive the car like insane people," have an "Inability to drive normally," and that "drivers from 'Texas' are considered to be the worst." People could identify drivers from Shymkent because of their license place, which used to (until very recently) begin with the letter "X." Some people indeed saw this very letter as the connection with the label "Texas," though it is perhaps more frequently connected with another term for people from Shymkent: "X-men" (see Figure 8.9).

Figure 8.9 is also of interest because of the clear racialization of this apparently criminally-minded man: he looks far more "Asian" than how most Kazakhs are popularly portrayed. As Table 8.1 indicates, there were various mentions of peoples' physical appearance—"black color of faces," "dark faces," "black color eyes"—and sometimes their cleanliness—"dirty people" (all students from Almaty). In general, though, explicit racism was largely absent from the accounts we collected. That said, our respondents were far more comfortable openly insulting individuals from South Kazakhstan through jabs at Uzbeks. As Nazpary has also suggested, southerners and villagers are "seen as being closer in culture and manners to Uzbeks (versus Almatians as closer to Russians)" and that all the negative characteristics explored here "are often ascribed by urban Kazakhs to Uzbeks."[43] One focus group discussion about "Texans" illustrates this:

Moderator: But on the other hand, they are viewed with caution. Why?

FG5P5: They cheat [*obmanyvayut*].

Moderator: Why—cheating?

FG5P5: They associate [*svyzalis'*] with Uzbeks.

[men in the group laugh together]

Moderator: It is influence of the Uzbeks, huh?

FG5P4: Well it's a border; it was always restless and it simply stayed that way.

Moderator: "It stayed that way." And everyone thinks so?

FG5P5: They are cunning [*khidryye*].

Moderator: Craftiness [*khidrost'*]—is it a trick they developed from trade?

FG5P5: They learned it from Uzbeks.

This alleged absorption of criminal or "foxy" behaviors from Uzbeks is based not just on spatial proximity, but actual association and interaction: "In my opinion their culture attributes are influenced by Uzbek people. Because many of them are foxy as Uzbeks" (student from Aktau). Or as another student explained: "In 'Texas' there are Uzbeks, since Uzbekistan is closer to the region. This brings to the idea that there is language deformation, Kazakh culture deformation, as well [as] very developed corruption!" (student from Semipalatinsk). By relegating these negative characteristics to a particular *space,* these narratives are indicative of a broader phenomenon that Jansson

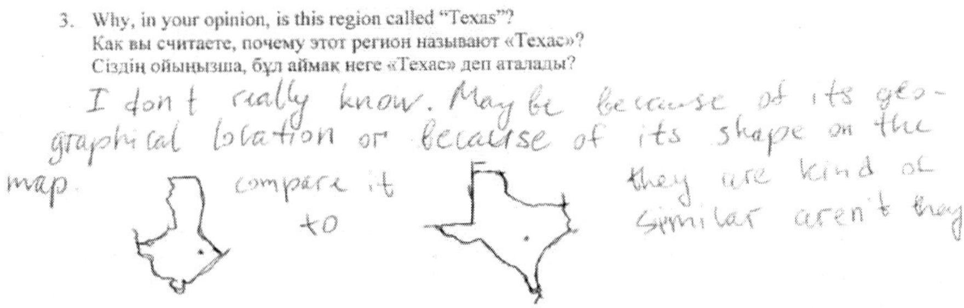

Figure 8.10 Example of One Answer Specifying Territorial Shape as a Reason for the Name Association. *Source*: Kristopher White.

describes as "spatializing" or "regionalizing" undesirable traits.[44] Johnson and Coleman develop this idea by exploring how places of internal otherness are not only constructed as repositories or spatial containers of backwardness, but that they consequently come to be seen as "impediments to national progress."[45] As such, by "hierarchicizing space" in this manner, "internal orientalist discourse represents a subordinate section of the state in a particular (unflattering) way so as to produce a national (i.e., state-scale) identity with desirable characteristics."[46] By writing off the ills of lawlessness, criminality, foxiness, and all manner of anti-social behavior, Kazakhstanis assert their own commitment to a particular vision of legality and honesty. Whether it is a "real" commitment is neither verifiable nor particularly relevant: such rhetoric is more about narrating one's own self as a reverent and truly *civil* subject.

Climate, Landscapes, Location, and Shape

We recognize that in many cases, our respondents were merely unsure about the origin of the South Kazakhstan–Texas connection. In fact, there were 112 discrete mentions of the phrase "I don't know" in the entire survey. Many were followed by an effort to come to some conclusion, but the expression of uncertainty was apparently important for speakers to qualify their statements and refuse authority on the matter. Figure 8.10 gives an example of precisely this—as well as illustrating the last theme we will briefly mention: explaining the Texas connection through physical geographic similarities. These answers—found through all our methods—were dominated by references to the heat and climate, desert landscape, location along the country's southern border, and the similar shape of the two territories' outline as viewed on a map.

As Koch discusses in her analysis of narratives about Kazakhstan's capital change, the most common answers to the survey question of why the capital was moved was Almaty's location is in a dangerous earthquake zone.[47]

She argues that this answer was likely selected frequently because it reflects an official narrative, but that of the many official reasons given by President Nazarbayev and his discursive machine, "This is arguably the most depoliticized: the move is constructed as something that had to be done for safety and on the basis of 'objective' physical geographic facts."[48] Writing off highly political questions to an issue of physical geography certainly has the power to diffuse potentially inflammatory discussions, and there were surely study participants who found this to be a quick way to dismiss our questioning. But once ideas like this start to circulate, people do also come to believe that physical geography is the explanatory factor. Of course, this leads to a sticky, ultimately unresolvable "which came first, the chicken or the egg" question, but in any case, these narratives were the least political tack a respondent could take.

DISCUSSION AND CONCLUSIONS: SPATIALIZING INTOLERANCE

In this chapter, we have argued that explaining why South Kazakhstan is called "Texas" is a political process, through which ordinary Kazakhstanis articulate situated geographical imaginaries about the independent state and its socio-cultural divides. Moving beyond the hitherto prevailing focus on the country's "Russian"/"Kazakh" divide and looking to divisions internal to the Kazakh nation, this study has been informed by the recent literature about how national identity formation occurs through discourses that need not be physically performed at international borders—that it is far more diffuse and connected to wider territorial imaginaries.[49] Although we have focused primarily on narratives about the region from actors with little or no contact with the place, we have noted that Shymkentsy are not irrelevant actors in this discourse. Rather, as Jansson also notes in his work on the U.S. South, many from the region seek to advance their own representations of the region.[50] Some no doubt strategically mobilize the Texas metaphor—extending it, and bringing it to life—whereas others may seek to actively negate it or seek to ascribe South Kazakhstan more positive traits. Furthermore, as Kazakhstanis are increasingly on the move in the years since independence, they are interacting more with their compatriots from different regions of the country.[51] For some, this has led to the break-down of certain stereotypes, whereas for others, it has led to their entrenchment.

Regions "are perpetually 'becoming' instead of just 'being,'" and as we noted in the introduction, the very act of defining a region is an act of power.[52] Regions, produced through the likes of popular metaphors like the Texas analogy, are, in Paasi's felicitous expression, "structures of expectations," which "are the basis for the narratives of identity, mobilisation of collective memory, and they also constitute the visible and invisible social 'gel' based on values, norms and ideologies."[53] As this case study illustrates, the modes of characterizing South Kazakhstan do indeed structure the expectations of ordinary citizens. Though they are far from static, popular imaginaries about Kazakhstan's internal divisions—both spatial and social—are still informed by certain binaries about rural/southern backwardness and urban/northern modernity. And yet, through ostensibly "innocuous" forms of expression, such as joking that Kazakhstan has its own Texas, speakers employing this narrative to denigrate certain internal others are spatializing their intolerance. By shifting the locus of criticism from an individual person to an abstract region, the act of spatializing intolerance obscures their outright prejudice. The veil of humor is assumed to obscure this ill-natured intolerance. And yet, this veil is readily transparent, and none of our interlocutors from Shymkent would be convinced that being called a Texan is a badge of honor, even if it is "just a joke."

NOTES

1. Thank you to Farida Tosayeva for her assistance on this project. From 2013–2014, this research was assisted by a Social Sciences Research Council Post-doctoral Fellowship for Transregional Research with funds provided by the Andrew W. Mellon Foundation, as well as a Central Asia Fellowship from the University of Helsinki's Aleksanteri Institute. Research from 2009–2012 was supported by the U.S. National Science Foundation (NSF) under Grant No. 1003836, as well as an NSF Graduate Research Fellowship, an NSF Nordic Research Opportunity grant, an IREX Individual Advanced Research Opportunity Grant, and a U.S. State Department Title VIII Grant for work at the University of Illinois Summer Research Laboratory on Russia, Eastern Europe, and Eurasia. Any opinions, findings, and conclusions or recommendations expressed in this material are those of the authors and do not necessarily reflect the views of the National Science Foundation, or any other granting organization. Any faults, errors, or omissions are those of the authors.

2. Jessica Allina-Pisano, "How to Tell an Axe Murderer: An Essay on Ethnography, Truth, and Lies," in *Political Ethnography: What Immersion Contributes to the Study of Power*, ed. Edward Schatz (Chicago: University of Chicago Press, 2009), 68–69.

3. David Laitin, *Identity in Formation: The Russian-Speaking Populations in the near Abroad* (Ithaca, NY: Cornell University Press, 1998).

4. For example Shonin Anacker, "Geographies of Power in Nazarbayev's Astana," *Eurasian Geography & Economics* 45, no. 7 (2004): 515–533; Jeff Chinn and Robert Kaiser, *Russians as the New Minority: Ethnicity and Nationalism in the Soviet Successor States* (Boulder, CO: Westview, 1996); Sally Cummings, *Kazakhstan: Power and the Elite* (New York: Palgrave Macmillan, 2005); Bhavna Dave, *Kazakhstan: Ethnicity, Language, and Power* (New York: Routledge, 2007); Robert

Kaiser, "Nations and Homelands in Soviet Central Asia," in *Geographic Perspectives on Soviet Central Asia*, eds. R.A. Lewis, R.R. Churchill, and A. Tate (New York: Routledge, 1992), 279–312; Robert Kaiser, "Ethnic Demography and Interstate Relations in Central Asia," in *National Identity and Ethnicity in Russia and the New States of Eurasia*, ed. Roman Szporluk (Armonk, NY: M.E. Sharpe, 1994), 230–265; Robert Kaiser, *The Geography of Nationalism in Russia and the USSR* (Princeton, NJ: Princeton University Press, 1994); Sebastien Peyrouse, "Nationhood and the Minority Question in Central Asia: The Russians in Kazakhstan," *Europe-Asia Studies* 59, no. 3 (2007): 481–501; Edward Schatz, "What Capital Cities Say about State and Nation Building," *Nationalism and Ethnic Politics* 9, no. 4 (2004): 111–140; Richard Wolfel, "North to Astana: Nationalistic Motives for the Movement of the Kazakh(Stani) Capital," *Nationalities Papers* 30, no. 3 (2002): 485–506; Zharmukhamed Zardykhan, "Russians in Kazakhstan and Demographic Change: Imperial Legacy and the Kazakh Way of Nation Building," *Asian Ethnicity* 5, no. 1 (2004): 61–79.

5. Kathleen Collins, *Clan Politics and Regime Transformation in Central Asia* (New York: Cambridge University Press, 2006); Edward Schatz, *Modern Clan Politics: The Power of "Blood" in Kazakhstan and Beyond* (Seattle: University of Washington Press, 2004).

6. For example Fredrik Barth, *Ethnic Groups and Boundaries: The Social Organization of Cultural Difference* (Boston: Little, Brown, 1969); Ernest Gellner, *Nations and Nationalism* (Ithaca, NY: Cornell University Press, 1983); David Knight, "Identity and Territory: Geographical Perspectives on Nationalism and Regionalism," *Annals of the Association of American Geographers* 72, no. 4 (1982): 514–531; Sankaran Krishna, "Cartographic Anxiety: Mapping the Body Politic in India," *Alternatives* 19, no. 4 (1994): 507–521; Anssi Paasi, *Territories, Boundaries, and Consciousness: The Changing Geographies of the Finnish-Russian Boundary* (New York: J. Wiley & Sons, 1996); Colin Williams and Anthony Smith, "The National Construction of Social Space," *Progress in Human Geography* 7, no. 4 (1983): 502–518.

7. David Jansson, "Internal Orientalism in America: W.J. Cash's the Mind of the South and the Spatial Construction of American National Identity," *Political Geography* 22, no. 3 (2003): 296.

8. Paasi, *Territories, Boundaries, and Consciousness*, 55.

9. Paasi, *Territories, Boundaries, and Consciousnes*, 64.

10. For example Dru C. Gladney, "Representing Nationality in China: Refiguring Majority/Minority Identities," *Journal of Asian Studies* 53, no. 1 (1994): 92–123; Gabriel Piterberg, "Domestic Orientalism: The Representation of 'Oriental' Jews in Zionist/Israeli Historiography," *British Journal of Middle Eastern Studies* 23, no. 2 (1996): 125–145; Louisa Schein, "Gender and Internal Orientalism in China," *Modern China* 23, no. 1 (1997): 69–98.

11. John Agnew, "Italy's Island Other: Sicily's History in the Modern Italian Body Politic," *Emergences: Journal for the Study of Media & Composite Cultures* 10, no. 2 (2000): 301–311; Militsa Bakić-Hayden, "Nesting Orientalisms: The Case of Former Yugoslavia," *Slavic Review* 54, no. 4 (1995): 917–931; Anthony Cardoza, "'Making Italians'? Cycling and National Identity in Italy: 1900–1950," *Journal of Modern Italian Studies* 15, no. 3 (2010): 354–377; Antonio Gramsci, "Some Aspects of the Southern Question," in *Selections from Political Writings (1921–1926)* (1926),

ed. Q. Hoare (London: Lawrence and Wishart, 1978), 441–462; Corey Johnson and Amanda Coleman, "The Internal Other: Exploring the Dialectical Relationship between Regional Exclusion and the Construction of National Identity," *Annals of the Association of American Geographers* 102, no. 4 (2011): 863–880.

12. Jansson, "Internal Orientalism in America"; David Jansson, "'A Geography of Racism': Internal Orientalism and the Construction of American National Identity in the Film Mississippi Burning," *National Identities* 7, no. 3 (2005): 265–285; David Jansson, "The Evil Empire Within: Southern Nationalism and the Washington Problem," in *Nation Within a Nation: The American South and the Federal Government*, ed. G. Feldman (Gainesville: University Press of Florida, 2014), 205–226; Mark E. Nackman, *A Nation Within a Nation: The Rise of Texas Nationalism* (Port Washington: Kennikat Press, 1975).

13. Tim Oakes, "China's Provincial Identities: Reviving Regionalism and Reinventing Chineseness," *Journal of Asian Studies* 59, no. 3 (2000): 667–692.

14. Jansson, "Internal Orientalism in America," 300; Johnson and Coleman, "The Internal Other," 864.

15. Agnew, "Italy's Island Other"; Jansson "Internal Orientalism in America."

16. Natalie Koch, "Bordering on the Modern: Power, Practice and Exclusion in Astana," *Transactions of the Institute of British Geographers* 39, no. 3 (2014): 432–443.

17. Johnson and Coleman, "The Internal Other," 868.

18. Anssi Paasi, "Regions and Regional Dynamics," in *The Sage Handbook of European Studies*, ed. C. Rumford (Los Angeles: SAGE, 2009), 471; Anssi Paasi, "The Resurgence of the 'Region' and 'Regional Identity': Theoretical Perspectives and Empirical Observations on Regional Dynamics in Europe," *Review of International Studies* 35, SupplementS1 (2009): 133.

19. Adam Nossiter, "Remembering Biafra: 'There Was a Country,' by Chinua Achebe," *New York Times*, November 1, 2012, accessed November 6, 2013, http://www.nytimes.com/2012/11/04/books/review/there-was-a-country-by-chinua-achebe.html.

20. Barry Popik, "Texas of Canada (Alberta province nickname)," *The Big Apple*, 1997, accessed November 6, 2013, http://www.barrypopik.com/index.php/new_york_city/entry/texas_of_canada_alberta_province_nickname/.

21. Charlie Mayer, "Welcome to Mongolia, the Texas of Asia," National Public Radio, November 14, 2005, accessed November 6, 2013, http://www.npr.org/templates/story/story.php?storyId=5012347.

22. Koch, "Bordering on the Modern," 437.

23. Robert Crews, *For Prophet and Tsar: Islam and Empire in Russia and Central Asia* (Cambridge, MA: Harvard University Press, 2006); Adeeb Khalid, "Backwardness and the Quest for Civilization: Early Soviet Central Asia in Comparative Perspective," *Slavic Review* 65, no. 2 (2006): 231–251; Joma Nazpary, *Post-Soviet Chaos: Violence and Dispossession in Kazakhstan* (London: Pluto Press, 2002).

24. Michael Billig, *Banal Nationalism* (Thousand Oaks, CA: Sage, 1995), 81.

25. Nursultan Nazarbaev, "Strategy 2030: Prosperity, Security and Ever Growing Welfare of All the Kazakhstanis." Official Site of the President of the Republic of Kazakhstan, 1997, accessed October 13, 2010, http://www.akorda.kz/en/kazakhstan/kazakhstan2030/strategy_2030.

26. On the Soviet articulation of the town-country divide, see Catherine Cooke, "Russian Responses to the Garden City Idea," *Architectural Review* 163 (1978): 353–363; N.A. Miliùtin, *Sotsgorod: The Problem of Building Socialist Cities* (Cambridge, MA: MIT Press, 1974).

27. Catherine Alexander, "Waste under Socialism and after: A Case Study from Almaty," in *Enduring Socialism: Explorations of Revolution and Transformation, Restoration and Continuation*, eds. H.G. West and P. Raman (New York: Berghahn Books, 2009), 148–168; Koch, "Bordering on the Modern"; Mateusz Laszczkowski, "Superplace: Global Connections and Local Politics at the Mega Mall, Astana," *Etnofoor* 23, no. 1 (2011): 85–104; Mateusz Laszczkowski, *"City of the Future": Built Space, Modernity, and Urban Change in Astana* (New York: Berghahn Books, 2016); Nazpary, *Post-Soviet Chaos*; Saulesh Yessenova, "'Routes and Roots' of Kazakh Identity: Urban Migration in Postsocialist Kazakhstan," *Russian Review* 64, no. 4 (2005): 661–679; Saulesh Yessenova, *The Politics and Poetics of the Nation: Urban Narratives of Kazakh Identity* (Saarbrücken: LAP Lambert Academic Publishing, 2010).

28. Alexander, "Waste under Socialism and after," 155.

29. Alexander, "Waste under Socialism and after," 155.

30. Nazpary, *Post-Soviet Chaos*, 166.

31. George Lakoff and Mark Johnson, *Metaphors We Live by* (Chicago: University of Chicago Press, 1980), 3.

32. Lakoff and Johnson, *Metaphors We Live by*, 157.

33. Jansson, "Internal Orientalism in America," 297; Edward Said, *Orientalism* (New York: Pantheon Books, 1978).

34. Natalie Koch, "Kazakhstan's Changing Geopolitics: The Resource Economy and Popular Attitudes about China's Growing Regional Influence," *Eurasian Geography and Economics* 54, no. 1 (2013): 110–133.

35. Paul Veyne, *Did the Greeks Believe in Their Myths? An Essay on the Constitutive Imagination* (Chicago: University of Chicago Press, 1988), 27; see also Harry G. West and Todd Sanders, *Transparency and Conspiracy: Ethnographies of Suspicion in the New World Order* (Durham, NC: Duke University Press, 2003); Luise White, *Speaking with Vampires: Rumor and History in Colonial Africa* (Berkeley: University of California Press, 2000).

36. The word *khidryi* has no easy English translation, so the variable use of foxy, cunning, or clever generally reflects this Russian adjective, which is used heavily to describe people from South Kazakhstan.

37. According to Nazpary, *membet* is a derogatory term for a "stupid and backward Kazakh from the *aul*" (i.e., village) and generally connotes the same set of negative character traits explored here, such as "being religious, traditional, backward, rich, cunning, Mafioso, violent, patriarchal, dishonest, bigoted." See, *Post-Soviet Chaos*, 169–170.

38. Author's fieldnotes, 2010.

39. Raymond Williams, *The Country and the City* (New York: Oxford University Press, 1973).

40. Nazpary, *Post-Soviet Chaos*, 156.

41. Agnew, "Italy's Island Other," 307.

42. See Koch, "Bordering on the Modern."

43. Nazpary, *Post-Soviet Chaos*, 169.

44. Jansson, "Internal Orientalism in America," 38.

45. Johnson and Coleman, "The Internal Other," 865.

46. John Agnew, *Geopolitics: Re-Visioning World Politics* (New York: Routledge, 2003), 21; Jansson, "Internal Orientalism in America," 297.

47. Natalie Koch, "The 'Heart' of Eurasia? Kazakhstan's Centrally Located Capital City," *Central Asian Survey* 32, no. 2 (2013): 134–147.

48. Koch, "The 'Heart' of Eurasia?" 143.

49. Anssi Paasi, "A *Border Theory*: An Unattainable Dream or a Realistic Aim for Border Scholars?" in *The Ashgate Research Companion to Border Studies*, ed. D. Wastl-Walter (Burlington: Ashgate, 2010), 11–31; Madeleine Reeves, "The Time of the Border: Contingency, Conflict, and Popular Statism at the Kyrgyzstan-Uzbekistan Boundary," in *Ethnographies of the State in Central Asia: Performing Politics*, eds. M. Reeves, J. Rasanayagam, and J. Beyer (Bloomington: Indiana University Press, 2013), 198–220; Madeleine Reeves, *Border Work: Spatial Lives of the State in Rural Central Asia* (Ithaca, NY: Cornell University Press, 2014).

50. Jansson, "Internal Orientalism in America," 312.

51. Yessenova, "Routes and Roots."

52. Paasi, "The Resurgence of the 'Region' and 'Regional Identity,'" 133.

53. Paasi, "The Resurgence of the 'Region' and 'Regional Identity,'" 133.

Part III

THE SOCIETY: NEGOTIATING CULTURAL CHANGES

Chapter 9

Building a Muslim Nation

The Role of the Central Mosque of Astana

Alima Bissenova

Astana's new Haziret Sultan mosque is one of the most magnificent and well-planned buildings in Astana. Named after the well-known Central Asian saint Ahmed Yassawi, who lived in the twelfth century and whose mausoleum is located and venerated in the city of Turkistan in Southern Kazakhstan, it was designed by a pair of Turkish and Kazakh architects, built by the Turkish "Sembol" company,[1] and officially opened on July 6, 2012, which is both Astana Day and the birthday of President Nursultan Nazarbayev. The mosque and its surrounding plaza are the most visited parts of Independence Square, which also includes the 90-meter-high Kazakh Eli monument, the Palace of Independence, the Shabyt Palace of Arts, and the Pyramid designed by the famous British architect Norman Foster. The mosque is located across the street from the Pyramid, which houses the Institute of Peace and Harmony and the Assembly of the People of Kazakhstan, and from to the gated and fortified building of the U.S. Embassy in Kazakhstan.

Haziret Sultan is the most-visited public building in the vicinity and the most accessible. On ordinary days, Independence Square is quite deserted, but there are always people going in and out of the mosque. The mosque itself has six entrances—the main, great-arched entrance, the women's entrance, the entrance for shops and offices, the entrance leading to the Qur'an reading room (*Qur'an oqytu*), the entrance for the ritual service of *neke,*[2] and one for the restaurant. On any given day, at least four entrances of the mosque are open, two entrances (to men's and women's prayer areas) remain open all night, and all six are open for Friday prayer. Unlike most public buildings in Astana, including the others at Independence Square, one does not have to show identification or to get a pass/ticket to get inside. Security guards at the entrance might ask you to remove your shoes before you step on the carpets or inquire about the purpose of your visit and then guide you to your destination within the mosque, but no document check is performed, and everybody is allowed into the mosque upon request.

According to the mosque certificate of occupancy (*tekhpasport*), a copy of which was shown to me by naib (deputy) imam, who has been part of the mosque administration since 2011, it has a praying space of 5,000 square meters, which translates into a capacity for 5,000 people (one square meter per praying person). However, as the same naib imam explained to me—and as I myself witnessed on several occasions, the capacity of the mosque can be increased by turning the building's many other spacious rooms and halls into prayer areas.[3] For instance, the halls of the second floor, where offices are located, are converted in this matter on holidays and some Friday prayers. Unlike other mosques in Astana, including the Nur-Astana Mosque built downtown in 2007, the enormous size of Haziret Sultan ensures that nobody has to pray outside during the cold months.[4]

The Haziret Sultan mosque also features a huge parking lot designed to accommodate 950 cars, which makes it easily the second-largest open parking area around a building in the city (after Khan Shatyr). However, even with such an enormous parking venue, getting the car in and out of the mosque area for Friday prayer remains an ordeal that needs additional regulation: a special unit of the traffic police directs traffic before and after the Friday prayer.

The official story of the construction of the mosque is complicated. Unlike the Nur-Astana Mosque, which is known as a "gift" from the emir of Qatar, Haziret Sultan was state-planned and largely state-funded from the very beginning. Any building constructed downtown on the Left Bank has to be approved by the Architectural Council under the president and, needless to say, erecting a mosque in the symbolic center of the nation—near the Kazakh Eli Monument—could not happen without the approval of the highest authorities, including the Architectural Council under the president and President Nazarbayev himself.

This well-planned site is one of the signs of the rapprochement between the state and Islam in the third decade of independence. However, the étatization of Islam goes beyond making the mosque part of the national landscape and a state-sanctioned public space. In many ways, the central mosque, like the other mosques in Astana, has turned into a state ideological apparatus; and in this function, it has been more efficient than many official state organs charged with promoting statist ideology.

RAPPROCHEMENT BETWEEN THE STATE AND ISLAM

Cooperation between the state and the Muslim community in Kazakhstan springs from mutual understanding and interest rather than Soviet-style control and rigid authoritarian state imposition. The state, in its quest to create its own public from which to generate support, realizes that it is far better to ride the wave of Islamic revival for its own purpose than to try and suppress it.[5]

That is why state authorities fund religious education in state-approved institutions at home and abroad and support religious enculturation of the masses at mosques. As evident from the first forum of imams (see Figure 9.1) held at the Pyramid on February 19, 2015, under the auspices of the Religious Board of the Muslims of Kazakhstan (DUMK)[6] but with explicit support from the Presidential Administration and the Committee on Religious Affairs, the state creates conditions for imams to advance and develop themselves by acquiring cultural capital and religious expertise and expects them to take on leadership roles in their communities.[7] For their part, the religious establishment and a wider religious community also aspire to fit into the state's modernizing project and to occupy a comfortable niche in the public realm in order to avoid accusations of "Islamic extremism," "backwardness," and "archaism." Like the situation of "too much honey" described by Maria Louw in her piece on the revival of Islam in Kyrgyzstan, in Kazakhstan too there exists resentment of growing Islamicization and the fear of the encroachment of Islamic customs and lifestyles on secular state institutions and a secular

Figure 9.1 Forum of Imams Held in the Palace of Peace and Harmony (Pyramid). *Source*: Alima Bissenova.

public.[8] The 2011 Law on Religious Activities that prohibited having (previously existing and mainly Muslim) prayer rooms in state offices and in public universities is a reflection of some of the fears of "excessive" expression of religiosity in public space.[9]

The issues concerning the role of Islam in social life are not bottled up—they are open for public debate, and arguments about competing (Islamic and secular) moral frameworks take place in a variety of forums, ranging from parliament to Facebook. For instance, one of the most visible issues around which different types of ideological persuasions mobilize is the phenomenon of polygamy, which continues to exist in the "gray" area between the secular legal framework that does not recognize it and religious and customary frameworks where instances of polygamous marriages are known and tacitly accepted. There have been several attempts to legalize polygamy in the Majlis—the lower chamber of parliament—starting from 2001 and most recently in 2013, but all have been thwarted by the parliamentary majority. In addition, there has been public outcry in the media and on the Internet against the normalization of polygamous relationships. For instance, a group of women bloggers have formed the so-called Anti-tokal'nyi Komitet (*Tokal* in Kazakh means the second wife, or the third, the fourth and so on); so one of the goals of the committee, at least at its inception in 2013, was to publicly criticize the phenomenon and shame the women who agree to polygamous relations.

Notably, during the fifteen months I observed at the Haziret Sultan mosque, following the sermons in person and on the Internet,[10] I never heard the imams leading the sermon take a stance for polygamy in the pulpit, even though family issues—marriage, divorce, responsibility of relatives toward each other, respect toward the parents, and so on—comprised about half of the topics discussed in the mosque. On most of the issues the message was quite conservative and in accordance with the teachings of the Qur'an and Sunna.[11] I also know that *aqad nikahs* (marriage vows or contracts) without state registration (including *aqad nikahs* for the second marriage if there is a written note from the first wife permitting second marriage) do take place in the mosque. But most likely the requirements of self-censorship of public speech and political correctness are much more pressing for the central mosque of Astana than for other mosques across the country—hence the silence on this important social issue, as well as on the important issue of hijab, which, while not prohibited in Kazakhstan, has remained an issue of contention between different parts of the public and even between different state organs. There have been instances when particular schools and university administrations, acting on the opinion of certain officials from the Ministry of Education, did not allow the wearing of headscarves in the classrooms. None of these verbal statements, however, made it into any legislatively endorsed prohibition. Eventually, in response to one case in Karaganda where a school director asked students to remove their hijabs, Minister of Justice Rashid Tusupbekov (also a former chair of the Highest Court Council and a former chief prosecutor) officially decreed that "Kazakhstani legislation does not stipulate any limitation on wearing hijab in educational institutions."[12]

While these issues of contention have not been tackled in public sermons, I was told by several imams and several mosque frequenters that they are often addressed in more "private" gatherings in the mosque such as "circles" with imams after the evening prayer and in face-to-face question-and-answer sessions. I asked one of the naib imams directly about their silence on such important issues as polygamy and hijab, and he replied that no good would come from stirring the public sentiment by making officials pronouncements to the whole country that would encourage Muslim women to wear hijab en masse and/or condone different types of polygamous marriages. However, the same naib imam emphasized that they are always there for the people who are living out these issues (related to hijab or polygamy) themselves and are ready to support them. While Astana imams continue to be more conservative "in private" with their trusted followers and more cautious in their "public" speeches and appearances, it is also a fact that Haziret Sultan and other centrally located Astana mosques are quite unique in their liberal decorum and

Figure 9.2 At the Entrance to the Women's Changing Room at the Haziret Sultan Mosque in Astana. *Source*: Alima Bissenova.

attempts to fit into the prevailing secular framework. The mosque has a women's dressing room outfitted with gowns and scarves (see Figure 9.2), which, while being super-convenient for female visitors of the mosque, also allows them to continue their secular lives outside and comfortably change in the

Figure 9.3 The Regular "Circle" with the Imam de jour (kezekshi Imam) after the Evening Prayer in Haziret Sultan. The view from the women's balcony. *Source*: Alima Bissenova.

religiously appropriate attire only when entering the mosque. This seems to be the overall atmosphere of the Haziret Sultan mosque—the mosque is comfortable for its parishioners—comfortable to park at, comfortable to change, spacious, with soft carpets on the floor inviting you to rest from the busy life outside—read, work on your laptop, or have conversation with the imam sitting in the "circle" after the evening prayer (see Figure 9.3).[13] The whole aura of the mosque helps to present Islam in Kazakhstan as a modern phenomenon suitable for modern life and contributing to the advancement of the individual and the whole society along the path of modernity.

ESTABLISHING ORTHODOXY: BETWEEN "GOOD" AND "BAD" ISLAM

Like many governments across the region and even the globe, Kazakhstan's government is also implicated in adopting the rhetoric of the global "war on terror" and contrasting "bad" extremist Islam with "good" moderate Islam.[14] While what is "bad" Islam is more or less clear—the Islam practiced by those who commit or condone terrorist acts, "good" Islam remains undefined. It is not an easy job to try to establish the body of "good" Islam that is clearly based on doctrinal principles yet simultaneously acceptable to the socio-political norms of "already existing" Muslim societies and Muslim-majority states. In his book on Islam in post-Soviet Uzbekistan, Johan Rasayanagam termed this predicament the "Imam's dilemma" when, for instance, Uzbek imams have to navigate between orthodoxy and state-promoted *ziyarat* (saint tomb visitation) practices.[15] Unlike neighboring Uzbekistan, however, Kazakhstan's government is not engaged in an all-out witch hunt for "Wahhabis"—a loaded term that groups all people who practice Islam differently from how it is prescribed by the state authorities—but they do not seek to establish the Caliphate and do not have other "anti-constitutional" goals.[16] At the same time, the boundary between "good" and "bad" Islam, however fuzzy, needs to be ideologically demarcated, and it is the responsibility of the state-supported religious authorities to establish and to police this border. So, as frequenters of Astana mosques can note, there is an ongoing ideological battle against so-called alien religious movements (*zhat dini aghymdar*), and imams of the mosques constantly remind their parishioners to stay on the right path not just according to Islam but also within Islam.

At the entrance to the main prayer hall of the Haziret Sultan mosque there are Soviet-style announcement boards with illustrations teaching the public how to pray "according to the Hanafi mazhab" (see Figure 9.5).

I heard different views about the degree of authoritarian imposition with which Hanafi orthodoxy is fostered at Haziret Sultan and other mosques in

Astana. Some interviewees considered it to be quite mild and merely limited to reminders during the prayer to adhere to the Hanafi style of *namaz*—not saying "amen" loudly after reading the Fatiha, not raising hands after the second *rakat*, not holding hands close to the chest (they should be on the level of waist), and not standing with one's feet too far apart.

Other interviewees, however, found this ideological policing irritating and even said that it caused them to deliberately avoid listening to the imams and attending their sermons. One pious Muslim told me that it is precisely for this reason of ideological imposition that he skips the sermons and only goes to perform his mandatory Friday prayer.

My own observation at the Haziret Sultan mosque has been that Hanafi styles are taught (usually after the mandatory Friday prayer See picture 9.4) to those among the public who do not really know how to pray at all. They are not rigidly imposed on worshippers who are acculturated in their prayers, even if slightly different from Hanafi ways. The imams of the central mosque are aware that a considerable part of their Friday prayer attendees are people who hardly know the external actions of prayer—so their prayer lessons according to the Hanafi mazhab are directed at those for whom the nuances of prayers of different schools are not really a principled matter. All three imams that I interviewed maintained that they see their primary role as general religious education of the masses rather than indoctrination according to one particular school within Islam.

However, once in a while, the mosque also sends a clear message about what kind of interpretation of Islam is completely unacceptable for Kazakhstani Muslims. In the course of one year, the mosque delivered three special sermons directly dedicated to battling "alien religious movements" (*zhat dini aghymdar*). One such sermon was preached by the head of the Youth Affairs Department of the Board of Muslims of Kazakhstan, Altynbek Utyskhanuly, on October 24, 2014. The sermon was entitled "The Danger Coming from the Proponents of Takfir"[17] (*Takfirshilerden tongen qauip*), and the movement said to practice such takfir was Dawa-Al-Hijra. "They are ready to call everybody who disagrees with them, *kafir*," said the imam. "They consider as *kafir* those who commit sins as well as those who follow government law." He continued, "If their own parents don't hold namaz and oraza—they also call them *kafir*!" The imam then argued that, unlike what *takfirshiler* say, the Qur'an teaches forgiveness and, if a person repents, Allah forgives even those who committed grave sins, with the exception of the great sin of *shirk*—believing in a deity other than Allah. The imam then went on to say how huge their damage to society was, particularly when they pit relatives and neighbors against each other and stir people to rise against their government by calling it a *kafir* government. "How can they call the government and the president that opened ten madrasas, that built Nur-Mubarak University and invited scholars

Figure 9.4 Instructions on How to Pray According to the Hanafi Mazhab. *Source*: Alima Bissenova.

from Al-Azhar to teach there, that built so many mosques where everybody can learn religion a *kafir* government?" he asked rhetorically.

Even if in the discursive field of differentiating between the "bad" extremist Islam and "good" moderate Islam, the imams have to follow the state's lead and give precedence to the matters of state security, there are some other fields in which imams take leadership in establishing orthodoxy without much interference and guidance from the state. One such field is teaching people to stay away from pre-Islamic folk traditions, different kinds of fortune-telling, and healing practices. Several sermons were devoted to understanding what type of traditional practices fit and what type of practices do not fit into the scripturalist framework. One of the sermons was actually called "Don't trust the fortune-teller, don't seek help from the healer!" (*Balgerge nanba, baqsygha barma!*) When denouncing these practices, the imams emphasize that they appear from the lack of religious education, and, if and when people read the scripture, they would understand why these practices are wrong. Notably, here the imams are going against the "bad" national folk traditions and are not afraid to take on some concepts that are dear to many Kazakhs—such as playing with the bones of animals and with *qumalaq* (sheep droppings, beads, or stones used in fortune telling).

INTEGRATING THE NATIONAL AND THE RELIGIOUS

In the course of my fieldwork, it became clear that the issue of interrelation and harmony between the national and religious traditions are at the core of imams' very own intellectual efforts to establish and propagate "good" Islam—Islam that is based on the orthodoxy recognized in the wider Muslim world and is simultaneously rooted in the body of so-called national traditions as well as fitting existing secular sensibilities and widespread notions of modernity and progress. The Muftiyat declared 2014 to be the year of "Religion and Tradition" (*Din men Da'stur Zhyly*) and a group of muftiyat scholars co-authored a book of the same title. While doing my fieldwork, I heard three very interesting sermons on this subject delivered at the Haziret Sultan.

Religion and Tradition

The first sermon was by the chief imam of Haziret Sultan mosque, Serikbai Qazhy. It was an "introductory" sermon on this issue and was called "The Interrelation between Religion and Tradition" (*Din men Da'stur Sabaqtastyghy*).

Serikbai Qazhy dwelled on the meaning of the Kazakh words *ghuryp* and *adet* that are both borrowed from Arabic *'urf* and *'ada*, respectively, and both connote "tradition." In Arabic, Serikbai Qazhy said, *al-'urf* means activities and practices that make good sense to the people and *al-'adat* means repeated and popular practices. The imam explained that there is a well-trodden place in shariat for *'urf* as Allah himself says in the Qur'an: Adopt forgiveness and enjoin the good (*'urf*) and turn away from the Ignorant.[18] The imam mentioned that *'urf* also counts as a source of sharia if it does not come against the primary sources of Qur'an, Sunna, and the consensus of Islamic scholars (*ijma*). The meaning of counting *'urf* among the sources of Sharia, according to Serikbay Qazhy, is because the practices of Muslim majorities in certain places could be trusted. He then quoted the companion of the Prophet, Abdullah ibn Masud, who said, "What Muslims count as good is also good before Allah." Serikbai Qazhy also stated that it is not a purpose of Islam to create a homogeneous society throughout lands because Islam recognizes that people are created in different communities with different customs, languages, and traditions.

Local Traditions and Cultures

The second sermon on religion and tradition was delivered by a guest speaker—the chief imam of the Karaganda central mosque.[19] The sermon was entitled "Islam and Local Traditions and Cultures." The imam started the sermon by challenging those who pit Kazakh tradition against Islam and saying that those who do that do not understand the spirit, the true meaning, and the history behind these traditions. "Kazakh tradition and Islam have been inseparable since the time when the Khan of the Turkic khanate, Karakhan, accepted Islam in the tenth century." He continued, "Kazakh tradition has been formed by Islam and has been inspired by Islam—unfortunately, many young [people] do not comprehend it today." He then gave several examples of misunderstanding of Kazakh traditions by some:

> A mother of a young man who studies Qur'an and Sunna came to me to complain that her son ordered her not to make *shelpek* [fried pita bread] in preparation for a *Qur'an oqytu* ceremony on Friday. This man told his mother that making shelpek is *bida'at* [innovation] … Astaghfirallah (God Forbid) … The problem is that this young man does not understand the meaning of making *shelpek*. Kazakhs make *shelpek* for charity and hand them out to poor people. Why? Because people's wealth was not measured with money but by the livestock and food they had. There were times during Kazakh history such as Aktaban Shubyryndy (White Heal Flight) when people were dying of hunger even though they had stored gold and silver. Even the richest could not exchange silver the size of a horse's head for one slice of bread. That is when the proverb came: "*Altyn kumis—tas eken, arpa bidai—as eken.*" [Silver and gold are only stones, but wheat and barley are bread] Then people understood what kind of things have the highest value. They say that the tradition of giving *sadaqa* and reading prayers goes against Islam but there is a Hadith when the Prophet said, addressing *sahaba*, [his companions)]: "Prepare gifts for the dead." "But what kind of gifts can we give the dead?" asked the puzzled *sahaba*. "Du'a [prayer] and sadaqa [charity]," replied the Prophet. So, our Kazakh ancestors were acting on the basis of this Hadith and were continuing the Islamic tradition in their own way.[20]

In similar vein, the speaker went on to defend other Kazakh traditions "under attack." One of the traditions that needed to be defended was the Kazakh tradition of *salem beru* (give salams by bowing to the in-laws) by the bride during her wedding. According to the speaker, some Kazakh Muslims also find this tradition un-Islamic and bordering on *shirk*. As the guest imam explained, this tradition is not about worshipping but about showing respect, as it is known that Allah himself asked angels to make *sujud* to the prophet Adam,[21] and this *sujud* was not intended as worship but as a sign of respect and recognition of authority.

The imam then went to say that some of the young Kazakh Muslims who travel abroad to other Muslim countries come back having adopted the style of costume and clothes of these Muslim nations without realizing that it might be a part of their "local" tradition and not necessarily the only correct Islamic way. Most often, the chief Karaganda imam noted, it happens to the "youth who did not see Kazakh *tarbiyat*[22] in their families" and thus do not recognize the Islamic foundation of their own traditional clothes.

Tradition and Sharia

The third sermon on the subject of religion and tradition was called "The Role of Tradition in Sharia" (*Sharighattaghy Adet-Ghuryptyng Orny*) and was delivered by Ruslam Kambarov, the naib imam of the Haziret Sultan mosque. While this most recent sermon was built on some of the common threads of the previous arguments made by Serikbai Qazhy Oraz and Berikqozha Qazhy, it also introduced a new way of thinking about tradition (*'urf*) in Islam—tradition as not only something that is passed down from generation to generation and has to be upheld no matter what, but as a constantly renewed and newly institutionalized set of practices and phenomena that should make sense to a Muslim society in a new context.

"*Dasturding ozyghy bar, tozyghy bar*" (some traditions go ahead of time and some do not withstand the test of time), he said, referring to a Kazakh proverb. As an example of such new traditions, the naib imam mentioned new ways of making trade and contracts that had not existed in the time of the Prophet but appeared later—for instance, giving guarantees for one's product that, according to the speaker, appeared in the time of Abu Hanifa. This sermon also dwelled on a Kazakh tradition of not marrying close cousins up to the seventh generation. "While marrying cousins is allowed in the Qur'an, the Kazakh way of arranging marriage is something that is in accordance with Islam and also makes sense to the majority of the people according to their tradition," the speaker said.

THE STRUCTURE OF THE SERMON: "ADDING FAT TO THE MEAT FROM THE RIBS"

A separate word needs to be said about the structural-organizational work that goes into preparing the sermons, about the imams who deliver them, and the audience who listens to them. The audience of the Friday sermons at the Haziret Sultan at times numbers up to 6,000 people and consists of mostly young-to-middle-aged people of different social strata and walks of life—from construction workers coming to prayer in their uniforms (sometimes shuttled to the mosque by the company buses) to the suave high-ranking officials and business people driving to the mosque in their SUVs and tapping away on their laptops while in the mosque. The imams who speak to this audience also tend to be young. The current chief imam of the Haziret Sultan mosque, Serikbai Qazhy Oraz, whose sermon on religion and tradition was cited earlier, has just recently turned forty, and the six current naib imams are younger than him, with three of them in their mid-thirties and three in their early thirties. None of the current imams have had a traditional theological education. The previous (inaugural) imam of the mosque, Kairat Zholdybai, had a bachelor's degree in Sharia from Al-Azhar, which is, in fact, very difficult to obtain—it might take up to a decade for non-Arabic speakers.[23]

Four out of six naib imams earned their Bachelor's degrees from the Otyrar Kazakh-Arab University in Shymkent and subsequent Master's degrees in religious studies (*religiovedenie* in Russian, *dintanu* in Kazakh) from various universities in Almaty and Astana—including Al-Farabi Kazakh National University and Eurasian National University. Serikbai Qazhy Oraz, the chief imam, has a Bachelor's degree in Islamic studies from Nur-Mubarak University, where several Azhari scholars teach, but he also spent several years in Al-Azhar and in Islamabad. He also has a law degree and a degree in economics.

Most of the naib imams have also studied briefly either in Turkey or in Egypt. All of them speak good classical Arabic, many speak Turkish and use Turkish materials to prepare for their sermons, and some speak adequate English. This broad educational background, in addition to linguistic expertise, as well as the experience of "having travelled abroad," particularly in the Islamic world, adds to their status and moral authority among the parishioners. The current nature of religious authority in Kazakhstan seems to constitute a marked change from how it was in Soviet times and even in the first decade of independence. The religious authority that the imams of the central mosque and the invited speaker imams wield (and some of them wield more authority than others depending on their qualifications is very "textual"—it comes from their knowledge and ability to quote from holy texts (I heard imams quoting the volume and page numbers from Ibn Taymiyya's collection) and to construct arguments with evidence from the texts (including the Qur'an, known collections of Hadith, and the body of Islamic scholarship). In addition to this textual scholarly knowledge, imams also have to possess extensive public presentation skills and eloquence in the Kazakh language.

All sermons at the Haziret Sultan and indeed most of the mosques in Kazakhstan, with a few notable exceptions of Uyghur and Uzbek mosques, are delivered in Kazakh. The general themes for the sermons are preapproved at the beginning of the year by the Board of Muslims of the Republic of Kazakhstan, particularly the Council of Ulamas and the Department of Sermons (*Uaghyz jane Nasihat Bolimi*).[24]

Thematically, most sermons explain matters of Islamic doctrine with an emphasis on spiritual development (repentance, forgiveness, occupying the state between fear and hope, being content and grateful) and the practice of Islamic propriety (living a pious life, abstaining from grave sins, building strong families, maintaining good relations with relatives and community).[25] The sermons also follow a mixture of the state national and religious calendars. For instance, on the eve of Independence Day, the imam spoke about what a blessing independence was for Kazakhs, particularly since they could now practice their own religion and traditions freely. On the eve of Constitution Day, the chief imam delivered a sermon explaining the importance of upholding just rule based on the constitution as well as following the law of the land for Muslims. On World War II Victory Day (May 9), the sermon was about the obligation to defend one's own country, and so on. At the same time, religious celebrations of Ramadan (*Oraza*), Kurban Eid, Maulid, and the holy months of Sha'ban and Rajab also get a series of sermons dedicated to explaining the meaning of these religious holidays. Political matters are usually never discussed, but sometimes things unwittingly take on political overtones. For instance, after the Paris Charlie Hebdo shooting, which happened on the eve of Maulid, the two sermons that were scheduled "according to the plan" talked about the exemplary life and the character of the Prophet Muhammad and the necessity to respect and venerate him and teach others through his example. So, it could be inferred from these sermons that any misrepresentation of the Prophet's life is really unacceptable to Muslims.

Even though the general themes of the sermons (and often times the *ayats* and *ahadith* that need to be cited) are pre-approved for the whole country, the imams still have considerable leeway in how they structure most of their sermons. According to the imams that I have interviewed, the need for pre-approval comes from the necessity to send a unified message to the Muslims of Kazakhstan and also from the fact that many imams at local mosques are not really that well-versed in Qur'an and Sunna. As one of the imams put it, "Village imams (*auldaghy imamdar*) might not have the necessary knowledge for such sermons."

The usual sermon starts with an *ayat* from the Qur'an, followed by some *hadith*, stories from the lives of the rightful Caliphs and companions of the Prophet and quotes from Islamic scholars. Following this, as one of the imams explained to me, imams are also encouraged to use excerpts from the religious works of Kazakh writers such as Abai and Shakarim as well as to use Kazakh proverbs. "We have to add some fat to the meat from the ribs,"[26] said one of the imams. "We have to explain the continuity between the religion and our traditional heritage." In addition to these scriptural references and allusions to Kazakh traditional ways, the imams often use examples from their own lives—what kinds of issues they encounter in their job and what they are approached with. For instance, Ghaziz Akhmet, whose sermon against the practices of healers and fortune-tellers I cited earlier, told the audience of Haziret Sultan that imams are besieged by people who come to share their visions with them—often visions of their dead relatives (*aruakh*), insisting that these visions have religious meaning. "I tell these people that what you see in your dreams are most likely to be *jinn* [supernatural creatures, made of smokeless fire, and demons] and not *aruakh*."

In his sermon on the importance of religious tolerance toward non-practicing relatives and compatriots, Imam Nurbek Yesmaghambet, an invited speaker from Almaty, related how he was often approached by people who complained of being shunned by their newly practicing relatives and sometimes their own children for being "bad" non-practicing Muslims. "This happens because of religious illiteracy," said the imam. "Had they read the stories of the life of the Prophet, they would have known how exceptionally kind the Prophet was to his many disbelieving relatives." The Prophet was particularly kind to his Uncle Abu Talib even though the latter is known to have not converted to Islam. "To be in agreement with relatives despite their shortcomings and sometimes despite their being *mushrik* [polytheist] was an example and the advice of the Prophet to his companions," continued the imam. "How does it compare to our young Muslims who turn away from their relatives and sever their relations?"[27] He then concluded the sermon by saying that if in the time of the Prophet the Prophet himself and his companions were kind to their relatives who repeatedly refused to follow their example, then contemporary Kazakh Muslim youth should also be tolerant and understanding of their parents and their relatives who are coming out of the experience of Soviet atheist indoctrination.

CONCLUSION

On May 7, 2015, the day of the Military Forces of the Republic of Kazakhstan and the eve of the 70th anniversary of the Victory in the Great Patriotic War, the largest military parade in the history of the country was held in Astana. As various military regiments and military machines—tanks and rockets—were parading through Independence Square, the Haziret Sultan mosque loomed large in the background. One regiment dressed in Red Army uniforms and carrying the Soviet red flag while marching before the grand white mosque might have looked particularly curious, but this strange visual mélange underscored the complex historic and cultural configurations of contemporary Kazakhstan—remembrance of the Soviet past, on the one hand, and the presence of the mosque conspicuously in the background for most important state functions, on the other.

As I argued throughout this chapter, however, the importance of the Haziret Sultan mosque in Kazakhstani politics goes beyond its physical manifestation in the national symbolic landscape. Much more significant is the powerful presence of Haziret Sultan as a place of recurring public speeches (sermons) that, unlike state-organized parades and meetings, gather only voluntary audiences and do not require wasteful expenditures. The people who come regularly to the mosque for prayers, sermons, and other rituals out of their own will are encouraged to continue to do so by both religious and state authorities. The religious authorities and state apparatus have their own goals of molding these people into their respective ideal publics and inculcating them with values fit for their own projects. While the religious leaders aspire to grow the number of their followers and to teach them the virtues of being good Muslims, the state authorities are concerned with turning these "good Muslims" into loyal constituents and "good citizens." From this arises the Kazakhstani imams' dilemma of how to make the goals of the state and religious establishment not only meet, but also overlap as much as possible. My analysis of the sermons delivered at the Haziret Sultan mosque underscores the efforts of the young imams to lead this process of integration and construct the body of "good" Islam based on the internationally recognized Islamic orthodoxy, on the one hand, and broadly defined "national" tradition on the other. Even if the imams' grasp of the widely declared Hanafi Islamic orthodoxy is incomplete, they actively seek and digest relevant textual sources and craft their sermons to reflect both the wisdom of Islam and the wisdom of the Kazakh people.

NOTES

1. The "Sembol" company has built many landmark buildings in Kazakhstan, including the transparent Khan Shatyr shopping center, Nazarbayev University, Rixos Almaty, and the Burabay Rixos Resort luxury hotels.

2. *Neke* is a Kazakh word originating from the Arabic *nikah* (Islamic marriage contract). In the announcements and signs at the mosque, many Arabic religious terms are kazakhified. For instance, the terms for different prayers are given only in the Kazakh version. The name of the mosque itself often appears in Kazakh-language sources as A'ziret Sultan rather than Haziret Sultan.

3. I personally observed this "enlargement" of the praying space during a Friday prayer on March 6, 2015, and a holiday Qurban Eid prayer on October 4, 2014.

4. Mosque officials roll out large carpets for this purpose. Pictures of Kazakhstani Muslims praying outside the mosque in cold weather and in the snow have often been circulated as a sign of steadfastness and exotic prayer situations.

5. We conceptualize the state not as a monolith but as a cumulative representation of several branches and agencies interacting with religions in their particular spheres.

6. The Religious Board of the Muslims of Kazakhstan (*Dukhovnoe Upravlenie Musul'man Kazakhstana*), also customarily called either muftiyat or DUMK, is an official institution that has roots in the Soviet era and branched out from the Soviet Religious Board of the Muslims of Central Asia and Kazakhstan in 1991. Since then, DUMK has grown in scale dramatically and now exerts considerable influence and power, overseeing most of the mosques in the country, several educational institutions, the Asyl Arna TV channel, three websites, and several print publications.

7. In several interviews with me, imams mentioned that the DUMK sends them abroad—to Turkey and Egypt to study. In April 2015, one of the naib imams of Haziret Sultan, Ghaziz Akhmetov, along with five other imams from Astana was sent to Egypt for a three-month training course. There is also an Imam Training Institute under the DUMK, which mainly trains regional and smaller district imams.

8. Maria Louw, "Even Honey May Become Bitter When There Is Too Much of It: Islam and the Struggle for Balanced Existence in Post-Soviet Kyrgyzstan," *Central Asian Survey* 32, no. 4 (2013): 514–526.

9. See Article 7 of the Law on Religious Activities and Religious Organizations (*Zakon RK o religioznoi deiatel'nosti i religioznykh ob"edineniiakh*) available at http://online.zakon.kz/Document/?doc_id=31067690.

10. The sermons of the Haziret Sultan are also available at www.muslim.kz and in CD format in the mosques.

11. In two 2015 sermons devoted to the issues of marriage and family, young people were advised to marry as early as possible and not to let financial and career considerations be an obstacle. Sermon from February 13, 2015, available at http://www.muslim.kz/kk/media/1044-gaziz-ahmet-neke-baqyttyn-bastauy.html.

12. "Zakonodatel'stvo Kazakhstana ne zapreshchaet nosit' hidzhab v uchebnykh zavedeniiakh." *Kazakhstan Today*, September 23, 2009, available at http://www.meta.kz/199882-zakonodatelstvo-kazakhstana-ne-zapreshhaet-nosit.html.

13. These circles after the evening prayer are usually for men but women also have their own activities in their quarters and can have their questions addressed to the imams in the men's section of the mosque in the time between the prayers.

14. Adeeb Khalid, *Islam After Communism: Religion and Politics in Central Asia* (Berkeley: University of California Press, 2007).

15. Johan Rasanayagam, *Islam in Post-Soviet Uzbekistan: The Morality of Experience* (Cambridge: Cambridge University Press, 2011), 139.

16. Johan Rasanayagam, "I Am Not a Wahhabi: State Power and Muslim Orthodoxy in Uzbekistan," in *Everyday Islam in Central Asia*, ed. Maria Louw (London: Routledge, 2007), 99–122.

17. *Takfir* refers to the practice of declaring other Muslims to be non-Muslims—that is *kufr.*

18. Chapter 7, verse 99.

19. Charismatic regional imams from Almaty, Karaganda, Atyrau, and other regions are often invited to give honorable "guest" sermons at Haziret Sultan.

20. Sermon delivered by Beqqozha Omirzaq Qazhy at Haziret Sultan mosque on March 22, 2014.

21. Chapter 2, verse 34.

22. *Tarbiyat* is a Kazakh concept also borrowed from Arabic and refers to the inculcation of values during the process of upbringing and education.

23. Alima Bissenova, "Central Asian Encounters of the Middle East: Islam, Nationalism and Post-Coloniality in Al-Azhar," *Religion, State and Society* 33, no. 3 (2005): 253–264.

24. It is also noteworthy that the head of the Department of Sermons has a PhD in Cultural Anthropology from the Al-Farabi Kazakh National University.

25. In the course of my fieldwork, there have been sermons entitled "Tawbe etuding Taghlymy" (The Art of Repenting), "Keshirimdi bolu—Kengshilik" (The Generosity of Forgiving), "Umit pen Urei arasynda" (Between Hope and Fear), "Iman jane Amal" (Faith and Action), "Shaytannyng Shyrmauyna Aldanba" (Don't be Deceived by Shaytan's Temptations), "Musulmannyng Sipaty" (The Character of a Muslim), "Namaz Bizge Ne Beredi?" (What Does Namaz Give Us?), "Neke—Bakhyttyng Bastauy" (Marriage, the Beginning of Happiness), "Zina Zardaptary" (The Consequences of Adultery), "Ata-Anangdy Qadirle" (Respect Your Parents) and other similar topics.

26. In Kazakh, "Bir qazy bir mai aralastyryp aituymyz kerek."

27. Sermon "Aghaiyn Tatu Bolsa" (When Relatives are Friendly) delivered on June 6, 2014.

Chapter 10

"The Spirit of Tengri"

Contemporary Ethnic Music Festivals and Cultural Politics in Kazakhstan

Megan Rancier

On June 7, 2014, the second annual "Spirit of Tengri" music festival took place in the urban cultural hub (and former national capital) of Almaty, Kazakhstan. Since its inception in 2013, this remarkable event has distinguished itself in several ways from the types of popular music events that typically take place in Kazakhstan. First, it is free and open to the public. Second, the festival explicitly stresses an "open air + live music" format. Third, the festival celebrates an international roster of artists and their distinctive musical styles. Designated "contemporary ethnic music" by festival organizers, the musical style could just as easily have been described as "world music"—a term historically fraught with identity politics, issues of representation, and uneven relations of power. However, the (admittedly ambiguous) genre of "world music" has also been discussed within ethnomusicology and cultural studies as particularly effective in expressing the position of the nation-state as both "inward-looking" and "outward-looking." In other words, music such as that performed at the Spirit of Tengri festival simultaneously articulates the unique aspects of individual national identities, while at the same time conveying a desire for commonality and connection with other nation-states. This is essentially the work that is being accomplished by the Spirit of Tengri festival—it enables Kazakhstan to represent itself as a modern nation that values its cultural roots, and it also provides a visual and sonic basis for imagining Kazakhstan as a major component of an interconnected, globalized world.[1]

In this chapter, I first make some brief remarks regarding the somewhat unorthodox research methodology underlying the information and analysis presented here. I then lay out the theoretical framework for my discussions, framed by studies of musical festivals, popular music, and the implications of both for conceptualizations of national identity and international relations. Next, I will describe the planning and realization of both the 2013 and 2014

Spirit of Tengri festivals, highlighting the spatial, visual, and, of course, musical structuring of each event; I will also provide some important points of comparison and contrast between the two events, pointing out how the significance of the festival appears to have changed markedly in the course of a single year. I will then provide extensive analysis of the musical styles represented at both festivals, offering some initial conclusions about why these styles of music are significant to the cultural—as well as the political—dynamics of Central Asia today.

METHODOLOGY

One of the unique aspects of this project has been the extent to which I have been able to gather data about the Spirit of Tengri festival through electronic methods. Because I was unable to travel to Kazakhstan to attend the event personally, I engaged in "virtual fieldwork"[2] by following the festival's Facebook page and combing through online news articles, video recordings, and interviews about the festival.

I will readily admit that, as a research method, virtual fieldwork presents a unique set of limitations, as well as advantages. On one hand, it cannot provide the complete, multisensory impression of a performance event that first-hand participant observation would enable. Likewise, because I could not interview festival producers and participating artists myself, the questions and answers provided in recorded interviews did not address all of the topics that I would be interested in exploring with these individuals, and I was unable to ask follow-up questions or request clarification of specific statements. Additionally, I must acknowledge the fact that because the information drawn from online sources is second-hand, there is always the possibility of a biased viewpoint—especially from the news sources whose owners served as a major sponsor of the festival.[3]

On the other hand, my utilization of these online resources has provided a very clear view of the festival organizers' desired public image for the festival; even if the public statements by producers and participants appear incomplete or subjective, the images and opinions chosen to represent the event clearly indicate the lens through which the festival is intended to be viewed by audiences. Second, engaging in "virtual fieldwork" helps to highlight the extent to which the festival has made effective use of technology—not only in terms of marketing and promotion, but also to cultivate a larger community around the festival through social media. Its online presence and multimedia resources serve as an extension of the festival's "outward-looking" viewpoint, accessing audiences not only within Kazakhstan or even Central Asia, but all over the globe.

THEORETICAL FRAMEWORKS

Music Festivals

Numerous folklorists, ethnomusicologists, and anthropologists have examined the significance of large-scale musical events as "a mechanism for preservation, interpretation, and celebration of the folk," as well as "an ideal place for multicultural encounter, both as an experience of the Other as well as of the Own."[4] Scholars have also explored the implications of music festivals for national conceptualizations of gender, interethnic relations within politically divided nation-states, and the cultural influence of international nongovernmental organizations, among many other issues that are too numerous to fully explicate here.[5] My main interests in applying the existing literature to the Spirit of Tengri festival concentrates on two main areas: how conceptualizations of "the folk" are presented and interpreted, particularly at a festival that prioritizes modernized (not traditional) folk music, and how the festival's emphasis on modernized folk music enables a "construction and deconstruction of old and new musical values" through the innovative presentations of various fusions between elements of traditional music cultures and more mainstream, globalized popular music genres such as rock 'n' roll, hip hop, and electronic dance music.[6]

On the first point regarding "the folk," Helen Regis and Shana Walton have explored the many contradictory ways in which "folk" culture is presented at the annual New Orleans Jazz and Heritage festival, pointing out the numerous complex implications of the term "folk." In their understanding of how the term is deployed at the New Orleans event, "folk" appears to simultaneously convey notions of heritage, the past, and the "other"; it is also perceived as inherently oppositional to mainstream culture and power structures.[7] In sum, to be "folk" in their interpretation means to be "authentic, native, and real," offering an experience of a worldview that stands outside the everyday to festival visitors. Folk festival performers receive the benefit of a raised profile and, often, the financial rewards of marketing their wares, while visitors gain a feeling of increased cultural capital through "the hipness of difference" that they experience at the festival.

At the Spirit of Tengri festival, however, the emphasis is not placed so much on traditional presentations of folk music, but on the modernization of traditional musical instruments and genres. As a festival of *contemporary* ethnic music, the festival includes no performances of "roots" musical traditions; instead, these traditions are presented through modernized re-imaginings and re-interpretations. Instead of prioritizing notions of authenticity and the origins of specific traditions, the Spirit of Tengri festival seeks to celebrate these traditions through modernized formats, with the hope that younger, urban listeners will become interested in the underlying traditional "roots" of the music. In the same way that "roots" music was regarded as "authentic, native, and real" at the New Orleans Jazz and Heritage festival, these underlying musical traditions are seen as the essential basis for the modernized styles performed at the festival; the frequent use of the word "roots" (Ru., *korni*) among festival participants and organizers to describe the "contemporary ethnic music" indicates their viewpoint that the power inherent in the original musical traditions carries over into modernized versions. Through this process, the various re-imaginings and interpretations of musical traditions presented at the Spirit of Tengri festival cultivate their own type of authenticity, and a powerful potential source of national pride.

Regarding the second point on old and new musical values, Baumann suggests that music festivals offer individual artists the opportunity to enact creative agency through the "negotiation of tradition and modern, authenticity and syncretism, of opposition, transformation, and economization of culture."[8] As numerous scholars of Soviet and post-Soviet cultural politics have noted, the encounters of these regions and populations with Soviet political and cultural modernity in the twentieth century resulted in several major shifts in musical production throughout Soviet territories, encompassing "a rule-setting bureaucracy," "a set of standardized formats and venues," "and the ubiquitous presence of official repertoire."[9] As Soviet cultural institutions began to shape a new form of musical nationalism, markers of ethnic identity (such as traditional musical instruments and folk songs) became grafted onto European classical forms, yielding hybridized musical practices such as national opera and folk instrument orchestras.[10] In the ensuing decades, officially sanctioned "national music" coexisted with burgeoning popular music scenes, which incorporated not only the slick, orchestrated sounds of Russian *estrada* (popular music), but sometimes also the more illicit styles of Western rock as well as traditional folk music elements:

> Some turned to the romantic-heroic world of rock, with its intimations of commodification. ... Others looked to tradition defiantly, searching for both homegrown roots and internationalist ties in musical styles associated with pro-communist days—an entirely different, though still somewhat romantic, version of modernity.[11]

Against the backdrop of Soviet cultural institutions (many of which continue to operate in Kazakhstan, as well as other formerly Soviet territories) and the Soviet philosophy of music as an emblem of national identity, as well as oppositional reactions to these institutions near the end of the Soviet era, the modernized "contemporary ethnic music" performed at the Spirit of Tengri festival may be understood as either a continuation of Soviet musical nationalism or as a more oppositional move away from mainstream *estrada* toward a more localized version of popular music.

Here we might re-consider Regis and Walton's description of the "folk" as "a form of symbolic opposition to power structures"—a sentiment echoed by Baumann when he notes that "the view of the local ... is rebellious, refractory, sometimes provocative. It does not lie down in the comfortable bed of the mainstream."[12] If contemporary ethnic music draws from folk and local musical traditions, but is essentially modern music, what is its resultant relationship with existing power structures? Does the presence of folk elements introduce an oppositional undercurrent to these modernized styles, or do the modernizing processes (e.g., electrification, amplification, and fusion with other musical styles) somehow neutralize the inherent rebelliousness of the folk? In other words, does the modernization of tradition represented by the Spirit of Tengri festival serve to challenge existing power structures or does it reinforce them? Can it do both? According to Baumann, this power dynamic must be observed on a case-by-case basis in the work of individual artists: "This negotiation of tradition and modern, authenticity and syncretism, of opposition, transformation, and economization of culture demands from each musician a special basis for decision making for each performance and each individual musical piece." A closer examination of participating festival artists later in this chapter will help to illuminate how these processes operate on an individual level.

World Music and the Nation-State

The search for "both homegrown roots and internationalist ties" mentioned by Slobin is a theme that echoes throughout the Spirit of Tengri festival, both in the musical expressions of the artists and the verbal commentary of organizers and participants, and it constitutes the second major area of theoretical significance in this article. In other words, what is the relevance of "world music"—broadly defined as music that is simultaneously traditional and modern, local and global—to expressions of nations, national identities, and perhaps even the geopolitical status and aspirations of nation-states?

In explaining the relevance of "world music" to the concept of the nation-state, musicologists Ian Biddle and Vanessa Knights have framed the question as a problem of finding a middle ground between the two concepts that are most frequently used to describe the main ingredients of world music: the "global" and the "local." Between these two extremes, Biddle and Knights place an entity that they identify as a "mediator" between global and local: the nation-state. In their view, the concept of the nation-state serves a crucial role in the performance and reception of world music because of its ability to both delineate between different nations and facilitate communication and connection between those nations:

> On the one hand, there is a recourse to a "new traditionalism," a tendency to cite and situate identities as based in a certain kind of "rootedness" in ethnicity, race, linguistic communities, the local and so on … a territorial, inward-looking sense of place. On the other hand, there is a tendency to celebrate a plurality of globalized cultures, a tendency often identified with so-called post-modern thought in which boundaries and borders becomes ever more blurred and ever more permeable … a translocal, outward-looking sense of place.[13]

In contrast to the scholars quoted previously, who seemed to prioritize folk music in terms of its potency and oppositional potential, Biddle and Knights specifically identify *popular* music as uniquely suited to reconciling the local and the global. In their view, popular music establishes a middle ground where performers can claim a national identity rooted in specific ethnic and historical terms, but also opens up that identity for exploration, connection, and possibly reevaluation within the context of other artists who are also expressing their own identities. In their words, "Popular music is perhaps *the* cultural product that has crossed (and continues to cross) boundaries and frontiers the most frequently, just as it has demarcated and consolidated local cultural spaces."[14]

Baumann describes a similar process whereby music at international music festivals moves from an "intracultural" concept of tradition and "authenticity," to a "transcultural" model that reflects the creation of new cultural phenomena via globalization.[15] Within this movement—away from the local and toward the global—ethnic and national markers remain but gradually become integrated into a dialectical and mutually beneficial relationship with globalizing forces: "Just as the local … draws on regional roots, the regional—in order to become recognized—has become dependent upon recognition via global strategies."[16] Thus there ensues a balancing act among world music artists to maintain *some* musical markers of difference, but not at the expense of alienating global audiences. By highlighting the different ethnic and national origins of the participating artists, but also emphasizing "contemporary ethnic music" over other genres, the Spirit of Tengri festival seems to embody this idea of the spectrum between "looking inward" and "looking outward." The artists can simultaneously display their own national roots, while also discovering sources of commonality between themselves and artists from elsewhere.

Obviously this type of musical negotiation of the local and global can benefit artists wishing to break into the "world music" market; however, it can also prove useful to individual nation-states in terms of internal nation-building, enhanced international profiles, and, perhaps, geopolitical influence in their respective world regions. As the host country of the Spirit of Tengri festival, Kazakhstan may be in a position to reap some or all of these benefits to varying extents. By promoting its own contemporary ethnic musical artists through the festival, Kazakhstan stands to gain a valuable cultural export, a draw for cultural tourism, a source of increased national pride, and recognition as a cultural—and, perhaps by implication, political—leader among formerly Soviet Turkic nation-states.

Now that the main theoretical questions of the chapter have been explored conceptually, let us look at the structure and content of the festivals themselves. These descriptions will provide concrete example of the concepts and questions explored above, illustrated by explanations of musical performances and commentary provided by festival organizers and individual artists.

THE FIRST ANNUAL SPIRIT OF TENGRI FESTIVAL (2013)

The Spirit of Tengri festival (see Figure 10.1) represented the culmination of many years of planning, diverse financial partners, and supporting organizations, and the highly skilled use of modern technology and social media. According to festival producer Zhan Kasteyev, discussions about creating a new type of music festival began in 1997, when Kazakh bands such as Urker were beginning to create new styles of popular music based on the combination of folkloric instruments and songs, Kazakh-language song lyrics, and Euro-American rock instruments and technologies. After fifteen years of what Kasteyev called "dreaming," TengriFM (a national radio station) and the STV television station established partnerships with sponsors including Global Building Contract, Tengri News, Massaget.kz (a Kazakh-language news and entertainment website), Meloman (a Kazakhstan network of music stores), and MEGA (a large high-end shopping center in Almaty).[17]

Kasteyev and co-organizer Batyr Kazybayev (president of the Alash Media Group in Kazakhstan) described the festival as an effort to revive interest in folkloric music and culture, as well as a desire for Kazakhs (and others) to re-discover their own "inner roots." By describing the music performed at the festival as "contemporary ethnic music," organizers seemed to also acknowledge the inclusion of music that was rooted in ethnic heritage, but not exclusively Kazakh ethnic heritage; it is a term that could be applied to any form of music that is at once traditional and modern. This musical style—which has also been described by individual artists with various terms such as "ethno-rock" and "ethno-jazz"—combines elements of folklore (most notably folk musical instruments and local-language lyrics) with techniques and styles more commonly associated with globalized popular music such as rock, hip hop, and jazz. This combination of traditional and modern defined the overall aesthetic for the festival: the venue featured replicas of nomadic artifacts such as *kiez yui* (felt yurts), *bal bal* stones (markers often designed with human faces and features), and petroglyphs such as those found in Tamghaly, all arranged within the decidedly twenty-first century space of a

Figure 10.1 Poster Advertising the First "Spirit of Tengri" Festival of Contemporary Ethnic Music.

concrete-and-stone pavilion located adjacent to the gleaming, modern MEGA shopping center.

Related to the incorporation of "ancient" and nomadic imagery at the festival is the name of the festival itself: "The Spirit of Tengri." Tengri is the name of the sky-god who is recognized as the central deity of nomadic spiritual practices called *Tengrism*, which encompassed both animism (nature-worship) and shamanic practices such as ecstatic trance rituals.[18] The figure of Tengri is recognized by many of the Turkic, nomadic, and formerly nomadic ethnic groups of Central Asia and Siberia. Among contemporary Central Asians, Tengrism is regarded by some as a Turkic national religion—a unifying element among the disparate Turkic peoples—while others view Tengrism more skeptically as a form of New Age spirituality or alternative medicine. Blue is considered the representative color of Tengri, and festival advertising consistently used various shades of blue; the fact that blue is also the color of the Kazakhstani national flag creates a conveniently multilayered visual symbol that interweaves traditional spirituality with patriotic sentiment.[19]

Of the twelve musical acts performed at the festival, five were from Kazakhstan (ethnically Kazakh), and one each from Kyrgyzstan, Sakha, Bashkortostan, Buryatia, Altai, Gornaya Shoria, and Tuva (see Table 10.1). As a result, the performers represented a wide swath of territory comprising not only sovereign nations but also two autonomous Turkic republics and four "federal subject" territories located within Russian borders. The artists on the festival roster were chosen through a process that took advantage of the increasing levels of Internet connectivity and social media usage by Kazakhstani music listeners. Songs of prospective participants were played on the TengriFM radio station, and listeners were asked to vote for

Table 10.1 List of Participating Artists in the First "Spirit of Tengri" Festival of Contemporary Ethnic Music (June 8, 2013).

Artist/Band Name	*Country/Region*
Aldaspan	Kyrgyzstan
HaPaNaSaSa	Kyrgyzstan
Naya	Kyrgyzstan
Qorlan Kartenbaeva	Kyrgyzstan
Roksonaki	Kyrgyzstan
Gulzada	Kyrgyzstan
Yuliana Krivoshapkina	Yakutiya (Sakha)
Agyrmak	Bashkiria (Bashkortostan)
Namgar	Buryatia
Bolot Bairyshev	Altai
Chyltys	Gornaya Shoria
Sainkho Namchylak	Tyva

Total artists: 12

their favorites on the festival's official website.[20] The artists who received the most votes were invited to perform at the festival. Some artists, such as Sainho Namchylak, were already internationally famous, while others, such as Qorlan Kartenbaeva, had achieved only local recognition. Some artists appeared in "national" dress from their respective homelands, while others did not. Performers were male and female (almost in equal proportions), and ranged in age from roughly 25 to 60 years old.

Despite the apparent diversity among the participating artists, a number of important unifying factors existed: Turkic ethnicity, nomadic heritage, a cultural legacy of animist or shamanic spirituality, and a musical style that combined traditional folklore with cosmopolitan sounds and technologies. These shared elements complemented the underlying theme of re-discovering and promoting "ethnic roots" while also clearly demonstrating points of commonality between representatives of various nations and cultures.

Musical Style

Although the overall style of music showcased at the Spirit of Tengri festival was branded "contemporary ethnic music," combinations of traditional and modern—folk and popular—local and global—have existed in many forms and under many names for at least the past 50 years. As globalization has intensified, so have hybrid musical forms that blend folkloric music with the globally mass mediated popular music styles of the day (whether it be rock 'n' roll, disco, pop, hip hop, or dance music). In Kazakhstan, these hybrid popular music styles have been variously named "folk-pop," "ethno-rock," or "ethno-pop," depending on the artist; the "ethno" prefix has been used by the Kazakh ethno-rock band Roksonaki to describe their music for at least 20 years.[21] More recently, the dombra virtuoso Asylbek Engsepov developed a hybrid style that he called DEKKO—an acronym of the musical elements that it blended together: dombra, *estrada*, *küi*, *komputer*, and *oryndaushi* (performer). The multi-instrumentalist Edil Husainov has also made extensive experiments combining traditional music for instruments such as the *sheng-qobyz* (jaw harp) and *sybyzgy* flute with electronic dance music; in 2005, one of his songs appeared on the internationally released album *The Rough Guide to the Music of Central Asia*.

In short, the hybrids presented at the Spirit of Tengri festival did not constitute a new phenomenon; rather, it can be understood as the most recent phase of an already well-established cultural practice: the creation of hybrid popular music styles based in Central Asian folklore. For example, Sainkho Namchylak has gained worldwide recognition and acclaim for her interpretations of Tuvan overtone singing, jaw harp playing, and folksong within more globalized styles of popular music. The Kazakh band Aldaspan, also featured at the festival, combines Kazakh sound sources such as *sheng-qobyz* and guttural singing with electrified *dombra* (and bass dombra) and a standard rock drum kit. As a third example, the Sakha vocalist Yuliana Krivoshapkina and the Kazakh DJ group Hapanasasa collaborated during the festival to create even further possibilities for "hybrid" styles of popular music with traditional singing, jaw harp, turntables, electronica, and percussion.[22]

As I noted earlier, popular music that blends traditional and modern elements appears to be a highly desirable (and widespread) form of musical representation for nations that wish to express their traditional roots, while also indicating their awareness of and integration into twenty-first century processes of globalization and cosmopolitanism. In addition, these artists create new and interesting music that seeks to attract younger listeners, presenting traditional music in a new way and encouraging increased interest in the folkloric source material. Several artists reinforced this sentiment in interviews with national media. For example, Sainkho Namchylak told Tengri News that "contemporary ethnic music reduces the distance between the ancient traditional songs and pop music."[23] Similarly, Rinat Ramazanov of the band Agyrmak stated that "[i]t attracts interest … all of these directions—even hard core, beatbox, mixers—we use them, namely with traditional folklore, to present it in a new way."[24]

Lastly, for the artists as well as the festival organizers, the "ethnic" content of these contemporary music styles offers a sense of connection—not only to the respective cultural heritages of individual nations, but to a larger community of Turkic and nomadic peoples. Several artists who were interviewed by local media expressed these types of sentiments:

> Gulzada (Kyrgyzstan): "In general, ethnic music—it unifies all peoples (*narodov*) because we have one root, and music—because it doesn't have nationality (*natsional'nost'*), it doesn't have language—music unites everyone."[25]
>
> "Agyrmak" (Bashkortostan): "I think that in recent times, really, there has been such a growth, namely in folk culture (*kul'tur narodnyi*) because the people yearn for it, they cannot forget about, as we say, their own roots."[26]
>
> Batyr Kazybaev (president of Alash Media Group): "In my view, the historic heritage of the Great Steppe has been undeservedly forgotten. Remembering, restoring, and reconstructing the great heritage and culture of the people sharing the same Tengri (sky) is very important for the national identity of all the people who have resided and still reside at the Eurasian continent. This is a very rich cultural layer that is full of unforgettable experience for almost everyone who touches it. That's why I think that remembering the roots is very important for Kazakhstan."[27]

This last quote especially highlights the nationalistic undertones (or perhaps overtones) of the "contemporary ethnic music" style. Music serves as a reminder of ethnic histories and cultural roots, and it also illuminates similarities between nations in terms of history, heritage, and in some cases perhaps shared struggles, as well.

Interestingly, producer Zhan Kasteyev pointed to a different motivation behind the re-discovery of ethnic roots through music: the creation of a locally rooted, but globally marketable, style of popular music:

> In the end it's already time that we find our own inner roots. Why did, let's say, the music of the Beatles, Led Zeppelin, the Rolling Stones, become popular throughout the world? Because it was their folk [people's] music. It's simply folk music—European, American. … In our case ours is here.

By characterizing folk music as a type of natural resource for global export to the international music market, Kasteyev points to a practical rationale behind the extensive investment of time and money into the Spirit of Tengri festival—the development of a culture-based industry, which Baumann describes as one of the "economic objectives of festivals": namely, the "establishment of a cultural marketplace."[28]

Shamanic/Animistic Legacies

Part of the feeling of connectedness among the participants in the festival was the common legacy of animist belief systems and shamanic healing rituals in all of the represented territories. Central Asian and Siberian shamanism has been extensively studied and well-documented by Russian and Western European scholars since the eighteenth century, but its presence in the music of so many contemporary artists indicates that these legacies continue to imbue creative expression with powerful messages and meanings. The "shamanic" references in the festival participants' performances remained limited to the use of particular vocal styles (guttural singing, imitation of birds and animals), instruments (frame drums), and song lyrics (e.g., Roksonaki's opening song, based on a shamanic incantation).[29] But although shamanism represented only one of the "ethnic" elements of the festival, it opens up many possible interpretations for *why* shamanistic sounds and imagery continue to inform popular music.

The figure of the shaman has embodied everything from a maniac or a charlatan to a primordial healer/priest or a mystical bridge to the spirit world; perhaps these associations appeal to the contemporary artists who are similarly seeking a link—not between the human and spirit worlds, but between the past and the present. Perhaps the ecstatic rituals practiced by the shaman also appeal to an underlying creative desire to step outside the limitations of everyday life, everyday expression, and to connect with a more "alternative" identity that rejects the conventions that have swept through Central Asia throughout the past several centuries. Animism is pre-Christian, pre-Islam, and pre-colonial; it is distinctly Central Asian and Siberian—not European, and not Russian. While none of the festival participants expressed outwardly subversive identities or sentiments, animist and shamanic concepts certainly provide a cultural precedent and potential creative outlet for such expressions. Recalling Regis and Walton's description of "folk" elements as "a form of symbolic opposition to power structures," perhaps the invocation of shamanic sounds and imagery present not only an experience of alternative spirituality, but also of voices and histories that have been politically and culturally marginalized since the early twentieth century.[30]

Technology

The role of technology in the Spirit of Tengri festival is also significant—not only because it serves the previously discussed goal of making connections (between tradition and modernity, and between various nations with Turkic ancestry), but because it extends the reach of the festival to the most crucial demographic for achieving its stated goals: young people. Not only were the performers for the festival chosen through mass electronic voting, but advertising and promotional recordings were also distributed online via the festival's Facebook page and official website. The performances at the festival—and the entire event itself—depended heavily on technologies such as sampling, special audio effects, and large-scale visual projections. Finally, the festival was recorded and later distributed in both CD and DVD formats. In addition, the festival's Facebook page extends the "community" of listeners and artists into digital space by posting media about music and spirituality, both in Central Asia and beyond. The Tengri FM radio show "Across the Universe," which features mainly traditional and New Age music, is also linked to the festival's Facebook page. If the goals of "contemporary ethnic music" (and events such this festival) are to bridge the gap between old and new, and to attract younger listeners to musical folklore, then clearly the continued use of all available technologies functions as a key factor in making these efforts successful.

THE SECOND ANNUAL SPIRIT OF TENGRI FESTIVAL (2014)

For the second festival, the location, geographical scope, and overall vision for the event shifted in several significant ways. In the first place, the 2014 festival was advertised as an "international festival of ethnic music"—still placing emphasis on the ethnic content of the performances, but now within the explicit context of a global community. This change reflected the recognition that among the thirteen performers on the 2014 roster, several arrived from outside Central Asia (see Table 10.2). In addition to the Kazakh, Kyrgyz, and various other returning performers from the 2013 festival, additional acts from the countries of Georgia (The-Shin), Turkey (Baba Zula), and Ecuador (Yarik) were included.

In contrast to the 2013 festival, when all of the performers could point to a shared Turkic or nomadic heritage, the connections between the 2014 performers appeared somewhat less obvious. As a result, the publicity for the event emphasized the universal aspects of the music and musicians. For example, in a televised interview General Festival Director Magauya Umorbekov explained, "When you come to the festival you necessarily feel this amazing, let's say 'vibration.' You—independent of whether you are familiar with the artists or not—you feel how it permeates inside very deeply—into our souls." It is comments such as these that seem to shape this festival as "outward-looking" as well as "inward-looking"—in other words, while part of the vision behind the festival is the promotion of each artist's respective cultural roots ("looking inward"), another part of this vision seeks connections between seemingly dissimilar peoples through a musical "vibration" that, presumably, is accessible for anyone to experience.

The 2014 festival took place outside the Palace of the Republic (Almaty's largest concert hall), at the intersection of Dostyk and Abai Avenues—a central location significant due to its historical use as a venue for state-sponsored programs and events during both Soviet and post-Soviet eras. With this politically significant building serving as a backdrop for the festival, the

Table 10.2 List of Participating Artists in the Second "Spirit of Tengri" Festival of Contemporary Ethnic Music (June 7, 2014)

Artist/Band Name	*Country/Region*
Aldaspan	Kazakhstan
Roksonaki	
Shaparat	
Gulzada	Kyrgyzstan
Agyrmak	Bashkiria (Bashkortostan)
Namgar	Buryatia
Bolot Bairyshev	Altai
Beluga Jam	Altai
Chyltys	Gornaya Shoria
Sainkho Namchylak	Tyva
Radykha Tyulyusha	Tyva
Baba Zula	Turkey
The-Shin	Georgia
Yarik-Ecuador	Ecuador

Total artists: 14

symbolic presence of the state was greatly expanded.[31] Additionally, the location of this building is particularly rich in national symbolism, surrounded by such nationally recognized landmarks as the Hotel Kazakhstan, the statue of nineteenth-century Kazakh poet Abai Kunanbayev, and the popular nearby Kok-Tobe park. This new location seemed to suggest that the 2014 festival was more warmly embraced by the official infrastructure of Almaty—and for good reason, since 2014 had already been declared "The Year of Almaty" by city officials. The festival received support from the mayor of Almaty, as well as its main sponsors Tengri FM and Kaspi Bank, and was incorporated into a larger official celebration of the city as "the cultural capital of the CIS."[32]

Another highlight of the 2014 festival was the introduction of a new type of modernized Kazakh folk instrument—the electro-zhetygen.[33] Traditionally, the plucked zither *zhetygen* has been utilized in folk ensembles and performed as a solo instrument; the electrified version featured a more compact, handheld structure (carried by the performer with a strap, much like a guitar) and a fingerboard that featured open strings on the left side, guitar frets on the right. The instrument was created in Moscow, brought to the festival by the Kazakh band Sharapat, and was featured in several local news stories about the festival. Of course, the modernization of folk instruments is not a new phenomenon in the cultural history of Kazakhstan (or any formerly Soviet state); however, the continuation of this practice is noteworthy. While during the Soviet period, folk instruments were "modernized" to more closely resemble European classical instruments, today the same process seems to make the folk instruments more closely resemble standard rock instruments like the electric guitar. For example, the group Aldaspan has also received media attention for incorporating an electrified dombra into their instrumentation—another seeming continuation of the Soviet practice of instrument modernization. I point this out not as a criticism, but as another example in my argument that the Spirit of Tengri festival creates a space for musical expressions that simultaneously "look inward" and "look outward"—a fact that serves as a parallel for the larger-scale processes that nation-states must also negotiate: how to maintain a unique national identity while also negotiating a foothold in the economic and geopolitical landscapes of globalization.

SIGNIFICANCE OF THE SPIRIT OF TENGRI FESTIVAL FOR KAZAKHSTAN

How we can understand the significance of this unique music festival within a larger context? In many ways, this event can be viewed as a proxy for Kazakhstan itself, which has been undergoing its own process of looking both inward and outward. On one side, we can look at the examples of so-called

Kazakhization in (for example) policies promoting Kazakh language use and education, as well as billboard campaigns aimed at encouraging Kazakh cultural pride. On the other side, Kazakhstan has been actively pursuing a greater leadership role in trade, tourism, and energy vis-à-vis Asia and Europe. This "inward/outward" vision is echoed in the country's most recent official statement on strategic development, *Kazakhstan 2050*, which "envisages a country in which ... Kazakhstan's traditional values, culture, and patriotism are preserved, while openness, ease of communication, and peaceful relations with the rest of the world underpin the respect that Kazakhstan commands on the international stage."[34] The specific mention of "traditional culture" clearly indicates the high value that the state places on culture as a strategic resource, one that (rather than promoting isolationism) facilitates "openness" with other nations. Futher, the use of the phrase "international stage" frames Kazakhstan's role in global geopolitics as a type of performance—a delicate balancing act between folk and modern, tradition and change, independence and interdependence. It is this very performance that, I would argue, is enacted on a microlevel in the "Spirit of Tengri" festival.

In conclusion, this festival is unique because its emphasis on contemporary ethnic music seems to eloquently articulate the "in-between" stage of development that Kazakhstan seems to find itself in at present. The country—like the music—is at once looking inward and outward: searching for connections with its own cultural roots while also seeking to establish its place within the global community. This search is reflected in the musical style featured at the festival, with its emphasis on rediscovering cultural roots, but through the medium of modernized folk music. At the same time, the international scope of the festival presents Kazakhstan as a member of a global community of nation-states that are both traditional and modern, local and global, rooted and cosmopolitan; as host country, Kazakhstan has placed at the center of this inward- and outward-looking cultural dynamic, possibly positioning itself as a leader of nation-states seeking a similar international image.

NOTES

1. Tanya Merchant has discussed an analogous situation in her examination of Uzbek pop music and nationalism, "Popping Tradition: Performing *Maqom* and Uzbek 'National' *Estrada* in the 21st Century," *Popular Music and Society* 32, no. 3 (July 2009): 373.

2. For a more detailed explanation of virtual fieldwork as it is utilized in the field of ethnomusicology, see Tim Cooley, Katherine Meizel, and Nasir Syed, "Virtual Fieldwork: Three Case Studies," in *Shadows in the Field: New Perspectives for Fieldwork in Ethnomusicology*, eds. Gregory F. Barz and Timothy J. Cooley (New York: Oxford University Press, 2008), 90–107.

3. "Elektrozhetygen vpervye prozvuchal na festival The Spirit of Tengri," *Tengri News*, June 7, 2014, http://tengrinews.kz/music/elektrojetyigen-vpervyie-prozvuchal-na-festivale-The-Spirit-of-Tengri-256650/; "Festival 'The Spirit of Tengri' eshche bol'she ob"edinit sem'i kazakhstantsev," *Tengri News*, May 31, 2014, http://tengrinews.kz/music/festival-The-Spirit-of-Tengri-esche-bolshe-obyedinit-semi-kazahstantsev-256234/; "'Roksonaki' na festivale The Spirit of Tengri ispolniat zabytye pesni predkov," *Tengri News*, May 26, 2014, http://tengrinews.kz/music/roksonaki-na-festivale-The-Spirit-of-Tengri-ispolnyat--zabyityie-pesni-predkov-255923/; "The Spirit of Tengri—The First International Festival of Contemporary Ethnic Music," *Tengri News*, June 10, 2013, http://en.tengrinews.kz/fotoarchive/464/; "The Spirit of Tengri Festival to Gather Artists from All Around Eurasia," *Tengri News*, June 5, 2013, http://en.tengrinews.kz/show_and_style/The-Spirit-of-Tengri-festival-to-gather-artists-from-all-around-Eurasia-19990/.

4. Helen A. Regis and Shana Walton, "Producing the Folk at the New Orleans Jazz and Heritage Festival," *Journal of American Folklore* 121, no. 482 (Fall 2008): 399; Max Peter Baumann, "Festival, Musical Actors, and Mental Constructs in the Process of Globalization," *World of Music* 43, no. 2/3 (2001): 10.

5. Wendy DeBano, "Enveloping Music in Gender, Nation, and Islam: Women's Music Festivals in Post-Revolutionary Iran," *Iranian Studies* 38, no. 3 (2005): 441–462; Ronit Seter, "Jerusalem and Tel-Aviv: Different News from Israel (Or, One More Step toward Peace): Three Contemporary Music Festivals," *Tempo* 59, no. 233 (July 2005): 46–51; Adriana Helbig, Nino Tsitsishvili, and Erica Haskell, "Managing Musical Diversity within Frameworks of Western Development Aid: Views from Ukraine, Georgia, and Bosnia and Herzegovina," *Yearbook for Traditional Music* 40 (2008): 46–59.

6. Baumann, "Festival, Musical Actors and Mental Constructs in the Process of Globalization," 14.

7. Regis and Walton, "Producing the Folk at the New Orleans Jazz and Heritage Festival," 408–409.

8. Baumann, "Festival, Musical Actors and Mental Constructs in the Process of Globalization," 26.

9. Mark Slobin, "Introduction," in *Retuning Culture: Musical Changes in Central and Eastern Europe*, ed. Mark Slobin (Durham, NC: Duke University Press, 1996), 2–3.

10. Marina Frolova-Walker, "'National in Form, Socialist in Content': Musical Nation-Building in the Soviet Republics," *Journal of the American Musicological Society* 51, no. 2 (1998): 331–371

11. Slobin, "Introduction," 6.

12. Regis and Walton, "Producing the Folk at the New Orleans Jazz and Heritage Festival," 408; Baumann, "Festival, Musical Actors and Mental Constructs in the Process of Globalization," 25.

13. Ian Biddle and Vanessa Knights, eds. *Music, National Identity, and the Politics of Location* (Burlington, VT: Ashgate, 2007), 5.

14. Biddle and Knights, *Music, National Identity, and the Politics of Location*, 7.

15. Baumann, "Festival, Musical Actors, and Mental Constructs in the Process of Globalization," 21–22.

16. Baumann, "Festival, Musical Actors, and Mental Constructs in the Process of Globalization," 19.

17. "Festival' sovremennogo etnicheskoi muzyki 'The Spirit of Tengri' (Almaty, 2013)." Recorded and edited by Rifat Serazhiyev, Egor Evdokimov /Artparovoz Production/. Producer A. Nuzhnyi, Artparovoz.tv©2013, http://www.youtube.com/watch?v=F9pOXheX4yk.

18. K.M. Baipakov and B.E. Kumekov, 2003. "The Kazakhs," in *History of Civilizations of Central Asia*, vol. 5, ed. Chahyar Adle and Irfan Habib (Paris: UNESCO Publishing, 2003), 108.

19. In her study of women's music festivals in Iran, DeBano notes that festival concert materials consistently utilized the three colors of the Iranian flag, which she interprets as "visually reinforce[ing] state ideologies in a very unique and meaningful way." See DeBano, "Enveloping Music in Gender, Nation, and Islam," 447.

20. "The Spirit of Tengri Festival."

21. "Festival The Spirit of Tengri."

22. Examples of each of these artists may be view on YouTube: Sainkho Namchylak: https://www.youtube.com/watch?v=f2R0edFkrw4 ; Aldaspan: https://www.youtube.com/watch?v=Iv3Xb1SeRiU ; Yuliana Krivoshapkina andHapanasasa: https://www.youtube.com/watch?v=qFZuEYMs4b4.

23. Asemgul Kasenova, "'Mamoi B'ork' okrestili pevitsy iz Tuvy na festival The Spirit of Tengri," *Tengri News*, June 9, 2013, http://tengrinews.kz/music/mamoy-bork-okrestili-pevitsu-iz-tuvyi-na-festivale-The-Spirit-of-Tengri-235751/.

24. 31 Kanal (31.kz) interview posted to "Spirit of Tengri" Facebook page on June 14, 2013, https://www.facebook.com/TheSpiritOfTengri.

25. "Festival' sovremennogo etnicheskoi muzyki 'The Spirit of Tengri.'"

26. "Festival' sovremennogo etnicheskoi muzyki 'The Spirit of Tengri.'"

27. "The Spirit of Tengri Festival to Gather Artists from All Around Eurasia."

28. Baumann, Baumann, "Festival, Musical Actors, and Mental Constructs in the Process of Globalization," 24.

29. "Roksonaki."

30. Regis and Walton, "Producing the Folk at the New Orleans Jazz and Heritage Festival," 408.

31. DeBano similarly notes the "powerful image of nation" projected by the use of the *Talar Vahdat* (Unity Hall) for a women's music festival in Iran. See "Enveloping Music in Gender, Nation, and Islam."

32. "Elektrozhetygen vpervye prozvuchal na festival The Spirit of Tengri."

33. "Elektrozhetygen vpervye prozvuchal na festival The Spirit of Tengri."

34. Aktoty Aitzhanova, Shigeo Katsu, Johannes F. Linn, and Vladislav Yezhov, eds. *Kazakhstan 2050: Toward a Modern Society for All* (New Delhi: Oxford University Press, 2014), 65.

Chapter 11

Return Migration from the United States

Exploring the Dynamics of Cultural Change in Kazakhstan

Douglas Blum

Post-Soviet Kazakhstan has been immersed in development and the accompanying sharp rise in urbanization and higher education as well as a massive increase in exposure to the outside world.[1] This, in turn, has created considerable tension—quite typical in the context of globalization—between modern values based on individual rights and traditional notions of deference or propriety.[2] As a broad generalization, such processes tend to result in "hybridity" according to which certain novel ideas are absorbed while others are revised or rejected.[3] Yet we still lack a sophisticated understanding of the personal, as well as interpersonal, processes and mechanisms through which hybridization occurs at the microlevel, including the meanings and consequences of new practices for those directly concerned. Return migration provides a useful and often quite vivid setting for addressing these questions, especially when it serves as a conduit for potent flows of cultural difference.[4] This chapter investigates the social process of globalization by exploring the thoughts and interactions of young Kazakhs who return home after living in the United States. Specifically, it considers the attitudes and experiences of these return migrants regarding gender equality, functional knowledge, volunteerism, self-sufficiency, openness, casual dress, and being nice to strangers. Along the way, it seeks to elucidate the practices involved in cultural borrowing and the negotiation of identity change.

The following analysis is based on ninety-two semi-structured personal interviews conducted in Almaty and Astana during 2011 and 2012. This included seventy-seven Kazakh return migrants, all of whom had spent at least three months in the United States and were between 17 and 27 years old. It also included 15 Kazakhs who had not traveled abroad, but who had interacted extensively with similar returnees from the United States. In addition, I conducted three group discussions with returnees and practiced participant observation in many everyday settings. Interviewees came largely from middle-class backgrounds and various regions of Kazakhstan.

In a nutshell, the results of this study suggest that foreign practices—even those generally taken for granted by citizens of the countries in which they occur—are inescapably associated with certain underlying values and identity constructs. Some are widely considered attractive, and therefore are frequently adopted and introduced back in Kazakhstan. Others encounter more extensive resistance, and return migrants who try to incorporate such practices into their lives may be unable to do so successfully. A fascinating question then becomes why certain practices are more readily transferable than others, as well as what sorts of arguments or justifications do, or do not, tend to facilitate uptake. The conclusion takes up this issue in an effort to briefly explain the observed patterns of cultural borrowing.

GENDER EQUALITY

Both before and since the fall of the USSR in late 1991, women in Kazakhstan have labored under the "double burden." They exercise at least nominal equality in the workforce while at the same time assuming all responsibilities for homemaking. Kazakh women have also traditionally been expected to defer to their husbands on all major decisions affecting the family and household. As part of this orientation, young women are taught to be generally demure and submissive in their dealings with men. Consequently, experiencing U.S.-style gender equality—which often happens when Kazakhs come to urban areas or college campuses in the United States—has a profound impact on many of them. One young woman, recounting her impression of the differences between gender roles in both countries, commented, "Girls are just as outgoing and expressive as guys; they are not shy." Another shared her main discovery: "I saw that men can do household chores."

Of course, such lessons do not remain mere abstractions, but often translate into new personal values and emotional commitments. Zarina was one such young woman, having developed starkly different perspectives across a wide range of issues while in the United States, and she offered a personal example of how her attitudes had shifted. As she recalled, "I heard women proclaim their independence. They're strong because of it." Zarina, too, came away from her experience feeling able to assert herself, even in a roomful of men. Or as another female returnee related the change in her own attitude: "If my girlfriends invite me to go out to a club but my boyfriend resists, but it is very important for me, I will say, 'I have to have freedom.'"

Kazakh men, not surprisingly, tend to have quite different reactions to the gender equality they witness in the United States. A typical attitude was voiced by Ilyas, a generally conservative young man who was enthralled by American efficiency and technological sophistication. For him gender equality was unquestionably appropriate insofar as it concerned matters in the workforce. "I mean, it's the twenty-first century!" he sputtered. "That's how it should be. People are equal." Obviously anyone who failed to recognize this fact was hopelessly outdated. At the same time, however, Ilyas insisted that "men should be dominant" in the household since this was essential in order to maintain basic notions of morality and male pride of place.

Post-return interactions are thus fairly predictable: few men promote gender equality in the private sphere, and those who do have scant hope of persuading their male peers to follow their lead. Indeed, such individuals may be derided as unmasculine. Almas J. was one young man who altered his views on these matters and tried to convince his old friends. He recalled them mocking him: "Hey, you are supposed to be in charge! Aren't you a man?" Anticipating such challenges, even those few progressively inclined males generally keep their opinions to themselves. In contrast, women returnees are not only more likely to discuss such issues with (mainly female) friends, but also to gain converts as a result. An example was related by Gaisha, a nonmigrant who said she was fascinated to hear that American men did not try to restrict their wives or girlfriends. As she explained, "Here a traditional man would never allow you going to a club without him. He will always call, try to control." Gaisha was convinced that the alternative was superior. "The West," she declared, "is a standard of how it should be." As a result of such interactions, it seems plausible that return migration will contribute to an ongoing shift in gender constructs, especially—or at least—among younger Kazakh women.

FUNCTIONAL KNOWLEDGE

Although it has improved dramatically since the mid-1990s, Kazakhstan's economy continues to suffer from high rates of nepotism and inefficiency. Yet the regime of President Nursultan Nazarbayev has strongly encouraged the acquisition of technological proficiency and other cutting-edge skills, and it has subsidized programs for travel abroad for this purpose. Inasmuch as the United States is widely regarded as the leader in global development, young visitors are eager to absorb and transmit their new practical skills, as a result of which they acquire status as well as income. In short, this is perceived to be a win–win proposition, benefiting the individual as well as the nation. As a result, the vast majority of visitors absorb functional knowledge voraciously and uncritically, despite the fact that implementing new practices back home often involves massive changes at every level of organization. In addition to adopting various skills, many returnees also embrace a Horatio Alger-esque image of limitless possibility. Erbolat, who studied and also completed a telecommunications internship in the United States, was one of many who articulated this sentiment. "For me nothing is impossible," he averred. "I know that it is possible to earn a million dollars if I want to."

Not surprisingly, in keeping with this outlook, the term "entrepreneur" carries immense cachet as an emblem of personal virtue. Arman Au. offered an example of this attitude, recalling with obvious pride how he "got the spirit of entrepreneurship" while living in America and decided to open his own business in Almaty. As he recounted, without appearing to boast, innumerable friends and acquaintances were impressed and even inspired by his knowledge as well as his gumption. Similar ideas were frequently echoed by other returnees using essentially the same stock phrases, such as "accept challenges" or "anything is possible."

Like returnees, nonmigrants also tend to express nearly unqualified enthusiasm for American know-how. As a result—and quite unlike other borrowed practices—there is little need for negotiation about the desirability of functional knowledge. On the contrary, returnees find that such ideas are almost unequivocally accepted by others. This appears to be equally true for specific technical skills and "businesslike" attitudes in general. Zhanar reported that she was perceived to be "more competitive and ambitious" since her time in the United States, which she considered an obvious compliment. Likewise, Aisha Bo. found her old friends remarkably eager to learn: "They try to listen to us. They try to get that drive [to succeed]." This combination of perceived power and unquestionable rightness offers a perfect example of Gramscian hegemony in action.

SELF-SUFFICIENCY

Almost all of the young return migrants in this study reported being strongly attracted to the American ideal of self-sufficiency. This refers to a range of practices constitutive of personal autonomy, understood both as a transcendent value and as a pathway to personal fulfillment. Enacting self-sufficiency therefore not only necessitates, but also lionizes, a departure from traditional notions of hierarchy and community.

A dramatic example of such views was provided by Kamila A., who came back feeling completely alienated from virtually all Kazakh customs, including those rooted in kinship or place. "We have really crazy traditions here," she said with disdain. "Like when somebody dies, we have to invite everyone over." For Kamila this was nothing short of ludicrous. "I don't feel like it. For people I don't even know?!" While less extreme or sweeping in their attitudes, many other returnees expressed reservations about doing their parents' bidding when this was at odds with their own preferences. Azamat was a young father who brought back with him a different understanding of family obligations. "Here [parents] continue to make the most important decisions—about us and our kids," he explained. "Like if they want us to do something related to the education of our children, you should listen to that. But in America I guess nobody cares. Once kids get married, they are not kids anymore." Azamat emphasized that he and his wife merely wanted to escape "excessive" parental influence in order to achieve independence, something that that they now regarded as an inviolable right. "We'll take into account their opinions, but we'll try to make our own decisions." To him this seemed like a balanced and unquestionably proper approach.

For many young returnees, the underlying essence of self-sufficient practice was a new sense of empowerment. Olzhas Y. described himself as a typical young Kazakh man. "I used to think I couldn't do anything by myself. If I went to a club I would go with ten guys, or if I was studying I would share notes." But all of this changed after he took the plunge and started working on his own. Soon enough he accepted the American way: "When you do something yourself, you get more confidence in yourself," he declared. For him there was no turning back.

For returnees, however, this attitude is a tough sell back home, often sparking disagreement with parents and extended family. Daulet was a fairly conservative individual who retained a number of key traditional values, but he ran into resistance due to his decision not to take a job at a Big Four accounting firm in Kazakhstan. "I didn't like [the firm's] attitude about their employees," he recalled. "They want you to be a slave for them, so I refused to work there. My mom was annoyed. She said, 'This isn't the US.'" Daulet stood firm, much to his mother's shock and dismay, but he also drew an important lesson from the experience: "I try to talk less about career planning and jobs with my parents," he confided. Of course, this in itself represents a sharp departure from established social norms, much like Azamat's definition of "excessive" parental involvement.

Younger Kazakhs appear more likely to be intrigued by the concept of self-sufficiency, glimpsing in it the prospect of a life free from traditional obligations. Arman T. worked in a retail store, but conversed with a close friend who had traveled to the United States. The lesson he drew from those conversations was that "in America every person can do what suits him." For Arman this was a liberating realization. As he explained, "I think for myself. I live on my own, away from my parents' village." Most nonmigrants, however, feel incapable of adopting such alien practices. Darkhan had heard tales of independence from his friends, but could not conceive of being able to enact such practices on his own. "Here people listen to their parents always, as long as they are alive," he explained. "About education, marrying, buying a house—the parents make these decisions." How could he presume to challenge the way things were? As his case demonstrates, the wider uptake of self-sufficiency is generally checked by conventional attitudes of deference (to parents and elders) and by other entrenched social obligations.

VOLUNTEERISM

Compared with other countries, Kazakhstan scores low on indicators of charitable giving.[5] Charity has traditionally been reserved for close or extended family, and most young travelers to the United States are mystified when they first encounter it.[6] As one young woman recalled, "It was completely foreign to me." The idea that someone would offer to work on behalf of nameless, distant others, while receiving nothing tangible in return, strikes many as the very definition of foolishness. And yet quite a number of returnees end up making charitable donations or engaging in volunteer work. Such individuals are clearly impressed by the deeply principled nature of charitable deeds, seeing in them an expression of a newfound commitment to Kazakh society as a whole. Kuralay, for example, explained that her motivation for participating was "just to help people, not for personal benefit." For her this was something of a revelation.

Another important reason for endorsing volunteer work is fealty to the nation-state, and many express their enthusiasm about the prospect of "doing something" for Kazakhstan. In this respect volunteering resembles the functional knowledge that returnees often endorse as a form of patriotism. The Nazarbayev regime has appropriated this concept in recent years and has begun to support charitable work as a means of augmenting state capacity. The most prominent example is the Bolashak Presidential Scholarship Program, which systematically promotes philanthropy on the part of its alumni. Regardless of precisely how it is construed, however, the key point is that many return migrants discover the social and/or emotional value of giving to others in need. For them these are fresh and profound realizations.

But once again, matters are entirely different back in the homeland. Few returnees even bother explaining volunteer work to people in Kazakhstan, since they correctly anticipate the negative, and even incredulous, reactions they are likely to encounter. As a result, many discuss the topic only with close friends and family. An example of this was Nargiza O., who managed to convince some of her old friends about the value of charity by discussing it in emotional terms: "I enjoy giving others something. It means that I am rich enough to share with others—rich not about money, but maybe about time or knowledge, experience, etc." Another occasionally successful approach involves appealing to nationalism. Thus one nonmigrant commented that she admired returnees' volunteerism: "I care about the future of Kazakhstan." For the most part, however, even optimistic return migrants soon abandon their efforts to gain fresh adherents. Anar came back from the United States brimming with idealism, but gave up trying to persuade others because, as she put it, "Our people cannot understand that someone can do something for other people for free."

OPENNESS

Another category of practice often commented upon is what Kazakhs refer to as "openness" or frank and honest expression. This includes comments that may be indelicate, brusque, argumentative, or controversial. Openness is therefore a marked departure from the traditional mode of discourse, which demands respect for convention and politeness to elders.

There appear to be several distinct rationales for enacting openness. Some returnees are drawn to it mainly for practical reasons; that is as a way of promoting beneficial change through debate. Zhanar, who (as noted above) was praised for being competitive, enthusiastically subscribed to this view, recalling how amazed she was to find that the U.S. classroom was a hothouse of intellectual exchange. This was the opposite of her experience growing up in Kazakhstan, where, as she put it, "students just sit there." Zhanar considered the U.S. system to be vastly preferable because, "In this [kind of] society it would be interesting to live. Maybe you would find a better opinion." A second reason for embracing openness stems from a new feeling of self-confidence due to having one's individual opinion affirmed, which then easily blends into the idea of freedom of speech. Aisha Bai had always been a proper young woman, but after visiting the United States found herself unwilling to sit docilely. Indeed, she had challenged the opinion of her aunt, who was the matriarch of her entire extended family: "My aunt criticized my mom. According to the traditional scenario, I was supposed to sit and be quiet and smile and promise to come back. But I said, 'If I don't come it's not because of my mom, it's because I don't want to come.' She was shocked. Since then she thinks that I'm unethical, that the U.S. spoiled me." For Aisha herself, taking such a stand would have been inconceivable in the past. Finally, a few return migrants enact openness simply in order to unsettle established attitudes and encourage free thought. Indira D. epitomized this approach with her sharp wit and progressive outlook. As she remarked, "Sometimes I like to mess with people. I try to push them out of their comfort zones because it might change their views or perspectives."

Yet while some returnees do take the plunge, most either reject openness or severely restrict its enactment. Bek-Ali explained that although he appreciated the benefits of honesty, and had become somewhat "more direct" since living in the United States, he nevertheless remained circumspect. "Here you have to be diplomatic," he emphasized, "you have to maneuver. I can't just say what I want, I have to formulate it." As a result, the vast majority of return migrants routinely engage in dissimulation. Aisha Bo. was aware of just how eccentric her post-U.S. views would appear, so she generally chose not to voice them. After all, why go around looking for trouble? As she noted, "The mentality here is different, and you just kind of need to adjust."

Despite such apparent discretion, the contrast in behavior is still often noticeable. Ordinary Kazakhs frequently observe that returnees tend to be unafraid of asking questions or expressing opinions. As one nonmigrant observed, "They always ask, 'Why?'" A small handful of nonmigrants are actually drawn to various forms of openness. One young woman described how she had modeled herself on a friend who had lived in the United States. "Now," she exclaimed triumphantly, "I can express myself. I am not afraid." But many who do experience openness react to it with hostility. This is especially the case if unfavorable comparisons are made between U.S. and Kazakh practices, something that is considered insulting to national pride. Others appear intimidated by the very notion of speaking out of turn in the presence of elders or superiors. And, of course, most nonmigrants have no opportunity to react positively or negatively, precisely because returnees tend to keep their unorthodox views under wraps.

BEING NICE TO STRANGERS

The typical Kazakh custom when encountering strangers on the street is to ignore them entirely. The notion of being polite, or even friendly, is quite remote from everyday consciousness. Consequently, numerous returnees remarked that after arriving in the United States they were flabbergasted, even disturbed, by the common practice of asking, "How are you?" Indira K.'s reaction was typical: "I used to freak out!" And yet Indira's ultimate decision was also typical. She grew to appreciate minor pleasantries for the cumulative difference they made in the social climate, and she became determined to incorporate such practices into her own life back home. "I don't want to lose the manners I gained in America," she stated.

Other returnees reach a range of different conclusions, all of which provide an insight into the social processes involved in enacting and transmitting cultural differences. Some, like Nargiza, decide to foster positive change in the social climate. "I try to treat everyone in a friendly way, and to be polite," she said. "Maybe people will change." Others know better than to even try, at least not more than once. Saltanat was charmed by American politeness, but left it behind. For her there was no point in trying. "In the U.S. you can easily say hi to someone you don't know. Here they think that you're stupid." And still other returnees seek a delicate balance between improving and inflaming local sensibilities. Bek-Ali, who as we have seen was careful about being "excessively" open, tried to find a happy medium here also. "Now I say hi in the elevator," he explained. "[But] I just say hi, I don't ask, 'How are you?'" This, he believed, would be going too far.

For the reasons already discussed, any immoderately friendly behavior stands out. If nonmigrants happen to know the particular returnee and understand the latter's reasons for behaving this way, they may be supportive. As one put it admiringly, "They have made progress." But most consider such conduct on the part of their friends to be unwarranted and even foolish. And not surprisingly, those who do not understand the reasons behind such bizarre conduct are unlikely to be so indulgent. In these ways the decision to be nice to strangers is rather similar to volunteering. A crucial difference, however, is that volunteering is done semi-privately and is generally received anonymously, if not gratefully, whereas being nice to strangers is performed in public and usually gets a frosty reception. As a result, many who do repatriate the practice soon decide to abandon it. Ainur Kh., a thoughtful and generous young woman, was one of those who initially felt strongly about the value of being friendly to others. After a few years, however, she reported that while she still tried to smile at strangers, she did so less often than previously, because "people look at me like I'm silly or crazy."

DRESSING CASUALLY

Most Kazakhs dress well, or at least appropriately, in public, which means sporting "European" styles and brand names. Beyond making a statement about status and fashion, clothing is also considered a barometer of decency. As one returnee explained, "You have to look a certain way if you want people to treat you normally." And yet return migrants often disappoint such expectations by dressing very informally. Damir was one who came back with a different attitude about this. "I just put on something comfortable," he shrugged. "I don't care." Many expressed similar views, often commenting that they were suddenly struck by the contrast with Kazakh attitudes, which, in turn, generates a critical reevaluation about what sorts of things ought to matter and why (or why not). A case in point was Ainur Kh. who became increasingly inclined to ruminate about social norms and their underlying assumptions. As she put it, "My old friends are more materialistic; I'm not.

I don't care how I look." In this way Ainur offers a perfect example of how returnees may consciously identify with specific clusters of alien values.

Yet while often insisting that they "don't care" what others think, in fact many returnees *do* care how they look. That is, they may intentionally wear casual or unconventional outfits as a way of publically rejecting superficiality and mindless conformism. Here again such acts tend to have a pedagogical flavor. Alma explained her own reason for putting on such unconventional sartorial displays. "Maybe some of them are thinking, 'Why didn't I ever think of wearing that before? Why wasn't I brave enough?'"

Regardless of whether the motivation is conscious or unconscious, anyone who fails to meet accepted standards of dress immediately stands out, and old friends are quick to observe and remark on this fact. Indeed, nonmigrants frequently comment that returnees are less well attired now than before they went to the United States. In a few cases, the reaction may be one of approval. Arman Au., a devoutly religious and deeply serious young man, chose to dress modestly as a way of rejecting worldly ostentation, and he laughed at the idea that "sometimes young people perceive me as a cool person," because of his casual style. Far more often, however, sporting American clothes is considered a betrayal of national identity. Rustam was one of many returnees who ran into this sort of resistance. "Some friends said that I love America," he recounted. "I asked why. They said, 'All your clothes, your style.'" Ostensibly aligning oneself with a foreign country is, of course, not value neutral. Because of similar reactions many choose to dress "properly" in order to avoid social friction. Anar had adopted numerous American attitudes, but had done so deliberately and with due reflection, as a result of which she was able to differentiate between relatively more or less central commitments. When she returned, her aunts were horrified by her lack of appropriately feminine attire. "I told them that I wore comfortable clothes in the U.S. They said, 'Forget your American clothes, we will buy you new clothes!'" In this instance, she decided to capitulate and to save her strength for more important battles ahead, like marrying a man of her choosing.

DISCUSSION AND CONCLUSIONS

As the foregoing discussion shows, certain U.S. practices and norms can easily be introduced and accepted, while others must be extensively adapted or "localized," and some can scarcely be enacted at all. In particular, practices that directly impact the reigning social order are more highly constrained than those that are purely personal or interpersonal. Thus, volunteer work may be dismissed as a harmless eccentricity, whereas acting in an unladylike way or refusing to defer to a man cannot be so easily excused. Some new practices are also substantially enabled by global norms, and returnees may consciously invoke ideas of human rights, freedom, and equality in order to justify their behavior. This is especially obvious with respect to gender equality. Yet the degree of enablement depends on the audience in question; in some circles the intrusion of supposed U.S. values may be resented.[7] Finally, the role of structural factors cannot be overlooked. The United States is widely considered to be the most powerful and developed country in the world, and acquiring commensurate knowledge is almost never problematized by returnees or their interlocutors—not to mention the fact that doing so is rewarded by employers and supported by the regime.

On an individual level, for those who spend time in the United States, the question is whether a given practice is considered attractive or offensive—and therefore whether borrowing is even attempted. A significant segment of the Kazakh community is repulsed by much of American culture, as a result of which their identities and cultural orientations remain largely unchanged. Olzhas, a generally conservative young man, who perceived rampant debauchery and hyper-individualism in the United States, ended up largely withdrawing and socializing with other Central Asian students while living abroad. As he explained, "We hung out together to prevent the influence of extremes." On the other end of the spectrum are those who experience a transformational change in outlook, involving not only a shift in particular attitudes but also in their very way of thinking and being in the world. Zarina was one such young woman, having been raised in a manner bounded by established notions of appropriateness. As she observed, "We were taught to accept things the way they are. Now I'm asking questions, of myself and about everything."

As a highly distilled version of a book-length project, the present chapter does not attempt to make an elaborate theoretical argument, but it may be worth noting that the analytical approach used here is rooted in critical theory and practice theory, both of which are concerned with the roles of agency and structure in the process of identity formation. In particular, it draws on the works of Margaret Archer[8] and Pierre Bourdieu[9] in order to gauge the significance of subjective ideas and of social constraints and enablements, as these bear on the introduction of U.S. values and practices. Archer and other critical theorists would emphasize the importance of "reflexivity" or mode of thinking, which may range from essentially replicative and conformist (like Olzhas in the above paragraph) to highly critical and introspective (like Zarina). In contrast, Bourdieu would stress learned repertoires of normalcy and their structurally anchored resistance to change, as well as the ability of astute actors to justify change at the margins.

Depending on how such questions are decided, there may be a greater or lesser degree of social adjustment. Of course, all return migrants receive approval for their U.S.-acquired practical skills and, in many cases, excellent jobs as well. The more problematic issue has to do with their underlying attachments and sense of self. Those who have retained basic values and identities are able to re-acclimate easily, while also preserving their previous relationships. Yet those who have undergone truly profound changes may experience extreme "return culture shock," and therefore have difficulty fitting back into their previous social milieus. Many in this latter group face frequent quandaries about whether, or how, to reveal their new preferences. This is true even of seemingly benign practices such as volunteering, and still more so of deeply divisive notions like gender equality. The result is often a difficult balancing act whereby returnees selectively conform and dissimulate in public, while also sustaining transnational ties through social media and seeking out like-minded others with whom to bond, strategize, and commiserate. This, in turn, has spawned the rise of artificial, Westernized settings such as coffeehouses, where such individuals congregate and where their deviant identities may be safely enacted.

In all of the above ways, return migrants actively mediate and instantiate cultural globalization, including knowledge compatible with global capitalism as well as individualism, value eclecticism, and an abiding tendency to question established social hierarchies and norms. Together with other sources and vectors of globalization, they are likely to play a disproportionately significant role in shaping Kazakhstan's development for years to come.

NOTES

1. Ronald Inglehart and Christian Welzel, "How Development Leads to Democracy: What We Know about Modernization," *Foreign Affairs* 88, no. 2 (2009): 33–49.
2. Ken Roberts, *Youth in Transition: Eastern Europe and the West* (Basingstoke, UK: Palgrave Macmillan, 2009).
3. Douglas W. Blum, *National Identity and Globalization: Youth, State, and Society in Post-Soviet Eurasia* (New York: Cambridge University Press, 2007).
4. Jane Jackson, "Globalization, Internationalization, and Short-Term Stays Abroad," *International Journal of Intercultural Relations* 32, no. 4 (2008): 349–358.
5. Legatum Institute, *Prosperity Index, 2012*, http://www.prosperity.com.
6. Ed Schatz, *Modern Clan Politics: The Power of "Blood" in Kazakhstan and Beyond* (Seattle: University of Washington Press, 2004).
7. Ulbolsyn Sandybaeva and Dametken Tolgambaeva, "Sotsial'naya Etika Prosmotra Fil'mov Sredi Molodezhi Kazakhstana" (paper presented at the ESCAS annual conference, Astana 2013).
8. Margaret Archer, *Realist Social Theory: The Morphogenetic Approach* (New York: Cambridge University Press, 1995).
9. Pierre Bourdieu, *Outline of a Theory of Practice* (New York: Cambridge University Press, 1977).

Bibliography

Adams, Laura and Assel Rustemova. "Mass Spectacle and Styles of Governmentality in Kazakhstan and Uzbekistan." *Europe-Asia Studies* 61, no. 7 (2009): 1249–1276.

Adams, Laura. *The Spectacular State: Culture and National Identity in Uzbekistan*. Durham, NC and London: Duke University Press, 2010.

Agnew, John. "Italy's Island Other: Sicily's History in the Modern Italian Body Politic." *Emergences: Journal for the Study of Media and Composite Cultures* 10, no. 2 (2000): 301–311.

Agnew, John. "The Impossible Capital: Monumental Rome under Liberal and Fascist Regimes, 1870–1943." *Geografiska Annaler* 80B, no. 4 (1998): 229–240.

Agnew, John. *Geopolitics: Re-Visioning World Politics*. New York: Routledge, 2003.

Agnew, John. *Globalization and Sovereignty*. Lanham, MD: Rowman and Littlefield, 2009.

Ahmed, Sara. *The Cultural Politics of Emotion*. Edinburgh: Edinburgh University Press, 2004.

Aiken, Jonathan. *Nazarbayev and the Making of Modern Kazakhstan*. London: Bloomsbury Academic Press, 2009.

Aitzhanova, Aktoty, Shigeo Katsu, Johannes F. Linn, and Vladislav Yezhov, eds. *Kazakhstan 2050: Toward a Modern Society for All*. New Delhi: Oxford University Press, 2014.

Akiner, Shirin. *The Formation of Kazakh Identity: From Tribe to Nation-State*. London: Royal Institute of International Affairs, 1995.

Akylbaeva, I.M., Z.B. Malgaraeva, and L.A. Umirzakova. Ethnic Identity Condition and Tendency: Materials of the Republican Scientific Practical Conference and "The Independent Kazakhstan: History and Experience" Devoted to the 20th Anniversary of Kazakhstan Independence, Astana 2011.

Aleprete, Michael. "Authoritarian Persistence in History's Aftermath." In *International Dimensions of Authoritarian Persistence: Lessons from Post-Soviet States*, edited by Michael Aleprete and Rachel Vanderhill, 1–10. Lanham, MD: Lexington Press, 2013.

Alexander, Catherine. "Waste under Socialism and After: A Case Study from Almaty." In *Enduring Socialism: Explorations of Revolution and Transformation, Restoration and Continuation*, edited by H.G. West and P. Raman, 148–168. New York: Berghahn Books, 2009.

Alexander, Gerard. "Institutionalized Uncertainty, the Rule of Law and the Sources of Democratic Stability." *Comparative Political Studies* 35, no. 10 (2002): 1145–1170.

Aliyev, Rakhat. *The Godfather-in-Law: Eine Dokumentation*. Vienna: Ibera Verlag, 2009.

Allina-Pisano, Jessica. "How to Tell an Axe Murderer: An Essay on Ethnography, Truth, and Lies." In *Political Ethnography: What Immersion Contributes to the Study of Power*, edited by E. Schatz, 53–74. Chicago: University of Chicago Press, 2009.

Anacker, Shonin. "Geographies of Power in Nazarbayev's Astana." *Eurasian Geography and Economics* 45, no. 7 (2004): 515–533.

Anderson, Benedict. "Introduction." In *Mapping the Nation*, edited by Gopal Balakrishnan, 1–16. New York: Verso, 1996.

Anderson, Benedict. *Imagined Communities*. London: Verso, 2006.

Anderson, Richard. "Look at All Those Nouns in a Row – Authoritarianism, Democracy, and the Iconicity of Political Russian." *Political Communication* 13, no. 2 (1996): 145–164.

Andrews, Emily. "Kazakhstan: An Ambitious Pension Reform." Social Protection Discussion Paper No. SP 0104, Washington, DC: World Bank, 2001. Accessed March 15, 2015. http://documents.worldbank.org/curated/en/2001/01/1620905/kazakhstan-ambitious-pension-reform.

Antonsich, Marco. "On Territory, the Nation-State, and the Crisis of the Hyphen." *Progress in Human Geography* 33, no. 6 (2009): 789–806.

Antonsich, Marco. "Searching for Belonging: An Analytical Framework." *Geography Compass* 4, no. 6 (2010): 644–659.

Appadurai, Arjun. "Disjuncture and Difference in the Global Cultural Economy." *Public Culture* 2 (1990): 1–24.

Appadurai, Arjun. "Sovereignty without Territoriality: Notes for a Post National Geography." In *The Geography of Identity*, edited by Patricia Yaeger, 41–58. Ann Arbor: University of Michigan Press, 1996.

Archer, Margaret. *Realist Social Theory: The Morphogenetic Approach*. New York: Cambridge University Press, 1995.

Aretxaga, Begoña. "A Fictional Reality: Paramilitary Death Squads and the Construction of State Terror in Spain." In *Death Squad: The Anthropology of State Terror*, edited by Jeffrey A. Sluka, 46–69. Philadelphia: University of Pennsylvania Press, 2000.

Aretxaga, Begoña. "Maddening States." *Annual Review of Anthropology* 32 (2003): 393–410.

Armistead, Louise (2013). "SFO Launches Criminal Investigations into ENRC." *The Telegraph*, April 25, 2013. Accessed May 7, 2013. http://www.telegraph.co.uk/finance/newsbysector/industry/mining/10017960/SFO-launches-criminal-investigation-into-ENRC.html.

Ashimbaev, D. *Kto est' kto v Kazakhstane. Biograficheskaia entsiklopediia*. Almaty: Credo, 2006.

ASRK. 2010. *Perepis'*. Astana: The Agency of Statistics of the Republic of Kazakhstan. Accessed March 30, 2011. http://www.stat.kz/p_perepis/Documents/Перепись%20рус.pdf.

Assenova, M. "Ablyazov Sentenced to Prison in UK for Contempt of Court." *Eurasia Daily Monitor*, February 27, 2012.

Ayaganov, B.G. *Politicheskie partii i obshchestvennye dvizheniia sovremennogo Kazakhstana*. Almaty: Ministerstvo pechati i massovoi informatsii respubliki Kazahstan, 1994.

Aygazin, Zhanybek. "Sistema pensionnogo maloobespecheniia." *Expert-Kazakhstan*, #6–7 (2012). Accessed March 15, 2015. http://expert.ru/kazakhstan/2012/07/sistema-pensionnogo-maloobespecheniya/.

Babak, Vladimir, Demian Vaisman, and Aryeh Wasserman, eds. *Political Organization in Central Asia and Azerbaijan*. London: Frank Cass, 2004.

Bach, Daniel C. and Mamoudou Gazibo, eds. *Neopatrimonialism in Africa and Beyond*. New York: Routledge, 2012.

Badie, Bernard, et. al. *International Encyclopedia of Political Science*. London: Sage Publications, 2011.

Baipakov, K.M. and B.E. Kumekov. "The Kazakhs." In *History of Civilizations of Central Asia*, vol. 5, edited by Chahyar Adle and Irfan Habib, 89–108. Paris: UNESCO Publishing, 2003.

Bakić-Hayden, Milica. "Nesting Orientalisms: The Case of Former Yugoslavia." *Slavic Review* 54, no. 4 (1995): 917–931.

Bank, Andre and Thomas Richter. "Neopatrimonialism in the Middle East and North Africa: Overview, Critique, and Alternative Conceptualization." Paper presented at the German Institute of Global and Area Studies workshop "Neopatrimonialism in Various World Regions." Hamburg, August 23, 2010.

Barker, Rodney. *Legitimating Identities: The Self-Presentation of Rulers and Subjects*. Cambridge: Cambridge University Press, 2001.

Barth, Fredrik. *Ethnic Groups and Boundaries: The Social Organization of Cultural Difference*. Boston: Little, Brown, 1969.

Bassin, Mark. *The Gumilev Mystique: Biopolitics, Eurasianism, and the Construction of Community in Modern Russia*. Ithaca: Cornell University Press, 2016.

Baudrillard, Jean, trans. *Simulacra and Simulation*. Ann Arbor: University of Michigan Press, 1994.

Baumann, Max Peter. "Festival, Musical Actors and Mental Constructs in the Process of Globalization." *World of Music* 43, no. 2/3 (2001): 9–29.

Beaman, Jean. "Boundaries of Frenchness: Cultural Citizenship and France's Middle Class North African Second Generation." *Identities: Global Studies in Culture and Power* 22 (2014): 1–17, doi: 10.1080/1070289X.2014.931235.

Beissinger, Mark. *Nationalist Mobilization and the Collapse of the Soviet Union*. Cambridge: Cambridge University Press, 2002.

Benjamin, Walter. "Paris, Capital of the Nineteenth Century." In *The Arcades Project*, translated by Howard Eil and and Kevin McLaughlin, 14–26. Cambridge, MA: Harvard University Press, 1999 [1939].

Bennett, Jane. *The Enchantment of Modern Life: Attachments, Crossings, and Ethics*. Princeton, NJ: Princeton University Press, 2001.

Beysembayev, Serik. "Tendentsii sotsial'no-demograficheskogo razvitiia kazakhstanskogo obshchestva (na baze sotsiologicheskikh issledovanii)." *Tsentral'naia Aziia i Kavkaz* 14, no. 2 (2011): 83–100.

Biddle, Ian and Vanessa Knights, eds. *Music, National Identity, and the Politics of Location*. Burlington, VT: Ashgate, 2007.

Billig, Michael. *Banal Nationalism*. Thousand Oaks, CA: Sage, 1995.

Bissenova, Alima. "Central Asian Encounters of the Middle East: Islam, Nationalism and Post-Coloniality in Al-Azhar." *Religion, State and Society* 33, no. 3 (2005): 253–264.

Bissenova, Alima. "Post-Socialist Dreamworlds: Housing Boom and Urban Development in Kazakhstan." PhD diss., Cornell University, 2012.

Bissenova, Alima. "The Master Plan of Astana: Between the Art of Government and the Art of Being Global." In *Ethnographies of the State in Central Asia: Performing Politics*, edited by Madeleine Reeves, Johan Rasanayagam, and Judith Beyer, 127–148. Bloomington: Indiana University Press, 2014.

Blum, Douglas W. *National Identity and Globalization: Youth, State, and Society in Post-Soviet Eurasia*. New York: Cambridge University Press, 2007.

Bogaards, Matthijs. "How to Classify Hybrid Regimes? Defective Democracy and Electoral Authoritarianism." *Democratization* 16, no. 2 (2009): 399–423.

Bourdieu, Pierre. *Outline of a Theory of Practice*. New York: Cambridge University Press, 1977.

Bowyer, Anthony Clive. "Parliament and Political Parties in Kazakhstan." Washington DC, Central Asia-Caucasus Institute and Silk Road Studies Program, April 2008.

Boyer, M. Christine. *The City of Collective Memory: Its Historical Imagery and Architectural Entertainments*. Cambridge, MA: MIT Press, 1994.

Bozdoğan, Sibel. *Modernism and Nation Building: Turkish Architectural Culture in the Early Republic*. Seattle: University of Washington Press, 2001.

Brownlee, Jason. "Durable Authoritarianism in the Age of Democracy." PhD diss., Princeton University, 2004. Accessed March 20, 2015. http://202.28.199.34/multim/3120423.pdf.

Brubaker, Rogers. "Nationalizing States Revisited: Projects and Processes of Nationalization in Post-Soviet States." *Ethnic and Racial Studies* 34, no. 11 (2011): 1785–1814.

Brubaker, Rogers. "Nationhood and the National Question in the Soviet Union and Post-Soviet Eurasia: An Institutionalist Account." *Theory and Society* 21, no. 1 (1994): 4–8.

Brynen, Rex, Pete Moore, Bassel Salloukh, and Marie-Joelle Zahar. *Beyond the Arab Spring: Authoritarianism and Democratization in the Arab World*. Boulder, CO: Lynne Rienner, 2013.

Buchli, Victor. "Astana: Materiality and the City." In *Urban Life in Post-Soviet Asia*, edited by Catherine Alexander, Victor Buchli, and Caroline Humphrey, 40–69. London: University College Press, 2007.

Buck-Morss, Susan. "Aesthetics and Anaesthetics: Walter Benjamin's Artwork Essay Reconsidered." *October* 62 (1992): 3–41.

Bukkvol, Tor. "Astana's Privatized Independence: Private and National Interests in the Foreign Policy of Nursultan Nazarbayev." *Nationalities Papers* 32, no. 3 (2004): 631–650.

Cardoza, Anthony. "'Making Italians'? Cycling and National Identity in Italy: 1900–1950." *Journal of Modern Italian Studies* 15, no. 3 (2010): 354–377.

Castells, Manuel. *Communication Power*. Oxford: Oxford University Press, 2009.

Centre for Social and Political Research. *Specifics of Interethnic Conflicts in Kazakhstan: Report of a Mass Population Survey and Focus Group Research.* Almaty: Centre for Social and Political Research 2009.

Chinn, Jeff and Robert Kaiser. *Russians as the New Minority: Ethnicity and Nationalism in the Soviet Successor States*. Boulder, CO: Westview Press, 1996.

Cohen, Margaret. "Walter Benjamin's Phantasmagoria." *New German Critique* 48 (1989): 87–107.

Coleridge, Samuel T. *Biographia Literaria*, vol. 1., 1817. Oxford: Oxford University Press, 1969.

Collier, David. *New Authoritarianism in Latin America*. Princeton, NJ: Princeton University Press, 1980.

Collins, Kathleen. "Economic and Security Regionalism and Patrimonial Authoritarian Regimes: The Case of Central Asia." *Europe-Asia Studies* 61, no. 2 (2009): 24–81.

Collins, Kathleen. "The Logic of Clan Politics: Evidence from the Central Asian Trajectories." *World Politics* 56, no. 2 (2004): 224–261.

Collins, Kathleen. *Clan Politics and Regime Transformation in Central Asia.* New York: Cambridge University Press, 2006.

Connerton, Paul. *How Societies Remember*. Cambridge: Cambridge University Press, 1989.

Connolly, William. *Capitalism and Christianity, American Style*. Durham, NC: Duke University Press, 2008.

Cooke, Catherine. "Russian Responses to the Garden City Idea." *Architectural Review* 163 (1978): 353–363.

Cooley, Alex. *Great Games, Local Rules: The New Great Power Contest for Central Asia*. New York: Oxford University Press, 2012.

Cooley, Tim, Katherine Meizel, and Nasir Syed, "Virtual Fieldwork: Three Case Studies." In *Shadows in the Field: New Perspectives for Fieldwork in Ethnomusicology*, edited by Gregory F. Barz and Timothy J. Cooley, 90–107. New York: Oxford University Press, 2008.

Coronil, Fernando. *The Magical State: Nature, Money, and Modernity in Venezuela.* Chicago: University of Chicago Press, 1997.

Crews, Robert. *For Prophet and Tsar: Islam and Empire in Russia and Central Asia.* Cambridge, MA: Harvard University Press, 2006.

Crowley, David, and Susan E. Reid, eds. *Socialist Spaces: Sites of Everyday Life in the Eastern Bloc*. Oxford: Berg, 2002.

Cummings, Sally. "The Central Asian Economies since Independence." *Slavic Review* 66 (2007): 755–756.

Cummings, Sally. "Eurasian Bridge or Murky Waters between East and West? Ideas, Identity, and Output in Kazakhstan's Foreign Policy." *Journal of Communist Studies and Transition Politics* 19, no. 3 (2003): 139–155.

Cummings, Sally N. *Kazakhstan: Power and the Elite*. London: I.B. Tauris, 2005.

Cummings, Sally. "The Kazakhs: Demographics, Diasporas, and 'Return.'" In *Nations Abroad: Diaspora Politics and International Relations in the Former Soviet Union*, edited by Charles King and Neil Melvin, 137–154. Boulder: Westview Press, 1998.

Cummings, Sally. "Legitimation and Identification in Kazakhstan." *Nationalism and Ethnic Politics* 12, no. 2 (2006): 177–204.

Cummings, Sally N., ed. *Power and Chance in Central Asia*. London: Routledge, 2002.

Cummings, Sally N., ed. *Symbolism and Power in Central Asia: Politics of the Spectacular*. New York: Routledge, 2010.

Dave, Bhavna. *Kazakhstan: Ethnicity, Language, and Power*. London: Routledge, 2007.

Dave, Bhavna. "Kazakhstan's 2004 Parliamentary Elections: Managing Loyalty and Support for the Regime." *Problems of Post-Communism* 52, no. 1 (2005): 3–14.

Davenel, Yves-Marie. "Cultural Mobilization in Post-Soviet Kazakhstan: Views from the State and from the Non-Titular Nationalities Compared." *Central Asian Survey* 31, no. 1 (2012): 17–29.

DeBano, Wendy. "Enveloping Music in Gender, Nation, and Islam: Women's Music Festivals in Post-Revolutionary Iran." *Iranian Studies* 38, no. 3 (2005): 441–462.

Dederer, Aleksander. *Strana i mir*, March 20, 2010.

Denison, Michael. "The Art of the Impossible: Political Symbolism, and the Creation of National Identity and Collective Memory in Post-Soviet Turkmenistan." *Europe-Asia Studies* 61, no. 7 (2009): 1167–1187.

Derbisali, Absattar Qazhy and Mukhammed Hussien Qazhy Alsabekov. *Qazaqstan Musylmandary Dini Basqarmasynyng 2000 Zhyldan Bastap Shyqqan Patualary Zhiyntyghynyng Bir Boligi*. Almaty: Kokzhiek, 2008.

DeWeese, Devin. "Sacred History for a Central Asian Town: Saints, Shrines, and Legends of Origin in Histories of Sayrām, 18th-19th Centuries." *Revue des Mondes Musulmans et de la Méditerranée* 8 (2000): 245–295.

Diat, F. "Olzhas Sulejmenov: *Az i Ya*." *Central Asian Survey* 1 (1984): 101–210.

Diener, Alexander. "Assessing Potential Russian Irredentism and Separatism in Kazakhstan's Northern Oblasts" *Eurasian Geography and Economics*, 56 no. 5 (2015): 469-492.

Diener, Alexander. "Diasporic Stances: Comparing the Historical Geographic Antecedents of German and Korean Migration Decisions in Kazakhstan." *Geopolitics* 14, no. 3 (2009): 462–487.

Diener, Alexander. *Homeland Conceptions and Ethnic Integration of Kazakhstan Germans and Koreans*. Lewiston, NY: Mellon Press 2004.

Diener, Alexander. "Kazakhstan's Kin-State Diaspora: Settlement Planning and the Oralman Dilemma." *Europe Asia Studies* 57, no. 2 (2005): 327–348;

Diener, Alexander. "National Territory and the Reconstruction of History in Kazakhstan." *Eurasian Geography and Economics* 43, no. 8 (2002): 632–647.

Diener, Alexander. "Transnationalism and Minority Territorialization in Kazakhstan." *International Journal of Central Asian Studies* 11 (2007): 86–102.

Domjan, Paul and Matt Stone. "A Comparative Study of Resource Nationalism in Russia and Kazakhstan 2004–2008." *Europe-Asia Studies* 62, no. 1 (2010): 35–62.

Dowell, K. "BTA v Ablyazov: The Secret Billionaire." *The Lawyer*, February 6, 2012. Accessed August 20, 2010. http://www.thelawyer.com/bta-v-ablyazov-the-secret-billionaire/1011246.article.

Égert, Balazs and Carol S. Leonard. "Dutch Disease Scare in Kazakhstan: Is It Real?" *The Michigan University William Davidson Institute Working Paper*, no. 866, March 2007.

Erdmann, Gero and Ulf Engel. *Neopatrimonialism Revisited: Beyond a Catch-all Concept*. Hamburg: GIGA Working Papers, 2006.

Erofeev, Viktor. *Khoroshii Stalin: Roman*. Moscow: ZebraE, 2004.

Evans, Peter. *Embedded Autonomy: States and Industrial Transformation*. Princeton, NJ: Princeton University Press, 1995.

Expert-Kazakhstan Magazine. "Roundtable with the Representatives of Pension Funds." February 28, 2011. Accessed March 15, 2015. http://www.enpf.kz/7409.

Faranda, Regina and David Nolle. "Boundaries of Ethnic Identity in Central Asia: Titular and Russian Perceptions of Ethnic Commonalities in Kazakhstan and Kyrgyzstan." *Ethnic and Racial Studies* 34, no. 4 (2011): 620–642.

Ferguson, James. *The Anti-Politics Machine: "Development," Depoliticization, and Bureaucratic Power in Lesotho*. Minneapolis: University of Minnesota Press, 1994.

Fierman, William. "Kazakh Language and Prospects for its Role in Kazakh 'Groupness.'" *Ab Imperio* 2 (2005): 393–423.

Fierman, William. "Language and Education in Post-Soviet Kazakhstan: Kazakh-medium Instruction in Urban Schools." *Russian Review* 65, no. 1 (2006): 98–116.

Fierman, William. "Language and Identity in Kazakhstan: Formulations in Policy Documents, 1987–1997." *Communist and Post-Communist Studies* 30, no. 2 (1998): 171–186.

Fierman, William ed. "Implementing Language Laws: Perestroika and its Legacy in Five Republics." *Nationalities Papers* 23, no. 3 (1995): 505–659.

Foucault, Michel. "Of Other Spaces." *Diacritics* 16, no. 1 (1986): 22–27.

Franke, Anja, Andrea Gawrich, and Gurban Alakbarov. "Kazakhstan and Azerbaijan as Post-Soviet Rentier States: Resource Incomes and Autocracy as a Double 'Curse' in Post-Soviet Regimes." *Europe-Asia Studies* 61, no. 1 (2009): 109–140.

Frolova-Walker, Marina. "'National in Form, Socialist in Content': Musical Nation-Building in the Soviet Republics." *Journal of the American Musicological Society* 51, no. 2 (1998): 331–371

Geertz, Clifford. "'Internal Conversion' in Contemporary Bali." In *The Interpretation of Cultures: Selected Essays*, 170–192. New York: Basic Books, 1973.

Geertz, Clifford. *Islam Observed: Religious Development in Morocco and Indonesia*. Chicago: University of Chicago Press, 1971.

Geiss, Paul Georg. "Central Asia: Changing Political Systems and Regime Types: In Between the Neopatrimonial and Bureaucratic-Developmental State in Central Asia." In *Presidents, Oligarchs, and Bureaucrats: Forms of Rule in the Post-Soviet Space*, edited by Susan Stewart, Margarete Klein, and Andrea Schmitz, 187–202. Farnham, Surrey, UK: Ashgate, 2012.

Gel'man, Vladimir. "Post-Soviet Transitions and Democratization: Towards Theory-Building." *Democratization* 10, no. 2 (2003): 87–104.

Gell, Alfred. *Art and Agency: An Anthropological Theory*. Oxford: Clarendon Press, 1998.

Gell, Alfred. "The Technology of Enchantment and the Enchantment of Technology." In *The Art of Anthropology: Essays and Diagrams*, edited by Eric Hirsch, 159–186. London: Athlone Press, 1999.

Gellner, Ernest. *Nations and Nationalism*. Ithaca: Cornell University Press, 1983.

Ginsburg, Tom and Tamir Moustafa. *Rule by Law: The Politics of Courts in Authoritarian Regimes*. New York: Cambridge University Press, 2008.

Gladney, Dru C. "Representing Nationality in China: Refiguring Majority/Minority Identities." *Journal of Asian Studies* 53, no. 1 (1994): 92–123.

Goss, Jon. "The 'Magic of the Mall': An Analysis of Form, Function, and Meaning in Contemporary Retail Built Environment." *Annals of the Association of American Geographers* 83, no. 1 (1993): 18–47.

Gottdiener, Mark. "The Consumption of Space and the Spaces of Consumption." In *New Forms of Consumption: Consumers, Culture, and Commodification*, edited by Mark Gottdiener, 265–285. Oxford: Rowman and Littlefield, 2000.

Gramsci, Antonio. "Some Aspects of the Southern Question." In *Selections from Political Writings (1921–1926)*, edited by Q. Hoare, 441–462. London: Lawrence and Wishart, 1926 [1978].

Grant, Bruce. "New Moscow Monuments, or, States of Innocence." *American Ethnologist* 28, no. 2 (2001): 332–362.

Grzymala-Busse, Anna. "Beyond Clientelism: Incumbent State Capture and State Formation." *Comparative Political Studies* 41, no. 4/5 (2008): 638–673.

Habermas, Jürgen. *The Inclusion of the Other: Studies in Political Theory*. Cambridge MA: MIT Press, 1998.

Habermas, Jürgen. *The Postnational Constellation: Political Essays*. Cambridge, MA: MIT Press, 2001.

Hacker-Cordón, Casino and Miley, Thomas J. Miley. "Operationalizing and Reconstructing the Theory of Nationalism." *CIDE* 198 (2007): 1–25.

Hale, Henry E. "Regime Cycles: Democracy, Autocracy, and Revolution in Post-Soviet Eurasia." *World Politics* 58, no. 1 (2005): 133–165.

Helbig, Adriana, Nino Tsitsishvili, and Erica Haskell. "Managing Musical Diversity within Frameworks of Western Development Aid: Views from Ukraine, Georgia, and Bosnia and Herzegovina." *Yearbook for Traditional Music* 40 (2008): 46–59.

Hennayake, Shantha. "Interactive Ethnonationalism: An Alternative Explanation of Minority Ethnonationalism." *Political Geography* 11, no. 6 (1992): 526–549.

Heyneman, Stephen. "Three Universities in Georgia, Kazakhstan, and Kyrgyzstan: The Struggle against Corruption and for Social Cohesion." *Prospects* 3 (2007): 305–318.

Highley, John and Jan Pakulski. "Elite Theory versus Marxism: The Twentieth Century's Verdict." *Historical Social Research* 37, no. 1 (2000): 320–332.

Hirsch, Francine. *Empire of Nations*. Ithaca, NY: Cornell University Press, 2005.

Holston, James. *The Modernist City: An Anthropological Critique of Brasilia*. Chicago: University of Chicago Press, 1989.

Hughes, James and Gwendolyn Sasse. *Ethnicity and Territory in the Former Soviet Union*. London: Frank Cass, 2002.

Ideologicheskie ustanovski i osobennosti identifikatsii naseleniia RK. Almaty: Strategiia, 2009.

Ilkhamov, Alisher. "Neopatrimonialism, Interest Groups and Patronage Networks: The Impasses of the Governance System in Uzbekistan." *Central Asian Survey* 26, no. 1 (2007): 65–84.

Inglehart, Ronald and Christian Welzel. "How Development Leads to Democracy: What We Know About Modernization." *Foreign Affairs* 88, no. 2 (2009): 33–49.

Institute of Eurasian Integration. *Sovremennoe sostoianie i tendentsii vsekazakhstanskoi kultury*. October 2014.

International Partnership for Human Rights. "A Sobering Reality: Fundamental Freedoms in Kazakhstan, Turkmenistan and Uzbekistan Twenty Years after the Soviet Collapse." Brussels, March 2012.

Ioffe, Grigory. "Understanding Belarus: Belarusian Identity." *Europe Asia Studies* 55, no. 8, 1241–1272.

Isaacs, Rico. "Informal Politics and the Uncertain Context of Transition: Revisiting Early Stage Nondemocratic Development in Kazakhstan." *Democratization* 17, no. 1 (2010): 1–25.

Isaacs, Rico. "'Papa'– Nursultan Nazarbayev and the Discourse of Charismatic Leadership and Nation-Building in Post-Soviet Kazakhstan." *Studies in Ethnicity and Nationalism* 10, no. 3 (2010): 435–452.

Isaacs, Rico. *Party System Formation in Kazakhstan: Between Formal and Informal Politics*. London: Routledge, 2011.

Isabayeva, Saule. "O kzakhom natsionalizme – na chistotu." *Central Asia Monitor* July 5, 2013, http://bit.ly/14ZFfVy.

Jackson, Jane. "Globalization, Internationalization, and Short-Term Stays Abroad." *International Journal of Intercultural Relations* 32, no. 4 (2008): 349–358.

Jameson, Fredric. *Postmodernism, Or the Cultural Logic of Late Capitalism*. Durham, NC: Duke University Press, 1991.

Jansson, David. "The Evil Empire Within: Southern Nationalism and the Washington Problem." In *Nation within a Nation: The American South and the Federal Government*, edited by G. Feldman, 205–226. Gainesville: University Press of Florida, 2014.

Jansson, David. "'A Geography of Racism': Internal Orientalism and the Construction of American National Identity in the Film Mississippi Burning." *National Identities* 7, no. 3 (2005): 265–285.

Jansson, David. "Internal Orientalism in America: W.J. Cash's the Mind of the South and the Spatial Construction of American National Identity." *Political Geography* 22, no. 3 (2003): 293–316.

Jensen, Nathan. "Economic Reform, State Capture and International Investment in Transition Economies." *Journal of International Development* 14, no. 7 (2002): 973–977.

Jessa, Pawel. "Aq Jol Soul Healers: Religious Pluralism and a Contemporary Muslim Movement in Kazakhstan." *Central Asian Survey* 25, no. 3 (2006): 359–371.

Jessa, Pawel. "Religious Renewal in Kazakhstan: Redefining 'Unofficial' Islam." In *The Postsocialist Religious Question: Faith and Power in Central Asia and East-Central Europe*, edited by Chris Hann, 169–190. Berlin: LIT Verlag, 2006.

Johnson, Chalmers. *MITI and the Japanese Miracle: The Growth of Industrial Policy, 1925–1975*. Stanford, CA: Stanford University Press, 1982.

Johnson, Corey, and Amanda Coleman. "The Internal Other: Exploring the Dialectical Relationship between Regional Exclusion and the Construction of National Identity." *Annals of the Association of American Geographers* 102, no. 4 (2011): 863–880.

Jones, Nathan Paul. "Assembling a Civic Nation in Kazakhstan: The Nation Building Role of the Assembly of the Peoples of Kazakhstan." *Caucasian Review of International Affairs* 2, no. 4 (2010): 159–168.

Jones Luong, Pauline. "Beyond 'Resource Nationalism'? Implications of State Ownership in Kazakhstan's Petroleum Sector." *PONARS Eurasia Policy Memo* no. 98, 2010.

Jones Luong, Pauline. *Institutional Change and Political Continuity in Post-Soviet Central Asia: Power, Perceptions, and Pacts*. New York: Cambridge University Press, 2002.

Jones Luong, Pauline, ed. *The Transformation of Central Asia: States and Societies from Soviet Rule to Independence*. Ithaca, NY: Cornell University Press, 2004.

Jones Luong, Pauline and Erika Weinthal. *Oil is Not a Curse: Ownership Structure and Institutions in Soviet Successor States*. New York: Cambridge University Press, 2010.

Junisbai, Azamat. "Are the Young Truly Different? Youth Opinion about Selected Social and Political Issues in Kazakhstan." Presentation at the international conference "Youth in Kazakhstan: Societal Changes, Challenges and Opportunities." George Washington University Central Asia Program, April 21, 2014.

Junisbai, Barbara. "A Tale of Two Kazakhstans: Sources of Political Cleavage and Conflict in the Post-Soviet Period." *Europe-Asia Studies* 62, no. 2 (2010): 235–269.

Junisbai, Barbara and Azamat Junisbai. "The Democratic Choice of Kazakhstan: A Case Study in Economic Liberalization, Intraelite Cleavage, and Political Opposition." *Demokratizatsiya* 13, no. 3 (2005): 373–392.

Kaiser, Robert. "Ethnic Demography and Interstate Relations in Central Asia." In *National Identity and Ethnicity in Russia and the New States of Eurasia*, edited by Roman Szporluk, 230–265. Armonk, NY: M.E. Sharpe, 1994.

Kaiser, Robert. *The Geography of Nationalism in Russia and the USSR*. Princeton, NJ: Princeton University Press, 1994.

Kaiser, Robert. "Nations and Homelands in Soviet Central Asia." In *Geographic Perspectives on Soviet Central Asia*, edited by R.A. Lewis, R.R. Churchill and A. Tate, 279–312. New York: Routledge, 1992.

Kalyuzhnova, Yelena. *The Kazakhstani Economy: Independence and Transition*. Basingstoke, UK: Macmillan, 1998.

Kamarov, Talgat. "NPP: Osnovnaia tsel' – sobliudenie interesov investorov i emitentov." *Exclusive Magazine*, November 21, 2013. Accessed March 12, 2015. http://exclusive.kz/talgat-kamarov-npp-osnovnaya-tsel-soblyudenie-balansa-interesov-investorov-i-e-mitentov.html.

Karin, Erlan and A. Chebotarev. "The Policy of Kazakhization in State and Government Institutions in Kazakhstan." In *The Nationalities Question in Post-Soviet Kazakhstan*, edited by Natsuko Oka. Chiba: Institute of Developing Economies, 2000.

Kassyamova, Didar, Zhanat Kundakbayeva, and Ustina Markus. *Historical Dictionary of Kazakhstan.* Lanham, MD: Scarecrow Press, 2012.

Kazakhstan Stock Exchange. "AFN okharakterizovalo nakopitel'nuiu pensionnuiu sistemu Kazakhstana po sostoianiiu na 1ogo fevralia 2008 goda." *Irbis*, February 14, 2008. Accessed March 12, 2015. http://www.kase.kz/news/show/1041816.

Kehl-Bodrogi, Krisztina. "Who Owns the Shrine? Competing Meanings and Authorities at a Pilgrimage Site in Khorezm." *Central Asian Survey* 25, no. 3 (2006): 235–250.

Kehl-Bodrogi, Krisztina. *Religion Is Not So Strong Here: Muslim Religious Life in Khorezm After Socialism.* Berlin: LIT Verlag, 2008.

Kemme, David M. "Sovereign Wealth Fund Issues and The National Fund(s) of Kazakhstan." University of Memphis, December 15, 2011. Accessed August 20, 2012, https://umdrive.memphis.edu/g-fcbe/www/docs/faculty/Kemme%20NFs%20of%20KZ%20Edited%2012–15-2011.pdf.

Kendall-Taylor, Andrea. "Purchasing Power: Oil, Elections and Regime Durability in Azerbaijan and Kazakhstan." *Europe-Asia Studies* 64, no. 4 (2012): 737–760.

Kennedy, Ryan and Adilzhan Nurmakov. "Resource Nationalism Trends in Kazakhstan, 2004–2009." *RUSSCASP*, April 2010.

Kenzheev, Nurakhmet. "Grigorii Marchenko nadeialsia na 2012 God." *Respublika*, June 10, 2011. Accessed August 20, 2012, http://comment-respublika.info/comment/showtopic/9316.

Kesici, Özecan. "The Dilemma in the Nation-Building Process: The Kazakh or Kazakhstani Nation?" *Journal of Ethnopolitics and Minority Issues in Europe* 10, no. 1 (2011): 1–58.

Khalid, Adeeb. "Backwardness and the Quest for Civilization: Early Soviet Central Asia in Comparative Perspective." *Slavic Review* 65, no. 2 (2006): 231–251.

Khalid, Adeeb. *Islam After Communism: Religion and Politics in Central Asia.* Berkeley: University of California Press, 2007.

Khalid, Adeeb. *The Politics of Muslim Cultural Reform: Jadidism in Central Asia.* Berkeley: University of California Press, 1998.

Khamidov, Alisher. "Kazakhstan Grapples With Reform of Sovereign-Wealth Fund." Eurasianet, August 4, 2014, http://www.eurasianet.org/node/69336.

Khliupin, V. *"Bol'shaia sem'ia" Nursultana Nazarbaeva. Politicheskaia elita sovremennogo Kazakhstana.* Moscow: Institut aktual'nykh politicheskikh issledovanii, 1998.

Khyupin, Vitaliy. "Kazakhstanskaia politicheskaia elita: mezhdu modernizatsiei i traibalizmom. Doklad na 2-om vserossiiskom kongresse politologov, Moskva, MGIMO, 22 aprelia 2000g." Mezhdunarodnyi evraziiskii institut, April 2000, http://www.iicas.org/page.php?id=105.

King, Charles and Neil Melvin. *Nations Abroad. Diaspora Politics and International Relations in the Former Soviet Union.* Boulder, CO: Westview Press, 1998.

Kjærnet, Heidi, Dosym Satpaev, and Stina Torjesen. "Big Business and High-Level Politics in Kazakhstan: An Everlasting Symbiosis?" *China and Eurasia Forum Quarterly* 6, no. 1 (2008): 95–107.

Knight, David. “Identity and Territory: Geographical Perspectives on Nationalism and Regionalism.” *Annals of the Association of American Geographers* 72, no. 4 (1982): 514–531.

Koch, Natalie. “Bordering on the Modern: Power, Practice and Exclusion in Astana.” *Transactions of the Institute of British Geographers* 39, no. 3 (2014): 432–443.

Koch, Natalie. “The ‘Heart’ of Eurasia? Kazakhstan’s Centrally Located Capital City.” *Central Asian Survey* 32, no. 2 (2013): 134–147.

Koch, Natalie. “Kazakhstan’s Changing Geopolitics: The Resource Economy and Popular Attitudes About China’s Growing Regional Influence.” *Eurasian Geography and Economics* 54, no. 1 (2013): 110–133.

Koch, Natalie. “The Monumental and the Miniature: Imagining ‘Modernity’ in Astana.” *Social and Cultural Geography* 11, no. 8 (2010): 769–787.

Koch, Natalie. “Sport and Soft Authoritarian Nation Building.” *Political Geography* 32, (2013): 42–51.

Koch, Natalie. “Urban ‘Utopias’: The Disney Stigma and Discourses of ‘False Modernity.’” *Environment and Planning* A 44 (2012): 2445–62.

Koch, Natalie. “Why Not a World City Astana and Ankara: Geopolitical Scripts in Urban Networks.” *Urban Geography* 34, no. 1 (2013): 109–130.

Koehler, Kevin. “Authoritarian Elections in Egypt: Formal Institutions and Informal Mechanisms of Rule.” *Democratization* 15, no. 5 (2008): 974–990.

Kolstoe, Pal et al. *Nation-Building and Ethnic Integration in Post-Soviet Societies: An Investigation of Latvia and Kazakhstan*. Boulder, CO: Westview Press, 1998.

Korteweg, Anna and Triadafilos Triadafilopoulos. “Is Multiculturalism Dead? Groups, Governments, and the ‘Real Work of Integration.’” *Ethnic and Racial Studies* (2014): 1–21, doi: 10.1080/01419870.2014.907925.

Krishna, Sankaran. “Cartographic Anxiety: Mapping the Body Politic in India.” *Alternatives* 19, no. 4 (1994): 507–521.

Kucera, Joshua. “No One Rigs an Election Quite Like Kazakhstan.” *The Atlantic*, April 2011. Accessed March 15, 2015. http://www.theatlantic.com/international/archive/2011/04/no-one-rigs-an-election-quite-like-kazakhstan/236817/.

Kudaibegenova, Diana. “National Identity Formation in Post-Soviet Central Asia: The Soviet Legacy, Primordialism, and Patterns of Ideological Development since 1991.” In *Social and Cultural Change in Central Asia: The Soviet Legacy*, edited by Sevket Akyldiz and Richard Carlson, 160–173. New York: Routledge, 2014.

Kudaibergenova, Diana. “Post Socialist Culture in Latvia and Kazakhstan: An Introduction to Reasons, Criticisms, and Perspectives.” In *National Identity: Time, Place, and People*. Riga: University of Latvia, 2012.

Kudaibergenova, Diana. *Re-writing the Nation: Elites, Networks and Narratives in Modern Kazakh Literature*. Lanham, MD: Lexington, 2016.

Kundera, Milan. *The Unbearable Lightness of Being*. Translated by Michael H. Heim. New York: Harper and Row, 1984.

Kuprianova, Anastasiia. “Pochemu na pensionnykh schetakh kazakhstantsev izchezaiut nakopleniia i kto na nikh polozhel glav?” YK-News.kz, February 2, 2015. Accessed March 12, 2015.

Kusherbaev, K.E. *Etnopolitika Kazakhstana: sostoianie i perspektivy*. Almaty, 1996.

Kuzio, Taras. "Nationalist Riots in Kazakhstan." *Central Asian Survey* 7, no. 4 (1988): 79–100.

Laitin, David. *Identity in Formation: The Russian-Speaking Populations in the Near Abroad*. Ithaca, NY: Cornell University Press, 1998.

Lakoff, George and Mark Johnson. *Metaphors We Live By*. Chicago: University of Chicago Press, 1980.

Landau, Jacob M. and Barbara Kellner-Heinkele. *Politics of Language in the Ex-Soviet Muslim States*. London: Hurst and Company, 200.

Laruelle, Marlene. "Cross Border Minorities as Cultural and Economic Mediators between China and Central Asia." *China and Eurasia Forum Quarterly* 7, no. 1 (2009): 93–119.

Laruelle, Marlene. "Olzhas Suleimenov." In *Russia's People of Empire: Lives Stories from Eurasia, 1500 to the Present*, edited by S. Norris, and W. Sunderland, 319–325. Bloomington: Indiana University Press, 2012.

Laruelle, Marlene. "Religious Revival, Nationalism and the 'Invention of Tradition': Political Tengrism in Central Asia and Tatarstan." *Central Asian Survey* 26, no. 2 (2007): 203–216.

Laruelle, Marlene. "The Three Discursive Paradigms of State Identity in Kazakhstan: Kazakhness, Kazakhstanness, and Transnationalism." In *Nationalism and Identity Construction in Central Asia: Dimensions, Dynamics and Directions*, edited by Mariya Omelicheva, 1–20. Lanham, MD: Lexington Books, 2014).

Laruelle, Marlene and Sebastien Peyrouse. *Globalizing Central Asia*. Armonk, NY: M.E. Sharpe, 2013.

Laruelle, Marlene and Sebastien Peyrouse. *Les Russes du Kazakhstan. Identité nationale et nouveaux Etats dans l'espace post-soviétique*. Paris: Maisonneuve et Larose, 2004.

Laszczkowski, Mateusz. "Building the Future: Construction, Temporality, and Politics in Astana." *Focaal: Journal of Global and Historical Anthropology* 60 (2011): 77–92.

Laszczkowski, Mateusz. *"City of the Future": Built Space, Modernity and Urban Change in Astana*. New York: Berghahn Books, 2016.

Laszczkowski, Mateusz. "'Demo-Version of a City': Buildings, Affects, and the State in Astana." *Journal of the Royal Anthropological Institute* 22, no. 1 (2016): 148–165.

Laszczkowski, Mateusz. "State Building(s): Built Forms, Materiality, and the State in Astana." In *Ethnographies of the State in Central Asia: Performing Politics*, edited by Madeleine Reeves, Johan Rasanayagam, and Judith Beyer, 149–172. Bloomington: Indiana University Press, 2014.

Laszczkowski, Mateusz. "Superplace: Global Connections and Local Politics at the Mega Mall, Astana." *Etnofoor* 23, no. 1 (2011): 85–104.

Laszczkowski, Mateusz and Madeleine Reeves. "Introduction: Affective States – Entanglements, Suspensions, Suspicions." *Social Analysis* 59, no. 4 (2015): 1–14.

Leftwich, Adrian. "Bringing Politics Back in: Towards a Model of the Developmental State." *Journal of Development Studies* 31, no. 3 (1995): 400–427.

Levi-Faur, David. "The Regulatory State and the Developmental State: Towards Polymorphic Comparative Capitalism." In *The Rise of the Regulatory State of the*

South: Infrastructure and Development in Emerging Economies, edited by Navroz Dubash and Bronwen Morgan, 235–245. New York: Oxford University Press, 2013.

Lillis, Joanna. "Kazakhstan Follows Thorny Path toward National Unity" Eurasianet., April 29, 2010. Accessed June 9, 2014, http://www.eurasianet.org/node/60952.

Lillis, Joanna. "Kazakhstan: Business Climate Grows Gloomy Amid Arbitrary Arrest Controversy." Eurasianet, June 9, 2009. Accessed August 20, 2012, http://www.eurasianet.org/departments/insightb/articles/eav061009.shtml.

Lillis, Joanna. "Kazakhstan: Corporate Retreat from LSE Raises Governance Questions." Eurasianet, December 4, 2013, http://www.eurasianet.org/node/67830.

Lillis, Joanna. "Kazakhstan: Landmark Eurasian Union Treaty Signed Amid Protests and Arrests." Eurasianet, May 29, 2014. Accessed March 15, 2015. http://www.eurasianet.org/node/68416.

Lillis, Joanna. "Kazakhstan: Nazarbayev Clan Set to Grow." Eurasianet, June 10, 2013, http://www.eurasianet.org/node/67097.

Linke, Uli. "Contact Zones: Rethinking the Sensual Life of the State." *Anthropological Theory* 6, no. 2 (2006): 205–225.

Linz, Juan and Alfred Stepan. *Problems of Democratic Transition and Consolidation: Southern Europe, South America, and Post-Communist Europe*. Baltimore, MD and London: The John Hopkins University Press, 1996.

Linz, Juan. *Totalitarian and Authoritarian Regimes.* Boulder, CO and London: Lynne Rienner, 2000.

Louw, Maria. "Even Honey May Become Bitter When There Is Too Much of It: Islam and the Struggle for Balanced Existence in Post-Soviet Kyrgyzstan." *Central Asian Survey* 32, no. 4 (2013): 514–526.

Louw, Maria. *Everyday Islam in Post-Soviet Central Asia*. London: Routledge, 2007.

Marat, Erica. "Nation Branding in Central Asia: A New Campaign to Present Ideas about the State and the Nation." *Europe-Asia Studies* 61, no. 7 (2009): 1123–1136.

March, Andrew F. "From Leninism to Karimovism: Hegemony, Ideology, and Authoritarian Legitimation." *Post-Soviet Affairs* 19, no. 4 (2003): 307–336.

March, Andrew F. "State Ideology and the Legitimation of Authoritarianism: The Case of Post-Soviet Uzbekistan." *Journal of Political Ideologies* 8, no. 2 (2003): 209–232.

Marchenko, Grigorii. "Prikaz No. 356 ob utverzhdenii grafika priema – peredachi pensionnykh aktivov i ob''iazatel'st v nakopitel'nykh pensionnykh fondov po dogovoram o pensionnom obespechenii v edinyi nakopitel' pensionnyi fond." National Bank of the Republic of Kazakhstan, September 24, 2013. Accessed March 15, 2015, http://www.afn.kz/attachments/9/22/publish22-1069604.pdf and http://base.spinform.ru/show_doc.fwx?rgn=63676.

Martinez-Herrera, Enric and Thomas J. Miley. "The Constitution and the Politics of National Identity in Spain." *Nations and Nationalism* 16, no. 2 (2010): 6–30.

Masanov, N. "Kazakhskaia politicheskaia i intellektual'naia elita: klanovaia prinadlezhnost' i vnutrietnicheskoe sopernichestvo." In *Evraziia: liudi i mify*, edited by S. Panarin, 365–380. Moscow: Natalis, 2003.

Matveeva, Anna. "Legitimising Central Asian Authoritarianism: Political Manipulation and Symbolic Power." *Europe-Asia Studies* 61, no. 7 (2009): 1095–1121.

Mazhitova, Evgeniia. "U sviazi Kulibaev - Masimov est' shansy." *Respublika*. November 27, 2009, http://www.respublika-kz.info/news/politics/6518/.

Mbembe, Achille. "Provisional Notes on the Postcolony." *Africa* 62, no. 1 (1992): 3–37.

McGlinchey, Eric. *Chaos, Violence, Dynasty: Politics and Islam in Central Asia*. Pittsburgh, PA: University of Pittsburgh Press, 2011.

McGlinchey, Eric. "Paying for Patronage: Regime Change in Post-Soviet Central Asia." PhD diss., Princeton University, 2003.

Médard, Jean-François. "L'Etat patrimonialisé." *Politique Africaine*, no. 39 (1990): 31.

Merchant, Tanya. "Popping Tradition: Performing *Maqom* and Uzbek 'National' *Estrada* in the 21st Century." *Popular Music and Society* 32, no. 3 (July 2009): 371–386.

Miley, Thomas J. "The Politics of Language and Nation: The Case of Catalans in Contemporary Spain." PhD diss., Yale University, 2004.

Miliùtin, N.A. *Sotsgorod: The Problem of Building Socialist Cities*. Cambridge, MA: MIT Press, 1974.

Molina, Fernando. "The Historical Dynamics of Ethnic Conflicts: Confrontational Nationalism, Democracy, and the Basques in Contemporary Spain." *Nations and Nationalism* 16, no. 2 (2010): 240–260.

Molodezh Kazakhstana 2014. Astana: Council for Youth Policy under the President of the Republic of Kazakhstan, 2014.

Mouffe, Chantal. *On the Political*. London: Routledge, 2005.

Moustafa, Tamir. *The Struggle for Constitutional Power: Law, Politics and Economic Development in Egypt*. New York: Cambridge University Press, 2007.

Mukhtarov, Daniyar. "Kazakhstan Works on Unifying Pension Funds." Trend Agency, November 14, 2013. Accessed March 12, 2015. http://en.trend.az/casia/kazakhstan/2211199.html.

Murphy, Alexander. "Territory's Continuing Allure." *Annals of the Association of American Geographers* 103, no. 5 (2012): 1212–1226.

Murphy, Jonathan. "Illusory Transition? Elite Reconstitution in Kazakhstan, 1989–2002." *Europe-Asia Studies* 58, no. 4 (2006): 523–554.

Murzakulova, Asel and John Schoeberlein. "The Invention of Legitimacy: Struggles in Kyrgyzstan to Craft an Effective Nation-State Ideology." *Europe-Asia Studies* 61, no. 7 (2009): 1229–1248.

Nackman, Mark E. *A Nation within a Nation: The Rise of Texas Nationalism*. Port Washington: Kennikat Press, 1975.

Navaro-Yashin, Yael. *Faces of the State: Secularism and Public Life in Turkey*. Princeton, NJ: Princeton University Press, 2002.

Navaro-Yashin, Yael. *The Make-Believe Space: Affective Geography in a Post-War Polity*. Durham, NC: Duke University Press, 2012.

Nazarbaev, Nursultan. *Evraziiskii soiuz: idei, praktika, perspektivy*. Moscow: Fond sodeistviia razvitiiu sotsial'nykh i politicheskikh nauk, 1997.

Nazarbaev, Nursultan. *V potoke istorii*. Almaty: Amatura, 1999.

Nazarbayev, Nursultan. "Strategy 2030: Prosperity, Security and Ever Growing Welfare of All the Kazakhstanis." Official Site of the President of the Republic of Kazakhstan,

1977, accessed October 13, 2010, http://www.akorda.kz/en/kazakhstan/kazakhstan 2030/strategy_2030.

Nazarbayev, Nursultan. 2014. "Address of the President of the Republic of Kazakhstan N. Nazarbayev to the Nation, January 17, 2014." Accessed June 29, 2014, http://www.akorda.kz/en/page/page_215839_address-of-the-president-of-the-republic-of-kazakhstan-n-nazarbayev-to-the-nation-january-17-2014#page.

Nazpary, Joma. *Post-Soviet Chaos: Violence and Dispossession in Kazakhstan*. London: Pluto Press, 2002.

Norris, Stephen. "Nomadic Nationhood: Cinema and Remembrance in Post-Soviet Kazakhstan." *Ab Imperio* 13, no. 2 (2012): 378–402.

Nutall, Clare and Ben Aris. "Kazakhstan Joins Growing List of State Pension Grabs." Stratfor, February 22, 2013. Accessed March 12, 2015. http://www.stratfor.com/the-hub/kazakhstan-joins-growing-list-state-pension-grabs.

Ó Beacháin, Donnacha and Rob Kevlihan. "Threading the Needle: Kazakhstan between Civic and Ethno-Nationalist State Building." *Nations and Nationalism* 19, no. 2 (2013): 337–356.

Oakes, Tim. "China's Provincial Identities: Reviving Regionalism and Reinventing Chineseness." *Journal of Asian Studies* 59, no. 3 (2000): 667–692.

Oka, Natsuko. "Ethnicity and Elections under Authoritarianism: The Case of Kazakhstan." *IDE Discussion Paper* no. 194, 2009.

Oka, Natsuko. "Everyday Corruption in Kazakhstan: An Ethnographic Analysis of Informal Practices." Interim Report for *Exploring Informal Networks in Kazakhstan: A Multi-Dimensional Approach*. IDE-JETRO, 2013.

Oka, Natsuko. "Neither Exit nor Voice: Loyalty as a Survival Strategy for the Uzbeks in Kazakhstan." Institute of Developing Economies Discussion Paper No. 286 (2011): 1–17.

Olcott, Martha Brill. *Kazakhstan: Unfulfilled Promise*. Washington, DC: Carnegie Endowment for International Peace, 2002.

Olcott, Martha Brill. "Kazmunaigaz: Kazakhstan's National Oil and Gas Company." *The James A. Baker III Institute for Public Policy Report*, 2007.

Osavolijk, Andriy. "Workers' Strikes Have Become Ever More Frequent in Kazakh Enterprises." *Open Dialogue*, July 22, 2013. Accessed March 15, 2015. http://odfoundation.eu/a/1213,workers-strikes-have-become-ever-more-frequent-in-kazakh-enterprises.

Ostrowski, Wojciech. *Politics and Oil in Kazakhstan*. New York: Routledge, 2010.

Paasi, Anssi. "A *Border Theory*: An Unattainable Dream or a Realistic Aim for Border Scholars?" In *The Ashgate Research Companion to Border Studies*, edited by D. Wastl-Walter, 11–31. Burlington: Ashgate, 2010.

Paasi, Anssi. "Regions and Regional Dynamics." In *The Sage Handbook of European Studies*, edited by C. Rumford, 464–484. Los Angeles: SAGE, 2009.

Paasi, Anssi. "The Resurgence of the 'Region' and 'Regional Identity': Theoretical Perspectives and Empirical Observations on Regional Dynamics in Europe." *Review of International Studies* 35, SupplementS1 (2009): 121–146.

Paasi, Anssi. *Territories, Boundaries, and Consciousness: The Changing Geographies of the Finnish-Russian Boundary*. New York: J. Wiley & Sons, 1996.

Peck, Anne E. *Economic Development in Kazakhstan: The Role of Large Enterprises and Foreign Investment*. Abingdon, UK: Routledge Curzon, 2004.

Perthes, Volker. *Arab Elites: Negotiating the Politics of Change*. Boulder, CO: Lynne Rienner, 2004.

Pew Research Forum. *The World's Muslims: Unity and Diversity*, 2012. http://www.pewforum.org/uploadedFiles/Topics/Religious_Affiliation/Muslim/the-worlds-muslims-full-report.pdf.

Peyrouse, Sebastien. "Nationhood and the Minority Question in Central Asia: The Russians in Kazakhstan." *Europe Asia Studies* 59, no. 3 (2007): 482.

Piterberg, Gabriel. "Domestic Orientalism: The Representation of 'Oriental' Jews in Zionist/Israeli Historiography." *British Journal of Middle Eastern Studies* 23, no. 2 (1996): 125–145.

Polat, Necati. *Boundary Issues in Central Asia.* New York: Brill, 2002.

Pomfret, Richard. *The Central Asian Economies Since Independence.* Princeton, NJ: Princeton University Press, 2006.

Pomfret, Richard. "Kazakhstan's Economy since Independence: Does the Oil Boom Offer a Second Chance for Sustainable Development?" *Europe-Asia Studies* 57, no. 6 (2005): 859–876.

Popik, Barry. "Texas of Canada (Alberta province nickname)." *The Big Apple*, 1997, accessed November 6, 2013, http://www.barrypopik.com/index.php/new_york_city/entry/texas_of_canada_alberta_province_nickname/

Privratsky, Bruce. *Muslim Turkistan: Kazak Religion and Collective Memory.* Richmond, UK: Curzon, 2001.

Quilian, Bo. "Kazakhstan's Role in Energy Sector of China is Increasing." *Munaishy Magazine*, November 4, 2008. Accessed March 12, 2015. http://www.petrokazakhstan.kz/eng/news/public/9.

Rabinow, Paul. *French Modern: Norms and Forms of the Social Environment.* Chicago: University of Chicago Press, 1989.

Ram, Harsha. "Imagining Eurasia: The Poetics and Ideology of Olzhas Suleimenov's *AZ i IA*." *Slavic Review* 60, no. 2 (2001): 289–311.

Rancière, Jacques. *The Politics of Aesthetics*. Translated by Gabriel Rockhill. London: Bloomsbury, 2004.

Rasanayagam, Johan. "I Am Not a Wahhabi: State Power and Muslim Orthodoxy in Uzbekistan." In *The Postsocialist Religious Question: Faith and Power in Central Asia and East-Central Europe*, edited by Chris Hann. Halle: Max Planck Institute, Studies in the Anthropology of Eurasia, 2006.

Rasanayagam, Johan. *Islam in Post-Soviet Uzbekistan: The Morality of Experience*. Cambridge: Cambridge University Press, 2011.

Reeves, Madeleine. *Border Work: Spatial Lives of the State in Rural Central Asia.* Ithaca, NY: Cornell University Press, 2014.

Reeves, Madeleine. "Materialising State Space: 'Creeping Migration' and Territorial Integrity in Southern Kyrgyzstan." *Europe-Asia Studies* 61, no. 7 (2009): 1277–1313.

Reeves, Madeleine, Johan Rasanayagam, and Judith Beyer, eds. *Ethnographies of the State in Central Asia: Performing Politics*. Bloomington: Indiana University Press, 2014.

Regis, Helen A. and Shana Walton. "Producing the Folk at the New Orleans Jazz and Heritage Festival." *Journal of American Folklore* 121, no. 482 (Fall 2008): 400–440.

Rico Isaacs, "Nomads, Warriors, and Bureaucrats: Nation Building and Film in Post -Soviet Kazakhstan." *Nationalities Papers* 43, no. 3 (2014): 1–18.

Ro'i, Yacoov "Central Asian Riots and Disturbances, 1989–1990: Causes and Context." *Central Asian Survey* 10, no. 3 (1991): 21–54.

Robbins, Bruce. "Actually Existing Cosmopolitanism." In *Cosmopolitics: Thinking and Feeling Beyond the Nation*, edited by Pheng Cheah and Bruce Robbins, 1–20. Minneapolis: University of Minnesota Press, 1998.

Roberts, Ken. *Youth in Transition: Eastern Europe and the West.* Basingstoke, UK: Palgrave Macmillan, 2009.

Roberts, Sean. "Doing the Democracy Dance in Kazakhstan: Democracy Development as Cultural Encounter." *Slavic Review* 71, no. 2 (2012): 308–330.

Robinson, Neil. "Institutional Factors and Russian Political Parties: The Changing Need of Regime Consolidation in a Neo-patrimonial System." *East European Politics* 28, no. 3 (2012): 298–309.

Robinson, Neil. "Patrimonial Political Economy and the Global Economy." Paper presented at ISA/ABRI Conference, July 2009.

Robinson, Neil. "Russian Patrimonial Capitalism and the International Financial Crisis." *Journal of Communist Studies and Transition Politics* 27, nos. 3/4 (2011): 434–455.

Rosenvalds, Juris, ed. *Parlamentārais diskurss Latvijā: Saeimas plenārsēžu datorizētā analīze,* Riga: Latvijas Universitāte, 2013.

Ross, Michael. *The Oil Curse: How Petroleum Wealth Shapes the Development of Nations.* Princeton, NJ: Princeton University Press, 2013.

Rumyantseva, Nataliya and Timothy Caboni. "Are Academics in Kazakhstan Capable of Self-regulation? A Study of Faculty's Normative Structure in the Midst of Higher Education Decentralization Reforms." *Tertiary Education and Management* 18, no. 1 (2012): 1–16.

Rustemova, Assel. "Kazakhstan: March-April Report." Central Asia Observatory, May 2013. Accessed March 12, 2015. http://www.asiacentral.es/uploads/kzmay13.pdf.

Rustemova, Assel. "Political Economy of Central Asia: Initial Reflections on the Need for a New Approach." *Journal of Eurasian Studies* 2, no. 1 (2011): 30–39.

Said, Edward. *Orientalism.* New York: Pantheon Books, 1978.

Sandybaeva, Ulbolsyn and Dametken Tolgambaeva. "Sotsial'naia etika prosmotra fil'mov sredi molodezhi Kazakhstana." Paper presented at the ESCAS annual conference, Astana 2013.

Saparova, A. "Sliianie i sliv. Metod Kelimbetova." *CentrAsia,* September 1, 2010. Accessed August 20, 2012, http://www.centrasia.ru/newsA.php?st=1283489700.

Sarsembayev, Azamat. "Imagined Communities: Kazak Nationalism and Kazakification in the 1990s." *Central Asian Survey* 18, no. 3 (1999): 319–346.

Satpayev, Dossym and Tolganay Umbetaliyeva. "The Protests in Zhanaozen and the Kazakh Oil Sector: Conflicting Interests in a Rentier State." *Journal of Eurasian Studies* 6, no. 2 (2015): 122–129.

Satpayev, Dosym. "An Analysis of the Internal Structure of Kazakhstan's Political Elite and an Assessment of Political Risk Levels." In *Empire, Islam and Politics in Central Asia*. Sapporo: Slavic Eurasian Research Center, 2007.

Saunders, Robert A. "Buying into Brand Borat: Kazakhstan's Cautious Embrace of Its Unwanted Son." *Slavic Review* 67, no. 1 (2008): 63–80.

Saunders, Robert A. "In Defense of Kazakschilik: Kazakhstan's War on Sacha Baron Cohen." *Identities* 12, no. 3 (2007): 224–255.

Schatz, Edward and Elena Maltseva. "Kazakhstan's Authoritarian 'Persuasion.'" *Post-Soviet Affairs* 28, no. 1 (2012): 45–65.

Schatz, Edward. *Modern Clan Politics: The Power of "Blood" in Kazakhstan and Beyond*. Seattle: University of Washington Press, 2004.

Schatz, Edward. "The Soft Authoritarian Tool Kit: Agenda-Setting Power in Kazakhstan and Kyrgyzstan." *Comparative Politics* 41, no. 2 (2009): 203–222.

Schatz, Edward. "Transnational Image Making and Soft Authoritarian Kazakhstan." *Slavic Review* 67, no. 1 (2008): 50–62.

Schatz, Edward. "What Capital Cities Say About State and Nation Building." *Nationalism and Ethnic Politics* 9, no. 4 (2004): 111–140.

Schedler, Andreas. *The Politics of Uncertainty: Sustaining and Subverting Electoral Authoritarianism*. Oxford: Oxford University Press, 2013.

Schein, Louisa. "Gender and Internal Orientalism in China." *Modern China* 23, no. 1 (1997): 69–98.

Schiek, Sebastian and Stephan Hansell. "Seeing Like a President: The Dilemma of Inclusion in Kazakhstan." In *Presidents, Oligarchs, and Bureaucrats: Forms of Rule in the Post-Soviet Space*, edited by Susan Steward, Margarete Klein, Andrea Schmitz, and Hans-Henning Schroder. Burlington, VT: Ashgate, 2012.

Schielke, Samuli. "Capitalist Ethics and the Spirit of Islamization in Egypt." In *Ordinary Lives and Grand Schemes: An Anthropology of Everyday Religion*, edited by Samuli Schielke and Liza Debevec, 13–45. Oxford: Berghahn, 2012.

Schlumberger, Oliver. *Debating Arab Authoritarianism: Dynamics and Durability in Nondemocratic Regimes*. Stanford, CA: Stanford University Press, 2007.

Schwab, Wendell. "Establishing an Islamic Niche in Kazakhstan: Musylman Publishing House and Its Publications." *Central Asian Survey* 30, no. 2 (2011): 22–42.

Schwab, Wendell. "How to Pray in Kazakhstan: The Fortress of the Muslim and Its Readers." *Anthropology of East Europe Review* 32, no. 1 (2014): 22–42.

Schwab, Wendell. "Islam, Fun, and Social Capital in Kazakhstan." *Central Asian Affairs* 2, no. 1 (2015): 51–70.

Schwab, Wendell. "Traditions and Texts: How Two Young Women Learned to Interpret the Qur'an and Hadiths in Kazakhstan." *Contemporary Islam* 6, no. 2 (2012): 173–197.

Seitenova, Aigul and Charles Becker. "Kazakhstan's Pension System: Pressures for Change and Dramatic Reforms." *Hitotsubashi Journal of Economics* 45, no. 2 (2004): 151–187, Accessed March 12, 2015. https://hermes-ir.lib.hit-u.ac.jp/rs/bitstream/10086/7665/1/HJeco0450201510.pdf.

Seter, Ronit. "Jerusalem and Tel-Aviv: Different News from Israel (Or, One More Step toward Peace): Three Contemporary Music Festivals." *Tempo* 59, no. 233 (July 2005): 46–51.

Shakhanov, Mukhtar. "A Report on Commission Proceedings and on Further Clarification of the Circumstances of the December 1986 Events in Alma-Ata." In *Conflict in the Soviet Union: The Untold Story of the Clashes in Kazakhstan.* Helsinki Watch. New York: Helsinki Watch, 1990.

Silverstein, Ken. "A Giant Among Giants." *Foreign Policy* (May–June 2012). Accessed August 20, 2012, http://www.foreignpolicy.com/articles/2012/04/23/a_giant_among_giants?page=0,5.

Sindzingre, Alice. *The Concept of Neopatrimonialism: Divergences and Convergences with Development Economics*. Hamburg: German Institute of Global and Area Studies, 2010.

Slobin, Mark. "Introduction." In *Retuning Culture: Musical Changes in Central and Eastern Europe*, edited by Mark Slobin, 1–13. Durham: Duke University Press, 1996.

Smith, Anthony. *Ethnic Origins of Nations*. New York: Wiley Blackwell, 1991.

Smith, Graham, Vivian Law, Andrew Wilson, Annette Bohr, and Edward Allworth. *Nation-Building in the Post-Soviet Borderlands: The Politics of National Identities*. New York: Cambridge University Press, 1998.

Soja, Edward W. *Thirdspace: Journeys to Los Angeles and Other Real-and-Imagined Places*. Cambridge, MA: Blackwell, 1996.

Solska, Magdalena. "Citizenship, Collective Identity, and the International Impact on Integration Policy in Estonia, Latvia, and Lithuania." *Europe-Asia Studies* 63, no. 6 (2011): 1089–1108.

Spehr, Scott and Nargis Kassenova. "Kazakhstan: Constructing Identity in Post-Soviet Society." *Asian Ethnicity*13, no. 2 (2012): 135–151.

Spencer, Jonathan. *Anthropology, Politics, and the State: Democracy and Violence in South Asia*. Cambridge: Cambridge University Press, 2007.

Spiritual Administration of the Muslims of Kazakhstan. *Qabirde Otyru, Uiyqtau, Qabirge Daretke Otyru, zhane Onyng Ustimen Zhuru Ukimi*, 2014. Accessed April 12, 2016, http://old.muftyat.kz/kz/fatwa/view?id=10.

Spiritual Administration of the Muslims of Kazakhstan. *Qabirstandy Ziyarat Etu Ukimi*, 2013. Accessed April 12, 2016, http://old.muftyat.kz/kz/fatwa/view?id=7.

Steen, Anton. "Elite and Mass Confidence in New Democracies – Towards Congruence? The Baltic States 1992–2007." *Historical Social Research* 37, no. 3 (2012): 12–47.

Steen, Anton. *Between Past and Future: Elites, Democracy and the State in Post-Communist Countries: A Comparison of Estonia, Latvia, and Lithuania*. Aldershot: Ashgate, 1997.

Stepan, Alfred. *The State and Society: Peru in Comparative Perspective*. Princeton, NJ: Princeton University Press, 1978.

Stewart, Kathleen. "Atmospheric Attunements." *Environment and Planning D: Society and Space* 29 (2011): 445–453.

Stewart, Susan, Margarete Klein, Andrea Schmitz, and Hans-Henning Schröder, eds. *Presidents, Oligarchs and Bureaucrats: Forms of Rule in the Post-Soviet Space*. Farnham, UK: Ashgate, 2012.

Strategiya Sociological Agency. "Osobennosti mezhetnicheskikh otnoshenii v Kazakhstane." May 2009.

Strategiya Sociological Agency. "Osobennosti identichnosti i konsolidatsii naseleniia Kazakhstana." March 2009.

Suyarkulova, Mohira. "Reluctant Sovereigns? Central Asian States' Path to Independence." In *Sovereignty After Empire: Comparing the Middle East and Central Asia*, edited by Sally N. Cummings and Raymond Hinnsbusch, 127–154. Edinburgh: Edinburgh University Press, 2011.

Svanberg, Ingvar. "In Search of a Kazakhstani Identity." *Journal of Area Studies* 4 (1994): 112–123.

Svanberg, Ingvar. "Kazakhs." In *The Nationalities Question in the Soviet Union*, ed. Graham Smith, 318–330. London: Longman, 1990.

Tasar, Eren. "Soviet and Muslim: The Institutionalization of Islam in Central Asia, 1943–1991." PhD diss., Harvard University, 2010.

Tasar, Eren. "The Official Madrasas of Soviet Uzbekistan." *Journal of the Economic and Social History of the Orient* 59, no. 1/2 (2016): 265–302.

Taussig, Michael. *The Magic of the State*. New York: Routledge, 1997.

Thrift, Nigel. *Non-Representational Theory: Space, Politics, Affect*. London: Routledge, 2008.

Todorov, Tzvetan. *The Fantastic: A Structural Approach to a Literary Genre*. Translated by Richard Howard. Ithaca: Cornell University Press, 1975.

Tololyan, Khachig. "Rethinking Diaspora(s): Stateless Power in the Transnational Moment." *Diaspora* 5, no. 1 (1996): 3–36.

Tussupova, Dinara. "Mass Media and Ethnic Relations in Kazakhstan." *Problems of Post-Communism* 57, no. 6 (2010): 32–45.

Tyan, Nick. "Kazakhstani Nation." http://www.academia.edu/3532663/Kazakhistani_nation2014.

Vale, Lawrence J. *Architecture, Power, and National Identity*. 2nd edition. London: Routledge, 2008.

Veyne, Paul. *Did the Greeks Believe in Their Myths? An Essay on the Constitutive Imagination*. Chicago: University of Chicago Press, 1988.

Wanner, Catherine. "Nationalism on Stage: Music and Change in Soviet Ukraine." In *Retuning Culture: Musical Changes in Central and Eastern Europe*, edited by Mark Slobin, 136–155. Durham, NC: Duke University Press, 1996.

Weber, Max. "The Types of Legitimate Domination." In *Economy and Society: An Outline of Interpretive Sociology*, 1922. Edited by Guenther Roth and Claus Wittich, translated by Ephraim Fischoff et al., 212–301. Berkeley: University of California Press, 1978.

Weber, Max. *Economy and Society: An Outline of Interpretive Sociology*. Berkeley: University of California Press, 1978.

Weber, Max. *The Protestant Ethic and the "Spirit" of Capitalism and Other Writings*. New York: Penguin, 2002.

Wedeen, Lisa. *Ambiguities of Domination: Politics, Rhetoric, and Symbols in Contemporary Syria*. Chicago: University of Chicago Press, 1999.

Wedeen, Lisa. *Peripheral Visions: Publics, Power, and Performance in Yemen*. Chicago, IL: University of Chicago Press, 2007.

Werner, Cynthia. "Gifts, Bribes, and Development in Post-Soviet Kazakhstan." *Human Organization* 59, no. 1 (2000): 11–22.

West, Harry G. and Todd Sanders. *Transparency and Conspiracy: Ethnographies of Suspicion in the New World Order*. Durham, NC: Duke University Press, 2003.

White, Luise. *Speaking with Vampires: Rumor and History in Colonial Africa*. Berkeley: University of California Press, 2000.

Williams, Colin and Anthony Smith. "The National Construction of Social Space." *Progress in Human Geography* 7, no. 4 (1983): 502–518.

Williams, Raymond. *The Country and the City*. New York: Oxford University Press, 1973.

Williams, Raymond. *Marxism and Literature*. Oxford: Oxford University Press, 1977.

Wolfel, Richard L. "North to Astana: Nationalistic Motives for the Movement of the Kazakh(stani) Capital." *Nationalities Papers* 30, no. 3 (2002): 485–506.

Wright, Gwendolyn. *The Politics of Design in French Colonial Urbanism*. Chicago: University of Chicago Press, 1991.

Yessenova, Saulesh. "'Routes and Roots' of Kazakh Identity: Urban Migration in Postsocialist Kazakhstan." *Russian Review* 64, no. 4 (2005): 661–679.

Yessenova, Saulesh. *The Politics and Poetics of the Nation: Urban Narratives of Kazakh Identity*. Saarbrücken: LAP Lambert Academic Publishing, 2010.

Zardykhan, Zharmukhamed. "Russians in Kazakhstan and Demographic Change: Imperial Legacy and the Kazakh Way of Nation Building." *Asian Ethnicity* 5, no. 1 (2004): 61–79.

Zepa, Brigita, et al. *National Identity in Latvia Report*. Riga: University of Latvia and Chicago: University of Chicago Press, 2011.

Zhusupov, S. "Dinamika Sociological Data 1999–2002." In *Politicheskaia analitika issledovaniia.* Almaty: "Arna-b." 1998–2001.

Zipes, Jack. "Breaking the Magic Spell: Politics and the Fairy Tale." *New German Critique* 6 (1975): 116–135.

Index

About the Editor and Contributors

ABOUT THE EDITOR

Marlene Laruelle is director of the Central Asia Program, research professor of international affairs and associate director of the Institute for European, Russian and Eurasian Studies (IERES) at the Elliott School of International Affairs, George Washington University. She explores contemporary political, social, and cultural changes in Russia and Central Asia through the prism of ideologies and nationalism. She has authored *Russian Eurasianism: An Ideology of Empire* (Johns Hopkins University Press, 2008), *In the Name of the Nation: Nationalism and Politics in Contemporary Russia* (Palgrave, 2009), and has recently edited *Eurasianism and the European Far Right. Reshaping the Russia-Europe Relationship* (Lexington, 2015). She has published, among others, *Europe-Asia Studies, Post-Soviet Affairs, Problems of Post-Communism, Nationalities Papers, Nations and Nationalism.*

ABOUT THE CONTRIBUTORS

Ulan Bigozhin is a PhD student in anthropology at Indiana University and a visiting scholar at George Mason University. He studies Islam, state-society relations, and sacred families in Kazakhstan. He will defend his PhD dissertation, "State, Shrine, and Sacred Families in Post-soviet Kazakhstan," in 2017.

Alima Bissenova is an assistant professor in the Department of Sociology and Anthropology at the School of Humanities and Social Sciences, Nazarbayev University. She obtained her PhD in 2012 at the Cornell

University, has a bachelor's degree in Kazakh language and literature from the Karaganda State University and a master's degree in Middle East studies from the American University in Cairo. In her current research, she investigates the social implications of post-Soviet development through the prism of the changing environment of major Kazakhstani cities, people's strategies at achieving and maintaining socio-economic status, and various methods of cultural capital accumulation. She is completing her first book manuscript, *Learning to Be Bourgeois: The Rise of the Middle Classes in Post-Soviet Kazakhstan.*

Douglas Blum is professor of political science at the Providence College. He has published on a variety of issues, ranging from the connections between ideology and foreign policy to problems of energy, geopolitics, and environmentalism in the Caspian Sea region. In recent years his research has centered on the connections between globalization and identity in the former USSR. His works include *The Social Process of Globalization: Return Migration and Cultural Change in Kazakhstan* (Cambridge University Press, 2016), as well as *National Identity and Globalization: Youth, State and Society in Post-Soviet Eurasia* (Cambridge University Press, 2007), and a volume from the project he directed, *Russia and Globalization: Identity, Security and Society in an Era of Change* (Johns Hopkins University Press and Woodrow Wilson Center, 2008). He received his PhD in political science from the Columbia University in 1991.

Alexander C. Diener is an Associate professor of geography at the University of Kansas. His research engages topics such as geopolitics, borders, identity, mobility, and urban landscape change through an area studies focus in the Central Asian states, Mongolia, and the borderlands of Russia and China. He is the author or co-author of three books, including *One Homeland or Two?* (Stanford University Press, 2009), and co-editor of three books, including *From Socialist to Post-Socialist Cities: Cultural Politics of Architecture, Urban Planning, and Identity in Eurasia* (Routledge, 2014). He has held research fellowships at the Kennan Institute of the Woodrow Wilson Center, George Washington University's Elliott School, Harvard University's Davis Center, and was the Regional Research Fulbright Scholar for Central Asia in 2011–2012.

Natalie Koch is assistant professor in the Department of Geography at Syracuse University's Maxwell School of Citizenship and Public Affairs. She specializes in political and urban geography, with a focus on geopolitics, nationalism, and authoritarian state-making. Her regional expertise is in the resource-rich countries of post-Soviet Central Asia and the Arabian Peninsula. She has authored numerous articles in journals such as *Political Geography, Urban Geography, Geoforum, Area, Transactions of the Institute of British Geographers*, and is the editor of the book, *Critical Geographies of Sport: Space, Power, and Sport in Global Perspective* (Routledge, 2016).

Diana T. Kudaibergenova is a cultural and political sociologist based at the University of Cambridge. Diana studies nationalizing regimes and power fields and theorizes how power elites establish hegemonic nationalistic orders. She conducted fieldwork in Latvia, Kazakhstan, Uzbekistan, Kyrgyzstan, and Ukraine and published on a range of issues related to nationalism and power relations. Her cultural sociology project deals with the processes of contesting and re-writing national discourses in a historical perspective, as well as with the study of globalisation and socio-cultural transformations. Diana completed her PhD and MPhil in sociology at the University of Cambridge and MA in international and intercultural relations at the University of Deusto in Basque Country in Spain.

Mateusz Laszczkowski is assistant professor at the Institute of Ethnology and Cultural Anthropology, at the University of Warsaw. He is the author of *'City of the Future': Built Space, Modernity and Urban Change in Astana* (Berghahn Books, 2016), the first ethnographic monograph of the Kazakhstani capital, as well as a number of publications in journals including *Social Analysis, the Journal of the Royal Anthropological Institute* and *City & Society*. His present research explores the politics of resistance against high-speed railway construction in Val di Susa, in the Italian Alps.

Sebastien Peyrouse, PhD, is a research professor at the Central Asia Program in the Institute for European, Russian and Eurasian Studies (George Washington University) and a senior fellow at the East-West Institute. His main areas of expertise are political systems in Central Asia, economic and social issues, Islam and religious minorities, and Central Asia's geopolitical positioning toward China, India, and South Asia. He has co-edited *China and India in Central Asia. A new "Great Game"?* (New York: Palgrave Macmillan, 2010), and has published a monograph, *Turkmenistan. Strategies of Power, Dilemmas of Development* (Armonk: M. E. Sharpe, 2011), and with Marlene Laruelle, *The 'Chinese Question' in Central Asia. Domestic Order, Social Changes, and the Chinese Factor* (London, New York: Hurst, Columbia University Press, 2011) and *Globalizing Central Asia: Geopolitics and the Challenges of Economic Development* (Armonk: ME Sharpe, 2012).

Megan Rancier received her PhD in ethnomusicology from UCLA in 2009, with a focus on Kazakh musical instruments and national identity narratives. Her doctoral fieldwork in Almaty, Kazakhstan, was supported by a Fulbright IIE Fellowship and Title VIII Research Scholarship. Her publications include an article in the journal *Ethnomusicology* and an album review in *Yearbook for Traditional Music*; she is also co-editing and contributing to a volume on the music of the Turkic-speaking world with Dr. Razia Sultanova (University of Cambridge). She currently teaches at the Bowling Green State University College of Musical Arts in Bowling Green, Ohio.

Assel Tutumlu is an assistant professor in international relations at Gediz University in Izmir, Turkey. She received her PhD in global affairs from Rutgers, State University of New Jersey under the supervision of Professor Philip Cerny, and fully supported by fellowships from various organizations. She also holds two master's degrees in international affairs from American University and in politics from the New School for Social Research. She mainly specializes in studying political economy of authoritarian regimes in Central Asia and beyond, but also writes on democratization, nation-building, and foreign policy issues. Her work appeared in *Europe-Asia Studies, Journal of Eurasian Studies,* and edited volumes from Sage, Lexington, and Nomos Press. Before working at Gediz University she held academic positions in Kazakhstan and the United States as well as professional titles at the United Nations, International Foundation for Election Systems, Kennan Institute of Advanced Russian Studies, and the Center for Non-Proliferation Studies.

Wendell Schwab received his PhD in anthropology from Indiana University and works at Pennsylvania State University. He studies Islamic media and Islamic traditions of learning in Kazakhstan. His work has appeared in journals such as *Central Asian Affairs, Central Asian Survey, Anthropology of East Europe Review*, and *Contemporary Islam*.

Kristopher White is an associate professor at the College of Social Sciences, KIMEP University in Almaty, Kazakhstan. He is a geographer whose recent research has focused on human-environment interrelationships in Central Asia and Kazakhstan. His recent publications have explored these issues in the Aral Sea basin. His forthcoming publications investigate regional imaginaries in Central Asia and the snow leopard and cultural landscape in contemporary Kazakhstan. His work appeared in *Environmental Crises in Central Asia: From steppes to seas, from deserts to glaciers* (London and New York: Routledge), *The Aral Sea: The devastation and partial rehabilitation of a great lake* (Berlin Heidelberg: Springer-Verlag), *Bulletin of Geography Socio-economic Series*, and *Journal of Eurasian Studies.*

Job # 38457